Plato's Individuals

Plato's Individuals

• *MARY MARGARET McCABE* •

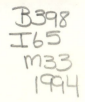

PRINCETON UNIVERSITY PRESS

PRINCETON, NEW JERSEY

Copyright © 1994 by Princeton University Press
Published by Princeton University Press, 41 William Street,
Princeton, New Jersey 08540
In the United Kingdom: Princeton University Press, Chichester, West Sussex

Library of Congress Cataloging-in-Publication Data

McCabe, Mary Margaret, 1948–
Plato's individuals / Mary Margaret McCabe.
p.   cm.
Includes bibliographical references and indexes.
ISBN 0-691-07351-1 (CL)
1. Plato—Contributions in concept of individuation.
2. Individuation (Philosophy)   I. Title.
B398.I65M33   1994
111'.82—dc20   93-42370

This book has been composed in Sabon

Princeton University Press books are printed on acid-free paper
and meet the guidelines for permanence and durability of the
Committee on Production Guidelines for Book Longevity of the
Council on Library Resources

Printed in the United States of America

1   3   5   7   9   10   8   6   4   2

For Kate, my beloved daughter

• C O N T E N T S •

THIS BOOK HAS taken a long time to write; during its parturition I have accumulated many debts of gratitude, both to institutions and to individuals.

From 1981 to 1990 I was a Fellow of New Hall, Cambridge; throughout that time I profited enormously from the vigor and the warmth of New Hall, and from the intellectual support given to me by all the other Fellows—my thanks. During that time I spent some sabbatical leave in the U.S.A., in 1984–85 as a Junior Fellow at the Center for Hellenic Studies, Washington, D.C., where I was also supported by the Fulbright Foundation, and in 1987 as a Perkins Junior Fellow in the Humanities in the Department of Classics at Princeton University. My warm thanks to all the institutions involved. Both in Washington and at Princeton I was very lucky indeed in my colleagues; both places enriched me immeasurably, and I am commensurately grateful. In 1990 I went to the Department of Philosophy, King's College, London; this has been very much my good fortune. To all my colleagues in London my grateful thanks for their tolerance, their friendship, and their philosophy (in particular, my thanks to Richard Sorabji, who makes ancient philosophy in London so exciting). My thanks, also, to the School of Humanities at King's for a small research grant to help me to prepare the final manuscript for press.

Chapters or sections of this book have been read at various different places—Princeton University, Cambridge University, the University of Pittsburgh, the Triennial Meetings of the Hellenic and Roman Societies. I thank the audiences on all those occasions for their comments.

Individuals are harder to count, since over the last ten years I have benefited so much from so many people: colleagues, friends, and students. May I offer a blanket thank-you here? I have recorded some particular debts in footnotes. Then I should like to mention those people in particular who have been concerned with this book. Several people have read and commented on drafts of the whole book; that was a thoroughly laborious business, and I am extremely grateful for the generous gift of their time to Dorothea Frede, Michael Frede, Keith Hossack, Geoffrey Lloyd, Richard Sorabji, and an anonymous reader for Princeton University Press. Without their comments this book would have been a poorer affair. Others have commented on different sections, or talked to me about various puzzles that worried me: Margaret Atkins, Myles Burnyeat, John Cooper, Nick Denyer, Rai Gaita, Chris Gill, Alan Lacey, Jonathan Lear, Mario Mignucci, Mark Sainsbury, Malcolm Schofield, Dominic Scott, David Sedley, Gabriel Segal, Scott Sturgeon. All of these people have helped me enormously. Of what appears here, they are blameless.

My more general debts should be recorded to David Furley, Andrew Ford, Froma Zeitlin, Elaine Fantham, and Joanna Hitchcock (formerly of Princeton

University Press). At Princeton University Press I have been lucky in my editor, Ann Himmelberger Wald, and my copyeditor, Joan Hunter.

Finally, my family has borne the brunt of all of this. My deep and lasting gratitude to Martin Beddoe, to Sarah and Edward McCabe, and to Kate, my daughter, to whom this book is dedicated, with love.

FULL bibliographical information is provided in the bibliography. The following abbreviations have been used in the text and notes:

Works of Plato, in the edition of J. Burnet, Oxford Classical Texts series (Oxford, 1900–1903):

Apol.	*Apology*	*Phil.*	*Philebus*
Crat.	*Cratylus*	*Pol.*	*Politicus*
Euthyd.	*Euthydemus*	*Prt.*	*Protagoras*
Euth.	*Euthyphro*	*Rep.*	*Republic*
Grg.	*Gorgias*	*Soph.*	*Sophist*
Hi.Ma.	*Hippias Major*	*Symp.*	*Symposium*
Parm.	*Parmenides*	*Tht.*	*Theaetetus*
Phd.	*Phaedo*	*Tim.*	*Timaeus*
Phdr.	*Phaedrus*		

Works of Aristotle, in the editions of I. Bywater, W. D. Ross, W. Jaeger, Oxford Classical Texts series (Oxford, 1897–1957):

Cat.	*Categories*
De An.	*De Anima*
Met.	*Metaphysics*
E.N.	*Nicomachean Ethics*
Phys.	*Physics*
An.Po.	*Posterior Analytics*

LSJ = Liddell, H. G., R. Scott, H. S. Jones, eds. *A Greek-English Lexicon* (Oxford, revised 1968).

DK = Diels, H., and W. Kranz, eds. *Die Fragmente der Vorsokratiker* (Berlin, 10th ed. 1960).

Plato's Individuals

· O N E ·

The Problem of Individuation

1. THE ARGUMENT OF THIS BOOK

Aristotle, they say, discovered the problem of individuation and, some say, solved it. Plato, they say, was interested first and foremost in what there is, not in the issue of how something that is, is a something. Not so, I shall argue. Plato was indeed centrally concerned with the problem of individuation—bequeathed to him by his predecessors—but both his account of the problem and his attempted solution are radically different from Aristotle's. In this matter, Aristotle has been the more influential in the philosophical tradition. Should he have been?

What do I mean by the problem of individuation? I argue below that when we try to arrange the world of our experience (whether sensory or intellectual), we suppose that certain items are basic. What is more, we imagine that basic items are countable, one by one. Further, we hope that each basic item is somehow or other one, unified, coherent within itself. On that account something will be individual because it is basic, unitary, and unified. Or we may consider the matter differently: something can be individuated by virtue of being the same as itself (both at a time and over some time) and different from other things. So individuals should be

1. basic;
2. one for counting (a unit);
3. unified;
4. self-identical and different from others.

But how do we know when we have got hold of an individual? There may be impostors, failures, parts of individuals that deceive us into individuating wrong. We regularly suppose that we can individuate by sorting things into kinds or types. If I can determine that this is one armadillo or one London bus, I can be sure I have my individual safe. On this account (which modern common sense prefers), individuation is by sortals—being one is being one of a kind (whatever kind we may choose); being the same (identical) is being the same one of the same kind and different from others of the same kind and others of other kinds, too. This principle has appealed to philosophers since Aristotle first formulated it; so I begin with the problems of individuation within the context of Aristotle's theory.

Plato, of course, came before Aristotle. How does he explain individuals? The rest of this book is an attempt to do two things: first, to argue that Plato was indeed worried by the problem of individuation; second, to explain his solution to it—one that is startlingly different from Aristotle's and that is of theoretical value in its own right.

Tradition associates Plato with a contrast between the particulars of the sensible world and the intelligible forms; and it is often thought that here lies the fixed center of his metaphysical views. I argue that, on the contrary, his account of what there is is determined not by the existence of forms but by his understanding of what makes something one something; individuals are, for Plato, both basic and primary. For Plato supposes that

1. Individuals are the basic components of the world, however that is constituted, because to be is first and foremost to be one.

2. So determining whether something is one is a prior question to sorting it into its kind. Being one something is basic and primary.

3. So being an individual is a primitive, irreducible feature of whatever entities there are. Being is being an individual.

As Plato develops his understanding of these issues, the problem of forms and particulars turns out to be a mere preliminary (Part I). Nonetheless, the contrast between forms and particulars is a preliminary to understanding the question, What is it to be an individual? that matters. In Chapters 2 and 3, I argue that while the theory of forms is introduced to explain the sensible world, it also features in a contrast between the composite and therefore perishable entities of the physical world and the simple eternal forms. Particulars have properties and participate in relations that render them complex, that make them difficult to identify over time, and that fail to supply a unifying principle to ensure that each is one (Chapter 2).

Individual particulars, as I characterize them, are *generous* collections of properties. Forms, as a consequence, are seen to be entirely simple entities, having no properties and standing in no relations that might impair their simplicity; I characterize them as *austere* (Chapter 3). This contrast, between generous and austere individuals, is a theme that runs throughout the book—and, I claim, throughout Plato's thought about what there is.

However, the austerity of forms (as Chapter 3 goes on to argue) becomes an impossible condition for them, as it marks their failure to explain particulars after all. Forms cannot be related to particulars in any way, they cannot be understood systematically, and they cannot be teleologically arranged, so long as they remain austere. At this stage in Plato's thought (midway through the *Parmenides*), there appears to be a crisis in Plato's thinking about forms. A crisis indeed there is, but it is a crisis for any account of being one at all (as I argue in Chapter 4). For the second part of the *Parmenides* embarks on an abstract consideration of "being one" that opposes these two modes: *either* something is one by virtue of the properties it has, *or* something is one in itself (prior to its having properties). But, Parmenides argues, both accounts of being one are paradoxical; the first allows any one to be hopelessly many, while the second suggests that any one is nothing at all.

This dilemma—between the generous and the austere conceptions of the individual—comes now, I argue, to dominate Plato's metaphysics. In the *Theaetetus* (Chapter 5) and the *Timaeus* (Chapter 6), the same contrast reappears, in each case rather differently presented (as bundles versus lumps in the *Theaetetus*; as slices versus stuffs in the *Timaeus*). In both cases, as in the second part of the *Parmenides*, the models of individuation break down and dialectic fails with them. Nonetheless, the repeated posing of the puzzle and the insistent counterpoise of the generous and the austere conceptions of individuation do produce understanding along the way—as Plato, and his readers, come to diagnose the assumptions that cause the impasse.

The difficulty, Plato suggests, is one that affects both the way the world is and the way we talk about it (Chapter 7). Both language and the world are arranged into basic items, their properties and the relations between them. Thus for words, no less than for things, remote austerity is intolerable (for speech and dialectic cannot take place); hopeless generosity is equally unbearable because speech becomes as flux-ridden and unstable as a generous world would be.

Matters come to a head in the *Sophist*. The remainder of the *Sophist*, the *Philebus*, and the *Politicus* offer a solution in terms of the claim that individuals are basic units. Any individual can be counted by virtue of its relation to other individuals, by its location among other individuals, by its difference from others, and by its minimal identity with itself. This (I call it the mesh of identity) provides a context-relative account of individuation (Chapter 8).

However, the context-relative account is a disappointing one in several ways. In particular, while it may explain how to count individuals—by differentiating them from others—it tells us little about how they are unified or made coherent. Individuals are still conceived on the austere model, as bare and basic units. And yet we do suppose (as the generous model of individuation revealed) that individuals have a richer account to be rendered than this. In particular, when we come to think of individual persons, the problem of unity becomes especially pressing, as does the fear that complex entities are liable to perish. Chapter 9 argues that Plato has a vivid and important theory of personal identity to give, which is the converse of the mesh of identity and which supposes that the individuation of persons may be absolute.

In the end, then, Plato attempts to answer the puzzles he has posed. He supposes that individuals as such are basic, and he suggests that either the relation between individuals, or the complex structure within an individual (especially an individual mind), explains how anything is one something. There are no sortals here—instead there are individuals per se.

2. NOTHING FROM NOTHING: VEHICLES OF CHANGE

Let us consider what the problems of individuation might be. Suppose we ask, What is there? There is the world and everything in it—people and palaces, tables and tortoises. There is everything we see, the middle-sized physical objects of our everyday experience. Yes, but what is there, *really*? Are these objects just shifting appearances in some other reality? Or is what we see what we get?

A pre-Socratic puzzle about change might lead us to suppose that what there is really, is different from what we see. If nothing can come from nothing (as Parmenides was the first to argue), then either there is no change at all, or something must persist thoughout the changes that seem to happen. If there is no change at all, then the world as we see it is unreal and to be rejected. But that consequence is a difficult one to live with; so perhaps we must allow for the possibility of change. In that case, we must be able to specify what underlies the changes that we see.[1] Thus, one strategy for determining what underlies change is to posit some basic stuff or stuffs:

> Wherefore some say that fire is the nature of things, some say earth, some air and some water, while some say several of these and some all of them. Whenever someone posits some such thing, whether one or many, he says that this and these many are all of reality, while everything else is an affection or a state or a disposition of them; whichever element they posit they say is eternal (for they deny that these change out of themselves), while everything else comes into being and is destroyed an infinite number of times. (*Phys.* 193a21–28)

In that case, the world comes in two layers: first of all there is reality, the genuine article that underlies change, and then, supervening on that, there are the various appearances of the physical world as it is presented to us. Thus, for example, Democritus could suggest that "by convention sweet, by convention bitter, by convention hot, by convention cold, by convention colour; but in reality atoms and void" (Democritus DK68B9).

For Democritus, what is real and basic is quite different from what we see; the two layers of the universe are quite distinct. For Anaxagoras, conversely, the basic reality is the same all the way through: "And since the portions of large and small are equal in number so there would be everything in everything. For it is not possible for anything to be distinct, but everything has a portion of everything" (Anaxagoras DK59B6).

The pre-Socratic physicists were anxious to maintain some sort of stability in the physical world; so they postulated basic stuffs. Their theories, then, had three features. First of all, the stuffs were supposed to *persist* underneath change; that the stuffs remain the same guarantees that superficial change is not frightening. Second, stuffs persist because they are *basic*, they underlie. Third, stuffs are thus *countable*: "Whenever someone posits some such thing, whether one or many, he says that this and these many are all of reality" (*Phys.* 193a23–24).

The trouble about these accounts of what underlies change in the cosmos is that they seem to preserve the possibility of change at too high a price. For it

---

[1] "In every case of coming to be . . . it is necessary that there always be something underlying . . ." (Aristotle, *Phys.* 190a13–16).

was common to the early physicists to suppose that reality is *other* than what we think it is; and they explain what we think there is in terms of something else. But we might reasonably object that they have thrown the baby out with the bathwater. They have given us something to underlie change, but they have done no proper explaining of the changes that we see. Instead, they argue that what we see is grounded in something else; the questions we reasonably ask about this world here are answered in terms of some other world, and that leaves our original questions unsatisfied.

The problem of change, however, is not limited to the vastness of the cosmos. Even when we deal with the particular items of our individual experience, change is threatening. Perhaps the individual particular may last some time, but not long enough to guarantee proper stability. Hobbes, after all, was not the first to worry about the problem of Theseus's ship.[2] The ship that transported Theseus back from his encounter with the Minotaur has been around for a long time; over and over it has been repaired so that all the original planks and spars and halyards have been replaced. Is this still the same ship? Suppose that what persists persists only relatively to some change; what reassures us that it persists at all? And if it does, how, relatively, can we explain what it is?

In any case, that something persists, even relatively, through change, may not be thought obvious. Change could be staccato, for example, as Heraclitus may have argued.[3] The world, on such a view, may be discontinuous, a series of separate episodes succeeding one another. In such a world, does anything persist through change? Can we even speak coherently of change?

Or, as Heraclitus may otherwise have argued, change could be a constant wearing away of whatever there is. Suppose that there is a uniform slippage in the world, albeit sometimes imperceptible. Whatever is thus and so now is, at the next moment, no longer thus and so. This is true (in such a world) of everything, in every respect. There is radical, total flux. In such a world is there anything but change?

Theseus's ship, staccato episodes, and radical flux all pose questions about the persistence of something over time, problems about diachronic identity. Perhaps we should continue to assert that identity is determined by persistence. For example, suppose that this book underlies the change of your turning the pages or returning it to the library. When, however, the book is burned by anti-Platonists next week, it is no longer the book that underlies the change, but rather, perhaps, the carbon of which it is composed and into

---

[2] Compare Cebes' worry that the soul, albeit lasting longer than the body, may eventually wear out (*Phd.* 87a ff.). Cf. M. Frede, "Individuals." A recent case in the Old Bailey concerned the sale of a vintage car. The price of the car was determined by its provenance—it was claimed that this was the car that had won Le Mans in 1932. The issue turned on whether, since the car had been mended so many times in the intervening period, this could reasonably be said to be the same car (even though there was no other that could fit the description on the bill of sale). The car was not a fake—but had it persisted through time?

[3] According to Plato's version in the *Theaetetus*; cf., in this book, ch. 5, secs. 2, 4.

which it disintegrates. In just this way the early physicists might have reduced identity to the basic stuff of the world, and so argued that stuff persists absolutely.

Stuff may persist—but is it identifiable? Does it actually reassure us when we worry about change? Aristotle reinvests in common sense, and reinstates the original question about change.[4] How, in the face of the prohibition on something coming from nothing, can we explain how Socrates was hairy and is now bald? Or how this armadillo, once smooth, is now warty? Or how that cat, once on the mat, is now in the coal bunker? How can there be any continuity in change?

A simple answer must be that *something persists* through the changes because there is something that underlies them. Suppose that the question about change is posed for particular cases: How can we explain this change from Socrates hairy to Socrates bald? If that is what we are worried about, it is little help to point out that some combination of earth, air, fire, and water underlies the change, that guarantees that something persists, but it does not tell us about Socrates (exactly the same answer could be given to the question about the cat). The answer of the early materialists, that is, is too general to help us with the problems of individual change.

Instead, if we stick to common sense, we might prefer to say that Socrates is what persists through the change from hairy to bald, the armadillo through the transformation from smooth to warty, the cat through the move from the mat to the coal bunker. So the answer to the question What underlies? will be relative to the particular change in question;[5] and it will be preferable for the answer to cite individual particulars as the persistent items underneath it.[6] In standard cases, after all, the individual particular lasts longer than its properties. Socrates turns up hairy before he turns up bald, the warts on the armadillo are late accretions to its hide, the cat sat on the mat before it decided on the coal bunker. The particular is relatively durable, compared to its properties; and that durability ensures that change is not a staccato series of episodes, but rather a continuous process, underlain by an individual particular —by the middle-sized objects of the physical world (*Phys.* 192b9; *Met.* 1028b8).

Aristotle insists that individual particulars, not stuffs, persist. And in this way he allays our anxieties about change. After all, we are concerned not so much about whether there will always be some underlying stuff (we do not habitually worry about the principle of the conservation of matter), but rather about whether this thing will persist long enough for the purpose in hand (that may be, for example, a worry about whether I will survive changes I undergo, or whether this book will last through a series of borrowings from the library). Without a proper notion of *what it is* that persists, we are no

---

[4] Cf. Owen, "*Tithenai ta phainomena*"; Barnes, "Aristotle and the Methods of Ethics"; Irwin, *Aristotle's First Principles*; Nussbaum, "Saving Aristotle's Appearances."

[5] Compare Aristotle's insistence on the relativity of matter, *Phys.* 191a8ff., 194b9.

[6] An individual particular is "this something," τόδε τι; cf. Aristotle, *Met.* 1028a27.

better off than we were with the early physicists. So the difficulty about change is at its most urgent for individual particulars; and it demands that we account for both persistence (identity over time) and individual identity (this particular thing is what persists).

Aristotle, suggesting that individual particulars underlie particular change, makes assumptions similar to those of the early physicists; but different in one vital respect. For Aristotle, what persists is, in the primary cases, something *of a particular kind* (a book, a person, a horseshoe crab). This then allows him to claim, first of all, that individual particulars endure relatively as such, they *persist relatively* to particular changes. Second, he argues that individual particulars are *basic*. Third, he supposes that they are *countable* (more readily countable than anything else). These three claims are all supported by the view that individual particulars can be sorted into kinds (especially natural kinds). Thus, Aristotle thinks that he can determine the identity of individual particulars, and their importance. And we may find ourselves agreeing with him.

3. THE GRAMMATICAL PREJUDICE

Why are individual particulars *basic*? Let us suppose—for argument's sake if nothing else—that the world out there is real. That, after all, is common sense enough; what we see is what we get. But then what we do see is multiform. As we look out on the world, there are different patches of this and that, some moving, some staying still, some like each other, some sharply distinct. How can we arrange what we see so as to begin the attempt to understand it? For arrange it we do, whether we are philosophers or not. Imagine, for example, drawing a map of the world you inhabit. How would you go about that? Would it be a map that reflected the spatiotemporal coordinates of the land-masses? Or a map that showed the populations of animals? Or a map that marked out important events? And would your map try to reflect some kind of universal standard of importance—containing only events, for example, that would be significant in world history? Or would it be thoroughly subjective, describing what happened to you, or displaying the animals you find attractive or absurd? Whatever the shape of the map, it will have principles of arrangement and selection. In particular, it will show what you think to be basic in the arrangement of the world (spatiotemporal coordinates, events, or living creatures). How may we decide what is basic?[7]

A short argument in Aristotle's *Categories* (1a16 ff.) offers one way of doing the trick. Aristotle points out, first of all, that language involves us in combining words together: "man runs," "pig rootles." And it appears obvious that these combinations are reflections of the way the world works. There is, therefore, regular correspondence between words and the world—the struc-

---

[7] Cf. Strawson, *Individuals*, p.31ff.

ture of our grammar tends, on Aristotle's view, to mirror the structure of the world.[8] This assumption I shall call the *grammatical prejudice*—the prejudice that our talk systematically and unconsciously reflects the world we inhabit, perhaps because the talk is the result of, directly caused by, the structure of the world.

But that assumption should allow us to divide the world up in just the same way as language describes it; language provides direct evidence for the way things are actually arranged. Take some simple sentences:

Socrates is bald.
This armadillo is lumpy.

Aristotle supposes that these sentences represent an asymmetrical structure: the predicate depends on, or is posterior to, the subject. The expression "is bald" is meaningless without the name "Socrates" that it qualifies; so, Aristotle says, "Socrates" is not said of "bald," but the other way around.[9] When we think about the world, therefore, this means that the bald is "in" Socrates, not Socrates "in" the bald; the lumpy belongs to the armadillo, not the armadillo to the lumps. So the world is composed of individual particulars that underlie their properties (Socrates underlies baldness), rather than consisting in more or less continuous stretches of property (Socrates is not just this piece of baldness plus another piece of fatness and another of cleverness).[10]

Is it reasonable to suppose that the world is divided up into objects and properties? Is Aristotle right to suggest that somehow objects are basic and their properties parasitic on them? And is he right to take those objects to be individual particulars like Socrates or this armadillo? The argument from common sense, perhaps, tells us that he is. Reflect, for example, on Socrates' life history. His baldness came upon him in late middle age, we may suppose; Socrates was there all along, but the baldness was a relative parvenu. When Socrates becomes bald, bald Socrates is not a completely new entity, replacing hairy Socrates; rather, Socrates the individual underlies, makes continuous, and makes sensible the replacement of the hairy property by the bald one.[11] The argument of the physicists, therefore, supports the argument from grammar—and tells us that objects are indeed basic.

Aristotle could, perhaps, mount three arguments to show that individual particulars are basic: the first is a linguistic argument, the second a physical one, the third metaphysical. The names of individuals, first, are the proper subjects of sentences; and they represent what underlies change. On this foundation Aristotle builds the theory of categories, which systematizes the contrast between substances and the attributes or affections of substance

---

[8] Cf. Aristotle, *Categories, De Interpretatione* passim, *Met.* 1005b19ff.

[9] Cf. M. Frede, "Individuals"; Hartman, *Substance, Body and Soul*, p. 19; and Aristotle, *An.Po.* 83a4ff.

[10] By "property" here, I mean just those features of a things classified in the categories other than substance; this argument does not apply to essential properties, or to the differentiae of species; see Aristotle, *Cat.* 5.; consider here Owen, "Inherence."

[11] Despite Matthews on "kooky objects," in "Accidental Unities."

(quality, quantity, place, etc.). And thus, second, he claims that individual particulars (substances) in the sublunary world are separable from their properties.[12] This, as I suggested, is a claim that can only be substantiated relatively. Individual substances underlie change—changes in their accidents and not in those features that constitute their essence. This gives us an understanding of the individual particular not, of course, as property-free, but as what is prior to property change and thus to accidents. The individual, in this way, is just what has the accidental features liable to change. Third, when we try to understand the world, we need to grasp its metaphysical arrangement. If we can only define some things in terms of others, then definables must be systematically arranged. Once again, the world is organized hierarchically, in terms of priority of definition; and here the definitions of natural substances come first (*Met.* 1003a33ff., 1034b20ff.).

This, then, gives Aristotle an answer to the Heraclitean complaint that if there is a new sun every day, perhaps there is a new Socrates as well. If properties are parasitic on their objects, the objects must be securely identifiable; they must persist as those objects over time. Once we can determine what something is, it is as such that its persistence is recognized and identifiable. In that case, if we can determine what something is at a time, we can decide whether it persists as such over time.

4. COUNTING THE WORLD, SORTING THE WORLD

Suppose that I am choosing a string quartet to play in an international competition and I have already chosen three players. What shall I do next? Choose one more. Now one of the problems of individuation is what makes the last member of my quartet just one member. After all, at this stage I will be disqualified from the competition if I mistakenly choose two more, since I need exactly four players. So I need to know how to get hold of just one individual player. Each player, after all, counts for one, none for more than one. My problems do not end there, however. I do not want just any old player, I want to make sure I get Gertrude, the violinist who played so well last week. So I need to know that she is still available, is still extant, is still alive, and has not been replaced, for example, in the same shell by some robot incompetent at fiddling. I need to know, then, that this violinist is the same violinist as that violinist. What is more, I must make sure not to commit myself mistakenly to Bertram (Gertrude's twin brother), who is quite hopeless at playing the violin (much better at percussion, which is inappropriate). I must make sure to hang on to the difference between this person and that person.

First we must be able to count: "Being one is the basis of being any number, for the first measure is the beginning; for the basic item through which we

---

[12] See Fine, "Separation"; Morrison "Separation"; and below, my ch. 3, sec. 5. For Aristotle's account of separation, see the description of mathematical abstraction, *Phys.* 193b33, and Lear, *Aristotle, The Desire to Understand*, ch. 6.

recognise some genus is the measure of that genus; so what is one is the beginning of what is known in each case. But what is one is not the same in each genus—in one case it is the interval, in another the vowel or the consonant, in another it is a weight and in another a measure of motion. But in every case what is one is indivisible either in quantity or in form" (*Met.* 1016b17–24).

To be one is: "most of all to be the first measure of each genus and especially of quantity, from which the other senses arise. For a measure is that by virtue of which a quantity is recognised" (*Met.* 1052b18).

What does Aristotle mean? Suppose I try to count a collection of things. In order to start I need some kind of "measure," some way of determining what is the unit for my count. So to count apples, I need an apple as a unit; to count armadillos, I need an armadillo as a unit. Then, and only then, can I say "one armadillo, two armadillos." So what happens when I count apples? To do so, I must first of all know what it is that I am counting (apples, not pips or segments of apple); and, second, I must identify the unit so described. I must be able to say what an apple is, if apples are to be counted; and I must recognize an apple (not muddle it with an armadillo) when I see it.[13] To establish the relevant unit, therefore, I need a sortal term as my measure. But for Aristotle, sortal terms correspond in the primary sense to natural kinds. So, if we believe Aristotle, the appropriate unit of measure is determined by the form or the essence of what is measured. Form explains the unit of measurement.

The practice of counting, then, brings together the question of formal unity (What is an apple?) and numerical unity (Which is the first apple?). This, then, involves both knowledge and perception; and allows me to differentiate between counting apples (there are ten in my basket) and armadillos (two in the corner). The question How many? is incomplete. I must ask How many apples? How many armadillos? or even How many monads? (*Met.* 1053a27ff.) for any answer to be sensible at all. But counting is of actual objects in the actual world. So the unit of counting is an object, an individual particular differentiated from others by its matter, rendered self-identical and whole by its form, and countable because it is one member of some kind. If I want to count sheep, I count them one by one; if I want to count universes, I still count them one by one; and the same goes for ideas, for grand schemes, for microbes, and for manholes.

5. Units and Unities

For something to be individual is for it to be one and only one; that is, individuals are both *units* and *unities*.[14] For in order for the single apple to be a unit for counting, it needs to have coherence and unity. That is, before I even

---

[13] Cf. *Met.* 1053a31ff.

[14] E.g., at Aristotle, *Cat.* 1b6; *Met.* 1034a8, 1038a16, 1041a18, 1043b35; cf. Owen, "Inherence," and Frede, "Individuals."

start counting, I must have some sensible idea of the unity of my measure. What is it for something thus to be a unity?

Unity, on reflection, may be a relative matter:

> Of the things which are said to be one in themselves, some are so called by virtue of being continuous, e.g. a bundle by tying and wood by glue; indeed a line, even if it is bent, is said to be one so long as it is continuous, and the same is true of each part (of the body), e.g. a leg or an arm. . . . "Continuous" describes what has motion that is essentially one and cannot be otherwise; and motion is one when it is indivisible—that is, indivisible in time. . . . Then in another way something is said to be one by virtue of the underlying substrate (whether ultimate or proximate) being indistinguishable in form. Something is indistinguishable when the form is indivisible in perception; thus wine or water is said to be one insofar as it is indivisible in form. Then things are called one whose account, which states the essence (the what it is to be something) is indivisible to someone indicating the thing to someone else (although every account is divisible in itself). For thus what grows and diminishes is one because its account is one. . . . In general, when the thought of something's essence is indivisible and cannot be separated either in time or in place or in account, such things are most of all one; and especially if they are substances. (*Met.* 1015b36–16b3)

If Aristotle is right, there are many different ways of being one, when we understand that in terms of something's being indivisible. Consider three cases he gives here: (1) unity by continuity, (2) unity of stuff, and (3) unity of form.

1. We might claim that something is indivisible because it is stuck together—as we can see from the fact that it moves all at once. For example, a bundle of sticks is one because it is tied together; a heap of matches can be glued together into a single lump of wood. This is one car, because it moves as a single object, even though it has various unnecessary attachments, such as a piece of string trailing behind. So long as it all moves at once, the car is one object, distinct from the bus from which it extricates itself as it reverses.

But the car's unity is not very strong just because it seems easily divisible. The string may fall off, or the hubcap roll away, and thus the "glued together" unity starts to disintegrate. If "moving all at once" is the principle of unity, it includes unnecessary attachments as well as accidental properties (the vivid purple of the car, the smelly exhaust of the bus); but there is nothing (except the glue or the rivets) that explains just why this object is a unity. Consider a bundle of sticks. Is it one bundle now, and then not a bundle at all when I extricate one of the sticks from the string that ties it together? What—we might well ask—makes this bundle now the same as (or different from) the bundle I hoisted before? Is glue, or string, enough to explain the identity of the bundle? And without understanding its identity, can I possibly understand what constitutes its unity?

2. Suppose, then, that objects that are merely glued together have an uncertain claim to be unities. Instead, we might insist on replacing the principle "moves all at once" with some better account of how this unit is internally

coherent. Now we might say (reverting to the early physicists again) that things may be one where they are simple in their underlying stuff. They should be, perhaps, homoiomerous. Water is one, because it is all the same stuff, its bits are homogeneous. Ask for water, and some water is what you get, not a part of some depleted whole. And this water is one if it all moves around together, that blancmange is one when it falls to the floor all in a single lump. Homoiomerous unities are one by continuity, as bundles are, but they have a better claim to be one (cf. *Met.* 1052a19ff.) because the stuff is the same, as well as the motion being continous (this is blancmange through and through).

But that criterion for unity is uncomfortable for two obvious reasons. If we are interested in unity because we want to arrange the world and the particulars in it, the insistence that unity is stuff is a depressing one. If the world coheres just because it is homoiomerous, then the objects of the world whose parts are dissimilar become (as the early physicists suggested) mere appearances in what underlies. But that account fails to take into account our interest in individual particulars that are, typically, coherent wholes, moving all at once but different in their parts, and held together by more than glue.

3. Think first of all about sameness. An antelope and an anteater are the same because they are both animals. Of course they are not the same animal, nor yet the same object. But if we are thinking about "animal" (cf. *Met.* 1052a30), then we will assimilate antelopes and anteaters, gnus and gorillas, hippos and humans. They have, that is, a kind of conceptual unity. How exactly? Consider these sentences: This antelope is an animal; That anteater is an animal. The genus allows us to sort these creatures, to say what they are, to show that they are one something or other; namely, one animal ("horse, man, dog are one something," 1016a27). But this is a weak case. The proper kind of conceptual unity is where the form (species, not genus) is the same. One "in form [is] that which is indivisible in knowledge and understanding; so that the principle of being one for substances would be primarily one" (1052a32). So when I tell you about this antelope, it has unity just because I can say "This is an antelope," and tell you exactly what it is, give you its essence, explain to you what it is *one of.* These natural items are one in the primary sense (1016b3).

Aristotle has several points to make, then, in answer to the question, What is it to be a unity? First of all, he exploits an intuition that unity is indivisible or *irreducible.* Second, he suggests that the unity of the species, tied as it is to the definition, is *definite.* Third, and consequently, specific unity is *essential,* not accidental.

How does this help with our original problems about individual particulars? Recall that to satisfy our anxieties about what there is really, individual particulars were to be persistent, basic, and countable. If unity is best explained by essence, do we have the individual particulars we want? Suppose I wish to find the last member of a set of eight Hepplewhite chairs. I need to know that the chair I buy at last is just one chair—the chair that matches the set (the same chair that was a member of the original set)—and not some other, apparently Hepplewhite but in fact a Victorian fake. And here further complications set in. I need to be sure, for example, that what I buy under the description "chair" is in fact a chair, not a bundle of sticks (a kit, perhaps, for making fake Hepplewhite chairs). And I need to be sure that this "chair" is not just a few cubits of wood (the stuff from which might be made a Sheraton commode). So my count of chairs is determined by what it is to be such a chair, and the unity of each chair is also determined by what it is to be such a chair—that makes sure that the chair is one and a coherent whole; and it gives us guidelines for working out whether it persists. In this account, then, of individuation, the central notion is essence or form; once we have grasped that, we can answer the questions about the world before us in a systematic way.

Recall the contrast between objects that are unified by being stuck together and those that are unified by form. Any particular could come under either classification, depending on how we think about it. Take this bunch of flowers—here we have rosemary and rue, eglantine and columbine, all tied together with string. This has the contingent unity of something haphazardly assembled, held together by a piece of string; when I wave one bit of the bunch around, the rest follows—it moves all at once. So it is one by continuity, just because it is tied together. But we might think of this, instead, *as* a bunch; under that description, it is individuated by what it is to be a bunch, and it is one because it is a bunch by virtue of its form (being a bunch), not by virtue of moving around in one piece. Contrast, then, the particular as an accidental unity, whose unity is explained by continuity, from the particular as an essential unity, whose unity is its form. Particulars are one accidentally, when they move all at once (accidents and all); but they are one essentially when they are considered just in terms of their formal or specific unity. So this armadillo (plus its warts, its snuffles, and its indigestion) is accidentally one because it ambles all together; but it is essentially one because it is an armadillo—its warts and its snuffles are irrelevant to its specific unity. And its essential unity is governed not by the criterion of "moving all at once," but by the criterion of "being an organic whole." Thus the essence of the particular both explains it and marks it off from parts of wholes and masses of stuff (*Met.* 1040b5ff.). So essential unity is fundamentally and primarily the unity of natural kinds (1041b29). In that case, of course, the analysis of unity coheres exactly with the analysis of substance: thus "being" and "being one" complement each other in the hierarchical account of what there is (1040b16ff.; 1045b3).

So unity, like being, is parasitic on essence: "being" is "being something or other," and "being one" is "being one something or other." It follows that "one is said in as many ways as being" (*Met.* 1030b10): Aristotle concludes that being and unity are transcendental predicates that apply across the categories and are modified by the categories.

Aristotle's predecessors, he complains, thought that unity was itself a substance (*Met.* 1053b11ff.), or else a simple property of substance. In just the same way, "being" was treated as something separate, apart from the many (1053b19), and "good" as a simple property of the objects in the world (*E.N.*

1096a11ff.). "One," "being," and "good," that is, were thought to correspond to real features of the real world, in themselves and unqualifiedly. Aristotle disputes this view. Instead, he argues, "being," "one," and "good" may only be understood when they are modified by some other term ("being an armadillo," "being one armadillo," "being a good armadillo")—especially in the category of substance, but subordinately across all categories. So unity per se is neither a substance nor a property. Unity, like being, qualifies substances and properties. This is a two-way relation. On the one hand, nothing is "just one," something is always one something or other—its unity and its being are parasitic on some feature of itself, essential or accidental. But on the other hand, for something to have a feature is for it to be something (or other) and primarily for it to be one something (or other). So the essence and the accidents of things must be, and primarily be, one: essences and accidents are thus parasitic on being and unity.

Thus, just as "being" is "being something or other," or "being good" is "being a good something or other," so "being one" is "being one something or other." If that is so, then to look for what is just one is misguided, since "being one" is always qualified by some further term. But in that case, we can readily see not only how unity is related to being, but why it is that Aristotle insists on the primacy of substance in the explanation of unity (*Met.* 1006b26). If "being one" is a predicate whose behavior mirrors that of "being," then not only will unity be distributed across the categories, but it will also[15] be focused upon the primary category, the category of substance (*Met.* 1003b1ff.). For the substance of something is *what it is*, and what it is is primarily what it is essentially, or necessarily, or by nature. On that account, the primary sense of being will reflect the essences of natural substances; and being one can be explained in terms of form and what it is to be something or other.

6. THE PROBLEMS OF INDIVIDUATION

If our world is founded on something basic, we need an account of what it is to be basic. Aristotle, I have suggested, rejects the physicists' answer (what is basic is some kind of stuff) in favor of the immediate and evident world before us. We, I think, do the same. As I run to catch the bus, I am not worrying about whether I shall reach one collection of molecules before another collection of molecules does; instead, I am anxious to get to the bus stop before the bus does. Our everyday encounters are not dominated by science but by common sense, and for that we tend to suppose that middle-sized individual particular objects are the basic pieces of furniture in the world. What is more, we adopt Aristotelian principles for counting and attributing unity; that is, for deciding

[15] At least according to the mature doctrine of Aristotle's *Metaphysics*; cf. Owen, "Logic and Metaphysics."

what counts as an individual. For we count, as he did, by sorting—buses, armadillos, and bald philosophers. And we sort by thinking not so much about simplicity or homoiomereity, but about principles that determine what makes a coherent whole. Like Aristotle, we tend to be essentialists when we answer questions about individuation:

1. What makes this one thing—not a bit of something? Here we have Quine's rabbit scuttling across a clearing. Why is it one rabbit, not merely a part of the rustic retreat? Why is it one rabbit, not merely two ears (and perhaps some legs)? Why is it a rabbit, and not just a collection of molecules? These questions inquire into its *internal unity*.

2. What makes this one thing distinct from whatever is next door to it? If two warthogs drink side by side at the water hole, why do they not coalesce into one? After all, some water, side by side with some more water, just becomes more water. These, we might say, are questions of something's being one among many, of its being a *unity within a context*.

3. What makes this a thing rather than, maybe, a property, or some stuff, or whatever is marked off by some spatiotemporal coordinates? Why does it matter to say that this is an armadillo and not merely some hardness of hide, or some armadillo-ish stuff, or whatever appears here now? These are questions about our principles for *being basic*.

4. What makes this thing now the same thing next week? How do I know that this racehorse is the same one as the racehorse that won yesterday? This is a question of *identity over time*.

How well can we answer these questions by looking to sortal terms, or to form, or to essence? Well enough, we may reply. This is (1) a whole rabbit; (2) one warthog rather than another; (3) an armadillo before it acquired the scars on its flank; (4) the same racehorse as the racehorse that won the Derby. Each answer relies on a sortal term (rabbit, warthog, armadillo, and race-horse). Nonetheless, there are at least two features that may be thought to be controversial.

First, is it right to claim that individuation or unity turns up just when (or most of all when) an individual is sorted as a natural kind? Chronologically, on Aristotle's view, unity and being something or other will turn up simultaneously; but from the point of view of understanding, unity is parasitic on substance, the membership of a natural kind. So we do not grasp items as *just one* before we grasp what they are *one of*. Is that correct?

Second, therefore, this account of individuation supposes that essentialism (and the Aristotelian theory of the categories) is a sensible account of the structure of the world. Is it? In the Platonic material, we may find several different attempts to explain individuation that may be thought to rival, and also to explain the origins of, the Aristotelian view.

The "problems of individuation" may be formulated as a difficulty about the individual items themselves, or about how we identify them. In fact, however, the problems of individuation pull apart into two separate issues. One asks what counts as an entity. The other asks what unifies an entity. So individuation concerns "being" and "being one." But these two notions are connected because we tend to suppose that entities are basic (more basic, perhaps, than properties), and that being basic involves being one (since pluralities are built upon units). So "individuals" may be understood to be basic entities; somethings; units; things that are one. Three pivotal terms are in play when we individuate: "one," "same," and "different." These terms, however, are not enough to distinguish individuals (violinists or chairs) from bundles (of nerves and sinews, or of sticks) or from stuffs (expanses of flesh, some wood). The underlying question, rather, is *what makes an individual a something*, rather than some somethings (a bundle) or some stuff.

Aristotle sees the key to individuation in specifying the "something"—for sorts individuate. Plato, I shall argue, is more interested in "one": he supposes that any one will be a something, and any something a one. In doing so, as I shall argue, Plato offers a radical alternative to the Aristotelian view.

7. Reading Plato

The interpretation of Plato's developing metaphysics I offer is not an orthodox one. You might object that it sits ill with the Platonic doctrines that others find in the dialogues (in particular, I suppose, with the view that Plato was first and foremost interested in the theory of forms). But the discovery of Platonic doctrines is a matter of interpretation; after all, what we actually find in the dialogues are not doctrines, but arguments, counterarguments, and puzzles. Many of the arguments are inconclusive or come under attack from another argument. Many of the puzzles remain unsolved. Many of the dialogues end in the impasse of aporia. How, amid all this, are we to determine "what Plato meant"? How are we to discern the doctrines hidden beneath the rampant uncertainty?

Three rough strategies are available to us. We may suppose that Plato's puzzles cover deep-lying certainty; or less well-hidden doubt; or something in between. Both the doctrinaire Plato and Plato the skeptic must, however, be interpreted from the dialogues—since the dialogues actually contain arguments—multifarious, multiform, some good, some bad, spoken by all sorts of characters, some virtuous, some vicious. Generally the arguments fail to provide us with a decisive conclusion.[16] How then do we interpret them?

The best arguments, you might be tempted to say, are deductive. They start from true premises, and proceed by valid inference to true conclusions; they are demonstrative. That kind of argument is a good thing for someone who wants to prove something directly. Then they succeed if the premises turn out to be indeed true, and the inferences indeed valid—for then they may be taken to have proved their conclusion. What this actually means, we might suppose,

---

[16] See, for example, the articles collected in Gill and McCabe.

is that this conclusion has been shown to fit in with all the other assumptions we have; and that it is thus consistent with everything else we believe.

Deductive arguments fail, however, when, despite the deduction, we do not believe their conclusion, which seems untenable or unbearable. For example, an argument to show the unreality of the external world might proceed with impeccable reasoning, from true premises, to a conclusion that we cannot tolerate. Here the argument might be thought to have failed psychologically or aesthetically, or even morally. We just do not like it, you might say. But then the philosopher's response to that sort of unease must be to argue back (it is always open to the antiphilosopher to close the book, or walk away from what disturbs him). He might reason thus: "The fact that I dislike this conclusion shows that it somehow conflicts with other, deeply held principles I hold; so now I must uncover those principles and bring them to bear on this argument. Then I might be able to show that the argument fails either because the premises, initially so plausible, are in fact false, or because the inferences, apparently valid, are in fact wrong." Thus philosophers vindicate their gut aversions (thank goodness, the world might turn out real after all).

Matters may be rather different when the argument seems deliberately to provoke the gut aversion: here we have *reductiones ad absurdum*, paradoxes and antinomy. A *reductio ad absurdum*, for example, works from premises that are believed to be true, through an apparently valid deduction, to an absurd conclusion. This will work best in a dialectical context: someone puts up a thesis, but the opponent argues that this thesis generates an absurd conclusion. So long as the inferences are valid, this strategy forces the exponent of the original thesis to rethink his premises, and thereafter to deny one or more of them—the opponent hopes that he will deny the thesis. Arguments like this are indirect.

Indirect arguments, however, run up against a difficulty. Any argument starts not from a single premise (even if a single premise is all that is stated) but from a collection of premises, some tacit or inexplicit. Suppose that Gabbitas advances the thesis that determinism is true. This might be something he holds along with the assumption that the external world is real, that it is accessible to reason, populated by persons, and so forth. If Thring shows against Gabbitas that his thesis generates an absurdity (suppose Thring could validly infer from this premise set that "determinism is true" is unstateable), he has cast doubt not on the claim that determinism is true, but rather on the collection of assumptions that Gabbitas holds. The absurdity only goes to show that Gabbitas's premise set is inconsistent, and does not point to which of the set should be rejected. Gabbitas's response to absurdity may be to reject the whole premise set (this might turn the determinist into a skeptic); or, more moderately, to abandon one of the least secure assumptions (which may or may not be the original thesis—the determinist might choose to abandon the claim that the world is susceptible to reason, not the claim that determinism is true). But which option he chooses is up to Gabbitas. For arguments like this are, in their classic cases, dialectical.

Dialectical arguments, then, have an importantly personal dimension. In a true dialectical context, the realignment of the premise set after a reductio is a matter for the person who holds that set of beliefs. Thring cannot make the decision about which of Gabbitas's assumptions Gabbitas should give up—only Gabbitas can do that. Now often we find philosophers arguing with themselves: so Prudence may advance a thesis to herself, and argue against it by reductio; but still it is Prudence who must work out which of her original beliefs should go in response to her argument with herself—the response may be a matter of decision, not straightforward inference. The classic example of this is the Socratic elenchus: there, Socrates declines to put forward any positive thesis, but insists that his interlocutor "say what he believes." The progress of the argument then depends on which assumptions the interlocutor finds impossible to abandon, and which he readily forgoes. Arguments like this, therefore, take place between two opposing views—and they presuppose, therefore, two complex theoretical positions lined up against each other (two sets of beliefs). This will be true, even if only represented as real, in philosophical fiction like Plato's no less than it is true and really real in the live battle between two members at a meeting of the Aristotelian Society.

Plato wrote dialogues in which one character is exposed to the questioning of another; he wrote fictional dialectic. But he also wrote real dialectic. Although Socrates is only a representation of what is real and the Eleatic Stranger is a fiction, Plato himself is real and so is his reader (so am I, and so are you as you read this). He plays upon the reader's self-conscious responses with all sorts of devices, such as irony and disavowal,[17] which activate our awareness both that the encounter between Socrates and his interlocutor is fiction and that the encounter between Plato and his reader is real. But then, what is going on is a dialectical encounter between Plato and his reader wherein we are examined for the consistency of our beliefs and assumptions. If that is what is happening when we read a Platonic dialogue, we are not, I suggest, justified in taking any indirect argument as the vehicle for Platonic dogma, or as camouflage for a grand metaphysical design. Any inferences about what Plato "really" thought must rest on the interaction between different arguments.

Plato uses indirect argument a great deal; it is, after all, not controversial to say that the historical Socrates argued in such a way, and that at times Plato's Socrates followed him. I shall argue further that many of Plato's arguments beyond the immediately Socratic are indirect or paradoxical. We cannot simply say that what these arguments do is hide some grand design, for the reasons I have mentioned; nor, except as a last resort, should we see them as skeptical: they are not so decisive. Instead, we might take the points they make seriously. Plato's arguments, therefore, can be read immediately as they stand, for or against the position they claim to investigate. Sometimes a villainous assumption is unmasked; sometimes we can only conclude that there is some

---

[17] Cf. here Vlastos, *Socrates*, chs. 1 and 4; Mackenzie, "Paradox."

mischief, somewhere; and sometimes there is real progress toward understanding what has been hitherto unclear. Whatever their effect, Plato's arguments all represent his, and our, painful progress toward understanding—progress we make just because, by their indirect character, Plato's arguments demand interpretation. This is the virtue of the dialogue form.

This has two consequences. First of all, as I have said, indirect arguments often show a set of premises to be inconsistent although they do not directly prove anything. That does not make them indeterminate; instead, they may uncover a belief set where one premise is more suspect than any other (as antecedent arguments may show), or where one premise is expressly hypothetical. But here a grander, second consequence of such a strategy becomes apparent. If indirect or dialectical arguments are to be effective, they must be both structured (interrelated) and systematic, in order to investigate the possibilities thoroughly. The end (or the interim conclusion) of such structured arguments may turn out to be a positive claim about something in particular; or it may, instead, offer some reflection on how we should go about thinking about some type of problem. In either case, the understanding we reach will be deep and complex just because the arguments call into question the whole structure of our thought. This consequence, I contend, was Plato's objective.

PART ONE

Preliminary: Plato's Middle Period Metaphysics

Particulars

WHAT DOES PLATO think there is? And what does Plato think—if indeed he thinks of it at all—of the problem of basic unities? Famously, Plato's account of what there is contrasts the particulars of the physical world and the forms. This contrast can be characterized (I shall argue in this chapter and its sequel) as a contrast between two sorts of individuals. Particulars, on the one hand, which are individuals of the common or garden kind, are complex and composite pluralities with a dubious claim to unity. They are "one under many."[1] Forms, on the other hand, are individuals, too, but they are individuals of a peculiar kind—utterly simple entities that are unities as such. They are "one over many." As we shall see, this contrast between two sorts of individuals is an extreme one—and one that raises difficulties for Plato's account of what there is.

Begin with the Aristotelian starting point—the world out there. Plato is notorious for his distrust of the physical, sensible world.[2] Why? Perhaps there is something wrong with our access to the physical world—maybe the problem is that the world is sensible, and sensation is fallible or otherwise flawed. Or perhaps there is something wrong with the world in itself; it is, for example, a mere appearance, or an illusion, not real and therefore not a proper subject for reflection. Plato's complaint may be an epistemological one, or an ontological one, or perhaps even both. In what follows I shall argue that Plato does not deny the reality of the sensible world but claims, instead, that it is epistemologically suspect just because it is not self-explanatory. But his account of the reality of the sensible world contains, I shall suggest, three features that will cause trouble:

1. Any feature of a sensible particular—whether a sensible property, a relation, or a value—is treated as a real, natural property of it (the thesis of *natural inherence*).

2. Some properties, notably relations and values, always occur in an individual particular along with their opposites (the thesis of the *compresence of opposites*).

3. As a consequence of (1) and (2), sensible particulars turn out to be thoroughly complex—and this complexity is later developed into an impossible condition for individuals.

---

[1] I owe this expression to Nick Denyer.
[2] This view of Plato can be documented from Aristotle onward: cf., e.g., *Met.* 987a33.

1. Socratic Definitions

Socrates began it all with his search for definitions (cf. Aristotle *Met.* 987b1, 1078b28). Definitions in ethics, not "nature," were the objects of Socrates' inquiry;[3] and if Plato is to be believed, Socrates never found any. Why not? Some have argued[4] that he could not find any definitions because he had no means of access to them, since he was so rude about the examples that the definitions might cover. Thus, perhaps, Plato portrays him in the *Theaetetus.* Theaetetus is attempting to define knowledge, and he offers some examples of knowledge (geometry and cobbling); but Socrates complains: "What noble largesse! When I asked you for one thing you have given me many; when I asked you for something simple, you gave me what is complex" (*Tht.* 146d4). In the *Theaetetus* this develops into a careful examination of what a definition should be like—or, more negatively, what it should not be. Especially,

1. it should not be circular or regressive—repeating the definiendum in the definition, but it should explain the definienda; and so

2. it should not merely be a list of the definienda—for that merely repeats, and fails to explain at all.

From none of this does it follow directly that definition is impossible.[5] But definitions might be a casualty of the claim that examples (any definienda) are so pernicious that we cannot really talk about them at all. Is Socrates' complaint that the examples are impossible to give? No—Socrates is looking for explanations, and he rejects examples *as explanations*. But the examples, nonetheless, are what he wants to explain: the definitions cover the definienda, rather than thrusting them out of reality altogether. Socrates' enterprise, as the *Theaetetus* gives it to us, is not based on the assumption that the everyday world is an illusion, but rather on the contrary assumption: that the everyday world is very much there, and needs to be brought under rational scrutiny.

So Socrates is not committed to the unreality of the external world (nor to its being in total flux either, or definition would be impossible anyway; *Tht.* 181c ff.); but he is worried that it is not self-explanatory. Examples are "many

---

[3] I disagree with Vlastos's extreme interpretation of Socrates' lack of interest in "the whole of nature," *Socrates*, ch.2. Although he was clearly not a physicist in the ancient sense, he was, I think, interested in epistemology and metaphysics, if only because his ethics are thoroughly intellectualist. Cf. Mackenzie, "Ignorance."

[4] See Geach, "Plato's *Euthyphro*." Geach argues for the "Socratic Fallacy": (1) examples are *no way* to answer the request for a definition; (2) because we cannot know which are the examples until we have the definition. This, Geach argues, lands Socrates in skepticism: (3) failing examples, we have no way of getting at the definition at all; so definition is impossible.

[5] See Burnyeat, "Examples," for an excellent rebuttal of Geach's complaint: while examples will not do the work of definitions, they can be adduced *as examples* while we are progressing toward the definition.

and complex" where the explanation should be "one and simple." Consider some earlier Socratic encounters.[6]

In the *Euthyphro*, Socrates tries to find out what piety is from Euthyphro, who claims to know. But when Socrates asks "What is the holy?" Euthyphro smugly replies: "What I am doing now." Socrates complains that Euthyphro could have given him a lot of examples like that (a complex of examples; *Euth.* 6c1ff.), but that none of the examples answers the question. Socrates is looking for "the one thing which explains why all these examples are examples of the holy"—they are examples, right enough, but not explanatory, because the examples, collectively, are many not one.

Why, nonetheless, should a series of examples not be explained by one of them? We might want to say that any collection of like things is made coherent by the paradigm case: so all the meters are members of the same set (the meter) because there is a standard meter that provides us with a central case to explain all the others (even if they should deviate just a little). But Socrates repeats his complaint in the *Meno*, when he tries to give an exemplary definition, of shape (74b ff). Suppose in answer to "What is shape?" we were to answer "circularity"; we should not then have explained *what is shape*, but only given *a* shape, since there are other shapes than circularity. And this objection seems to hold even if "circle" is indeed a paradigm case of a shape. For even when we cite a paradigm,

> We always arrive at many; but don't do that to me. Instead, since you call all of these many things by a single name, "shape," and since you say that there is none of them that is not a shape, even although they are opposite to each other, tell me what is this thing which includes the circular as well as the straight, which you call "shape," and say is no less a circular shape than a straight one. . . . For when you say that, you don't mean that the circular is no less circular than straight, nor the straight no less straight than circular. (*Meno* 74d–e)[7]

What Socrates is after is not an example, but an answer to "what is the same over all cases"; he is looking for the "one over many." But cases of shapes will not do—for those cases do not apply universally to the set, or if they did they would generate a contradiction.[8]

On this account, the trouble with examples, even paradigm cases, is twofold. First of all, they are too thin: the paradigm case will fail to deal with the

---

[6] I make no apology for using the *Theaetetus* as some kind of evidence for what Socrates thought. It is clearly a self-conscious echo of Socratic procedures; and in this matter in particular it is reinforced by evidence from earlier dialogues. But this comparison should be used with care; cf. Burnyeat, "Socratic Midwifery."

[7] Socrates turns this trick, of course, by substituting "the circular," as the putative definition of "shape," for "shape" in expressions like "the circular shape."

[8] Socrates attacks Laches on the same front: if courage is "standing in the front line," what of courage in retreat? This example will not cover all cases; but that is just what a definition must do (*Laches* 191e).

complexity of a definiendum such as courage. Second, they do not look like *explanations* at all. If I offer a circle as a paradigm case of shape, then I cannot treat it as I should a definition (as Socrates' substitution experiment shows). Suppose, on the one hand, that I want to understand what circular shape is, my citing (or pointing to) the paradigm circle will get me no further forward with *understanding* (even although I may have before me a jolly good example). Worse still, if I use this paradigm to explain "straight," the explanation degenerates into incoherence. So the trouble with paradigms is not that they are not examples of the definiendum, but that they cannot explain it—the paradigm is itself in need of the explanation we seek.

This failure of examples to explain is exacerbated by a further feature of the examples themselves. Consider piety again. If (as Euthyphro subsequently suggests) the holy is what is loved by the gods, then anything that is holy is also unholy. For the gods (like anyone else) dispute about what they value— and as is the way of the gods, if one likes something, another hates it (what Hera loves, Aphrodite loathes). So if what is holy is defined as what is loved by the gods, then the definition will apply equally to what is holy and what is unholy, at the same time. And that will not do for definitions: definitions cannot be plural or complex in this way. Nonetheless, Socrates argues, it is a general feature of the examples of the things he is trying to define. Any case (of piety or of beauty or of courage) is in itself incurably many, never just one. The trouble with examples, on that view, is not just that they are one member of a plural set, one among many, but that each is itself many. So in the *Hippias Major*, he points to the way in which a beautiful girl is also ugly compared to a goddess, while the ugliest of monkeys is lovely too, when set side by side with a pipkin: "The wisest of men appears a monkey beside a god—both in wisdom and in beauty or anything else? Shall we agree, Hippias, that the most beautiful girl is ugly compared to the race of gods?" (*Hi. Ma.* 289b).[9]

Any example of a property (or at least of one of these evaluative properties) is no less an example of the opposite property. But then, no example is the "one over many" that will define and explain what we do not yet understand —the property itself.

Examples, then, will not do as definitions.[10] Socrates argues that they are

[9] I follow Burnet's text here, but see Woodruff, *Hippias Major*, p. 54. This point is made by the "other" Socrates, the offstage character of the *Hippias Major*; but the Heraclitean point he makes seems entirely consistent with what we may ascribe to Socrates (e.g., *Charmides* 161a–b; *Laches* 193d) and what Plato would say in, for example, the account of value in the *Symposium* or the *Republic*. See again Irwin, "Plato's Heracliteanism"; we need, as Irwin suggests, to rethink what Plato thought about Heraclitus. We should do well to rethink Heraclitus, too. Cf. Mackenzie, "Heraclitus."

[10] But the expression "example" is rather a confused one; at times Socrates speaks of particular examples (Helen, this grubby gorilla) and at times of types of example (the characteristic behavior of Scythians in battle, the circle). How far does his failure to distinguish between type and token vitiate his objection to examples in definition? Not at all. He has, to recapitulate, two objections to examples: (1) that they are too thin to function as definitions, and (2) that they are characterized by opposites. Both will be true of type and of token. 1. Neither an actual nor a general

the wrong sort of thing to produce in definition. This does not entail that they are not proper things themselves; nor does it enmesh us in Geach's difficulty—that we cannot grasp any examples before we have the definition, and so we cannot use examples on our way to understanding. We do have examples (token or type) that are indisputable examples—but they just are not definitions. Any of these examples is tricky not least because it is not only an example of what we are trying to define, but it is also an example of the opposite. This means that it cannot be "that by virtue of which all the F things are F"; it also means that there are no paradigm cases, since any case of F, on this argument, is also a case of not-F. But to say that no example is a paradigm case does not threaten the example's claim to be a genuine example; examples, for Socrates, are perfectly proper, so long as we do not confuse them with definitions.

2. NATURAL INHERENCE

Socrates just may not have been interested in the status of the physical world. Plato, however, held a wider brief and, if Aristotle is to be believed, was worried about the nature of "sensibles." Like Socrates, Plato has problems with our knowledge of the phenomenal world. The *Phaedo* offers a complex attack on the relation between the world and our understanding of it. Here Plato tries to show why reliance on perception limits our understanding of the world—and he insists that the problem is both epistemological and ontological. Not only is there a massive gulf between perception and understanding, but also the objects of perception themselves escape understanding because they are the objects they are. The arguments about what there is complement the arguments about how we understand what there is; Plato concludes that there is such a thing as proper understanding just if there are things that are properly understood.

These arguments, however, should be read in context. The *Phaedo* dramatizes Socrates' last hours before his sentence of death is carried out. It is hardly surprising, then, that Socrates' last arguments are consolations for dying. Death, it appears, has no sting because the soul is an immortal entity, and death merely relieves our souls of the burden of the body. So *my* death has no sting because *my* soul marches on afterwards; if it is not my soul that survives, of course, I shall not be consoled. The whole dialogue is designed to show how individual souls could be entities of the immortal sort, and individual as well—and Plato argues for this by pressing an analogy between souls and the

---

paradigm case will do to explain a virtue—neither Euthyphro's "what I am doing now" nor Laches' "standing firm in the battle line." 2. Any token, no more and no less than any type, will be characterized by opposites just if it is enmeshed in the relations and values of the phenomenal world (see below, sec. 3). This compresence of opposites does not render either type or token unreal or illusory; but it does render them bad explanations, on Socrates' view.

incomposite forms, which remain constant and eternal. This is the "affinity" argument, whose influence is felt throughout the dialogue.[11] So the consolation for dying rests on an ontological distinction between physical particulars and souls and forms. Souls are neither physical nor perishable, as bodies are. Instead, they are imperishable and nonphysical, like forms: the affinity argument takes the strain of the proofs of immortality. The downgrading of sensible particulars, therefore, is crucial to the success of the dialogue.

But what exactly is Plato's complaint about sensible particulars? Is it just that they change constantly?[12] Or that they are unreal, or illusory; or that they are the object of passing perception, not the rigors of reason; or that they are contradictory? As it turns out, he argues neither that they are unreal nor that they are in flux. Instead, his objection is that sensible particulars are cognitively unreliable; and this objection has its ontological counterpart in the claim that sensible particulars are *complex*—which is why they are perishable. Plato's account of their complexity is based on the claim that all their properties, even relational or evaluative ones, are *real* (this I shall call the thesis of *natural inherence*).

The affinity argument depends on a strict contrast between forms and sensible particulars: "Surely what has been put together and what is composite by nature is liable to be affected thus—namely to be divided just where it was put together; while if there is anything that is incomposite this, if anything, is liable to remain unaffected thus? . . . Therefore whatever is always (the same) in the same respects and likewise is most likely to be incomposite, whereas things that are one way at one time, another way at another, and are never (the same) in the same respects—these are composite?" (78c).

Focus first of all on the nature of the composite, susceptible, dissoluble objects—which turn out to be sensible particulars. The affinity argument argues from their composite nature to their liability to destruction. Plato is not arguing that because these objects change (or are in flux) and must ultimately be destroyed, so they must have changeless counterparts that will

[11] For example, in the last argument (*Phd.* 102b–106c) Socrates exploits the established difference between forms and particulars to show that while particulars, which are composite, may change and be affected, neither forms nor souls change or are affected since they are incomposite. This "cleverer" rerun of the affinity argument is supposed to show, again, that the soul's simple nature renders it imperishable and immortal.

[12] He was influenced, apparently, by the Heracliteans, who persuaded him that "all sensible things are always flowing and there is no knowledge of them" (*Met.* 987a33). How far was flux Plato's problem? See Irwin, "Heracliteanism," and also Nehamas, "Imperfection"; Bolton, "Plato's Distinction"; Kirwan, "Plato and Relativity"; Vlastos, "Degrees of Reality"; Jordan, *Arguments for Forms*; Fine, "One over Many"; and now M. Frede, "Being and Becoming." Frede offers a tempting interpretation of γίγνεσθαι as a Platonic term of art to mean "only temporarily to take on and display the character if an F without ever being an F," p. 48. I think, against Frede, that Plato's account of *becoming* shifts from the middle to the later dialogues. In the *Phaedo* and the *Republic*, it represents one of the ways in which opposites turn out to be compresent; in the *Theaetetus* and the *Timaeus*, it represents the way in which anything (in the phenomenal world) is only a *such*, never a *something*. Cf. below, ch. 2, sec. 3; ch. 5, sec. 4; ch. 6, sec. 5; and above, ch. 1, sec. 2, on Theseus's ship.

survive—that, indeed, would hardly be an argument at all. (He might just as well say: Everything we see changes; not everything can change; so there must be more than we can see. The second premise is wildly question-begging, and certainly not enough to protect us against the fear that in fact everything does perish in the end.) Instead, he argues that the fact that sensible particulars are composite must be the explanation of the fact that they change; further, from the composite nature of sensibles he argues that there are incomposite entities, which may thus be assumed not to change. This allows us to suppose that souls are imperishable.

What is it that makes physical objects composite, and why are they thus liable to be destroyed?

Imagine some physical object—a eucalyptus tree—and suppose that we accept the common-sense view that this eucalyptus tree is an object existing in the physical world. That is, the tree is there in the garden whether or not I or anyone else see it; it is *real*. And it has a life history of its own; it is independent of the various perceivers who may come across it at one time or another. Now that might be true because time and space are real, and this tree has a unique position in spatiotemporal coordinates; or it might be so because the tree is made of atoms, and those (perhaps unlike the secondary appearances)[13] are really what there is. But the common-sense position insists that what there really is is a tree (not just atoms, or merely coordinates); the tree is real. We see it; and it is just what we see (with some reservations about the mistakes we may make about it on seeing it). But it is not there because we see it; instead, we see it because it is there. It is independent.

By analogy, and still on common-sense assumptions,[14] we can say several things about its perceptible properties—it is glaucous, aromatic, bitter to the taste, smooth to the touch. We know that it is glaucous or aromatic because we see it and smell it—but it was *really* glaucous, etc., all along, before we ever encountered it.

What if I want to measure it? If I say that it has a particular size, it is fifteen feet tall, I have compared it, perhaps, to some real or notional (fifteen-foot) ruler, and claimed that it is the same size as that. So is its size a real property of it, just like its smell or its taste? Perhaps—but it is not so obviously a matter of direct perception when we say that it is taller than the berberis growing beside it, or smaller than the telegraph pole. To make such claims about its relations with other things, it seems we have to make more subtle judgments than the ones involved in such terms as "glaucous." After all, when we compare two items in size, the comparison itself seems to be something we do, rather than being some connecting thread (comparative size) stretching between the two items (what if we compare Etna with Everest?). So it is not at all obvious that the relations in which my eucalyptus tree stands to other things (taller than the berberis) are a feature of the eucalyptus tree considered in itself.

---

[13] As Democritus might claim, DK68B9.

[14] I set aside here, as not a matter of "common sense," theories such as a reductionist account of color; but on this, see Foster, *Immaterial Self*, p. 5ff.

Certainly, the tree has some size, but perhaps its relations with other trees (or even its relation to my ruler) come from its context, its being next door to the berberis, or from my judgment as I decide whether it needs pruning. Its color may be a physical property of the tree, but is its relation to the berberis a physical property in the same way? Is that just a matter of its own height?

Perhaps, furthermore, I declare that the eucalyptus tree is a fine tree, while I condemn the telegraph pole as an eyesore. When I say "the eucalyptus is excellent," do I point to a real property of the tree, its excellence? It is at least controversial to claim that the excellence of the tree is an actual, real, or natural property of the tree, rather than some value that I bestow on it in praise; and surely the telegraph pole does not actually have the tear-jerking property of onions. It has become a modern commonplace to argue that values are not facts.[15] Even if we concede, such an argument might go, that there are objective facts of the matter (the eucalyptus tree grows in the garden), the value we put on them is not a natural feature of the world, but an expression of our own attitude to what there is in the world. The eucalyptus tree is excellent just if I (or someone else) find it so, and deplorable likewise.

So, on this simple analysis, there are three categories of predicate and three types of corresponding property, feature, or aspect of a physical object at issue here. First, there are common or garden *perceptible properties* (grey, for example, or odoriferous); second, *relational properties* (larger than, for example); and third, *values* (excellent, for example). We might be tempted to classify them into two: on the one hand, there are real properties, genuine features (out there) of the objects; on the other hand, there are features or aspects that are somehow dependent (on an observer, perhaps, or supervening within a context). How does Plato see these contrasts?

The modern thought that facts and values are quite different in source has, of course, an ancient counterpart, in the debate about whether value is to be understood by nature or by law (or convention). For example, Protagoras could sensibly argue that benefit is relative to whoever is benefited: "I know many things which are harmful to men—food and drinks and drugs and thousands other such, and many which are beneficial; and some things which to men are neither, but are harmful or beneficial to horses; or some which are only so to cows, or to dogs" (*Prt.* 334a).[16]

He could later be taken (by Plato) to have meant that people's values can be changed by the skillful rhetorician, so that values are taken to be subjective: "Whatever seems just and beautiful to each city, is so to that city, just so long as it thinks so; but when each of their opinions are harmful, the wise man exchanges them for good ones, making them both be and seem so to them" (*Tht.* 167c).[17]

---

[15] The modern tradition begins with Hume, and persists; cf., e.g., Moore, *Principia Ethica*, p. 13.

[16] Compare, of course, Heraclitus, DK22B9, 13, 111.

[17] There are many other examples: cf., e.g., Antiphon, DK87B44, or Plato's own portrayal of Callicles, *Gorgias* 483a ff.

But two different claims should be distinguished; they may or may not occur together.

1. Value is *relative* to its beneficiary (one man's meat is another man's poison). Value may also be comparative (Marilyn Monroe was more beautiful than Mary Pickford). In either case, value is understood *as a relation* (it does not follow from this that value is either subjective or arbitrary).

2. Value is always relative *to some valuer* (beauty is in the eye of the beholder). This view supposes that values, possibly unlike facts, are the constructs of human or other minds;[18] this I shall call *subjectivism*.[19]

The claim that values are relations (1) turns out to be a thesis that Plato will accept, as we shall see later. It is subjectivism (2) that he attacks, on the grounds that it fails to explain why we value whatever we value, and thus runs the risk of value being hopelessly arbitrary. This objection, in turn, leads him to suppose that values, even if they are relative, are real properties.

Socrates started the attack.[20] When Euthyphro tries to define "the holy" as "what is loved by the gods," Socrates complains that it is absurd to suppose that pious actions are pious because the gods love them, rather than god-loved because they are pious.

> But if, my dear Euthyphro, the god-loved and the holy were the same thing, and the holy were loved because it is holy, then the god-loved would be loved because it is god-loved; if, on the other hand, the god-loved is god-loved because it is loved by the gods then the holy is holy because it is loved. But now you see that they are the other way round, and completely opposed to one another. For on one view something is such as to be loved because it is loved; on the other something is loved because it is such as to be loved. When you are asked, Euthyphro, what the holy is, you are liable not to be showing me its essence, but rather some affection of it, that this happens to what is holy, that it is loved by all the gods." (*Euthyphro* 10e–11a)

The difficulty that Socrates finds with Euthyphro's account is that it fails to explain why the gods should love whatever it is they do love. The explanation cannot appeal to the fact that the gods love it (because that confuses explanation and explanandum); and yet it cannot appeal (as Socrates implies that it should) to the object of the gods' affections just because this—namely, what is holy—is still itself undefined. Socrates' defeat of Euthyphro relies on the assumption that a proper definition of value must cite some feature of what is valued or risk triviality; even the ideas in the mind of god must be explained by some feature of reality out there.

[18] They occur by convention, νομῶι.

[19] This is to skirt the issue of what sort of subjectivism is offered by such an account of value. It could be mild, and allow for intersubjective value, or extreme, and tantamount to solipsism. See here Mackie, *Ethics*.

[20] Dating is not crucial here; but see Appendix A. I assume that the *Euthyphro* is Socratic, and the *Lysis* transitional between the Socratic group of dialogues and middle Plato. Cf. Mackenzie, "Impasse and Explanation," for this and for a detailed analysis of the *Lysis* argument referred to below.

Plato then takes up the same point. In the *Lysis* (217a ff.), Socrates is investigating what feature of "the friend" (*to philon*) is the explanation of others' attitudes toward it. He rejects the subjectivist view (that value is in the eye of the valuer) on the grounds that this cannot explain why we value something in the first place. In the *Symposium* (210a ff.), Diotima describes our progress from appreciating one stage of beauty to a higher one as being affected by the beautiful things we come across. We advance from enjoying the beauty of Alcibiades' body, to the beauty of Socrates' mind, thence perhaps to Hammurabi's code ("beautiful institutions"), and thence maybe to Pythagoras's theorem ("beautiful pieces of knowledge"). Eventually we have a sudden vision of the form of the beautiful, an object that is incomparably beautiful by nature; and here we reach the end of the ascent (*Symp.* 211b6).[21] The whole process works just because we are brought into contact with things that are already beautiful before our encounter with them. Alcibiades is beautiful just walking down the street before we ever set eyes on him; and Socrates' mind would have been beautiful whether or not anyone had ever wondered at him.

So value, to be comprehensible, must come from the valued, Plato suggests; otherwise, there is no explaining it at all. That something is beautiful should explain why we love it; it is absurd to argue that it is beautiful because we love it, since that makes our loving it in the first place inexplicable. The valuable feature of the valued object explains why we value it because that feature is the cause of our attitude.

Now it is no argument against this naturalist view of value that something may be valued one way by one person, another by another. Values may be relations between the valuer and what is valued without the value itself becoming unreal or arbitrary. Suppose that Rembrandt's *Night Watch* is a fine painting, from my point of view, but a disastrous failure from the point of view of the burghers of Amsterdam who commissioned it. Suppose, further (with Plato), that its beauty is a feature of it that causes me to like it; and its uncomfortable realism a further feature that causes the burghers to hate it. Then the painting will be beautiful-for-me and also hateful-for-the-burghers; and these may be real features of the painting, not ideas in the minds of me and the burghers. Indeed, the various real features of what is valued will explain the variety of values a variety of people put upon them, without thereby making illusory the beauty—or the hatefulness—of the objects out there in the world.[22] Or so, at least, it could be argued if we want to claim that the world explains why we value what we value. Further, it may explain how values can differ from person to person and culture to culture—nothing about cultural difference implies the unreality of the explanatory features of the real world.

[21] See below, ch. 3, sec. 3, on this story as a solution to Meno's paradox.

[22] The argument I attribute to Plato here should be distinguished from one that said that certain nonevaluative facts about the world (e.g., the use of certain colors in a painting) generate or cause an act of evaluation by the observer. This account allows the value to be created by the observer over and above the facts of the matter out there—which, although the facts cause or trigger the evaluation, still does not fully explain it. Plato's view, I think, is that the real world does fully explain the different values that you or I put on particular objects in the world; thus, the value is entirely real or natural.

What is more, we might also concede that values might be comparative, and still be natural. Even if Mary Pickford is less beautiful than Marilyn Monroe, she still has the edge over Quasimodo—and that because of her own (albeit lesser) beauty. (The same analysis, after all, could be given of color; even if this daffodil is less yellow than that tulip, both are yellow, nonetheless.)[23] Once again, that seems to be Plato's view: the ascent of beauty in the *Symposium* relies on (a) the real beauty of beautiful things and (b) the relativity of that beauty; they can be "rank-ordered" as we climb up the ladder (e.g., *Symp.* 210b7).

Values, then, may be relative to the valuer, and they may be comparative. For both reasons, values will turn out to be relations between the valuable thing and something else. But then if value is a relation for either or both of these reasons, and if values are real features of the world, then at least some relations will be real. The *Night Watch* actually has the property of beautiful-to-me as well as the property of hateful-to-the-burghers. Mary Pickford really is prettier-than-Quasimodo, and Marilyn Monroe prettier-than-Mary-Pickford. These evaluative properties must be real for them to explain the value; but they must also be relations to explain the differences between people's aesthetic views or between the contexts in which they appear; so relations are conceived as real properties of things in the world, as real inherent features of what is valued.

Now this assumption may have come easily to Plato, who supposes that other types of relation are also real features of the relata.[24] Hence, for example, he can say of the case where Simmias is taller than Socrates: "Simmias is not naturally taller than Socrates by virtue of being Simmias, but by virtue of the tallness which he happens to have; nor is he taller than Socrates because Socrates is Socrates, but because Socrates *has smallness in relation to* his tallness" (*Phd.* 102c; my emphasis).

Simmias is taller than Socrates, smaller than Cebes. But suppose that Simmias grows so that, instead of being smaller than Cebes, he is now taller than him.[25] What then has happened to his smallness (vis-à-vis Cebes)?[26] There are, Socrates suggests, two possibilities. Either Simmias's smallness (vis-à-vis

---

[23] This will be reasonable even if there are difficulties with vague terms.

[24] Compare, however, Owen, "*Peri Ideōn*," followed, e.g., by Nehamas, "Predication": they suppose that Plato's problem with relations should best be understood as a linguistic one, with incomplete predicates. But this seems wrong; Plato's problems were first and foremost with reality ("things," e.g., Plato, *Crat.* 436; *Euthyd.* 277e ff.), and only secondarily with the difficulties of language. On this, see now Burnyeat, *Theaetetus*, esp. p. 151. See below ch. 4, sec. 5.

[25] This is how I take "on the approach of the opposite" at *Phd.* 102d ff.—that Simmias's smallness vis-à-vis Cebes has come under threat, and so must give way. A different view might be that Simmias's smallness vis-à-vis Cebes withdraws when we start to consider his tallness vis-à-vis Socrates (that is, this argument is about compresent opposites, and not about change). But that would not, I think, be enough to establish Socrates' conclusion, that the soul must withdraw on the approach of death; in that case withdrawal is literal; in the case of compresence of opposites it merely goes out of mind. On the imagery of this passage, cf. O'Brien, "The Last Argument."

[26] This argument may work for other properties than relational ones, of course; it will reflect any property change. However, as we shall see, the compresence of opposites limits the kind of properties thought to be at issue; cf. below, sec. 3.

Cebes) has withdrawn, or it has perished. If it withdraws, then it must be lurking around somewhere else—and that would be absurd[27]—so it must have perished. Conversely, forms (and like them souls) cannot tolerate becoming the opposite of what they are, so they must withdraw (and hence survive, somewhere else). Socrates infers from this that forms (and souls) are immortal.

This argument stands or falls by its premise: Either Simmias's smallness (vis-à-vis Cebes) has withdrawn, or it has perished. But that rests on whether the option "withdraw or perish!" is a live one for anything (whether form or particular or property), on the approach of its opposite. If Simmias's size relative to Cebes is merely a matter of some observer's perspective on the two men, the question "What happens to the smallness?" would be a silly one— there would be no such thing as his smallness to lurk or to disintegrate as Simmias reaches the growth surge. The option "withdraw or perish!" would not be live for an idea in the mind of the observer. What is more, the symmetry between forms (which cannot perish and so must withdraw) and properties like largeness (which cannot withdraw and so must perish) would be lost if largeness cannot reasonably be said to perish (but rather, be forgotten, or become irrelevant when the observer changes his point of view, or his mind). For forms to withdraw, properties too must be the sorts of things that might "withdraw or perish"; my idea of Simmias's smallness (vis-à-vis Cebes) certainly cannot withdraw, and it can only perish in a rather dubious sense; so the parallel must be between real forms and real properties in the relata.[28]

Perhaps—we might argue against Plato—relations are not properties at all; perhaps they are not features of the relata, but merely a supervenient arrangement of the relata. Relations, on that view, may be radically different from either things or properties, since they do not have any independent ontological status at all. This leaves open, of course, the question of what status they do have: they might be an arrangement of what there is; or they might be a relationship that we perceive in what there is. In the latter case, but not the former, relations will be mind-dependent. On the contrary, says Plato, relations are mind-independent; and they are inherent properties of the relata (so that Cebes has largeness vis-à-vis Simmias). Thus at *Republic* 476e ff. he argues for a complex view of reality corresponding to our cognitive states; throughout, the assumption seems to be that the properties and accidents of things and their relations and their value are a part of that external reality. Now the equal sticks and stones of the phenomenal world may be thought to have a causal (and hence real) effect upon the mind when they prompt recollection (*Phd.* 73ff.); the same may be said of the way in which beautiful objects provoke the lover to love them (*Symp.* 210ff.). If relations and values are

---

[27] It is worth bearing in mind that Plato has here a proto-Aristotelian view of properties inhering in a subject, and not surviving separately.

[28] I discover that N. P. White has reached this conclusion separately, in "Plato's Metaphysical Epistemology," and compare Castaneda, "Plato's *Phaedo* Theory of Relations." White, however, supposes that real relations are derelativised in the particulars; this I take not to be the case. See below, sec. 3.

thought to affect the mind, then they are not inventions of the mind, but real pieces of the furniture of the world. I shall call this naturalism about properties, values, and relations the thesis of *natural inherence*. (Hereafter I shall often write indifferently of "properties".)

Any object in the sensible world that has naturally inherent properties is bound to be complex, because it has a collection of properties. So it is a consequence of this naturalism that Plato may infer, from the fact that all physical objects stand in various relations to other physical objects, that they are composite, in contrast to the incomposite and austere forms (*Phd.* 74–79). How, then, does this complexity of physical objects come to seem problematic?

3. THE COMPRESENCE OF OPPOSITES

When Plato discusses particulars, he focuses upon their properties. Once again, Socrates lurks in the background. Recall the discussion of definition in the *Meno* (73e ff.). When Socrates attempts to explain the problem of definition by example, he cites shape and color, the properties of physical objects, rather than horse or hyena, the natural kinds that have shape or color. In the early dialogues, more strikingly, Plato is troubled by such Socratic questions as What is piety? and What is courage? because he wants to explain how individual actions may be characterized as pious or courageous by offering an account of what piety or courage is.

Disputes, Socrates suggests, are not omnipresent (*Euth.* 7b ff.). Some properties of things are subject to dispute; but the actions themselves that are so characterized are not subject to argument. He takes it for granted that people do sacrifice to the gods or stand in the battle line, and never suggests that the actions themselves need explaining. Rather, it is the value of the actions that causes trouble (*Euth.* 5b). Moreover, for Socrates, it is only the evaluative properties of things that cause such trouble—weight, for example, or density can be decisively measured and dispute allayed.

Plato extends the difficulty. He predicates his discussion of the education of the philosopher kings in the *Republic* on an account of the constitution of the physical world—which is all that the "lover of sights and sounds" can appreciate. The trouble with these characters is that they are limited to the multiform appearances of the physical world—the plurality that is beautiful and ugly, just and unjust (*Rep.* 476a, 479a). But these fumblers are not just restricted to evaluative plurality; they get things like mathematics wrong, too. In particular, they find themselves dealing with the double that is also half, the large and the small, the light and the heavy, and all such things as those; and here, no less than when they deal with value, they find themselves (all unawares) at a disadvantage, prone to vacillate and disagree, liable to all sorts of error.[29]

---

[29] The interpretation of this argument, *Rep.* 476e–480a, is thoroughly disputed. See especially Annas, *Republic*, ch.8, versus Fine, "Knowledge and Belief." More below, ch. 3, sec. 3.

To put this in Aristotelian terms, the puzzle is not to explain the essences of kinds, but rather to explain their accidents. Both the existence and the nature of the objects that have the properties are taken for granted. There is, then, no question whether there really are sticks and stones out there in the world; the problem, rather, is how we account for their properties. To express the equivalent point in terms of grammar, Plato is not worried about the subject terms in a sentence, but about the predicate terms—their application and their explanation—and not just any predicate terms, but only the worrying ones: values (just, unjust, etc.) and relations (double, half, large, small) (*Rep.* 479a; *Phdr.* 263a ff.). For it is in these cases alone, he argues, that particulars suffer from the *compresence of opposites*.

Consider first the *Phaedo*'s argument to show that learning is recollection.

> We say, I suppose, that the equal is something; I don't mean a stick to a stick or a stone to a stone or anything else like that, but something else besides all these things, the equal itself. Do we say that it is something, or nothing?—We say so, by Zeus, amazingly so.
>
> And indeed we know it, what it is?—Certainly.—Whence did we get the knowledge of it? Surely from the things we mentioned just now, when we see sticks or stones or any other equal things, from them we get in mind that, which is different from them? Or doesn't it seem to you to be different? Consider it this way, too. Surely equal stones and sticks, while remaining the same, sometimes appear equal to one and not to another?—Certainly.
>
> Well then, is it ever the case that the equals themselves appear to be unequal to you, or equality to be inequality?—Never, Socrates.—Therefore these equals are not the same as the equal itself. (*Phd.* 74a–c)

This argument can be schematized as follows:

1. We perceive sticks equal to sticks.
2. We know what "equal" is.[30]
3. We get the equal in mind[31] from the sticks and stones.
4. The sticks and stones "appear equal to one and not to another."
5. The equal never appears equal to one and not to another.
6. Therefore the sticks and stones are different from the equal.

Suppose that I see two elephants, of exactly the same height. "Jumbo is equal to Nelly,"[32] I say. What is before me is a single case of equality; and yet this

---

[30] This looks true for anyone: the fact that we can formulate the proposition "this stick is equal to that stick" shows that we have the concept equal, over and above the sticks. There is, however, no ontological commitment here.

[31] The Greek is ἐπίστασθαι; there thus appear to be two sorts of "knowledge" here. We know what equal is independently of the sticks and stones (this is the object of one knowledge); but we get our knowledge of it now from the example before us, in the sense that we get it in mind from this example (here we have the other knowledge). The language here takes us directly back to the point made at *Phd.* 73c; there is no suggestion here that we can derive our concept of equality from the sticks and the stones. Quite the reverse—we had that all along.

[32] This is frequently misunderstood as "Jumbo is like Nelly"; Plato is talking about a quantitative, not a qualitative, relation here.

case (my saying "Jumbo is equal [in size] to Nelly" indicates) allows me to think of "the equal itself," to think of the general, and no longer of the particular. But this general concept is not immediately before me, since I am confronted not just by a particular case, but by a case that is somehow *vexed* (equal to one and not to another). So for this to *remind* me of "the equal" indicates that "the equal" is not identical with this case, nor directly derivable from it. On the contrary, I had the concept of "equal" all along, and I Recollect it in the particular case.

With the help of this sequence (as I shall argue in the next chapter), Plato concludes that the form equal is a transcendent entity, which we Recollect in our ordinary speech. The argument turns on the nonidentity claim at (6); and this relies in turn on the problem with the particular case at (4). So Socrates makes a point here about the nature of the sensible world and our knowledge of it to generate the conclusion that all knowledge is Recollection. The objects of the sensible world, he claims, do not give us a direct or immediate grasp of, for example, "what it is to be equal." Yet we can always come up with statements like "this stick is equal to that stick"—from perception (cf. *Phd.* 75b)—and recognize at the same time that they fall short of what it is to be equal.[33] How, if not from the sticks themselves, could we grasp the idea of equal that we consistently use? We must, Plato concludes, have had the knowledge of "what it is to be equal" in our minds all along, knowledge that we recollect when we say "this stick is equal to that stick."[34]

For this argument to work, Plato must show that the sensible examples[35] of equality are inadequate to show "what it is to be equal." This, it seems, is because "equal stones and sticks, while remaining the same, sometimes appear equal to one and not to another" (*Phd.* 74b7–9). Plato could be complaining that the objects of the phenomenal world are inadequate

 a. because they *change* ("*sometimes* appear") and are thus unknowable; or
 b. because they are *appearances* ("sometimes *appear*") and thus deficient or even indeterminate; or
 c. because they are somehow or other *complicated* by being "equal to one and not to another"—whatever that involves.

Now the problem is surely not the problem of change or flux (a). The objects do remain the same, presumably, over time, so that they are not in total flux. Moreover, the proviso that they remain the same seems to exclude this being even a problem of moderate change: Socrates is not making a point about how

---

[33] This is to interpret "we say, I suppose, that this stick is equal to that stick" as a general, and fairly innocuous, reference to our ordinary modes of speech, and not to some esoteric Platonic doctrine. See Appendix B.

[34] This is one interpretation of a thoroughly vexed argument: for other interpretations, cf., e.g., Gosling, "Similarity"; Bostock, *Plato's Phaedo*, p. 72ff.; Penner, *Nominalism*, p. 57ff.

[35] Individual particulars—tokens, I think, not types; vide ἄλλα ἄττα ἰδόντες at 74b5; and compare here Gosling, "*Republic* V," laboriously countered by F. C. White, *Particulars*, ch 3. Plato needs to show that no individual case of equality will supply the paradigm of equality directly, so that equality must be Recollected. For a rather different account of the whole issue of the compresence of opposites, cf. Irwin, "Plato's Heracliteanism."

this stick could suffer some trivial change and still stay the same stick; nor is he confronting the sorts of problems that beset Theseus's ship. The difficulty here is not one of the stick's identity over time.[36] Or suppose that the claim is that any stick, by its very nature, is bound to be equal at one time and not at another. Why? Why should a pair of sticks not persist as equal so long as they persist? And if they are subsequently destroyed, this appears to be a difficulty about their being sticks, not about their being equal. The emphasis of this passage, however, is on the unreliability of "equal," not of "stick." Indeed, there seems to be no problem with the stick at all. Instead the difficulty seems to rest on the difference in the stick's intermittent ("sometimes") appearances.

So perhaps Socrates is suggesting that the equal sticks and stones are "mere appearances" (b); that is, that they are not independent entities but either secondary appearances of entities that exist in their own right (whatever entities those might be) or else illusions—there is nothing real there at all. Now that, of course, would render the whole argument lamentably question-begging. (As "Of course, we all know that the world is full of mere appearances, but there must be some fixed realities; so there are forms for us to Recollect. . ."; any serious-minded dialectician would simply block this at the first move. Do we know that the world is full of mere appearances? What warrant, especially in a pre-Cartesian frame of mind, do we have for doubting the reality of what is out there, and doubting it without any preliminary skirmish on behalf of naive realism?)[37] Moreover, that interpretation of the sticks and the stones will not do either. Socrates is not arguing that these sticks and stones seem to be equal when in fact they are not,[38] but that the sticks "appear and are equal to one, but do not appear, nor are they, equal to another." So the problem must lie in the conjunction "equal to one *and not* to another"; hence, (c) the difficulty is that the sticks are *complicated* by being "equal to one and not to another." This stick, that is, suffers from the compresence of opposites; and this renders it cognitively unreliable (so that we must Recollect equality itself).

It is still not clear why the compresence of opposites should be a problem. First of all, to what is the stick equal or unequal? The Greek is obscure—does it mean (1) "equal from one person's point of view and not another"? or (2)

---

[36] This excludes the variant reading, "equal at one time and not at another," which simply saddles Socrates with a factitious contradiction (this equal stick turns out [later] to be an unequal stick) instead of a puzzle.

[37] Compare Descartes's negotiations with common sense in the *First Meditation*.

[38] Cf. Mackenzie, "Impasse and Explanation." The problem here is how we take "appears/seems"—as epistemic (this stick seems equal to that, and it is) or nonepistemic (this stick appears equal to that but it is not). The Greek won't help: for although φαίνεσθαι is epistemic when it occurs with the participle, and nonepistemic with the infinitive, this sentence is elliptical anyway, and lacks participle or infinitive. Either interpretation will do for the positive ("appears equal to one"), but only the epistemic will make sense of the scope of the negative ("does not appear equal to one, and is not"). But then this argument cannot be dealing in a sense of appears that will allow the conclusion that the sticks are mere appearances, which uses the nonepistemic sense of appears. The same point should be borne in mind when interpreting *Rep.* 476a.

"equal in one respect and not in another"? or (3) "equal to one stick and not to another"? Is Plato making a point about (1) *relativism* (everyone's view of a given pair of sticks is different); (2) the *imperfection* of the physical world (any given pair of equals will not be equal in every respect); or (3) the *structure* of the phenomenal world (any stick is involved in relations of both equality or inequality)? His account of the compresence of opposites, I shall suggest, rests on his assumptions about the complexity of the physical world in which the particulars occur. As a consequence, he seems to subscribe to all three accounts whereby particulars are qualified; but the focus of his attention, I shall argue, is the third.

Second, how strong a point can Plato make about the phenomenal world? Does he mean to say that this difficulty (whatever it is) constantly and permanently attaches itself to objects in the sensible world? In that case, he has a strong premise for his argument—possibly a premise too strong to defend:

> Equal (sticks or stones) are always equal to one and unequal to another.

Or perhaps he means to say that this is an intermittent feature of the sensible world—

> Some equal (sticks or stones) are equal to one and unequal to another.

In that case, the premise may be too weak to sustain the argument that phenomenal objects are so problematic that there must be some other objects to explain them. The weak premise only points to some sticks and stones whose equality is suspect. Marginal cases, however, are not frightening enough to send us flying to the protection of forms; perhaps the marginal cases are to be explained by central, but still phenomenal, examples of equality. So for the argument to go through, Socrates needs a strong premise—but not so strong as to be implausible.

1. Suppose that his claim is a relativist one—the world being however it is, the particulars appear differently to different people. But in that case, we risk particular properties becoming hopelessly relative or subjective, so that truth and determinacy disappear. Therefore (the argument would run), there must be some stable entities free from relativism. *Ex hypothesi*, they are not entities in the physical world, so they must transcend the physical world—and thus there are objective, nonrelative forms.

This argument could be underpinned by total relativism—the claim that any feature of the real world is a "feature-for-me," only to be understood relative to the perceiver. Only total relativism, it might be thought, dismisses objective truth for the phenomenal world, so only total relativism is strong enough to underpin this sort of argument for a theory of transcendent forms. But total relativism (like Protagoreanism)[39] is a very strong claim; perhaps we should prefer a weak sort of relativism (surely it is only in my eyes that the Mona Lisa is unattractive: beauty is in the eye of the beholder). Now, although

---

[39] Cf. Plato, *Tht.* 151–71, and Aristotle, *Met.* 1009a6ff.

this thesis may be more appealing for values than for relations such as equal, we might still be persuaded that any judgment that this pair of sticks is equal is incurably relative to the judge, since someone else from a different perspective may find the sticks unequal. So (generalizing) any such judgment will be true for someone when it may be false for someone else; no case of equality in the sensible world is reliably perspective-free.

It could of course be objected that differences of perspective may not always deliver different judgments; relativism of this sort may not be strong enough to show that any sensible example of equality is puzzling by being equal to me but not to another. When it comes to values, however, the thought that any value is relative to a valuer is persuasive.

2. Or perhaps the argument rests on a specific claim about the imperfection of the physical world. It is indeed true, Plato must then be arguing, that any stick is only equal to some other stick in one respect; there must (strong premise again, for the argument to go through) be some respect in which they are not equal. Now this premise seems at first implausible (at least so long as we avoid the mistake of reading "same" for "equal"). There is no reason to believe, and plenty of reason to disbelieve, the claim that a pair of rulers are not equal to each other in every respect, even if they do not occupy the same space. Indeed, here the sheer enormity of the premise would render foolish an argument that should run from the obvious to the controversial (that there are forms).

But we should continue to keep in mind Socrates' insistence that while the sticks remain the same, they appear "equal to one and not to another"—the difficulty arises from this qualification. Now I have argued above that relations such as equality should be understood as properties; but they are nonetheless relative properties. This could mean two different things:

a. The objects have the properties, but relatively (e.g., this stick has some degree of equality, but it does not have equality absolutely); or

b. The objects have properties that are themselves relative (e.g., this stick has, entirely adequately, the property of equal-to-that-stick; while at the same time it lacks the property of equal-to-that-stone, it has the property of unequal-to-that-stone).

Now (a) might be thought to underpin the claim that sensible instances of the form are imperfect, because they only have a part of equality, not all of it; they have some equality, but not equality itself. Their failure lies not so much in the imperfection of the equality they have but in its incompleteness, testified by the fact that they are unequal to something else.

3. But why should it be true that every instance of equality is thus incomplete? Suppose, instead, via (b), that just as Simmias has the property of largeness vis-à-vis Socrates, so this stick has the property of equal-to-that-stick. This does not mean that the stick has the property Equal but only relatively, but rather that the property the stick has is itself determined by the relation "to-that-stick." Its property, then, is not equality imperfectly instantiated, but equality-to-that-stick instantiated adequately.

Now consider what might be thought to follow from specifying this property (equal-to-that-stick) for this stick. The specification is incurably comparative: it is to that stick that this stick is equal. But then it might be thought to follow from this positive claim that there is something else to which the stick is *unequal*; thus, the significance of limiting the stick's equality to that stick may be that in some other relations it is unequal. That is, if this stick is equal-to-that-stick, then *there is something else* to which this stick is unequal.

Now this might be thought to be a commonplace feature of any predication:[40] when I make the claim that this holly is green, I am marking the holly off from all sorts of other things that are not green. It is, we might say, a feature of ordinary predication that no predicate applies universally (if it did it would be somehow meaningless). So, for any predicate, if it describes this object here, there is some object that it fails to describe. But Socrates' problem with the sticks, if it is read as "equal to one stick but not to another," is not one about ordinary predication, nor about negated predicates, but specifically about the relations (such as "equal") in which some particular may stand. But then the difference between an ordinary predicate ("green") and a relational one ("equal") may become clear. For ordinary predication may suggest that there is something somewhere that fails to have the property in question; but this relational predication suggests that this particular itself has both the property in question (equal-to-that-stick) and the opposite property (unequal-to-some-other-stick). So if we are considering each individual particular in itself, it may have ordinary properties without also having their opposites in some respect or another (the holly is just green). But when it comes to relational properties, its having one relational property might seem to imply that it also (in some other respect) has its opposite.[41] Consider, thus, a world where many things are interrelated, and suppose it to be like the world of our sensible experience. That is a world not of uniformity but of difference —where the objects are not symmetrical (like atoms or billiard balls) but disparate and lopsided: rabbits and elephants and four-horsed chariots.[42] In this world each particular will be enmeshed in a variety of relations to other particulars; and thereby any particular, by having one relational property in one respect, will readily be thought to have its opposite in another. This, let us say, is a *contextualizing* feature of relations. The context will not render some relatum a natural contradiction (since each property is suitably qualified; equal-to-b does not contradict unequal-to-c), but it will render it cognitively

---

[40] I am grateful to an anonymous commentator for Princeton University Press for focusing my attention on this problem.

[41] One might, as my anonymous commentator did, come up with counterexamples. Suppose that we are dealing with the series of the positive integers and the relation "less than": *one* will be less than 2, 15, 436, but there will be *nothing less than one*. Plato's examples, however, are less outré ("equal," "same," "different"); and in these cases the construal I suggest is plausible.

[42] A point about modality here. The necessity of this compresence of opposites is a feature of *worlds like this one*, not of any possible world. Plato, of course, does not explain modality in terms of possible worlds—since, after all, he denies that there is more than one world; see chap. 6, sec. 2.

unreliable. After all, if I am trying to find out what "equal" means, my looking to examples in the natural world, all of which will be characterized by both equal and unequal (albeit in different respects), will be of little or no help. I might, for example, get hold of the wrong property (unequal-to-c) in my attempt to grasp equal. In just that respect, therefore, Socrates could conclude (at *Phd.* 74d ff.) that the sticks and stones will fall short of what it is to be equal; they fail to explain the equal, just because they are characterized by both equal and unequal (albeit in different respects) at once.

To recapitulate, if Plato's objection to particulars is that they are "equal to one *and* not equal to another" (etc.) , we should interpret his complaint as being not about the reality of the sensible world, but about its reliability when it comes to understanding and explaining it. Now particulars may suffer from the compresence of opposites either because they are irretrievably perspectival (1); or because they only possess whatever relational properties they do possess relatively (2); or because they are naturally contextualized within their world (3). But several passages suggest that it is the third that lies at the heart of Plato's understanding of the compresence of opposites and that best explains his problems with the first. For Plato represents the difficulty directly as one about the individual particulars having opposite properties, rather than as one about their having those properties in some qualified way; and he does so both for ordinary relations and for values.

The argument to establish the complexity of sensible objects includes the claim that particulars, which are completely unlike forms, are "never in the same respects in any way the same as themselves or to each other" (*Phd.* 78e3). Now one way of reading this remark would be to interpret it as a flux thesis—the particulars are always changing—but then it directly contradicts the earlier claim that the particulars do in fact remain the same (74b8). Central here is the modality of the distinction. The forms are *always* as they are; the particulars are *never* in the same respects the same as themselves, and so forth (cf. 78d6, e3; 79a10, c6, d5.) Does this mean that the particulars are in flux? No. The particulars are represented as enmeshed in unstable relationships not *over time*, as they would be in a state of flux, but rather *at a time*.[43] But those unstable relations are contextualized (they are related thus both to themselves and to each other) and universalized (they are permanently thus). This is the strong premise that is needed for the Recollection argument.

Likewise at *Republic* 479a ff., Socrates deals with the relations double and half, large and small, heavy and light:

> About these many beautifuls things, my friend—shall we say that any of them is something which does not also appear ugly? Or of the just things, any which does not appear unjust?. . . . And what of the many double things? Do any of them appear and less half than they appear double . . . or likewise for large and small things, light and heavy, each can be said to be no more what we say they are than

---

[43] οὐδέποτε at *Phd.* 78e3 means "at any time" rather than "at one time and at another"; for the latter we should expect ἄλλοτε—compare a different thesis at *Tim.* 49d4.

they are their opposites. . . . So each of the many things is no more what someone might say it is than it is not so.

Glaucon agrees; like the child's riddle, what is large is also small, what is light
is also heavy—they "work both ways, and none of them can be clearly understood to be whatever it is any more than it is not, to be both any more than it is
neither" (Rep. 479c3–4).

Here again the particulars are thought to suffer from compresent opposites
by their very nature (or by the nature of the structured world); and this affects
our *understanding* of the properties or relations they instantiate.

A similar and connected assumption appears in the last argument of the
Phaedo. Here Socrates has been discussing the criteria for proper explanation,
and he concludes that explanation is impossible in two limiting cases: either
when we have two opposing explanations for the same explanandum (addition *and* division explain two);[44] or when the same explanation accounts
for opposite explananda (the head explains Simmias's being taller than Socrates *and* Socrates' being smaller than Simmias) (96e ff.). In the latter case,
Socrates supposes (rightly) that the tallness of Simmias and the smallness of
Socrates are *correlative*—and thus they are bound to turn up at the same time
(vide, e.g., 102c). Here the compresence of opposites consists not so much in
Simmias being both tall and small (taller than Socrates and smaller than
Phaedo), even although he does turn out to be so, but in the fact that Simmias's
being taller than Socrates needs explaining at the same time as does Socrates'
being smaller than Simmias. But anything that explains both at once will look
absurd (like the head), because it does not really explain at all. It fails as an
explanation because the explananda are both correlatives and opposites; here
we have compresent opposites that cannot be explained by something that
explains both. Cases like this are, then, just like the sticks and the stones,
cognitively unreliable.

So instances of relations such as equal or large are not enough to explain
what it is to be equal or what it is to be large; to understand the "what it is" we
need to look further than cases where the opposites turn up at once. Further,
Plato suggests that the compresence of opposites will be a problem no less for
values than it is for relations.[45] Why should that be so? I have suggested that
values, for Plato, just are relations, in two ways.

1. If this statue is beautiful, its beauty is relative to anyone who finds it so.
This is true even though its beauty is a natural property of the statue—so that
it turns out to have the property beautiful-for-me, which reflects a relation it

[44] This is where the type/token business may be thought to get a hold. Socrates does not mean
that for any token two it is explained both by one being added to one and by an original one being
halved. Rather, he wants to suggest that either explanation may operate for a given two; and to
infer from that that neither explanation properly (exclusively) explains "two" (the type). But this
shift does not, I think, affect the point. Socrates is making a perfectly sensible claim—that
explanations should not be random, or impossible to generalize from case to case (i.e., impossible
to universalize the tokens into a type, when it comes to explanation).

[45] Compare Rep. 479aff., where no distinction is made between the two types of property.

has to me. But if evaluative properties are relational like that, then they also suffer from the compresence of opposites, just because values are generally—in this world, at least—relative. So this statue will turn out to be no less ugly-to-someone-else than it is beautiful-to-me, as a consequence of the vexed nature of evaluative properties. This was Socrates' point at *Euthyphro* 7ff.; it is picked up by Plato, for example, at *Republic* 479a ff.[46] Thus, the perspectival features of values can be construed as relations.

2. If this woman is beautiful, she can only be relatively beautiful; even Helen is bound to be superseded by some goddess. If this potbellied pig is ugly, by parity of reasoning, some uglier beast is always going to turn up. Now this is a substantive thesis about the nature of valuable things: nothing in this world is absolutely beautiful, or absolutely ugly; any beautiful woman is only comparatively, relatively so, and any ugly creature likewise. So the pig may have the property uglier-than-the-cat; but he will also have the property prettier-than-the-slug, and Helen will have the property more-lovely-than-Lavinia while at the same time she is plain compared to Aphrodite (Socrates at *Hi. Ma.* 289; cf. the hierarchy of beauty at *Symp.* 210b ff.). All values in this world, therefore, are qualified, but they are so by virtue of the fact that any value is comparative ("beautiful compared to the gorilla?"); so values are relative and thus liable to the compresence of opposites.

On this account, then, Plato construes values as crypto-relations. This may put a different complexion on the arguments Plato offers for the imperfection of the valuable things in this world. One view might be that Plato just noticed that all values are somehow tarnished and grey—nothing is really as lovely as we should like it to be. So—on such a view—he postulates something that is as beautiful as it can be, and that suffers from none of the imperfections we can see in the physical world—the form. The form "first of all is always and never becomes or ceases to be nor grows nor diminishes; next it is not beautiful in one respect, ugly in another, nor at one time as opposed to another, nor is it beautiful in relation to one, ugly in relation to another, nor is it beautiful here, ugly there, beautiful to some people, ugly to others . . . but itself by itself, with itself, single in form it is always" (*Symp.* 211a1–b5).

Diotima's strategy, clearly enough, is to infer the existence of the form of the beautiful from the fact that the objects of the sensible world are, as the form is not, beautiful in one respect but ugly in another, beautiful at one time but ugly at another, beautiful in relation to one thing but ugly in relation to another, beautiful here but ugly there, beautiful to some people but ugly to others. This inference has been interpreted as a move from the imperfection of the sensible world to the perfection of the intelligible world. But if that is what it is, the inference is a bad one; that values are relative to times, or persons, or respects does not imply that they are defective (in the respects in which they are indeed valued).

Consider a different interpretation.[47] To secure the inference to the form of

---

[46] Hence the use of νόμιμα at *Rep.* 479d4.

[47] Cf. Nehamas, "Imperfection," who suggests that particulars thus "fall short of being such as" F.

the beautiful, I suggested, Plato needs to show not that values are generally relative, but that they are always so—that any value, instantiated in the physical world, will be a case of the compresence of opposites. Now we might construe Diotima's list of the ways in which something may be both beautiful and ugly as an argument that value is relative (not that it is deficient). Suppose that I say "the *Night Watch* is beautiful to me." This registers both what I think of the painting and my recognition that the burghers hated it; it does not impugn or affect my judgment that it is beautiful. If you say "the blue of the windows at Chartres is lovely now," you suggest that it was once less so [48]— and so on. Diotima's point could be generalized; any judgment of value is context-specific; this means that such a judgment is relative to its context, and fails to apply without that context. But that feature of value judgments will make evaluative properties relations (to a context, however specified); and that will make them subject to the compresence of opposites. What it will not do is to make values imperfect.

These passages argue, then, for the compresence of opposites in individual particulars on the grounds that both the relational and the evaluative properties they have must always be understood in some relation. So while forms possess the characters they possess in an absolute and hence unqualified way, particulars may possess their properties with any of the qualifications mentioned; that is, over time, in respect, in different relations, in different parts, or from different perspectives. But these qualifications are construed relationally. Thus forms are "themselves by themselves," *auta kath'auta*, while particulars have irregular relations *with other particulars* no more and no less than they have irregular relations *with themselves* (*Phd.* 78e3). This renders them cognitively unreliable. It also, as the *Phaedo's* argument about souls reveals, renders them composite, while the forms are incomposite.[49] Why should the real complexity of particulars, over and above their cognitive unreliability, be problematic?

4. COMPLEX INDIVIDUALS

In the affinity argument of the *Phaedo* (78b ff., repeated in the last argument, 102a ff.),[50] Plato insists that particulars are tricky for ontological, not epistemological reasons; and that forms are correspondingly ontologically pure.

[48] As apparently it was; I owe this example to Anthony Savile.

[49] My insistence that this is a matter of properties, and the real complexity of the particulars, should make it clear that I do not construe the problem as merely grammatical; of diagnosing, perhaps, the way in which some predicates are "incomplete" ("equal" always means "equal-to-something," even if the qualifier is unexpressed). But compare Owen, "*Peri Ideōn*," p. 172.

[50] As I have pointed out, the last argument relies on the premise that the option "withdraw or perish" is a live one. That means that *apart from souls* there must be both items that perish (such as, as I argued above, naturally inherent properties) and items that withdraw. The latter option is made genuine by postulating forms, which cannot perish, but must withdraw. So the underlying strategy of the argument is to show that souls are like forms in always taking the "withdraw" option at the approach, among other things, of death. This, effectively, is an affinity argument.

This is not an argument to contrast appearance and reality; nor should it be confused with the epistemological argument that precedes it (the Recollection argument). For the problem with compresent opposites is restricted to just some properties (such as "equal," "larger than," or "beautiful"); it is not a general difficulty attached to objects as such.[51] But in the affinity arguments Plato looks to objects as a whole, and argues that *complex objects are destructible* and thus inferior to simple objects.

Suppose that any particular is a collection of properties naturally inherent in it (a collection that may be as sinister as you like, from an epistemological point of view, or else fairly innocent—the issue of compresence does not turn up in this argument as an epistemological problem). The particular will thus be a complex, and destructible. Why? Because it is liable to disintegrate *at exactly the points where its parts are stuck together (Phd. 78c)*; conversely, an incomposite entity has no point of weakness and is indestructible.[52] Sensible particulars, therefore, die; forms and souls survive.

So Plato argues from the unity of an object at a time to its ability to persist over time. In general, his claim is that when something is complex and plural it cannot persist forever; when something is simple and one, it does persist, just because it is not liable to come apart at the seams. Is his argument plausible? Why should a composite entity be weak at the points where it is stuck together?

Two different comparisons may be in order here. First, compare an atom of mercury and a molecule of cinnabar.[53] The atom is (in some sense, and without counting its subatomic particles) hard to split just because (or just insofar as) it is a simple entity. But the molecule is easy to divide (by heating) into its component atoms (of mercury and sulphur), just at the point where it is joined together. Now consider the contrast between a walrus and some water. Both are physical objects, and so liable to the ordinary accidents of physical life. The walrus is a complex physical object—one snout, two tusks, several whiskers, and so on—while the water is simple. Try siphoning off some water and the remainder stays water, but remove the walrus's vital organs and the walrus is defunct. So in this case the simple entity (the water) seems easy to divide, while the complex one, separated at the joints, ceases to exist.

But the various contrasts between an atom, a molecule, some water, and a walrus all involve different accounts of the constitution of each thing. An atom is (again without considering its subatomic structure) something that is simple and uncuttable ex hypothesi; its simplicity and its atomicity go hand in hand, and they are its principle of individuation, too. The molecule, by contrast, is built up of such simple entities, and is vulnerable, therefore, to being cut just where they join. Its structural principle *is* just that it is composed of

---

[51] Cf. Owen, "*Peri Ideōn*," and Alexander, *In Met.* 82.11–83.6, on the restricted scope of the forms; cf. below, ch. 3, sec. 4.

[52] This argument may apply to properties at a time or over time; cf. *Phd.* 78c6.

[53] My thanks to Keith Hossack here.

atoms; it is individuated by specifying what that composition is. The water is another thing again—this is a mass, some stuff. A measure taken away from the original mass makes not a great deal of difference; it is individuated by being just some more water. The walrus, by contrast, has a strong principle of individuation—its organic complexity—that makes division lethal for it. If we think about this in terms of parts, the water is simple because its parts are the same (more water); the walrus is complex because its parts are different (it is an organic whole).

Now the question is this: how far is Plato justified in thinking that being composite makes what is composite liable to dissolve at the places where it is joined? Both simple objects (the atom and the water) are such that either they *resist* division by virtue of being simple, or they find division innocuous (there is always some more water left). But complex objects, contrariwise, are destroyed by division just where their different parts join together (the molecule divides into its elements, the organic unity of the walrus is destroyed). Examples such as these might encourage us to agree that destruction of a complex object occurs because it is complex, and takes place at the joints.[54]

This account of the destruction of an organism, however, owes its force to the idea that an organism is perishable if its organic nature is divided; the walrus is destroyed if the features that make it a walrus are separated off, and not if it merely loses some accidental property. So, it might be thought, Plato can only argue that complex organisms are liable to perish if they come apart at the joints, once he has distinguished between essential features of a thing and accidental ones. And, indeed, in the last argument of the *Phaedo*, Socrates contrasts Simmias and his accidental property, large, with fire and its essential property, hot (103c ff.); in the *Republic*, he points to the difference between a finger being a finger and its being smaller than another finger (523c ff.). Thus, fire will not tolerate the approach of the opposite of heat and still remain what it is; snow will not remain behind to become hot. In cases such as these, complex organisms will be destroyed when their essential properties are lost. But does it follow from this that simple entities are indestructible? Surely not—and Socrates bases his final argument for the deathlessness of soul not so much on the simplicity of its nature as on the fact that it possesses life as an essential attribute. So the contrast between essence and accident will not account for the claim that composite entities are destructible, simple ones are not.

Instead, Plato has often been supposed to base his argument for the perishability of physical objects on their liability to change; this may be why Aristotle thought that he was worried about flux. When Socrates insists that a physical particular is composite, he may be pointing to its changing properties; these properties make it vulnerable not so much because there are many of them, but rather because they are liable to come and go. This may be

---

[54] Compare, here, Plato's imagery for proper collection and division in terms of the articulation of an organic whole, *Phdr.* 265e.

particularly pressing if we worry about "aspect-change." In its strictest sense, and at its most puzzling, the compr: esence of opposites is a problem about properties at a time: this rabbit now is smaller than the dog, but larger than the mouse the dog is chasing. However, this can be construed more loosely as a change in aspect: [55] for example, suppose we look at the map and determine, first, that Cambridge is north of London, and, next, that Cambridge is south of York. Cambridge has had these comprescent properties (north of London, south of York) all along, but we notice them one after the other. Then, more loosely still, as I drive along the Cambridge ring road, I am, now north, now west of Cambridge; Cambridge has aspect change, too, from being to my south to being to my east.[56] While this is not a case of comprescent opposites at a time but over time, it still looks pretty indeterminate: will Cambridge in this example provide me with an explanation of "what it is to be east"? (Compare the case of the dog, once a small puppy, who has grown now to be bigger than the rabbit; will this case of "large" [any better than the stick, the stone, or the middle finger] be self-explanatory? Surely not.) The original problem of the comprescence of opposites is not primarily a difficulty about change, but it may be thought to include diachronic and aspect change (e.g., at *Phd.* 102b ff; *Symp.* 211).

However, that something is composed of more than one part does not imply that it acquired one part later than another, nor that any of its parts is liable to change. Conversely, being changeable does not imply of itself that something is complex. Why should not a simple entity simply change or dissolve at an instant? If Plato wants to argue that if physical objects are perishable then there must be imperishable souls, why should he drag in the issue of simplicity and complexity? We must, surely, diagnose a different strategy and different assumptions than the problem of flux.

Plato's puzzle of the comprescence of opposites shows that he thought that any individual particular in the physical world is enmeshed in a complex of relations and values. The assumption of natural inherence, further, treats these relations and values as properties of the individual particular itself. So any particular has a multitude of properties over and above the ordinary properties immediately accessible to perception; and all these properties may be treated as natural parts of it.[57] But if the properties and the relations of something are parts of it, can it lose them, or have them altered, with impunity? How far, if this is so, can a physical whole resist destruction? Reflection on Plato's suggestion that simple objects may be indestructible may show what his underlying assumption is. If something is simple, it has no parts, but it is just a single unit. In that case, it has a principle of coherence (its bare unity) that will explain its survival as such. On the other hand, a complex

[55] Again, see Irwin, "Heracliteanism," here.

[56] The problem of "mere Cambridge change" that affects Cambridge here will be discussed further below (see ch. 5, sec. 3, and ch. 8, sec. 9); cf. here Geach, *God and the Soul*, p. 71ff.

[57] Some interesting work on Plato's approach to mereology is being done by Verity Harte, University of Cambridge.

entity, as a physical particular may be, will be a whole composed of its parts. But what principle holds those parts together? Any collection, to be unified, must have a unifying principle—say, "that it be one." Its being governed by that principle will ensure that it is one. In Plato's terms, this will mean that it has the property of unity; and that property will be one of the collection of natural properties that it has. But then the principle that should coordinate the collection of properties will be itself one of the properties to be coordinated. And then there will be nothing to ensure that this individual does not come apart at the joints (the ties have become what is tied).

Plato does not give an account of the connecting principle over and above the properties of something. Perhaps this is why he supposes that the points at which one (nonessential) property is joined to another will be points of weakness. This allows his argument to proceed not from the changeability of things to their liability to destruction, but from their compositeness to their weakness.

So he polarizes simple entities (souls, he hopes, and forms) and complex ones (the ordinary objects of the sensible world); thus, he opposes items that are "many," and items that are "one." Now that contrast is in fact ambiguous in a Platonic context.

It may reflect the difference between the many instances of a form, and the one form itself (e.g., *Rep.* 596a). Perhaps, then, the point would be that particulars are inferior because they are not universals (but instead are involved in many universals?). This seems not only an implausible claim (why should the fact that particulars are not universals mean that they are inferior?), but dangerously circular. For somehow the complexity of particulars is thought to be a reason for postulating universals; but that reason cannot then be the claim that particulars are instances of universals—if it is not to be trivial.

Instead, the *Phaedo* needs the contrast between "*a many*" and "*a one.*" Socrates, for example, is "a many" because he has many different characters, properties, relations. This reflects not his falling under a universal,[58] but his having many properties all collected together into a whole, Socrates himself. Socrates, as I shall say, is *generously* endowed with properties. The form of the beautiful, by contrast, is just one, a single, simple, uniform item, not at all characterized by plurality. The form, as I shall say, is an *austere* unity.

Now let us recapitulate. Plato supposes, I have suggested, that the sensible world is real, and that it actually contains the particulars it seems to contain. These—the individual particulars of the sensible world—are doubly problematic. First, they instantiate opposite properties at once (opposites qualifiedly, that is); so they need explaining because they are cognitively unreliable. Second, because the properties they have are agglomerated together into a collection that has no principle of unity, any individual particular is a plurality and as such is liable to change and perish. So individual particulars are

---

[58] Plato's account of essential properties does not give us an Aristotelian sort.

ontologically suspect just insofar as they are composite.[59] Sensible individuals have only a dubious claim to unity.

In this chapter I have argued that this consequence follows from three features of Plato's account of individual particulars:

1. He supposes that relations and values are real properties of their possessors (natural inherence, sec. 2 above).

2. These properties are still relative, however and so liable to the compresence of opposites (sec. 3 above).

3. So entities that suffer from the compresence of opposites are complex and therefore destructible (complex individuals, sec. 4).

Now, throughout the middle period Plato continues to suppose that sensible particulars are genuine individuals—look, we can count them, point to them, pick them out (Socrates, Simmias, this finger, that stone). Particulars can figure as "one under many." However, once the contrast between complex (generous) particulars and simple (austere) forms has been made—and the argument advanced that complexity renders particulars destructible, simplicity renders forms eternal—it becomes evident that while Plato can explain the particulars being *many*, he has no account to give of their being one. Instead, he is forced to suppose that identity, unity, and persistence derive from the simplicity of being a bare unit. So perhaps, in order to understand "being one," we need to turn our attention to the forms. The next chapter will argue that this would be a mistake.

---

[59] Notice here Plato's imagery: he describes such items as *monsters* (τέρατα) at *Phd.* 101b, *Parm.* 129b, and *Phil.* 14e. Compare Aristotle, *Phys.* II.8, where the trouble with monsters is made clear: they are disconnected *and thus* inexplicable—both because they come from unexpected sources (a mule would count as a monster because it comes from parents that are of different species; cf. *Pol.* 265d ff.), and because they are badly put together, like Empedocles' mutations.

Forms

PARTICULARS may be infuriatingly complex. But forms—Plato is supposed to have thought—are simple, sterilized by the exercise of pure thought. Are not forms paradigmatic unities? And if they are, then surely forms will be basic, forms will have thoroughgoing identity over time (they are eternal), and forms will be countable and determinate. Forms should be individuals in the most absolute terms.

Consider, first of all, how Plato establishes that there are forms and how he analyzes their nature. As the previous chapter anticipated, there are two separate strands of argument: one is epistemological, and appeals to forms as the explanations that particulars need; the other is ontological, and supposes forms to be entities of a simple, imperishable kind.

1. KNOWLEDGE AND THE SEPARATION OF FORMS

The epistemological arguments are the first to appear.

How can you look for what you do not know? How can you start an inquiry when you cannot even formulate the objective? If you know what you are looking for, there is no point in looking for it; if you do not know what you are looking for, you cannot even begin the search (*Meno* 80d–e).[1]

Meno's paradox of inquiry has often been thought a mere fallacy,[2] but let us give it a run for its money. Notice, first, that it is a paradox—the inquiry "Can we inquire?" surely cannot be answered "no" without contradicting itself. Further, confronted by the paradox that denies the possibility of inquiry, we immediately inquire, What has gone wrong with the argument? How can I reinstate my ability to question? And notice, second, that it is a puzzle about motivation (about *reasons*). If I know (all there is to know) about something, then I have no reason to inquire into it; if I know nothing about something, the reason to inquire into it can get no purchase on my mind at all.

First of all, the paradox looks like a mistake. Suppose the object of inquiry is Q. Socrates starts with the following disjunction:

  i) Either I know Q or I do not know Q—

---

[1] N.B., there are worries about the construal of the argument, too; cf. Moravcsik, "Learning as Recollection." I regret that Gail Fine's excellent paper in Kraut's *Companion to Plato* came to my attention too late for detailed consideration here.

[2] The fallacy has been variously diagnosed; cf., e.g., Scott, "Paradoxe"; Nehamas, "Meno's Paradox"; Vlastos, "Anamnesis." The claim that this is "merely" a fallacy is thought to be supported by Socrates' comment that it is "eristic" (80e2). But that, of course, means that the argument is contentious, not that it is trivial.

which looks trivially true. But then he treats this as expressing:

i*) Either I know Q completely or I am utterly ignorant of Q.[3]

Suppose, for example, that Q is a body of knowledge, such as "the dates of the English kings and queens." Although I could tell you about some of this body of knowledge (I can do so for William the Conqueror or Elizabeth I), there are areas where I am completely at a loss (Stephen and Matilda, for example, or William and Mary). But in this case, neither do I "completely know" Q, nor am I totally ignorant of it; and from the lamentable gaps in my knowledge I can formulate the firm purpose of amendment. In cases like these—and cases like these, after all, are those where our interest in inquiry is the greatest—the paradox seems frankly wrong because it equivocates on two senses of "know" ("know completely" vs. "have in mind").

If there are two senses of "know" (or two sorts of knowledge, if you prefer) in play here, how does the paradox come out if we use just one sense, consistently? This will give two interpretations of the argument:

i**) Either I completely know Q, or I do not completely know Q.
ii**) If I completely know Q, there is no point in inquiring into it.

That seems true, and reasonable. I might, if I know all there is and ever will be to know about nuclear physics, cheerfully *contemplate* what I know; but I cannot be motivated to inquire into it when I already have it licked.

iii**) If I do not completely know Q, I cannot start to look.

This is false (as in the case of the English kings and queens); so this version of the paradox is incomplete, and the paradox broken.

The alternative version is lopsided, likewise:

i***) Either I have Q in mind or I do not.
ii***) If I have Q in mind, I cannot be motivated to inquire into Q.

False. If I think to myself "nuclear physics is my project of self-improvement for today," I have Q in mind, but not yet licked.

iii***) If I do not have Q in mind, I cannot formulate an inquiry into Q.

True, surely. If I cannot even imagine the subject of my inquiry, the inquiry itself cannot take place (serendipity does not count here—the paradox is about deliberate inquiry).

Both versions of the paradox, therefore, allow for the possibility of some awareness, some kind of cognitive grip on the subject of my inquiry, which is neither complete knowledge nor total ignorance, and which can be used to

---

[3] This looks most plausible in cases where Q is a single (simple?) object—then I might be said either to know Q (to have a complete mental grip on Q) or not to have Q in mind at all. This approach to Meno's paradox turns up in the *Theaetetus* (cf. ch. 5, sec. 6, and ch. 9, sec. 8); on this issue see Russell, "Knowledge by Acquaintance," and comments by Burnyeat, *Theaetetus*, p. 75ff.

express the object of my search. Once we inquire carefully into the paradox, we can see that the vague notions we may have in mind all the time can be turned into questions and can mark the beginnings of an inquiry (just like the ordinary process of recalling a forgotten event). But the effects of the paradox do not end there—three problems still remain.

First, how can I understand what it is to "know completely"? How, when I do *completely* know, do I know that I know? What is it like to reach the end of an inquiry? How, when I know Q, do I recognize that Q is what I was looking for?

Second, how, if I am completely ignorant of Q, can I begin to think about it? How, when at one time I do not have Q in mind, can I then get Q in mind? What is involved in "getting something new in mind"?

Third, how can we specify Q so that it is possible to have it in mind without knowing it completely? My examples have been "bodies of knowledge." We might have a grip on an arm or a leg without having got hold of the whole organism, and yet, just because it is an organism, and because the arm is connected to the shoulder, the shoulder to the neck, and so on, hanging on to the arm will allow my knowledge to develop. But what if Q is *either* a simple object *or* a disconnected collection of objects? In the first case, to have Q in mind may be the same thing as knowing it completely; in the second case, there is no guarantee that having one member of a disparate collection of things in mind will lead me to knowing the rest.

Consider the problem of ignorance first. How do we get "new" knowledge, independent of other things we already know?

Suppose I am sitting in the garden and Q, hitherto unknown to me (under any description), trundles across the lawn. I see Q, and thus I get Q in mind. How? The question "What reason did I have to look for Q?" is redundant; I had no reason to look for Q, no motive at all. Instead, Q *happened to me*; Q affected me by appearing in my visual field and impinging on my optic nerve (and so on). I perceived Q not because I decided to perceive Q, but because Q acted upon my perception.

This empiricist answer to the paradox looks reasonable enough; it cancels the paradox's appeal to motive by citing the *cause* of my perception (Q). This works, however, only if the cause is thought to be a real one;[4] if empiricism is to give a short answer to the paradox, it is done by claiming that the real objects of perception affect the senses (and hence the mind—this is how we "get Q in mind"). So I can come by "new" knowledge by being affected by the external world.

Socrates' answer to the paradox, however, is not a straightforwardly empiricist one. Instead, he offers the theory of Recollection: "Insofar as the soul is immortal and has been born many times, and it has seen everything both here and in Hades, there is nothing which it has not learned; so there is nothing

---

[4] Compare Descartes's thought experiment; the evil demon causes me to think that I see, etc., *First Meditation*.

surprising about its ability to remember about virtue and other things, which it has known before. Since all nature is akin, and the soul has learned everything, there is nothing to prevent it, once it has recollected one thing (what men call learning) from rediscovering all the rest, if it is brave and untiring in the search" (*Meno* 81c–d).

Socrates' theory is enmeshed in myth, but his answer to our question (How do I get something new in mind?) is clear enough. For the theory of Recollection breaks the paradox by suggesting that inquiries of the sort Socrates and Meno are engaged in do not start from no knowledge at all. The mind of the inquirer is not empty, it is no tabula rasa; instead it is full, even if the "knowledge" it contains is not fully conscious, and needs to be recalled.

Suppose we try to detach the mythical bits and pieces from this theory. We could construe it as a theory of innate ideas: no inquiry is really new, for our souls are things of the sort that are full of information, or ideas or whatever.[5] On this account, the paradox simply fails to bite.

But we might object to this because the answer is still pretty opaque—or grants too much to the paradox and puts too much into the mind. This answer, in the end, will take all the fun out of inquiry ("Oh well, I knew that all along"), and will take all the dangers of error away. What is more, by packing the mind full of everything conceivable, this answer supposes that the real world does not impinge on us at all. In short, it turns out to be violently antiempirical (recall that some accounts of Plato's objections to particulars suppose that he was, just so, violently against the sensible world).

But that interpretation of the theory of Recollection is not supported by further scrutiny of the text. For Socrates insists that the soul "has seen everything both here and in Hades," so that "there is nothing which it has not learned." Now *this* learning cannot be Recollection (since this is what explains the fact that we do Recollect); this learning is true learning, learning from scratch (as opposed to "what men call learning," which is in fact Recollection). What we learn is a whole body of knowledge (all of nature, naturally connected together). But how? "The soul has seen everything." At first, this looks innocuous (we dull empiricists agree that learning takes place by seeing); but reflect once again on the context (and on the trouble Socrates had with definitions). The problem is not, How did I get this cat in mind?—which is answered by the mechanics of perception—but rather, What is virtue?—a question about an a priori matter, which is not susceptible to sense perception. Nor, according to Socrates, can it be derived from sense perception, directly or indirectly (by induction or some such process).[6] On the contrary, Plato suggests here,[7] such knowledge is indeed a priori; we get it in mind in the

---

[5] On innate ideas compare Locke, *Essay Concerning Human Understanding* I; Leibniz, *New Essays on Human Understanding*, bk.1 ; and see also Scott, "Platonic *Anamnesis*."

[6] Recall his complaints about examples; see ch. 2, sec. 1.

[7] I take this passage to represent the shift away from the historical Socrates toward Plato's own views; nonetheless, there is a good deal of continuity, as I suggest, between Socrates' problems with definition and Plato's theory of forms.

underworld. So is his proposal that although we can see the things in this world, we have innate ideas about what we cannot see (and those are what we Recollect)? Not a bit of it. His claim is that, just as we see things here, so we "see" things in the underworld. The content of our Recollection includes not only perceptible objects from this world, but also virtue and things like that. We *see* the things in the underworld.

What does Socrates mean by that? Is he proposing that we have an "inner eye," the eye of the soul, or that we have some kind of intuitive grasp of the things, like virtue, that we cannot directly perceive? Surely, to talk of intuition is to miss the point of the soul "seeing everything." In the context of Meno's paradox, sight breaks the puzzle about the *reason* for inquiry by citing a *cause* (Q impinged on my vision). Socrates' claim that the soul sees things in the underworld must be interpreted, surely, in the same terms: that the "things in Hades" affect the soul (my discarnate shade does not need to go and look for virtue, virtue encounters my soul, affects it, as physical perception would).

But then recall the price the empiricist pays (in the face of the skeptic): he supposes that the world, which can affect us thus, is real (even if it is not exactly as it appears to us). If we ask the Socrates of the *Meno* how we can inquire into virtue, his answer is that we Recollect it from before. How did we learn it before? On pain of a vicious regress, Socrates cannot say "we Recollect it from before"; instead, he suggests that we encountered it at some point in our discarnate lives. It, then, must be independent of us, the sort of thing that affects us, not any kind of innate idea (even if we are born with the idea *of it* in our minds).

That is as far as the *Meno* will take us (there is no mention of forms here). But the theory of Recollection in the *Phaedo* goes further in trying to explain "getting in mind." Here (*Phd.* 73c ff.), Socrates argues from a series of claims about ordinary recollection to the theory of Recollection.[8] Ordinary recollection will give him two (contentious) premises:

1. If we see *x* and get in mind *y*, where *x* is "of a different knowledge from *y*," then we have recollected *y*.
2. If we are reminded of *y* by (seeing) *x*, and *x* and *y* are like each other, we notice how far one falls short of the other.[9]

Then Socrates presses the distinction between the ordinary objects of perception (equal sticks and stones) and our general concepts (the equal itself):

3. We know what equal itself is.
4. We get our knowledge of equal from the ordinary objects of perception.
5. The sticks and stones suffer from the compresence of opposites.
6. The equal itself does not suffer from compresence of opposites.
7. So the sticks and the stones are not the same thing as the equal itself.

---

[8] Cf. Appendix B.
[9] For an account of this "falling short," cf. ch. 2, sec. 3.

At first glance, these could be taken to form a simple empiricist argument for the induction of general terms from particulars. But for such an argument, the premises and the conclusion should be reversed; Socrates should be arguing for 4 from 5–7, and not the other way about. Instead, his objective seems to be, first of all, to prove the nonidentity of the equal sticks and equal itself (so that, of course, cannot be the assumption in play from *Phd.* 74a9), and then the explanation of our understanding of equality in terms of the theory of Recollection. Now, if I see one thing and get in mind another, this is taken to be a case of ordinary recollection; by analogy here, seeing the equal sticks and stones and getting in mind the equal itself is a case of Recollection, provided that Socrates can show that the equal sticks and stones are not identical to the equal itself (that is, provided that he can show, in the expression of *Phd.* 73c8, that they are not "of the same knowledge"). He does that by arguing that although I "get my knowledge" of the equal itself from the sticks and the stones, they are not sufficient for my knowledge of the equal itself. They could not be so, because they are not the same thing as the equal itself (the sticks are both equal and unequal; the equal itself cannot be). So my knowledge of the sticks and the stones is provided by ordinary perception; and from that,[10] triggered by that knowledge, I Recollect the equal itself. This, then, so far from being an argument for induction, is an argument against it; sensible particulars merely trigger the use of the ideas that we have, they do not generate universals at all.

At this stage, what *is* the equal itself? The argument has not shown a great deal; it has contrasted the concept of equality and shown that this concept is not merely a universal derived from sense-data. In doing so, it has shown that "the equal itself" and the particular equals are nonidentical; but that in itself tells us nothing about the ontological status of the equal itself. Consider this: we might cheerfully claim that this yellow football and the universal yellow are nonidentical on the grounds that the football does not exhaust all the yellow there is, and we would still not be making any grand ontological claim about yellow (which might just be "all the yellow, ever").[11] Or we might confidently maintain that my idea of justice is not the same thing as yours, nor the same thing as that decision of a court or some other distribution of birthday cake, without implying that my idea of justice is independent of my having it in mind. For two items to be nonidentical, that is, does not show that either or both of them are pieces of objective reality.

The next phase in the argument, I think, attempts to rectify that by exploiting the second condition of recollection (2, above). The equal sticks are not

---

[10] The preposition ἐξ (at *Phd.* 74b4) may be what causes the trouble in this passage. Once we bear the context in mind—namely, the earlier discussion of remembering—it is easy to see that when Socrates says that we know what the equal is, and that we get this knowledge from the equal sticks and stones, he does not mean that we acquire the knowledge of the concept from the particulars, but rather that we get (or get again) in mind the knowledge of equality that we already have (compare the same use of "get," λαμβάνειν, at 73d1).

[11] See here Quine's parsimonious account of universals, *Word and Object.*

identical to equality itself because they are both equal and unequal. However, this does not make them the sort of thing that will give us knowledge; for knowledge, as Socrates has taught us, should not be ambiguous or equivocated, nor should it fail to explain. If, then, we know what equal is, what we know must be unequivocal and unambiguous, free from context or qualification. So it cannot be derived from the objects of this world or from sensation; so we must have known it all along. But what have we known all along? Something that is like the equal sticks and stones, as they are to it (since it is by likeness that they remind us of the equal itself); but something that is not deficient, where the equal sticks and stones are. They fall short of the equal itself (by being both equal and unequal); the equal itself, however, suffers no such fate, and does not fall short of being equal in any way at all. Could it, then, be a universal like yellow? Or an idea of mine, like my idea of justice? Surely not. If such an equal was either a universal or an idea I got into my head, what would be its origin? It would be derived from the sensible particulars: and this argument would turn out (after all) to be an argument for induction. But the reverse is true; this argument proceeds by denying induction and then postulating the theory of Recollection. The idea of equality cannot, therefore, be derivative from the sensible particulars (like the universal), nor from my inspection of them (like my ideas).

But could it be an innate idea, complete and permanent? Or is it an object independent of any mind? Return to the puzzle about the sticks and stones—a puzzle about how they could give us knowledge of the equal itself; and keep in mind the answer, that they can only trigger Recollection of the equal itself, since they are inadequate to give proper knowledge. This argument is based, like its counterpart in the *Meno*, on the assumption that we do come to know things—but not from the sensible world alone. Now if "the equal itself" here is merely an innate idea, Plato has simply denied that there is any coming to know (we know everything all along). What is more, he would then break the back of the immortality argument; for at a crucial stage in what follows, Socrates shows that the soul must have prenatal existence, because otherwise there would be no time at which it could have learned the concepts that it has (*Phd.* 76c; the moment of birth, after all, is the moment when we *forget*, not the time at which we learn). Now a theory of innate ideas cannot make this point (the individual is just born with a soul made like that, full of ideas); instead, it requires a theory that the soul *acquires* ideas, and that it does so in a preincarnate existence. But then the ideas that it acquires are not in it all along, so they must be independent of it.

> But Socrates did not make the universals separate, nor the definitions; but they [sc. the Platonists] separated them. (Aristotle, *Metaphysics* 1078b30–31)

How far does this argument of the *Phaedo* present a claim for "separate" forms?[12] Forms are independent of, and prior to, sensible particulars; and

---

[12] This is a controversial issue; cf. Fine, "One over Many," "Separation"; Morrison, "Separation."

forms are independent of, and prior to, minds. Now at the very least, this means that any form is independent of, and *thus separate from*, any given particular and any given mind.[13] For example, the form of large is separate from, because it is not identical with, this large elephant—so much the argument from the sticks and the stones has shown. And the form of large is separate from my mind as I look at the large elephant before me—so much the argument from Recollection has shown. But that claim is rather a mild one; perhaps large is a universal that does not depend on any particular instantiation or imagination, but nonetheless needs *some* instantiation, and must be an idea in *some* mind. Does Plato's argument give us any stronger beer than this rather commonplace theory of universals (which could, what is more, be shared by Plato and Socrates, contrary to Aristotle's account)? Plato might mean either of two things. Consider the contrast thus:

1. There are forms, whether or not there are instantiations of them, and whether or not anyone knows anything about them. There is always a form of equal, no matter what happens in the world. This will be *uncompromising* separation.

2. While forms must be instantiated (and thus accessible to some mind)—there is always something equal, somewhere or other—they are not dependent on any one example, which may perish or change without the form itself being affected. This is a *compromised* separation.

How are we to determine which is Plato's view?

2. Simple Forms and Explanation

Forms are what particulars fail to be. This will be so for both epistemological reasons and ontological ones. First, explanation is possible (Plato supposes). Forms explain, particulars do not. If particulars fail to provide explanations *because* they are subject to the compresence of opposites, then forms, which succeed in explaining, must be *free from compresence*. Second, particulars are complex items, and so are subject to change and decay. Forms, by contrast, are simple items and thus are both constant and eternal. Any particular is a many; any form is *just a one*.

Forms serve as *explanations* for vexed terms (e.g., at *Phd.* 100d ff.). Particulars are cognitively fishy, because they suffer from the compresence of opposites. Forms are postulated as just what is not cognitively fishy. Now that will matter only for properties that introduce compresent opposites to particulars —especially, that is, relational and evaluative properties. To solve the problem, Plato needs little more than a theory of universals, since he merely has to be able to answer the question, How did we come to know what it is to be equal? This question could be answered by a theory of universals, a theory of innate ideas, or some kind of nominalism.[14]

---

[13] Contrast Aristotle's different account of separation at *Phys.* 193b33ff.

[14] Cf. Penner, *Ascent from Nominalism*, ch.1.

But nominalism is an option that Plato does not take, even in the earlier stages of these arguments—and for two reasons. First, as I have argued, he treats relations and values as real natural properties of what is valued. We might find it easy to explain our use of vexed terms such as "equal" or "beautiful" by looking to the ideas that we have. So our understanding of "equal," for example, may be a universal, constructed from many instances. This universal, we might suppose, is mind-dependent, and has in itself no objective existence. However, once concede that "equal" is a real property out there in the world, and it may be easy to suppose that its explanation has the same status, and is just as real as its instances. Second, Plato seeks not merely to explain the terms we use, but to account for the appearance of the properties in the world. In that case, if the explananda are real, the explanation must also be real, since it is responsible first of all for the existence of the explananda, and only thereafter for our being able to talk about them.[15] But an innate idea could hardly cause real beauty out there in the world; nominalism is only an option either if we are only interested in mind-dependent properties (if beauty is in the eye of the beholder) or if we are only worried about how we come to call something beautiful irrespective of how it became so.[16] The former is not in tune with the naturalism that Plato espouses; the latter explains nothing about the world, only about our attitudes to it—and thus fails to answer the questions that Plato poses in the first place: "By virtue of what is this action pious?" "By virtue of what do we call this action pious?" The answers should cite a real entity, because Plato thinks that the explanation of why it is pious is also the explanation of why we call it so; but not conversely.

For a form to explain, then, it must be real. Moreover, in order that the form explain, rather than itself needing an explanation, it should be free from the compresent opposites that are its explananda. Only then will the theory of forms conform to Socrates' "simple-minded explanation": "the beautifuls are beautiful by virtue of the beautiful" (*Phd.* 100d).

Socrates arrives at this formula by objecting to various alternative modes of explanation. The pre-Socratic materialists tried to answer the question, Why?—grand questions, such as Why is the world the way it is? Why do things change? Why is this a man?[17] And the man on the Piraeus ferry also asks "Why?"—"Why is my brother fatter than me?" "Why is Demos's donkey larger than mine?" But no one so far has come up with a satisfactory way of answering these questions: for any answer seems to be somehow or other equivocated. Either we offer the same explanation for different explananda (Demos's donkey is larger than mine by a hand, but my donkey is smaller than

---

[15] The claim that an explanation is real may look strange to the modern eye. But we should bear in mind that "explanation" translates the Greek αἰτία, commonly rendered as "reason, cause"; in that case, an explanation could readily be a piece of the furniture of the world.

[16] I shall return to this issue; it is worth noting here that Plato's central problem is not how we use language but how the world is constituted.

[17] Cf. here Vlastos, "Reasons and Causes."

Demos's by the same hand), or we offer opposite explanations for the same explananda. ("Why two?" can be answered either as "division of a one in half" or as "addition of one to another one")[18] So the first requirement for explanation is that it should *fit* the explananda: hence, "the beautifuls are beautiful by virtue of the beautiful" matches the explanation ("the beautiful") exactly to the explananda ("the beautifuls").

But this explanation, however appropriate, turns out to be banal, or even tautologous. Surely, must not any explanation do some explaining—and not just reiterate the explananda? Now Socrates' simple-minded explanation is not (of course) as simple minded as all that: the "beautiful" that explains the "beautifuls" is not a particular (one of the explananda) but the form, beautiful. There is no tautology here, although perhaps there is banality.

Recall the two versions of "separate" forms. When Socrates mentions the beautiful, he may mean either a form that is uncompromisingly separate (from all particulars and all minds) or one that is compromised (separate only from a particular particular or a particular mind). The first looks like a theory of transcendent forms; the latter more like a theory of universals.

Now if "the beautiful" is the universal that includes all the beautifuls, how far does it *explain* them? "Why the beautifuls?" I ask—and what do I want to know? I might be asking the extent of the class of beautifuls—in which case the universal is a suitable reply, if dull. The beautifuls are all members of the class of beautiful because they all fall under the universal "beautiful." That tells me nothing about how they come to be beautiful, nor about how I come to understand them as beautiful; all it does is tell me about the extension of the class. And yet (to go back to Socrates' question once more), the issue is not the extension of the class (the list of examples), but rather the *explanation* of the class—the account of *why* they are beautiful, not just *that* they are. The explanation of the class explains how these beautifuls come to be beautiful— not by virtue of themselves (tautology and failure of explanation here), nor by virtue of something quite different from themselves (the ugly, for example),[19] but by virtue of the beautiful, which *is not one of them*, and not (for the explanation to work) dependent on any of them at all. And for the explanation to appeal to me, or to anyone else, the explanation must be something that I *come to understand*—not something that I invent or derive from abstraction. So the beautiful is separate from both the instances of beauty (and would thus exist even if it were not instantiated) and from the minds that understand beauty (it would exist even if no one had a clue about what beauty

[18] It is tricky to formulate precisely Socrates' objection here. He is not claiming that anyone actually says of any particular two that it is formed both by the division of one in half and by the addition of one to one; rather, he is offended by explanations that vacillate or fail determinately to answer the question in hand. If, on being asked "Why two?" (a question about two in general), I say "Oh, well, either by dividing one in half, or by adding one to one," my explanation may be correct—but at the expense of providing an explanation that can be applied to cases. Cf. Mackenzie, "Impasse and Explanation," and ch. 2, sec. 3.

[19] Cf. here the *Lysis*'s attempt on this problem, which produces just that sort of answer, and concludes that it is absurd; *Lysis* 218ff.

is, or what counts as a beautiful thing). The forms, to explain, must be uncompromisingly separate. This I shall take, in what follows, to be the fundamental claim of this theory of forms: that forms are, in this uncompromising sense, *nonidentical* with particulars, and that forms are uncompromisingly mind-independent. These forms are real; they are transcendent.

Recall the problem with particulars. They suffer from the compresence of opposites—the equal sticks are always somehow unequal—and so demand explanation. So if forms explain, they should be free from the compresence of the property they explain; no form suffers the compresence of *its own* opposite. The form equal is never unequal, the form of beauty is never ugly, the form of large is never small. Now what does this tell us of the nature of the form? This question could be framed in two different ways:

1. Is the form equal, which cannot be unequal, consequently equal? Is anything that cannot be unequal, equal? (Does even the question make sense? Equal, we must continue to remember, is a relation—"equal to something or other." To what would the form equal be equal?) Does the form have the property that it explains (might it be *self-predicating*)? Or perhaps, is the form just the property it explains? Or could it simply be exempt from properties altogether? On the one hand, we could understand the form as the essence of, for example, equality; so it is either paradigmatically, perfectly equal, or it is just what it is to be equal, and thus its nature *is* equality. Or, on the other hand, we might understand it more formally, as it were: the form just is the explanation of the property (just as *The Origin of the Species* is the explanation of evolution); and as such it neither is, nor has, the property, even although it is a mind-independent entity.

2. Does the form have any other properties (whether or not it has "its own" property)? If Plato objects to the way in which particulars are irredeemably contextualized in relations with each other, must he deny any context to the forms? In that case, no form should suffer from the compresence of *any* opposites. The form equal would then no more be both large (larger than some other form) and small (smaller than a third form) than it may be both equal and unequal.

The epistemological argument precludes only the compresence of the form's own opposite, since it complains that the particular suffers compresence of that particular pair of opposites—and hence is unreliable in that respect. So the form must not suffer from the compresence of its own opposite; but this neither implies nor denies that it has the property it explains, or that it just is what it is to be (whatever it explains). Further, it is irrelevant to that epistemological difficulty whether or not that particular suffers from the compresence of some other, hitherto unconsidered pair of opposites. On that ticket, there seems no reason to saddle Plato with the view that forms, *qua* explanations, must be free from all compresence.

However, forms are not only explanations; they are *simple objects*, austere and indestructible, analogous to souls. This assumption is the clearest and first evidence that Plato thought that forms were neither concepts, nor ideas, nor universals, nor immanent in particulars. For when he uses the affinity arguments in the *Phaedo*, he needs to show that souls are separate from bodies in the sense that they survive the separation from the body—and death loses its sting. But then any soul, and any form, will be individual, not universal (what survives is Socrates, or you, not just a world soul—no consolation otherwise).[20] It will be capable of existence independent of particulars and bodies; and it will be capable of such existence *just because* it has the simple austerity that resists destruction (there are no seams where death could tear a form apart). In that strong sense, both forms and souls are separate, mind-independent substances, free from the compresence of opposites. They are also, on this argument, quite simple (souls are as like them as possible), so that they have no properties at all. They are just "themselves by themselves," just one.[21]

A passage from the *Republic* may serve to confirm Plato's insistence on the simplicity of the forms. Plato is describing the process of dialectic, by reflecting on the problem of compresence. Socrates and Glaucon compare three fingers: the little finger and the ring finger and the middle finger. They agree that each is no more and no less a finger, irrespective of its properties. Socrates begins:

> "For in all these matters, the soul of the ordinary person is not compelled to ask the mind 'what is a finger?' For sight never signifies a finger simultaneously to be the opposite of a finger. . . . So such an item is unlikely to provoke or arouse the mind to thought. . . . Well, now; does the sight adequately see their largeness or smallness, and does it make no difference to the sight whether the finger in question is in the middle or at the end? And likewise for fatness and thinness or softness and hardness in the case of touch? And the other senses likewise—won't they show such things deficiently? Doesn't each of them do this: first the sensation which is directed at the hard must be drawn up at the same time at the soft, and it reports to the soul that it senses the same thing as hard and soft? . . . So, in such cases the soul must be at a loss about what sensation signifies by hard, if it says that the same thing is soft; and likewise for the sensation of light and heavy, what is light and heavy, if the heavy signifies the light and the light heavy? . . .
>
> "So it is likely that in such cases the soul first tries calculation and thought, since it is provoked to consider whether each of these reported items are one or two. . . . Therefore if there appear to be two, then each will appear to be different and one. . . . If each is one and both are two, then mind will think the two separately; for it would not think inseparable things were two, but one. . . . But we said that sight saw large and small, not separate but collapsed together. . . . But for the sake of clarity the mind when it thinks must sees large and small, not collapsed together, but separate, differently from the way sight sees

[20] It was pointed out to me by Myles Burnyeat and Malcolm Schofield that this is exactly Plotinus's account of the consolation of philosophy. I reply that it is hardly consoling; and that in any case the *Phaedo*'s arguments are emphatically concerned with personal survival.

[21] See ch. 2, sec. 4, for a detailed discussion of this argument.

them. . . . Therefore from this experience it first occurs to us to ask 'what is the large?' or again 'what is the small?'. . .

"So some things provoke thinking, and some do not, where the provocative things are those which occur to sensation at the same time as their opposites; and things which don't do that, do not rouse thought. . . . Well, then, which group does number and the one fall into? . . . We may work it out from what we have agreed. For if the one is sufficiently seen itself by itself, or grasped by some other sensation, it would not drag us to reality, as we said in the case of the finger. But if some opposite always is seen along with it, so that it appears no more one that its opposite, then it will need some judgement, and the soul must be at a loss in this matter and investigate it, moving the thought in itself and asking itself what is the one itself; and thus the study of the one would be one of those things which lead and turn us to the vision of what is."

"But," Glaucon said, "this is especially what the sight of one does; for we see the same thing as both one and infinite in number at the same time." (*Rep.* 523c–525b)

Once again, Plato approaches the problem with particulars from an epistemological point of view; but now the epistemological problem is firmly tied to the ontological thesis that sensible particulars are complex entities. He argues—with autobiographical insight—that the problem with particulars is "psychagogic." If we consider the middle one of three fingers, which is large and small, the compresence of opposites (large and small) drags the soul upward to thinking about "what is large?" (though not "what is finger?"—which is adequately answered by sensation). But when the soul starts to ask itself that question, a further problem arises: how, confronted with this middle finger, can we identify "large" at all (grasp it, itself by itself), in order to ask "What is large?" Surely the large and the small are collapsed together—and thus defeat us before we even begin. Before we ask "What is large?" then, we must sort out "the large," which, in its manifestations, appears both one and many. The large is itself subject to the compresence of opposites, namely, one and many; so the primary question the soul must ask is not "What is large?" but "What is one?" before any dialectic can get off the ground. For our question cannot begin to be settled until the item about which we ask the questions is itself a determinate one something, itself by itself.

This passage, then, moves the compresence of opposites up a level, by acknowledging that not only particulars, but also the properties of particulars, may suffer compresence. At the first stage, compresence is necessary for the irritation that provokes dialectic; but then the source of the irritation must be removed before any further progress is made. The compresent opposites must be distinguished and identified in order to feature in any well-formed question. Look at the assumptions that are at work in this passage.

Plato suggests that being "one itself-by-itself" is a necessary feature of any nonvexed item, so that any explanandum must be determined in this way before the explanation can occur. What is more, the "one not many" requirement on proper explananda is itself liable to occur as a vexed property, as a case of the compresence of opposites. Consequently, we may ask a quite *general* question—"What is one?"—which needs an answer before any other, more substantial questions can be answered. But this demand betrays three assumptions:

1. Plato supposes that *being one* is fundamental or basic—the questions about individuation must be asked first.

2. "Being one" is understood absolutely: something is one, simpliciter (not one *giraffe*, one *finger*). Hence the dialectician must inquire into, and understand, *what one is* before he can let his attention wander to sticks or fingers or hippopotami.

3. What is more, this problem of being one is entirely general—being one is basic to anything that is anything. So the inquiry into what makes something one, or how a something is one something, will cover not only sensible particulars but also the entities of the intelligible world—souls and forms.

Now this account gives some general requirements about the nature of the objects of inquiry, and thus some conditions on the nature of forms. Any inquiry is provoked by the compresence of opposites—whether in a particular finger or in a form such as the large. But no inquiry can be conducted successfully if its objects remain "collapsed together"; and this will be true both for forms such as large and for forms such as one. Any form, Socrates finally suggests, will be many and not one so long as any compresence of opposites is admitted to it at all: thus, the inquiry into largeness is impossible without a prior inquiry into one; and that inquiry can only be carried out if the one is just one, and not in any way many. Any form, we may conclude, needs to be a simple entity if it is to serve as the proper object of inquiry; forms, whatever their natures, must exclude the compresence of any opposites.

So Plato offers a thoroughgoing contrast between the ontological status of particulars and that of forms. The arguments for the simplicity of the form do require that the form be free from *all* compresence. These arguments, as we have seen, rested on the assumption that the properties, relations, and values of a particular constitute its being many (particulars have a *generous* nature). In that case, the form, being just one, cannot have any of those properties, relations, and values; and in that way it maintains its singularity. This I call the *austere* nature of the form. Now austerity could be required in one of two quite different ways:

First, it may be a demand for *purity*. If Plato supposes that any form just is what it is to be (equal, large, whatever), then the form may have the simple nature of whatever property it explains. This account would tell us the difference between one form and another; but it might not meet the condition that forms should be just one, if being one itself is counted as a property of the form.

Second, it may be a demand for the forms to be *simple entities,* and not composite in any way. This account would tell us nothing of the individual nature of different forms, but it would meet the demand that no form should be in any way composite, where being one itself counts as a property of any form.

Now of course it seems sensible to say that no form is either larger or smaller than anything else; to suppose otherwise is to make the mistake of treating forms as if they were physical objects. So we might be ready to concede that forms are free not only from "their own" compresence, but also from the compresence of *some* other properties too. But forms are to be simple. To reemphasise the point, this seems to be a very strong claim, that any form is absolutely simple and unitary, not possessed of any features that would render it many in any way; forms are austere. Remember now the thesis of natural inherence with which, I have argued, the middle-period metaphysics began. This involved two claims:

1. that properties are real features of their objects;
2. that relations and values are properties.

But, when it comes to simple forms, these claims cause trouble.

What of relations such as "sameness" or "difference"? Are we to say, for example, that no form is both the same as itself and different from everything else?

What of values? Any form—according to the teleology of the *Republic*—will be unqualifiedly good. To be valuable, for a form, is not to suffer from compresence, just because the forms are unqualifiedly valuable. But I have suggested that Plato has a naturalist approach to value. In that case, the form's goodness will be a feature of the form over and above its being a form. Will that impugn its austere singularity?

If forms are responsible for the real nature of things (or the properties of things), how are forms and particulars related? After all, if relations are real properties, they will constitute real properties of forms no less than of particulars—and then any form will have many properties, and be a many, not a one.

3. UNDERSTANDING AND TELEOLOGY

Remember Meno's paradox: How can I begin an inquiry? How am I motivated to start to wonder? And how, when I have reached the end, do I know that I have the right answer? Plato argued that inquiry was possible when Recollection is triggered by our experience in this world. But the theory of Recollection looks pretty fanciful, and it gives nothing more than an hint of the answer to the second question. (We know we have the right answer in the same way that we recognize the return of full memory after the vague naggings of half-recall: "Where have I seen that woman before?" The question troubles me until I suddenly recall, beyond the possibility of doubting, that she sold me a hat last week). Meno's paradox remains troubling as Plato's theory of knowledge develops, especially since the theory of Recollection is absent from the major dialogues of the middle period.[22]

At the same time, the *Phaedo*'s account of explanation adds a further worry. Complaining about the deficiency of his predecessors' accounts, Socrates says: "In truth it does not occur to them that everything is tied and held together by the good and by what is necessary. I therefore would gladly become a student of anyone who offered any such explanation whatever. But since I was deprived of that, and was neither able to find it myself nor to learn it from others, would you like me to give you a demonstration of the second voyage I made in the inquiry into explanation?" (*Phd.* 99c5–d2).

Socrates was looking for an explanation that was universal (of "everything") and systematic ("tied together"); such an explanation, he supposes, would also be teleological, since the structure would be determined by what is both necessary and good. The objective then is what we might call cosmic teleology—the thesis that the whole cosmos is tied together in a single *structure*; because it is structured, it is good.[23]

One response to Socrates' ambition is the skeptical one. Socrates is far better off, we might say, to offer the formal explanations of his second voyage than to steer for the impossible destination of teleology. After all, the skeptic complains, teleology is cloud-cuckoo-land, the wishful thinking of those who want the reassurance that the universe is not in fact a heap of random sweepings, nor our role in the world the product of accident and contingency, of no particular use, purpose, or good at all. If Socrates wants to provide us with a consolation for mortality, he needs a stouter argument than the sentimental optimism of the teleological account.

But reflection on the way Plato deploys teleological arguments provides a response to this skeptic. Plato's interest in teleology may best be explained in terms of his metaphysics and his epistemology; it is significant, then, that Socrates is *frustrated* in his teleological ambitions in the *Phaedo*, the work in which we most expect to find consolation for mortality. Instead, we should look to the *Symposium* and the *Republic* to see how the interest in teleology is an interest in explanation, rather than the hope that we are not part of a random muddle. The underlying drive toward teleology is the view that explanation works by system, and cannot be based on what is random or contin-

---

[22] The history of the theory of Recollection is a vexed one; it turns up again in the *Phaedrus*, later than and, I argue (Mackenzie, "*Phaedrus*"), critical of the doctrines of the *Republic*; but we should not therefore suppose that it is implicit in the dialogues in between—especially the *Symposium* and the *Republic*: that is, to suppose that Plato is merely a doctrine monger, and not a paid-up arguing philosopher.

[23] Socratic or Platonic teleology should be distinguished from the Aristotelian version, which explains "the best" in terms of the flourishing of individual species. For Aristotle, the goodness required by teleology comes from the functioning of the members of the species (this is, as it were, linear teleology); for Plato, the goodness comes from the structure, the order of a complex whole; compare the arguments about the ordered soul at *Gorgias* 504ff. But see Furley, "Rainfall"; Sedley, "Teleology"; and McCabe, "Myth."

gent. Teleology provides a universal structure; and that, insofar as it is ordered, is bound to be a good thing.

So three questions remain outstanding:

1. How does inquiry begin and proceed?
2. How does inquiry terminate?
3. How can explanations be made systematic and teleological?

The questions are connected. The *Meno* had suggested that everything we come to know is connected ("all nature is akin"); but the *Phaedo's* (later) version allows for piecemeal, even haphazard recollection; and it does not require the ordered investigations of dialectic. So if knowledge is piecemeal and not systematic, there may be no connection at all between one piece of knowledge and another; consequently, the purposes of philosophical inquiry will be frustrated.

The *Symposium* is about love: but it is love of a rational sort. Diotima, the priestess from Mantinea, offers Socrates an account of how we make progress in love—and thus at the same time come to know what we failed to see before. We see a beautiful boy in the street and we want him, we desire him;[24] then we realize (the more the merrier) that many boys are better (more collectively beautiful) than just one. Then an encounter with Socrates encourages us to believe that beautiful minds are better than beautiful bodies; and thus we ascend through the hierarchy of beautiful things (souls, institutions, sciences, etc.) until suddenly we come across the form of the beautiful, which is beautiful unqualifiedly, itself by itself, eternal and single in form (*Symp.* 210a ff.).

The ascent of love attempts to answer the question How do we make progress in knowing? by supplanting two crucial features of the *Phaedo* account.

First, inquiry is motivated not by the cognitive triggering of recollection, but by the appetitive impulse of love. Alcibiades smites us with his (real) beauty, and his beauty ignites a correlative lust. But lust being the greedy creature it is, we move in its grip from the particular to the general (all the beautiful bodies we can find); and thence up the ladder through the more refined sorts of beauty and the more recherché sorts of desire. Once again, the motive first to inquire is replaced by a cause (Alcibiades' beauty) and supplemented by a familiar psychological phenomenon (appetite, desire).

Second, we can now progress in knowing. It is, Diotima supposes, a commonplace that desire tries to maximize its objects.[25] If I desire chocolate, then

---

[24] The "ascent of love" is both a philosophical theory and an account of the structure and expectations of Athenian aristocratic culture. The latter does not, I think, affect our assessment of the former. Cf. here Dover, *Greek Homosexuality*.

[25] This part of the theory makes it clear that we are not talking about love in one of its modern senses, which is specific to some individual object. If I love Rudolf Valentino, that cannot be generalized to my loving all men, or all silent movie stars. But if I desire this after-dinner mint, then there is, it could be argued, some description under which my desire is generalizable: "I desire chocolate." "I desire sweet things." "I desire whatever I cannot have," etc.

my desire is not for this single after-dinner mint, but for the whole box (unless this desire is qualified by a countervailing desire, to avoid nausea). If I desire beauty, then two beautiful objects are better, more satisfying than one. Equally, I will desire what is more beautiful more than what is less beautiful, and a larger group of more beautiful items more than a smaller. But then desire can become a rational plan for living if I can deliberately pursue what is more desirable. To be more satisfied, therefore, I need to find out what is more beautiful, and how it can be multiplied—and so on up the ladder of love. Rational erotics, then, proceeds by following the interconnections, the structure of what is known.

Inquiry happens, and it works, because our encounters with beauty out there in the world activate our desire for more; that desire is progressively satisfied as we accumulate more and more "beautifuls," until eventually we emerge at (are transformed by) the pinnacle, the form of the beautiful that is the final stage in the ascent. So progress up the ladder of love is made, first, because the beautiful objects affect us (they have beauty naturally inherent in them); second, because we desire them (they are good to have); and third, because they are connected with each other in a single structure of beauty.

This approach is made more general, and connected more directly to the problems of philosophical understanding, in the central books of the *Republic*.

Socrates says that philosophers should be kings. Why? Because philosophers know, while everyone else only believes. Why should that make philosophers better at being kings than anyone else? Because knowing is a state of mind (not an individual cognitive episode) that will allow the philosopher to be right in affairs of state, and to promote the interests of the citizens with prudence and success.[26]

Socrates offers an argument (*Rep.* 476e ff.) to convince the "lover of sights and sounds," the mere believer, of the truth of his claim. His argument proceeds in two separate stages.[27]

In the first stage (476e–478e), Socrates uses the common assumptions of the ordinary man (someone who will be, in Socrates' sense, a believer) to derive a contrast between knowledge, belief, and ignorance. Knowledge is a capacity of soul, and so is belief; but the former is infallible, the latter fallible. Knowledge is about what is, ignorance is about what is not; and so belief is about what both is and is not (or about what lies between complete being and complete not-being).[28] In the second stage (479a–480a), Socrates explains,

---

[26] The detailed interpretation of the argument of *Rep.* 476e ff. is thoroughly controversial; I leave that aside here, and refer my reader to Annas, *Plato's Republic*, ch.8, and Fine, "Knowledge and Belief." In what follows I am rather closer to Fine than to Annas.

[27] Socrates' remark at *Rep.* 478e7, "with these things agreed as a foundation . . . ," marks the move from stage 1 to stage 2, which brings in the forms.

[28] I construe "what is," etc., in the first stage as a generic descprition of what is true, so that knowledge is about truths, while belief is a muddle of truth and falsehood. In the second stage of the argument, but no earlier, Socrates produces the theory of forms (of "what is") as an account of knowledge. It is only by this stage of the argument that the lover of sights and sounds might be brought to concede such Platonist premises. Cf. Appendix B.

by an argument from the compresence of opposites, that the infallibility of knowledge can only be explained by something fixed and reliable—the forms.

Socrates insists that knowledge and belief are capacities.[29] A capacity is different from an action. Today I stood on my head: that was an action. Tomorrow I shall have the same capacity for standing on my head: I could repeat the action. Capacities have as their objects classes of action, not particular events—and this will be true no less of cognitive capacities than it is of athletic ones. Suppose, then, I say that knowledge is a capacity that has truth as its object. What do I mean? Surely I am saying that knowledge is a disposition to get things right. It is not only a matter of being right now, but the capacity to do it again and again—tomorrow, the next day, and the week after.[30] Ignorance, contrariwise, is the cognitive state of the person who is persistently wrong, pigheadedly misguided (certainly not someone we should want to rule over us). And belief is the cognitive capacity where we *may or may not* get things right; its object is the class of truths and falsehoods. Belief, unlike knowledge (and unlike the persistent wrongness of ignorance, too), is thoroughly unpredictable. The believer may be right, but then again he may be wrong—you pays your money and you takes your choice. But if that is his state of mind, he will be bad news as a ruler, for he will not be able to tell whether he will be right next time; and when it comes to foreign policy, or the intricacies of economics, next time is what matters. Predictive certainty demands a state of mind that will always be right, and knowledge is the only state of mind that guarantees predictive certainty.

But *how* does knowledge afford us that guarantee? By *Republic* 478e, Socrates has made the vital distinctions between the two states of knowledge and ignorance; but he still has to explain *why* knowledge gets it right. At this point, he returns to the theory of forms and to a rerun of the argument of the *Phaedo*. Again he debates with the believer, who does not admit the theory of forms (479a4). Any of "the many beautifuls" also appears ugly, what is just appears unjust, what is double appears half, and so forth. Any of these things no more is what someone says it is than it is not so. So none of these things can be thought strictly either to be or not to be both these properties or neither.[31] But then this surely means that such items lie between being and not-being, since they are more murky than being, clearer than not-being. So these many beautifuls roll around between being and not-being.

---

[29] See *Rep.* 477c1ff; compare the discussion of affections of the soul at *Rep.* 511d7.

[30] That our expression "knowledge" is not a capacity word of the same sort is, of course, no counterargument; we are dealing here with the Greek ἐπιστήμη.

[31] There is a nest of compresent opposites here, lurking amid Plato's echoes of Parmenides. First, I take Burnet's punctuation to be wrong, and would delete the comma after "strictly be thought"; this gives an incomplete, not a complete use, of "is." The subject is "the many"; the copula is both affirmed and denied; and the predicate term is both affirmed and denied, and neither affirmed or denied. Boiled down, Socrates allows the following possibilities: *x* is {F and not-F}; *x* is not {F and not-F}. His point is that *x* cannot be strictly thought to be F simpliciter, both because of the negation of the copula *and* because of the negation of the predicate term (the compresent opposite).

However, this does not guarantee that knowledge is a state of mind, a permanent cognitive disposition suitable for a ruler. The philosopher might, for example, be able to get hold of the form of beautiful (and tell the citizens all they need to know about the relative merits of bodies and mathematical theorems), but still be vague about the form of justice, so that when it comes to dividing the spoils of war or the silver from the mines, the philosopher is just as inegalitarian as anyone else might be. How does Plato make sure that his philosophers have a comprehensive sort of knowledge? How does he give them *understanding*? At *Republic* 505a, Socrates says: "You have often heard that the form of the good is the greatest object of learning, by virtue of which just things and the rest become useful and beneficial. Now you know, I suppose, that this is what I was going to say, and, furthermore, that we do not know the form of the good properly; but even if we have as much knowledge as possible of all else, so long as we lack knowledge of the good, you know that our knowledge will do us no good—as nothing else would, without the good."

The good is what makes all knowledge hang together, and be worth having. But unfortunately, we do not know the good. How can we even understand the theory that we are offered about it? Imagine, Socrates suggests, that it is like the sun, which is the offspring of the good (*Rep.* 507a ff.). The sun, by casting its light, makes the objects of the sensible world visible; so it connects us,[32] who see, to the visible world (507e). So the good sheds truth on the objects of the intelligible world and makes them accessible to our understanding (508c–d): the objects of knowledge make us understand them, so long as they are illuminated by the truth. Thus, the form of the good is the supreme entity, the cause of our understanding the rest. But the sun does not just make things visible, it makes the living things in the world grow; likewise the good makes the intelligible things be what they are, and so the good is itself beyond being (509b).

This passage is pretty mysterious: What does it mean for the form of the good to be beyond being? How can it shed truth on the other forms?[33] Yet the allegory of the sun does give us some immediate illumination. First of all, Plato persists in a causal account of understanding: so he continues to claim that the objects of knowledge are mind-independent, separate forms. But now Socrates has improved on his earlier account by offering the analogy with the natural world. For physical nature here is enlightened and flourishes all together; the world is a systematic whole, ordered by the best. Likewise, intelligible nature is made coherent and systematic by the form of the good, which also makes it knowable in the first place: what is known, then, is known as a whole, as a connected and teleological system—or else it is not known at all. Knowledge, that is, is understanding—a rich and coherent grasp of the system

---

[32] The "yoke" imagery of *Rep.* 508a1 embellishes the "tying together" of *Phd.* 99c.

[33] Again, I leave these details of interpretation aside; but, here cf., e.g., Annas, *Plato's Republic*, ch.10.

of truth and reality. The philosopher is a knower of this sort—or else he fails to be a philosopher at all. There is no piecemeal knowledge (or if there is, it is trivial and worthless). Proper understanding is structured; proper understanding is a fixed and infallible state of mind.

This vivid teleological picture of understanding is clarified by the sober analysis that follows—the divided line (*Rep.* 509d ff.). Here, "states of mind" are classified in ascending order, in four sections:

1. *eikasia*, the state of mind in which we are unable to tell the difference between an image and reality, is the first. Here Plato may have in mind the distorting effect of poetic imagery and the theater, where the audience blurs suspended disbelief and direct access to reality. Exactly so, the television soap opera persuades its viewer that it is true, not imaginary; the line between fact and fiction disappears, and the audience is trapped in "imagination," *eikasia*.[34]

2. *Pistis*, the converse state of mind, in which we are able to distinguish the facts of our world from its fictions, is the second. Plato seems to be emphasizing not the distinction between different types of objects for our cognitive states, but rather our own cognitive ability to discriminate between the true and the false. This higher state of mind, *pistis*, improves on *eikasia* just by getting these distinctions right; it follows from this that both *pistis* and *eikasia* are cognitive attitudes toward a complex of data that must be assimilated and distinguished, and not merely be the one-to-one relation of acquaintance.

3. Next, we have *dianoia*, the hypothetical stage, of which mathematics is an example. Here one connects hypotheses and conclusions (e.g., at *Rep.* 510b), and the criterion of truth can only be coherence ("they treat their hypotheses as true," 510c6; "they end consistently," *homologoumenōs*, 510d2), since there is no way of confirming either hypothesis or conclusion other than by its fitting into the whole system (cf. *Phd*, 100a ff.).

4. The philosopher whose state of mind is *noēsis* moves, by contrast, beyond hypotheses to the unhypothesized beginning whereupon he may confirm and connect everything that depends on that beginning, "and thus he reaches the end" (*Rep.* 511b). This is a closed system, where the various elements of understanding are interconnected and interdependent. And it is a system that is uniquely true; hence, it is anchored to the ultimate principle, "the unhypothesized beginning."

---

[34] Here again, my interpretation is controversial. Some commentators, for example, suppose that εἰκασία is defined simply by its objects, literally interpreted—shadows and reflections in water. Here, there is no question of what the viewer sees these *as*; instead (this interpretation supposes), whenever I see a shadow, I am, *eo ipso*, in a state of εἰκασία. If my interpretation of the argument at the end of Book 5 is at all plausible, then this will not do as an account of εἰκασία— for it describes not a state of mind but an individual cognitive event, and it has nothing much to do with truth and falsehood. The crucial point must surely be cases where I muddle the image with what the image is of—and thus the issue is what I see the image as. And then that may be a state of mind—the state of mind where I regularly muddle image with reality. Plato's bugbear in this respect, of course, is the theater.

Here is one of Plato's accounts of dialectic (*Rep.* 511b). Inevitably, there is massive disagreement, both about the interpretation of the divided line and its relation to the sun analogy. But for present purposes, just two points are needed—and they are largely undisputed.

First, here the *Republic* meets the desideratum of the *Phaedo*—a coherent and universal explanation for "everything" (hence, "and thus he reaches the end," 511b8). I have suggested that at each stage of the divided line, cognition is defined in terms of its grasp (or otherwise) of the *structure* of what is understood; at least all commentators will agree that at the top of the line understanding must be of a complex system. If the divided line does fit closely with the sun, moreover (as *Rep.* 509c–d implies), that system is also teleological, made coherent by the overriding form of the good.

Second, this account, even more than its predecessors in the *Phaedo* and the *Symposium*, points to a close connection between epistemological arguments and ontological ones. The system is not imposed on the world by minds; instead, the system is a part of the complex ontological structure of forms and particulars. Plato supposes, that is, that the structure of understanding corresponds to *and is caused by* the structure of what there is. Once again, the *Republic* meets Socrates' challenge in the *Phaedo*, to give a proper explanation.

So how are forms now characterized? If each form is a piece of the teleological whole, then it will be both valuable (good) and enmeshed in the structure. Arguments in both the *Phaedo* and the *Republic* seem to demand that any form should be just one, austere and itself by itself. But the teleological account of philosophical understanding requires that forms have properties (in the wide sense of "property" that I have suggested in the previous chapter); for they have a value, and they are interrelated. And to that extent they are neither austere nor "themselves by themselves"; instead, they are a part of the unique system of what is intelligible and real.[35]

The forms are postulated in the middle period to dissolve the trouble with particulars. When Plato is looking for simple explanations, or when he is seeking the paradigm of a simple entity, the nature of the forms is directly contrasted with the nature of particulars. Particulars turn up in a complex of relations; they are essentially contextualized. Consequently, forms are understood as context-free. So while particulars are *generous* individuals, objects

---

[35] To anticipate: the account of structured understanding in the middle period reappears in later dialogues as the classifications derived from collection and division (e.g., at *Phdr.* 265; *Soph.* 219ff.; *Pol.* 262ff.). Now it is a matter of considerable dispute whether this method of analysis collects and divides separate forms, or merely classifies kinds (whether they be universals, or ideas, or whatever). But whatever it is that is collected and divided, the product is a structure where the individual terms are understood *by being interrelated*. Sophistry is the conflation of different terms (*Soph.* 230d), but true dialectic is to understand just how different "ideas" are connected and distinguished, to understand the κοινωνία γενῶν. So Plato's view of understanding remains true to the *Republic* picture: understanding is systematic, not piecemeal, formulated by the interrelations of what is understood. This, as we shall see, is a vital feature of Plato's changing metaphysics.

with many properties, values, and relations, forms are simple and incomposite, *austere* individuals. But the teleological account of forms suggests that, so far from being contrasted with particulars, the forms are analogous to them, when they are considered together, as a structured whole. At that point, forms, like particulars, become enmeshed in relations and value; and for that reason each form, too, might be thought to be a many.

4. THE THEORY OF FORMS

What Is a Form?

In the *Phaedo* and the *Republic* Socrates talks about forms in a haphazard and often allusive way. But a theory of incomposite single forms is directly advanced in the *Parmenides* by the young Socrates in the face of Zeno's paradoxes and the views of Father Parmenides; and Parmenides attacks it with enthusiasm.[36] Socrates makes two claims about forms: an *existential* thesis: "Don't you think *that there is* some form of likeness itself by itself, and again some other form opposite to it, what [it] is [to be][37] unequal? (128e5–129a2). . . . If someone were first to divide off the forms that I mentioned just now, *separately* themselves by themselves, such as likeness and unlikeness and plurality and the one and motion and rest and all such things. . ." (129d6–e1); my emphases); and a *characterization* of the forms: "Next, if someone showed that they [the forms] were able to *mingle together in themselves, and divide from themselves*, I should be amazed. . ." (129e2–3; my emphases).

Think about *separate* forms first. The language that Socrates uses to describe his forms places stringent requirements upon their ontological status. The standard description of particulars is that they are "many," *polla* (129a3; 131a9, b1, 9; 132a1), at the same time that they are, individually, "each," *hekaston* (131d1, 4; 132c10). By contrast the forms are one, *hen*, and individual, *hekaston* (131a9, b1, 6, 7, c9, 10; 132a1, 2, 3, b2, 5, 7, c4; 133b2; 135a2, b8). Forms no less than particulars are described as "somethings," *ti*, *atta* (130b3, 8, c2, d4, e5; 133b2, c4; 135a2).

The relation between the two types of entity is described by the adverb/preposition *chōris*, "separate." The relation is a symmetrical one: the forms are *chōris* the particulars, and the particulars are *chōris* the forms. Plato uses the preposition *chōris* trivially enough to mean "without," "apart from" (*Apology* 35b9; *Charmides* 157b6; *Crito* 44b7; *Symposium* 173c4); and this usage turns up also in the *Parmenides* itself (131a5; 140a1). Sometimes "x cannot be *chōris* y" signifies that y is a necessary condition of x (e.g.,

---

[36] There is a (another) minefield here. How seriously are we to take the *Parmenides*' attacks on the theory? Seriously, I suggest, if the arguments are to any extent compelling—and so, I shall suggest, they are. Reading the *Parmenides* at all is a tricky business; compare, famously, Vlastos's "record of honest perplexity" with any of the more dogmatic accounts either before or since.

[37] My additions in parentheses—Socrates here uses the "ὅ ἔστιν" expression canonized at *Phaedo* 75c ff.

Timaeus 28a5, 61c8; *Sophist* 238b8, 249c1). However, *choris* does not merely signify a relation; it also tells us something of the nature of at least one of the relata. Thus, for example, the soul, when it is separate[38] from the body, is as such "itself by itself," *auto kath'auto* (*Phd.* 67c6).[39] Now (as I have argued), Socrates' soul is separate and "itself by itself" insofar as it survives when he dies; and this is only a consolation for dying if the soul that survives is determinately Socrates (rather than, perhaps, returning to some soul receptacle). This suggestion, that what is separate is also determinate, is borne out by the general use of the participle *chōrismenon* to describe determinate items: so, for example, the separation of "skills," *technai* (*Rep.* 522b7; *Politicus* 303d1; *Philebus* 55e1), of people (*Symp.* 192c1), or of virtues (*Meno* 87d5). This develops, in later dialogues, into a technical term to describe different classes, properly distinguished (*Pol.* 262e3, 280b8, etc; cf. *Soph.* 253d6 and compare *Rep.* 595a9), so that "separate" implies "determinate." And when entities, not classes, are described as separate, their determinacy (e.g., *Rep.* 453c5; *Tim.* 24b2, 73b8) is coupled with the view that what is separate is an individual, "one," "something," *hen, ti* (*Meno* 87d5; *Phd.* 97b3; *Rep.* 524b10; *Euthydemus* 284a4), with an individual "nature," *phusis* (*Soph.* 245c9).

Think, first of all, how different the claim that forms are *separate* will be from the claim that forms are *different* from particulars. If, for example, my idea of bliss is quite different from yours, that tells us nothing of the ontological status of either; neither may ever be instantiated, neither may be very definite, neither may be thought of as having any real properties (apart from the tricky property of vagueness, perhaps). Or if we argue that my idea of bliss is different from this glass of water, the reality of the glass of water carries no implications for the realization of my fantasy. But were I to say that my idea of bliss is *separate* from that music, then, in Plato's terms, the bliss must be somewhere around after all. The logic of the separation relation includes, but is not included by, nonidentity. So forms are not identical to particulars, *and they are separate as well*—real, determinate somethings (not masses, concepts, or properties). Thus:

> 1. Forms are *self-subsistent*, not mind-dependent. This is a consequence of the argument from explanation, as we have seen; and it is duly expressed by the *symmetry* of the *chōris* relation. Thus forms are *separate*.
>
> 2. Forms are not masses, but *determinate* separate items. This will be a consequence of the argument for the affinity of forms and souls. Therefore, forms are *countable* individuals (either because each is a simple entity, or because the nature of each is different from the nature of any other).
>
> 3. Forms are "ones"—they are single unified items. The argument for incomposite forms (as opposed to composite particulars) demands that each form be just one—an austere individual.

---

[38] Here Plato uses the cognate verb, χωρίζειν.
[39] Compare *Rep.* 609d ff.; *Soph.* 227c9; and *Phd.* 78.

4. If forms are "somethings," they are not "suches": that is, they are not themselves properties, but at best they are the *possessors of properties* (although even that may be disallowed by their austere individuality at 3 above). On this count, they are basic entities.

On all these grounds, then, forms are characterized as individuals, and individuals par excellence. The two-world thesis of the *Parmenides* is presented as a thesis about two types of individual: forms and particulars. And it is *as such*, I shall argue, that it comes under Eleatic fire.

Forms are characterized differently from particulars. Individual particulars characteristically possess properties; and that makes them many. Indeed, particulars *are always* characterized by opposites. Sensible individuals, such as Socrates and Zeno, partake in both likeness and unlikeness; after all, considered in relation to each other, "thee and me" are bound to be *both* like *and* unlike (129a2–3; cf. 129a8, d1). And such a state of affairs is not only tolerable, but necessary, for the objects contextualised in the phenomenal world. So *particulars*

1. are both like and unlike (129a1–2);
2. are both like and unlike *themselves to themselves* (129a8); and
3. are both one and many (129c4–d6).

But how far can *forms* possess properties? Particulars are characterized in these different ways; but to be like particulars—on Socrates' account in the *Parmenides*—is fatal for forms. So for *forms*,

4. the form like cannot be unlike (129b1–3)—no form can be characterized by its own opposite;
5. so the form one cannot be many, nor can the form many be one (129b7);
6. no forms can exhibit these opposite properties *in themselves* (129c2);
7. nor can forms mingle and separate *among themselves* (129e2–3).

If the trouble with particulars is the compresence of opposites, then the form cannot suffer from that; hence (4) and its special case (5). More generally, however, by contrast with condition (3) for particulars, no form can be both one and many. Particulars can be one and many—one with many parts (this large articulated lorry), one among many others (that man in the queue). But forms are just themselves in themselves, just one (hence 6). And, most strongly of all, (7), they cannot intermingle and separate: not only do they resist their own opposites, but they also resist the properties imparted by other forms; they do not *interpredicate*. These requirements are said to ensure that the forms are "separate," *chōris*, and "themselves by themselves," *auta kath'auta*; (129d7); and they imply that the forms are just one each, not many.[40]

---

[40] Teloh and Louzecky spotted the focus of attack in the arguments here, but did not follow through the consequences of that for the reading of the *Parmenides* as a whole.

So Socrates' theory of forms wants both forms and particulars to be individual substances; and it allows properties to particulars but not to forms. This is consistent with the characters of forms and particulars in earlier dialogues, as we have seen. Sensible individuals, first of all, are conceived in a *generous* way such that each may (or must) admit a multiplicity of properties. Forms, by direct contrast, are conceived in an *austere* way so as to exclude altogether any multiplicity or variation; they are "themselves by themselves," *auta kath' auta*. *Both* accounts of the nature of individuals, as the rest of the dialogue is designed to show, come to grief; and with them we lose the power of discourse.

Why should Socrates insist on the individual status of both forms and particulars? The answer to this question has an Aristotelian flavor. For it appears that Plato attributes to particular individuals (to sensible "ones" or "somethings") a certain priority.

In the middle period, as we have seen, although sensible particulars are troublesome because they have compresent opposites, nonetheless there are trouble-free underlying entities—sticks and stones, or fingers—that are fixed in the sensible world, and that allow the possibility of sense-perception and hence cognition. Thus, in the opening passages of the *Parmenides*, Socrates, in all his plurality, is still *one under the many*, the individual who carries the properties in question.

The forms are thought to be individuals for different, intellectual reasons. Plato inferred from the compresence of opposites in particulars that forms are single-formed, *monoeideis*; and their singularity is thought to give them priority when it comes to explanations so that they are *ones over many*. Hence, in the *Parmenides* Socrates is committed to two sorts of thing: on the one hand, sensible individuals; and on the other, intelligible individuals, the forms. This pair of assumptions, "one under many" and "one over many," dominates the entire dialogue, as Plato tries to come to grips with the specification of such individuals.

What Is a Theory?

Plato thinks there are forms. How far does he hold a *theory* of forms? Is his commitment to these ideal individuals systematic enough to merit the title of "theory"? Many of Plato's arguments mention particular forms (equal, beautiful, good). Now obviously enough these are theoretical items—they are not sensible, visible, obvious objects, but constructs offered as explanations of particular problems (this stick equal to that; Alcibiades' beauty). But a theory needs to do more than invent theoretical entities; it needs to make theoretical claims about them. Suppose that I believe that there is a fairy at the bottom of my garden who is responsible for my tomatoes' ripening. That belief would constitute a theory if I thought that all ripening tomatoes in anyone's garden owe their flourishing to some local genius. One crucial thing about a theory, that is, is that it should be *universalizable* from case to case, and systematic in that way (or else that there should be rules for limiting its application—for example, only the fairies at the bottom of the gardens of people whose surname begins with M ripen the tomatoes).[41]

Socrates' simple-minded explanation in the *Phaedo* is still too piecemeal, I suspect, to satisfy such conditions for theory. But there is a moment in the closing passages of *Republic* X that looks more promising: "So shall we begin our discussion from there, by our accustomed method? We are accustomed to posit a form as one something in each case, for each set of many to which we give the same name, are we not?" (596a).

Socrates goes on to suggest that there is a form of bed, of table; anything that shares a common name has a corresponding form. Now this looks like quite a different argument for forms than the argument from affinity or the argument from explanation. For here Socrates suggests that linguistic considerations underlie our postulating forms. In order to account for any universal, we need a form—one word, one form.[42] And that, of course, could hardly be more universalizable.

The argument from names works for all sorts of cases. When a carpenter makes a table or a bed, he looks to the form of table or bed. And the form, of course, antedates his doing any sawing or hammering, for he did not invent it; it was there already (*Rep.* 596b). If anyone made the forms, it was god, the amazing craftsman who fashioned everything that grows and lives, and even the earth itself, everything in the heavens and beneath the ground.[43] Now any bed may have many counterparts, and many imitations. But no form is more than one; for if there were two, there should need to be a third to give the form to the first two, and so on. There is, therefore, just one ideal bed, not more than one.

The one over many thesis, as it is presented in the *Republic*, emphasizes that, in order to avoid a dangerous regress, there should be *exactly one and only one form* for each collection of many things. When we want to *count* the number of forms there are, then, we count the names there are—there are just that many forms; the theory is fully universalizable.

That, however, is not all there is to a theory, especially to a theory that offers theoretical entities. "Entities are not to be multiplied beyond necessity."[44] Aristotle, far earlier than William of Ockham, recommended ontological parsimony; and the same interest in simplicity is to be found in the early

[41] Some might find this condition for theory unpalatable, as Keith Hossack points out to me. However, it is clearly *Socrates'* view that theories need to be universalizable at *Parm.* 130e.

[42] See Fine, "One over Many," for a sane account of this passage.

[43] It is worth bearing in mind the cagey way in which Socrates puts this thesis. He attributes incredulity to Glaucon; and then modifies his thesis: "in some way there is a creator of everything, and in some way not": 596d3–4. This sort of caveat turns up in the *Timaeus*, too; cf. ch. 6, secs. 1, 6.

[44] Kneale and Kneale, *Development of Logic*, p. 243; there is no evidence that William of Ockham ever wrote the canonical formula of his razor *entia non sunt multiplicanda praeter necessitatem*. Ockham's razor it remains, even if the ontological economy it recommends is, as I argue here, very much a part of early theoretical thinking.

monists.[45] Think again about the fairies at the bottom of my garden. Suppose that I want to persuade you that they are what cause my tomatoes to ripen; you, a skeptic, will be more likely to believe a theory with fewer theoretical moving parts, fewer fairies, less hierarchy in the ethereal world, than you will believe something grossly complicated. Socrates—if Aristophanes is to be believed—saw just this point. If the clouds explain all there is to be explained—rain, growth, and everything else we see—what need is there for the Olympian pantheon as well? (Aristophanes *Clouds* 311ff.). Economy is the watchword in theory; be mean with your entities, and your theory will be all the better for it.

At *Parmenides* 130b–d, Parmenides asks Socrates about the scope of his theory, a question that recalls the universal scope of the argument from names in *Republic* X. How many forms are there? Socrates insists that there must be forms of likeness, one, many (the relations), and of just, beautiful and good (the values). He is doubtful, however, when it comes to the forms of man, fire, or water, and, he is positively dismissive of the "silly" forms—hair, mud, dirt: "No way, said Socrates—but they are just as we see them. It would be nothing short of absurd to suppose that there are forms of these things. And yet I worry lest I should adopt the same principle about everything—and then when I get to that stage I run away in terror lest I tumble into a pit of nonsense and am destroyed" (130d3–7).

Now this passage is often read as a piece of sentiment on Socrates' part; he thinks, perhaps, that forms ought to be fine and shining exemplars, and is thus anxious to exclude mud and garbage. But that account fails to explain his hesitation over man or fire; and it misses the point of the dilemma in which he finds himself. He is pressed, he says, by the thought that he should adopt the same principle for everything—and that makes him think that there should be forms of the "sillies." Why? Because theories should be *universalizable*. But why then does the fact that we can see hair and dirt mean that there may not be forms for them? Not because they are trivial or grubby, but rather because they are unnecessary. After all, hair and mud are "just as we see them"—they are directly accessible.[46] Theories should be *economical*: that will press Socrates in the opposite direction, toward the view that we should only postulate forms where we must. And where would that be? Where there is the danger of compresent opposites—that is, for relations and values. And it is for relations and values that forms are imperative for Socrates.

This argument (if such it is), then, constitutes an account of the theory of forms as a theory. For it shows how Socrates must reconcile the principle that any theory should be universalizable (or universalizable within specifiable limits) and the demand that theories should be economical. In what follows in the *Parmenides*, the demands of economy continue to be felt. Plato, no less

---

[45] This, I suppose, is where Thales, about whom we know very little except "water," scores over Anaxagoras's "everything in everything."

[46] Compare the argument about direct perception at *Tht.* 163b ff.

than Aristotle, anticipates Ockham's razor: Plato's ontology is the head to be shaved.

Aristotle hoped that his account of individuation would explain both what made something one and how it was countable. Principles of individuation, that is, should explain something's being a unity and its being a unit. Plato's theory of forms, as it is presented in the *Parmenides*, starts with a strong claim about how any form is a unity (austerely) and a puzzle about counting them (there should be as few as possible). But recall how this pair of questions about individuals is already involved in the original specification of the contrast between forms and particulars. Particulars are both one and many—Socrates is one man with four limbs, ten fingers, and so forth; and Socrates is one man among many. But forms are never one and many, but just one. Can this sort of individual be specified? And can it be counted? Parmenides' attack on Socrates' theory asks both questions; and hears a negative reply.

5. FORMS AS SEPARATE SUBSTANCES

What is it like for something to be a nonphysical, mind-independent substance—*and* to be unified and single, "just one itself by itself"? Parmenides attacks this on two fronts:[47]

1. He tackles the relation between forms and particulars, and shows that this, however it may be construed, has unwelcome consequences for the nature of the form (*Parm.* 130e–131e).

2. He attempts to construe forms as thoughts (*nōemata*) and concludes that, thus, both forms and particulars are internally incoherent (132b–c).

The argument in (1) has two stages. If particulars are large by participating in (*metalambanein*) largeness, what is the nature of that participation? The particular participates either (a) in the whole form or (b) in a part of the form:

a. But if in the whole form, then the form, which is one, will be in each of the many. But then the form that is one and the same will be as a whole in each of the many, which are separate from each other; and so it will be separate from itself (131b).

b. But if in a part of the form, then the form will have parts. But then the form will no longer be one. Moreover, the part of the large itself that is in a particular large thing will be smaller than the large itself, so that the large thing will be large by virtue of something smaller (than the large itself)—which is absurd.[48] And the part of the small that makes the small particular small will be smaller (because a part) than the small itself—which is no less absurd.

Socrates attempts to slip out from under these consequences by offering

---

[47] Cf., e.g., Cornford, *Plato and Parmenides* ad loc.; Allen, *Plato's Parmenides* ad loc; Vlastos, "Third Man Argument"; and Mignucci, "Third Man Arguments."

[48] The puzzles of *Phd.* 99ff. explain why this is thought to be absurd, a τέρας.

(rather halfheartedly) an analogy between a form and a day (131b3). Parmenides changes the analogy to a sail (131b8), and draws his conclusion about partition with no difficulty. Had Parmenides accepted the day, would Socrates have been any better off? Socrates needs to persuade us that there are such things as mind-independent, nonphysical substances, which are not subject to partition or reduplication. Now Parmenides' sail is a physical object, and a bad analogue for a form; but a day seems no better. How can we individuate a day? Is it measured by the light? By a clock? By my perception, or yours, of what has happened in it? If it is a stretch of time, its claims to be independent and separate (for example, from the events that it "contains") are pretty thin. And if it is relative to someone's perception of it, then it must be badly cast as an explanation of that perception, or of the events that happen to the perceiver. Days are not physical things (and so Socrates' analogue improves on Parmenides' sail); but they look dangerously like thoughts.

Suppose that forms are thoughts (2), which occur nowhere but in minds (or souls, *Parm.* 132b5). Then perhaps they could be one and immune from partition or reduplication. But, says Parmenides, each form must be a thought of something, something that is, and that is one. But then that something will be the form (and prone to the previous difficulties). Moreover, the particulars will thus be composed of thoughts; so they will either think, or be thoughtless —either of which is absurd.

This argument may look specious, but it has hidden strengths. Explanations, Socrates had insisted in the *Phaedo*, come before our understanding them; and they come before the explananda, too—for it is *by virtue of* the explanations that the explananda are the way they are. The theory of transcendent forms, after all, comes from that demand. But then Socrates does no good by suggesting that forms may be thoughts, since thoughts fail to meet the priority conditions for explanations; instead, as this argument shows, the explananda come first, and the explanations collapse altogether.

Socrates comes to grief in his attempt to specify a mind-independent substance that is just one, and that can resist the dangers of partition or reduplication. Those dangers are generated by the participation of particulars in forms, all right; but the problem lies deeper than the immediate needs of the theory of forms. For Socrates has no paradigms to offer of nonphysical substances of the type he needs. (After all, in the *Phaedo*, the paradigm was the form itself, on which the assumption was based that souls too might be nonphysical, and yet substantial enough to survive death.)

The contrast between the sail and the day turns out to be a significant one. Socrates' forms must be mind-independent *and* they must be austere individuals. Suppose we try to understand forms as separate substances *like* physical objects (sails, or fingers, or sticks and stones). How then are we to understand the relations in which any form must stand to anything else? The problem with particulars arose because relations and values are construed as real properties of them. But then if forms are objects like that, they, too, will suffer from the plurality that infects the sensible world; and then we are back with the original difficulty, forms or no forms. If forms are specified as mind-independent, they risk their austerity. Try, instead, specifying them as something that is not involved in real relations with the real world—like a thought. Thoughts may be austere single units, as the forms need to be, but they lack the reality the forms need to do their job—of explaining the nature of the particulars, which are so problematic. If, then, we have to choose between the sail and the day as an analogue for forms, we are stuck; either (as the sail) forms are complex and real, or they are simple and unreal. Neither option will do.

6. Counting Forms

Recall the fatal conditions for forms. They may not be characterized by their opposite (suffer from their own compresence); and they may not interpredicate, be characterized by some other form. They may, of course, be characterized by themselves—at least unless there is some other reason for ruling out self-predication.

Parmenides now tries a different tack to show that forms are *both one and many* (the two Third Man Arguments [TMAs]: *Parm.* 132a–b, 132d–133b). In the previous section he showed that forms, if they were anything at all, turned out to be *one under many*, single items possessed of a plurality of properties. Now he reaches his absurd conclusion by showing that each form is *one among many*; this consequence is as lethal for the original theory. For, in contravention of the original postulate, forms are both one individual (*hen hekaston*) and many (indeterminate in number; cf. 132b2, 133a2).[49] Forms would thus be like particulars in a fatal way—any form would be *a many*, no less than a one (we shall see how this is a noxious, not an innocent, consequence for forms). But in that case the forms may need explanation no less than the particulars; while *as* explanations, they start to look superfluous. So perhaps they should be eliminated?

The interpretation of both TMAs is a notorious minefield.[50] There are three main areas of dispute.

1. What is the logical structure of the arguments? Are they valid or otherwise? Are they intended to be deductive; or are they *reductiones ad absurdum*? Following on from that,

2. What is the relation between the two arguments? Does the second merely recapitulate the first, or offer a different point altogether?

3. And what is the target of the arguments? If they show that there is some-

---

[49] And compare the treatment of numerical indeterminacy later in the dialogue; 144a; 158c; 164c; cf. ch. 4, sec. 3.

[50] Among the many, see especially Vlastos, "Third Man Argument"; Sellars, "Third Man"; Strang, "Third Man"; Cohen, "Third Man"; Schofield, "Likeness"; Mignucci, "Third Man Arguments."

thing wrong with the assumptions of the theory of forms, exactly what is wrong? And is the villainous assumption dispensable, or does the whole theory collapse?

Third Man Argument (TMA) 1

Parmenides' first TMA begins:

> I think that you postulate each form to be one from considerations such as this: whenever there seem to you to be many large particulars, perhaps there appears to be a single, same, character to someone who is looking at them all, whence he supposes the large to be one.
>
> True.
>
> What then of the large itself and all the other large things? If you look at them all in the same way in your mind, does not there appear to you to be some one large again, by virtue of which all these large things are large?
>
> It seems so.
>
> So another form of largeness has appeared, besides that largeness itself (that we got before) and the things that partake in it; and over all those again another one appears, by virtue of which all of them are large; and indeed no longer is each of your forms one, but infinite[51] in number.
>
> (*Parm.* 132a–b)

To schematize, I offer a fairly standard interpretation of this argument. It has three basic premises attached to the theory of forms, and derived from earlier dialogues.

> O. Each form is (just) one.[52]

This premise is open to various interpretations. What do we understand by the form's being one? Many commentators insist that the form is unique (and therefore vulnerable to an infinite regress). But such an assumption seems unnecessary (as well as dangerous); there is no immediate reason why a collection of cloned forms should not explain the particulars just as well as one unique form. What is more, the scene-setting discussion with Zeno requires a different interpretation. Here, Socrates demands not uniqueness, but stark unity: the form must be *just one*, an austere individual. We have seen how some earlier arguments for forms (apart from the teleological arguments) imply such an austere conception. Here the idea seems to be that to explain some many, you need a one, something that is *a unity*.[53]

> NI (Nonidentity). A set of f particulars are f by virtue of the form F-ness; and the form is not a member of the set of things it explains.

This premise does not carry a very strong ontological commitment. NI does not tell us, for example, that forms are really real, particulars mere appear-

---

[51] Indefinite? ἄπειρον.

[52] Here "one" is predicative, and the "is" a copula, not existential; cf. Mignucci.

[53] Mignucci, "Plato's Third Man Arguments," p. 161, suggests that we understand the form to be "one and the same," which I take to imply that it must be a self-identical individual.

ances; or even that forms exist independently of minds (although Plato does want such ontological commitment, as we have seen, for other reasons). But it does tell us that the explanation[54] of something is not also one of its own explananda (for reasons outlined in *Phd.* 99ff.); NI is not, that is, about particulars as such, but about explananda—hence Parmenides' emphasis on "by virtue of." And that thesis about explanation lies at the heart of the theory of forms.

    SP (Self-Predication). F-ness is itself f.

At first sight, this premise appears to be *obviously* inconsistent with NI—and then it is hard to see how the argument could get off the ground at all. But, first, reflection on the passage makes it clear that SP is, if anything, implicit (e.g., as in "if you look at them all *in the same way* in your mind"), not explicit. Second, if SP (rather than some different thesis, e.g., of self-identity:

    [SI, "the form F-ness *is what it is to be* f"])[55]

is in play here, we may see from earlier passages why Plato should espouse it. Recall the teleological account of forms. Here the desire to know, and the progress toward philosophical understanding, happen because what is understood is ordered by the good; and the form of the good (or the beautiful) stands at the pinnacle of understanding. But then the form of the good must, for this explanation of understanding to work, be itself desirable. So it must be good, it must itself have the value it imparts to the rest of the structure, albeit supremely so. So the form of the good must possess that property of goodness. SP, on that account, is not an absent-minded assumption, but a central part of Plato's metaphysical epistemology.

    Given these premises, the argument is easy to reconstruct. Suppose that we take a set of particulars, all the particulars that are f. Since they need explaining, there must be a form, F-ness, which is not itself one of the explananda (by NI). But that form, since it too is f (via SP), can be thought of as a member of a group that also contains all the f particulars. But then that group also needs explaining (if the first group did), and not by one of its members (by NI)—so there must be another form. But then the form F is both one (as at O) and many (since each stage of the argument offers an explanation of things that are f). And that, Parmenides implies, will not do.

    What is objectionable about the conclusion that the form is one and many? Several accounts, I think, are possible.

    1. What we thought was just one in number turns out to be infinite in number. This, I suppose, would be absurd if it were characterized as an

---

[54] Cf. Mignucci here on the forms as explanations for a collection of particulars already identified (the collection of particulars is not the means to making the identification, on pain of the Socratic Fallacy).

[55] I shall discuss this further below. Notice that SI may be the claim that the form is the essence, or the nature of F; and this itself may bring some sort of SP with it. On this, cf. Nehamas, "Self-Predication," and thence Vlastos, "Self-Predication."

infinite regress. But would Plato object to an infinite regress? Unlike Aristotle, he has no prima facie objections to infinity, at least up till now.

2. What we thought was just one in number turns out to be infinitely many. This might be construed as a contradiction (F-ness turns out to be one and many in number)—but wrongly so. It is not some particular F-ness that turns out to be both one and many; each member of the set of F-nesses is one, while the set itself has many members—no contradiction here. (And, what is more, Plato would surely not fall for that one—look at Socrates' remarks about himself being one member of a group at *Parm.* 129d1).

Both (1) and (2) offer conclusions that are only apparently absurd. They turn on the question of *counting* forms—and suggest that Plato's problem is "How many forms are there for each set of particulars?" Yet this question might, on some views, be thought to be marginal. What does it matter if there are many (cloned) forms to explain the large things, so long as the explaining is done by each form at its proper level?[56] If the conclusion is (1) or (2), it seems, the TMA may turn out to be innocuous to the theory of forms (and Plato's strategy in putting it forward thus one of clearing away misunderstanding, not directly attacking the theory itself).

That, however, will not quite do. Particulars (like Socrates) are allowed to be one under many (complex individuals) *and* one among many (countable); but the second is connected to the first. For Plato, remember, relations are real properties. So if this stone is one among many boulders, its being "one among many boulders" will be one of its many properties, one of the features that make it a complex item or a generous individual. If, however, something is forbidden to be many in any respect (as forms are required to be austere individuals), then it cannot enter into relations that would make it one among many, since those relations would pluralize it and destroy its austerity. But then (2) turns out to be dangerous for the form F-ness. If there is more than one F-ness to explain the f's, each F-ness will be related (somehow or other) to the others; each will be one among many and (on the thesis of natural inherence) therefore many, not just one. On that basis, the conclusion of the argument is genuinely inconsistent with the assumptions of Socrates' theory.

If that is the correct interpretation of the conclusion, then the premise set must be under attack by means of the dialectical and indirect approach of a *reductio ad absurdum*. Which premise is the target? Traditionally, SP is thought to be the villain; since after all NI is at the ontological heart of the theory of forms. But the construal of the argument I suggest has a wider target than SP. For the argument shows how if the form is understood as self-predicating, then, *eo ipso*, it will become involved in other relations and other contexts, because now it will be subject to the invasions of predication and the attributions of properties. As a consequence, it becomes one among many. And that is enough for it to lose its austerity, and to cease to fit the criteria laid

---

[56] This is the issue that has flummoxed the commentators often enough, e.g., Vlastos, "Third Man Argument."

down for forms. But then the danger for forms is not self-predication alone, but any predication that will impugn its austere unity.

Third Man Argument (TMA) 2

Socrates tries a new tack (or is it?):

> These forms stand like paradigms in nature, while the other things are like them and are their copies, and the participation of particulars in forms is nothing but their being likened to them (the forms).
>
> So if something is like the form, is it possible for that form not to be like that which is likened to it, insofar as it has been made like to it? Or is there any way in which something like is like what is not like it?
>
> No.
>
> Surely is is absolutely necessary for what is like something that is like it to partake in the same one thing?
>
> It is necessary.
>
> And that which likes partake in to be like, surely that is the form itself?[57]
>
> Absolutely.
>
> Therefore it is not possible for something to be like the form, nor for the form to be like something else; otherwise, some other form will always appear besides the form, and a new form will never stop turning up, if the form is like what partakes in it.
>
> You speak the truth.
>
> So it is not by likeness that the particulars participate in the form, but some other mode of participation must be found.
>
> It seems so.
>
> (*Parm.* 132d–133a)

Is this a new argument? Socrates' strategy might be a sneaky one: TMA 1 indirectly attacks SP (the most popular candidate for the villain of the piece); Socrates purports to drop SP in the argument that follows, but then covertly reintroduces it in the suggestion that the relation between form and particulars is one of likeness. After all, if the large particulars are like the form large in their being large, then the form will be large too, surely?[58] Thereafter TMA 2 proceeds with the same premise set as TMA 1 (O, NI, and SP) and exposes the same inconsistency.

That would be a disappointing result. But in TMA 2 the relation that connects forms and particulars—likeness—is classically a relation explained

---

[57] Schofield, "Likeness," rightly retains the MSS εἴδους at e1 and glosses Socrates' first move as the claim that any likeness involves a form, his second that the form is the form of likeness.

[58] Some have supposed that the likeness relation is not symmetrical—from Proclus 915.3ff. onward. And this view persists, despite Owen's sharp words on the subject in his *"Timaeus,"* p. 69–71. But Owen must be right—the relation copy/original is not symmetrical; but if *a* is like *b*, then (in that respect at least) *b* is like *a*.

by a form (vide 129a1, 130b4). This thought might supply a different reading of TMA 2. Take as its premises the following:

> O. The form is just one.
>
> NI. The explanation is not one of its own explananda.
>
> L. The relation between forms and particulars is the likeness relation, implied by the particulars being copies of the forms.

Suppose that we take a group of particulars {the f's} that need explaining. By NI they are to be explained by a form (F-ness) that is not one of the explananda. What is the relation between form and particulars? Irrespective of the property (being f) explained by the form, which may or may not belong to the form as well (that is, irrespective of the truth or otherwise of SP here), the relation between form and particulars is one of likeness (by L). But then the group {F-ness, f's} all have the property of likeness. That then needs explaining by some form that is not one of the original relata {F-ness, f's}, by NI again. So there is a form Likeness, and its related particulars {F-ness, f's}, which are all like each other. What then is the relation between Likeness and its related particulars {F-ness, f's}? They must be like each other (by L). So now we have a new group of likes {F-ness, f's, Likeness}. What explains them? Some form of Likeness that is not one of them (Likeness'), via NI. And then, by L, Likeness' and {F-ness, f's, Likeness} are like each other; so that they must be explained by another form Likeness"—and so on. Once again the original form (F-ness), which explains the original group {f's}, will turn out not to be just one but one among many (and a motley crowd at that—{F-ness, Likeness, Likeness', Likeness," etc.}).[59]

On this interpretation of TMA 2, the argument does have something fresh to contribute to Parmenides' attack on the forms. For here *any* interpretation of the relation between forms and particulars is liable to be tricky, just because the form's entering into a relation with anything (including its own explananda) violates the austere premise, O. The difficulty is brought out by adopting likeness as the account of the relation between forms and particulars, since likeness is familiar as a relation that requires a form. The issue, that is, is not self-predication at all, but *interpredication*; and the attack is on the notion that a form could be the possessor of any properties; if it is to be an austere individual, it cannot.

So the two TMAs attack the nature of the forms from the aspect of their relations with each other. If the theory of forms supposes that forms cannot interpredicate, then forms will be austere in the fashion I have described. But if that is so, it is difficult to see how the forms can function at all.

This interpretation of the two TMAs, some would argue, is quite wrong. So far from being a serious attack on the nonidentity assumption of the theory of forms (as I have construed them, cumulatively, to be), they are a defensive exercise, designed to clear up misunderstandings about the theory of forms. In

---

[59] Compare Schofield, "Likeness," and Mignucci, "Third Man Arguments," both of whom interpret the argument without an SP premise.

particular, Plato wants to point to the mistake of treating the forms as self-predicating, where we should suppose them, instead, merely to be self-identical:

SI. The form F-ness is what it is to be f.[60]

Certainly, SP is a dangerous premise. Plato is committed to this, it is often thought, as a consequence of the "simple-minded answer" at *Phaedo* 100d, where he is anxious to establish a clear connection between explanation and explananda by giving them *the same name*. So "the beautiful itself is beautiful," interpreted as the view that the form has the property that it explains. But, argue Plato's defenders, this need not follow from the simple-minded answer; all Plato needs, to retain his account of explanations, is the claim that forms, rather than being self-predicating, are self-identical; this makes sense of the statement "the beautiful is beautiful" without giving rise to the difficulties of the TMA.

Let us disregard the objection that I have already made—that Plato's teleology demands that some forms at least be self-predicating. Consider instead whether we are any better off with SI. What is meant by the claim that forms are self-identical? It may be thought that SI gives us the claim that the form is the essence (the nature, the "what it is to be")[61] of what it explains; so that each form *just is* the property it explains. Now this account of the nature of a form needs—if my interpretation of the agenda of the *Parmenides* is correct—to be consistent with the demand that any form is an austere individual. However, this consistency may be far to seek, for three reasons:

1. TMA 1 may not produce an absurdity with SI as a premise; but TMA 2, which attacks any relation between forms (even construed as essences or natures) and particulars on the basis of NI alone, does. For TMA 2 shows that any relation between forms and particulars must have both forms and particulars as relata; but then if relations themselves are explained by forms, and if no relation can be explained by either of the relata (by NI), then any relation between form and particular or between one form (F-ness, Likeness) and another (Likeness, Likeness', etc.) must be explained by some further form. So any form, to be related to particulars, will turn out to be one among many; and that, on the assumptions of the *Parmenides*, is absurd.

2. SI presupposes that we have some grip on the notion of the identity of an individual (indeed, I wonder whether it is only individuals that we should readily admit to being self-identical in the first place; neither a mass nor a

---

[60] On the choice between SP and SI, see Allen, "Predication"; Nehamas, "Self-Predication"; Vlastos, "Self-Predication." Nehamas tries to defuse the difficulty by characterizing the form as "what it is to be f" and the particulars as "f by participating in the form." The use of *f* in each expression is univocal, although "is" (in "the form *is* what it is to be f" versus "the particular *is* f") is ambiguous. This ingenious solution to the problem of SP takes no account, in my view, for the direct reason for SP that Plato has—namely, his teleology. Nehamas's interpretation also attributes a confusion to Plato—between having a property and being a property—which the arguments, e.g., of *Phd.* 102ff., seem to me to preclude.

[61] I am grateful to an anonymous commentator for Princeton University Press for focusing my attention on the "forms as natures" construal of SI.

property has a "self" to which it may be related).[62] However, if the earlier arguments attack the notion of an austerely self-identical individual, the present arguments cannot then be saved by invoking just that opaque notion. Put this another way. If the danger of the TMA is that it imports plurality and indefiniteness (numerically) and indeterminacy and incoherence (via the one and many conclusion) to the forms, and thus threatens their individuality, then the theory cannot be saved by falling back on a different thesis, that these individuals just are self-identical. For that thesis is already in doubt.

3. In any case, will even this account of the forms as natures allow them to be different from each other, distinct and self-identical, without thereby becoming many? If all relations, including those of identity, are subject to the thesis of natural inherence, even this account of forms will be inconsistent with the demand that they be austere. Now that may mean that the austerity demand is too strong; but that demand is, as I have argued, central to the argumentative strategy of this part of the *Parmenides*. Without its explicit rejection, SI is as tricky as SP.

This leads to a further and wider question, to which we shall return. Has Plato distinguished, or is he defeated by, the contrast between the "is" of identity and the "is" of predication?[63] How successfully is he able to separate

"Socrates *is* the husband of Xanthippe"

from

"Socrates *is* bald"?

And how successfully *should* he be able to separate them?

7. Forms as the Objects of Knowledge

If forms are austere individuals, Parmenides has suggested so far, they seem to be unspecifiable. Next he turns his attention to the forms as objects of knowledge (*Parm.* 133b–134e). The final stretch of argument begins with a fresh assertion of the premise—that form are individuals (*hen, hekaston, ti,* 133b1). Yet this, predicts Parmenides, may rule them out as the objects of knowledge. But then the forms are redundant; and then—the attack implies—the theory of forms itself collapses in a heap.

The argument comes in three stages:

1. forms cannot be related to the world of particulars (133b–e);
2. forms cannot be known, except to god (134a–c); and this
3. implies the remoteness of god from us (134c–e).

But if 1, 2, and 3 are true, the forms cannot exist.[64]

---

[62] Compare, perhaps, Plato's arguments about the indeterminacy of stuff in the *Timaeus*; see ch. 6, sec. 5.

[63] Cf below, ch. 4, secs. 3, 4, 8; ch. 7, sec. 3; and ch. 8, sec. 2.

[64] Notice that this argument will only go through with the addition of an Ockhamesque

Consider first of all the claim (1) that the forms are separate and themselves by themselves (*Parm.* 133c). In that case, they are not at all "in us." (For Parmenides' argument not to be outrageously question-begging, this does not mean that there are no instances of forms in our world; but rather, and consistent with Socrates' original thesis, that the [separate] forms themselves do not belong "down here." These forms are transcendent.) So if the forms are interrelated at all, those relations must be contained within and among the forms; they will have no relations with particulars. In just the same way, the relations in our world are between particulars, and not between particulars and forms. Thus, a slave is the slave of a master and not of "the master itself, what it is to be a master"; whereas mastery is of slavery, and slavery of mastery. So things related in this world are related to each other, and not to a form; interrelated forms are related to each other and not to particulars; the two orders are *completely* separate.

So what? Parmenides exploits two levels of absurdity in this exchange. First, he builds on what has gone before—earlier he had questioned whether any sense at all could be made of the relation between forms and particulars; now he takes Socrates' defeat there for granted. If a particular slave is the slave of a particular master, we are thrown back on the phenomena of this world for explanations, and not allowed to escape with talk of another world altogether. Second, by drawing a parallel between the relation between a slave and a master, and the relation between slavery and mastery, he shows the anomaly of treating forms in any way like particulars. To suppose, that is, that they enter into familiar relations with each other is ridiculous. As Socrates had predicted at the outset, it would be amazing to find forms interrelated; and amazing it turns out to be.

A particular case of the interrelation of forms (2) will be the relation between knowledge itself and truth itself. Knowledge itself will be related to its proper objects, the forms. But the forms are not "down here." So our knowledge will be related to our truth, and to our own objects of knowledge, and will have nothing to do with the forms at all. So the form of beauty will be unknowable by us—likewise the form of the good and any other form.

This argument is crucial to understanding Plato's catholic approach to relations, and his puritan attitude to forms. Here "being known" represents a relation between the knower and the known, and is restricted to proper sorts of relata. Once again, therefore, only particulars are related in the way proper to particulars; while forms are related in their own restricted way. The final absurdity of "knowledge itself being of truth itself" takes us once again back to the premise of the whole argument—that the interrelation of forms is bound to be absurd. What Parmenides shows us with progressive emphasis is just why that should be so; knowledge itself is not merely a reproduction of particular knowledge at a higher level, any more than mastery is a special kind of master. On the contrary, such items, if there are any, simply do not partici-

---

premise—if forms are so remote as not to do the job for which they were postulated, *then there are none.*

pate in normal relations with other items. Instead they are, as Socrates originally supposed, austere. But in that case they are ill fitted to be related to us and to our problems about knowledge and explanation.

The last arrow (and the most devastating? 134c4) in Parmenides' quiver is the "god's eye view" argument (3), which reappears in slightly different form in the *Sophist* and the *Cratylus*. If there is "knowledge itself," it must be far more precise than our kind of knowledge. In that case, only god is fit to know it. But if god knows the forms, then he is related to them, and not to us, since the two orders of relata are quite distinct and separate. In that case, god cannot know us, any more than we can know the forms; and yet it is absurd to exclude god from any knowledge at all.

The same strategy turns up here again; if the forms are remote and austere, then knowledge of them must reflect that remoteness and austerity. But then the same will be true for the person who has that knowledge; he too must be remote and austere. Once again, the absurdity cashes in on two features of the theory of forms. First, it suggests that interrelations between forms (and god) are impossible to conceive without merely replicating (in a silly way) the interrelations of this world—which were, after all, what we were called upon to explain. Second, it suggests that the forms, austerely conceived, cannot be thought of as known at all, since being known itself brings them into relation with something; and that is disallowed by the austerity premise itself.

That feature of this argument is brought out more clearly in the versions that turn up in the *Cratylus* (439–40) and the *Sophist* (248–49).[65]

In the *Cratylus*, Socrates starts with the postulate that there are two sorts of thing (the argument has turned to the discussion of knowledge derived from things, not names)—particulars of the phenomenal world, and forms. The former are constantly in flux; the latter are eternally fixed and stable. Socrates imagines the fate of "the beautiful itself" and argues (1) that it cannot be known if it changes and (2) that it cannot be known if it is impassive, because then becoming known would change it.

> But the beautiful itself, we should say, is surely the sort of thing that is always such as it is?
> Necessarily.
> [1] But if it were in flux, would it be possible to talk about it correctly, if it always slipped out from under, saying first that it is "that" and secondly that it is "such"? Instead, surely it must become something else even as we speak, and slip out from under and no longer be thus?
> Necessarily.
> How then could that, which is never the same, be a something? For if it ever were the same, at that very time it would clearly fail to change. (2) But if it were always the same, and were the same thing, how then could it change or move at all, since it must not change out of its own form?

[65] A detailed interpretation of the texts of these arguments may be found in Mackenzie, "*Cratylus*"; I discuss the *Cratylus* further below, in ch. 7, sec. 5, and the *Sophist* in detail in chs. 7 and 8.

In no way.

But then [sc. if it never changed] it could not be known at all. For at the approach of someone who was coming to know it it would become other and different. (*Crat.* 439d–440a; my enumeration)

So phenomenal particulars are unknowable by nature (1); and the forms cannot come to be known (2). For there is no coming to know a fixed and immutable object, since coming to be known would affect the object. So forms can only be permanently known; or not known at all.

This argument clearly exploits both the claim that knowledge is a relation naturally inherent in its relata; and a mild version of the austerity thesis—the claim that forms are impassive and cannot be affected. Moreover, like its companion in the *Parmenides*, the *Cratylus* argument suggests that knowledge is either total (the god's eye view) or totally absent; in which case, the conclusion runs, the forms fail to perform the function for which they were postulated, and there is thus no point in postulating them at all.

The *Sophist* argument makes the same kind of point.

Eleatic Stranger: I see what you mean—that if coming to know is an action, then what becomes known must, as a consequence, be affected. And according to this argument being, as it becomes known by knowledge, insofar as it becomes known just so far does it move in respect of being affected—which we said should not happen to what is at rest. (*Soph.* 248d–e)

If becoming known is becoming affected, then forms, which are impassive, cannot become known.[66] The Eleatic Stranger (ES) treats becoming known as a real affection of the object that becomes known and uses this assumption to explode the claim of the friends of the forms that forms are what is known. If they cannot become known, they are no use when it comes to knowledge, at least so far as we are concerned. Austere forms, once again, will not do.[67]

The attacks on forms in the critical period, then, exploit the tension between their austere status as individuals and their functioning within the structure of explanation and understanding. To reveal that tension is of course to offer a challenge: how, if not by virtue of the ordered relations of forms, is understanding to be understood? After these arguments, is understanding necessarily tied to the existence of forms? This is the problem of Plato's late epistemology, and it is a vexed topic of debate. But there is a further, and neglected, difficulty. At *Phaedo* 78d, the particulars were said to be "never so to speak in any way according to the same things, both in relation to themselves and in relation to each other"—the particulars are enmeshed in context. But the forms are divorced from context, and that will be the trouble. The

[66] Cf. ch. 7, sec. 2.

[67] Becoming known, some may object, is merely a Cambridge change for what becomes known, and does not involve a real change as well. This will be discussed further below, at ch. 5, sec. 3, and ch. 8, sec. 9. In "Putting the *Cratylus* in its Place," I responded to this objection by pointing out that if forms are objects of knowledge in themselves, then becoming known can hardly be an affection that is incidental, nor one in which they are causally inert.

particulars, as the *Phaedo* thesis makes clear, are generous in their possession of properties; the forms must be utterly austere.

To recapitulate, the thought that forms are austere individuals, utterly simple individual entities, comes from three interconnected claims about the forms. First, they function as real explanations for the puzzling particulars as the phenomenal world. Second, as such they are themselves not in need of explanation. So forms, unlike particulars, do not suffer from the compresence of their own opposite; nor, it seems, from the compresence of any opposites. Where particulars, then, are context-bound, the forms are context-free. Third, forms are, as we should like souls to be, incomposite simple entities; so each form is just one and not at all many. Forms, that is, are austere individuals.

The arguments against forms have turned on their characterization as individuals; and the account of particulars also presented them, in a different way, as individuals. So over and above the question What things are there? is a further, more general and more abstract question raised by the tension between forms and particulars. What is it to be an individual? If the contrast between forms and particulars rests on the difference between two conceptions of an individual—what is just one versus what is the possessor of properties—how in general are these two conceptions to be resolved? Suppose that we turn away from specific individuals (forms and particulars) to consider the problem of individuation itself; how can that problem be explained, understood, and solved? The second part of the *Parmenides* begins to tackle just that question.

PART TWO

The Problem Emerges

The One and the Others

1. Ones and Manies

Plato proposes, then, that there are two sorts of thing: forms and particulars. And he thinks that the difference between the two can be characterized as the difference between ones that are also many (particulars) and ones that are just one (forms). But he thinks that for two reasons. First, he supposes that particulars are many because they possess an indeterminate number of properties, and that all those properties can reasonably be described as parts of the particular. This will be true whether the property in question is common or garden (green, slimy), or relational (as large as the cat next door), or evaluative (thoroughly unpleasant to look at). (This, you may recall, is the thesis of natural inherence.) Second, particulars are especially many because they are subject to the compresence of relational and evaluative opposites (if the toad is fatter than the frog, there is something somewhere—perhaps some hippopotamus—than which it is thinner, and so on). Forms, conversely, are meant to explain the compresence of opposites, and so cannot suffer from it. It seems, moreover, that they cannot suffer from any pluralization at all—they are just one, in contradistinction to the indefiniteness of any particular. So characterized as one and many, a form is an austere individual (just one), and a particular is a generous individual (one and many).

Particulars manifestly exist; they are out there in the world—and Plato was not the sort of skeptic to deny that, however tricky he may have supposed the world out there to be. Forms, however, are theoretical entities, postulated to solve the problems of particulars. So they may or may not exist, depending on whether argument can sustain them. The question of their existence, however, seems to stand or fall by whether they can be shown to be the sort of individuals Plato suggests them to be. If they are not austere individuals (the arguments of the first part of the *Parmenides* suggest), then there is no point in having them at all. And yet austere individuals, it seems, are too austere to do the job for which the forms were invented; and otherwise they degenerate into generosity.

The *Parmenides* opened with a series of Zenonian puzzles. If there are many, they must be both like and unlike. But that is impossible, since likes cannot be unlike nor unlikes like; so it is impossible that there are many (127e). So there is just one. Socrates, however, claims that his theory of forms can rescue us from the paradoxical world of the monist. For the pluralities of the sensible world (you, me, the toad in the garden) are like or unlike by virtue of their participation in the form; this allows them to be qualifiedly like or unlike, and thus to be many without paradox. But forms themselves cannot be qualified, so that they must be free from opposites (both, as I have argued, their own opposite and any other). Socrates thus defends manifest plurality from the austere one of Elea only at the price of offering some austerity of his own, the forms.

But this suggests that the problem he faces is wider than just the attack on the forms. For the forms were postulated to mitigate the difficulties of sensible particulars; and if the forms are vulnerable, so those difficulties will reemerge. But what exactly is the problem with particulars that Socrates escapes by postulating forms? One diagnosis of Zeno's puzzle might be simply that he has dropped the qualifiers that complete "like" and "unlike." He may, for example, have argued thus: "This elephant is like that telegraph pole; and it is unlike the post-office van. So this elephant is both like and unlike. So this like is unlike. But that is a contradiction. So there is no elephant, just the Eleatic one."

Now why would Socrates need the theory of forms to avoid this conclusion? It would be an easy matter to point out (as indeed he could, cf. 129a ff.) that the elephant is like in one respect, unlike in another, and leave Zeno standing. But that strategy would leave untouched Zeno's conclusion, which is not the skeptical claim that the world is full of contradictions (so that we cannot understand it at all) but instead the radical ontological claim that just because the world is confusingly plural, it is not there at all. Zeno's argument turns on the contrast between the contradictory nature *of plurality* and the blissful purity of the one. Socrates consoles him by showing how plurality is not so bad after all—provided we postulate forms. So what follows is already focused not on Zeno's factitious contradiction, but on the difficulties faced by plural entities, difficulties apparently solved by having pure ones. Instead of monism, Socrates offers a two-world thesis, expressed as a claim about two different sorts of individual: there are particulars, which are one and many (generous individuals, as Zeno points out), and there are forms, which are just one and austere. The forms seemed to mitigate the problems of generosity. What then happens to the individuation of particulars if the forms are gone?

Once Parmenides has got his teeth into the theory of forms, this problem reemerges with renewed force. Particulars without forms are absurd (as Socrates seems to concede to Zeno). But forms, too, suffer from the kind of contradictions attributed to particulars, if Parmenides' arguments are valid against them. On that account, then, both forms and particulars are absurd. In particular, they are absurd because we seem unable to talk about them sensibly. But the alternative offered by Parmenides and Zeno seems just as bad. For if we find ourselves in the arms of the Eleatic one, there is nothing left to talk about; monism (as Zeno allows) is as absurd as pluralism. Neither provides us with a satisfactory account of how many things there are, just because neither shows us how to talk about the individuals we postulate. Thus, the first part of the *Parmenides* ends with a dilemma (135a–c). Parmenides, the Eleatic who does not believe in forms, urges that without forms we lose the power of dialectic; against him Socrates, the exponent of the theory of forms, allows that the theory makes no contribution to the explanation of particulars. It looks as though counting and reason stand and fall together.

What exactly is at stake here? Think about the structure of the closing dilemma, and the emphasis of Zeno's original worry about the contradictions in the sensible world. The dilemma starts from a disjunctive premise—either there are forms or there are not. But each disjunct implies that there is no dialectic; and that conclusion is intolerable. Why? Not, surely, because life is intolerable without forms (Parmenides, for one, could not have conceded that), but rather because life is intolerable without dialectic. What is more, to show by dialectic that dialectic is impossible seems to be at least self-refuting. We must, then, find our way out of the dilemma—but in order to rescue dialectic, not forms. And that, of course, should be done by dialectical means, which may provide if not a deductive, then a pragmatic defense of dialectic.

In what follows, I shall argue that Plato turns his attention away from forms as such and from particulars as such. For transcendent forms are—on the interpretation I offered in the last chapter—entities that fail to supply the explanations they promise if they are conceived as simple individuals. Particulars, on the other hand, need explaining because they are complex individuals. What Plato badly needs is to consider What is an individual? as a general question, leaving open the issue of which entities qualify. And that general investigation, I argue, is on hand in the second part of the *Parmenides* (hereafter *Parmenides* II), continues in the *Theaetetus* and the *Timaeus*, and is brought to a satisfactory conclusion in the *Sophist*. The agenda from here onward, that is, is not the viability of the theory of forms, but the nature of individuation. What is one?—as *Republic* 523 had predicted—is the question that demands an answer first.

2. Dialectic and Gymnastic

After his dilemma about forms, Parmenides seems to offer us some consolation. The dilemma is, apparently, avoidable by someone clever, unlike the naive young Socrates (135a7ff.). What Socrates needs, then, is training in the art of dialectic; only then will he be able to see his way out. And that is what is promised in the sequel—a piece of gymnastic.

> "What then will you do about philosophy?" said Parmenides. "Whither can you turn while these matters are unknown?" "I cannot see that clearly at the moment." "Well, it is premature to try to define what is beautiful and just and each one of the forms, before you have gone into training, Socrates. Indeed I thought that when I heard you talking with Aristotle here earlier. But it is a noble and divine impulse, this one of yours to argument; so drag yourself towards what is thought to be useless and is described by the many as claptrap, and train yourself on that while you are still young. Otherwise, truth will escape you."

"What sort of training, Parmenides?" Socrates said. "The kind you have heard from Zeno—with this exception. I enjoyed hearing you say to him that you were not prepared to think about visible things, nor to confine your wanderings to them, but rather to those things which someone might grasp in argument and where he might suppose there to be forms." "That is because I think it easy to show that in the sensible world the same things are like and unlike or anything else at all." "Quite right," he said. "But it is necessary to do this as well, for each thing hypothesised to be, not just to consider what follows from the hypothesis, but also if the same thing is hypothesised not to be, if you want to be better trained." (*Parm.* 135c–36a)

There follows a long and exhausting treatment of two hypotheses: "If one is" and "If one is not." Each hypothesis is treated from two different perspectives: "If one is, what is true of it?" and "If one is, what is true of the others?"—"If one is not, what is true of it?" and "If one is not, what is true of the others?"—generating four stages in the argument.[1] Each stage is then treated in two movements (or three, in the case of the first), to reach either a negative conclusion, that nothing can be said of what is hypothesized, or a positive one, that anything can be said of what is hypothesized. Both negative and positive conclusions are absurd.[2] The negative one concludes (as Parmenides' dilemma had) that what has been (exhaustively) mentioned is unmentionable. The positive one concludes (as Zeno's paradoxes had) that what has been hypothesized is contradictory. The four stages and their movements may be schematized:

> *First Hypothesis*: "If one is":
>> Stage I: "If one is, what is true of it?":
>>> movement a. 137c–142a (negative);
>>> movement b. 142b–155e (positive);
>>> movement c. coda 155e–157b.
>> Stage II: "If one is, what is true of the others?":
>>> movement a. 157b–159a (positive);
>>> movement b. 159b–160b (negative).
> *Second Hypothesis*: "If one is not":
>> Stage III: "If one is not, what is true of it?":
>>> movement a. 160b–163b (positive);
>>> movement b. 163b–164b (negative).
>> Stage IV: "If one is not, what is true of the others?":
>>> movement a. 164b–165d (positive);
>>> movement b. 165e–166c (negative).

The entire exercise culminates in a terminal aporia:

[1] The antinomies have been carefully discussed in recent years. See especially, Cornford, *Plato and Parmenides*; Ryle, "Plato's *Parmenides*"; Owen, "Notes on Ryle's Plato"; Schofield, "Antinomies"; and most recently, Meinwald, *Plato's Parmenides*.

[2] The absurdity is important, cf. Schofield, "Antinomies"; and contrast Cornford's introductory remarks, *Plato and Parmenides*, p.104, which imply that the second part is intended to solve the problems of interpredication announced at 129d.

"Let it be said, then, that, as it seems, whether the one is or is not, in every respect and in every way both in relation to themselves and each other the one and the others are and are not, appear and do not appear." "Very true" (*Parm.* 166c).

The interpreter is then left with a thorny problem. What exactly is the point of the gymnastic session? And how do the arguments about "the one" relate to the arguments of the first part of the dialogue?[3] And what is this "one" anyway?

It is, first of all, reasonable to suppose that there is some underlying unity to this dialogue (not least because it is about "the one," passim).[4] Consider first of all its structure. It falls, formally, into three parts: the opening encounter between Socrates, Parmenides, and Zeno; the discussion about forms; and the gymnastic session. There is, clearly enough, an underlying unity of theme: how can dialectic deal with ones and manies without succumbing to Eleaticism? There is also a striking literary connectedness. The dialogue opens with a "Chinese whispers" effect: Cephalus tells an unidentified audience (as Plato tells his reader) of the meeting between Socrates and the Eleatics; but Cephalus had the story from Antiphon, who had it from Pythodorus.[5] This frame introduces the arguments; but the terminal aporia fails to return to the frame, so that we are left within the dialectical exchange. This effect draws the reader into the argument and emphasizes the continuity of the dialogue as a whole. So the dialogue is presented as fitting together, as coherent as well as continuous, and not as a piecemeal collection of arguments.

One explanation of the unity of the dialogue might be that the whole discussion is about forms.[6] The first set of arguments is about forms in general; the gymnastic session takes one particular form (the form One) and investigates that in detail. This could generate an optimistic view or a pessimistic one. The optimist would suppose that Plato saw that there were some difficulties with his theory, but did not regard them as lethal (even if they were seriously worrying).[7] So he continued to postulate a (transcendent) form for the gymnastic session, which has the effect of showing how forms are in fact

[3] It is, I think, a counsel of despair to suggest that this dialogue is not by Plato at all; but compare Brandwood, *Chronology*, on Ritter, p. 85. Once again, I shall insist that stylometric tests beg the question about which literary devices are unconscious and which are not; cf. Mackenzie, *Cratylus*, and Appendix A. I remain unabashed by the criticisms of Ledger, *Recounting Plato*. Owen, of course, deals with this one in style, "*Timaeus*," p. 66.

[4] Compare Socrates' remarks about the unity of a speech or a written work, *Phaedrus* 264c. Cf. Mackenzie, "Plato's *Phaedrus*."

[5] The Chinese whispers effect appears also in the *Symposium*; but there, unlike the *Parmenides*, the frame is closed at the end, as one of the narrators, Aristodemus, reappears in the story.

[6] Thus, for example, Allen, *Plato's Parmenides*, p. 183—although very often exponents of this line of interpretation are not entirely clear what is meant by (what kind of ontological commitment is involved in) postulating forms. The crucial thing about forms must be their separation, which I have construed as transcendence; if Plato shifts from talking about transcendent forms in the first part to talking about universals or concepts in the second, I take him not to be talking about the same things.

[7] Cf. especially, Vlastos, "Third Man Argument" here: the *Parmenides* is "the record of honest perplexity."

mentionable and can in fact have predicates (the positive treatments of the hypotheses, that is, are sensible, not absurd). The pessimist, on the other hand, will observe that the form One is in just as much difficulty if we can say anything whatsoever about it as it is if we cannot even mention it. On that view, the gymnastic session ends, as the encounter between Socrates and Parmenides ended, in aporia; and Plato may have known how to extricate himself—or he may not. On either view, the gymnastic session may not offer a serious philosophical contest; instead it may be protreptic, merely, the fitness exercises that will limber Socrates up for the grown-up job of rescuing the theory of forms.

But this is sheer romanticism, a misguided wish to saddle Plato with a "great theory."[8] At the literary level, it ignores all the irony of the contrast between Socrates and the clever man who will see things clear in the light of the forms. When does Plato ever recommend someone unequivocally as a clever man (recall the modest irony of Socrates' "I know that I know nothing")?[9] Indeed the theory of forms itself is described as simple-minded (*Phd.* 100d); how simple-minded, then, to undervalue the power of the arguments marshaled against the theory here in favor of a remark robbed of its irony. What is more, we risk anachronism with "mere" gymnastic. Hardly—Socrates will be completely trained (*teleōs gumnasamenos*) when he has gone though an extraordinary task (*amēchanon pragmateian*), a race wherein Parmenides will be the aged racehorse trembling before the fray (137a). But the training is for the sake of the race; and so the gymnastic, which is also a race, is valuable in its own right, a weighty play (*pragmateiōdē paidian*).[10] Then *Parmenides* II is serious philosophical stuff; it should have a serious connection with the first part of the work.

Stage I: If One Is, What Is True of It?

The first hypothesis of *Parmenides* II is "if one is." In the first stage this is treated in two movements with a coda. The first movement ends in the conclusion that the one cannot even be mentioned, let alone known or understood; the second, from showing that both of a series of a pair of predicates apply to one (indeed that any predicate at all may be applied to it in any respect; 155c), infers that we can mention, perceive, believe, or know the one. Both conclusions are absurd. The first violates the law of the excluded middle; and it seems to be self-refuting because it rules out speech altogether (the conclusion claims that we cannot even mention the hypothesis we have been discussing). The second, on the contrary, rules in everything—we can say whatever we like about the one, without restriction (in particular, without let or hindrance

---

[8] Or, worse, to suppose that he only had one theory, without which he is nothing.

[9] And see now Vlastos's excellent discussion of irony, *Socrates: Ironist and Moral Philosopher*, p. 21ff.

[10] Compare Plato's puns at *Euthyd.* 278b ff. and *Phdr.* 265, 276, on the relation between παιδιά and παιδεία.

from the law of noncontradiction).[11] Of what one can these conclusions be reached?

Compare two different treatments of the parts of the one in the first stage.

1. *The denial of parts to the one* (*Parm.* 137c–139b; my translations generally omit Aristotle's responses).

> If one is, then the one cannot at all be many. So it must have no part, nor be a whole. For a part is a part of a whole, and a whole is that from which no part is missing. Either way the one would be made of parts, whether it were a whole or had parts. Either way, then, the one would be many and not one. But it must not be many but itself one. So it is not a whole and has not parts. . . . [So it has no beginning, middle, or end; it is indefinite, formless, in no place, and neither moving nor at rest.]

This argument is run on a restricted reading of "one" in the hypothesis "if one is." All the deductions that follow suppose that for something to be one rules out any pluralization at all; and that is taken—as the arguments exhaustively show—to include ascribing any predicates, or attributing any relations or any properties to this one. If it is *just* one, then nothing is true of it, and nothing can be said of it at all.

2. *The attribution of all parts to the one* (*Parm.* 142b–143a).

> If one is, it cannot be and not participate in being. So the being of the one is not the same as the one, or else this would not be the being of that, nor would that, the one, share in this; instead it would be the same thing to say "one is" as to say "one one." But the hypothesis is not "if one one" nor its consequences, but "if one is." So "is" signifies something different from "one." So when someone says "if one is," they mean just that the one partakes in being. But then the one is the sort of thing that has parts. For if the "is" is said of the one that is, and the "one" is said of what is one, and the being and the one are not the same, but belong to the thing which we have hypothesised, namely the one being, then it, being one, must be the whole, and being and one must be its parts. But each of those parts is not merely a part, but a part of the whole. So whatever is one is whole and has parts. Now each of the parts of what is one, the one and the being, will not be lacking: the one will have being [as a part], and being will have one [as a part].[12] And each of these parts in turn has being and one, and the least part comes to be out of two parts and so on forever—whatever is a part itself always has these parts, so that one always has being and being always has one. So necessarily it keeps becoming two and is no longer one. Thus what is one is indefinite in number.

[11] The contradictions here, that is, are serious and not trivial, like Zeno's. For example, the one is the same and not the same as itself; compare the terminal ἀπορία, which asserts that the one is and is not *in every respect and in every way*: this is in startling contrast to the qualification of opposites in *Rep.* and *Phd.*

[12] Cornford, *Plato and Parmenides*, p. 130, remarks that "the sense is certain though the reading is dubious."

Here Parmenides' strategy is quite different. He appeals to the semantic difference between "one" and "is" to generate a one with parts; he assumes, that is, that any ascription of a predicate (including, perhaps, "existence"?) to the one signifies some real feature of the one. In that case, to say that the one *is* pluralizes the one, and its parts likewise. Upon that assumption is built the rest of the second movement of the first hypothesis, and the contradictions that result.

On reflection these contrasting assumptions are familiar. The first, that the one is just one, so that nothing at all can be said of it, is the demand that "one" be treated austerely. The second, that "if one is" legitimates any predication to "one," in particular the predication of opposites, is generous in its ascription of properties. But the contrast between the generous and the austere hitherto has reflected the contrast between particulars (which are generously endowed with properties of all sorts) and forms (which austerely are just what they are). The difference, that is, between generous individuals and austere ones is a difference in ontological level. But here that difference has disappeared, and the (same) one[13] is treated first austerely, then generously. Why? This question should, perhaps, be approached through another. What is this one we are dealing with here?

Both optimists and pessimists supposed that the second part of the *Parmenides*, despite the conclusions of the first,[14] hypothesizes a form ("the form one," "unity itself," "the one itself") and explores the consequences to it of various logical maneuvers. After all, discussion is promised, not of visible objects, but of those things that we might grasp in argument (*logos*) and where someone might postulate there to be forms (*Parm.* 135e).[15] Thus, at various stages of the argument Parmenides' terminology suggests the theory of forms (e.g., *tou henos autou*, 137b2). More significantly, perhaps, the argument treats its subject both as an object ("unity itself") and as what imparts unity (the property "unity"); such a dual role, it is often thought, could only be performed by a form.

Prima facie, however, the sense of such a move is puzzling. We might wonder why, having offered a difficulty for the forms that cannot (even on the traditional view) be solved by any but the best trained, Parmenides should persist in maintaining the discredited thesis before the training has even begun. And it is hard to see why Parmenides would be misled into thinking that this is *his* one (*Parm.* 137b3), which excludes plural properties altogether.

Parmenides compliments Socrates on resisting Zeno's paradoxes: "You were not prepared to think about visible things, nor to confine your wanderings to them, but rather to those things which someone might grasp in argument and where he might suppose there to be forms" (*Parm.* 135e). This does

---

[13] Cf. Owen, "Ryle's Plato," p. 98, who insists that the subject must remain the same from treatment to treatment.

[14] Or perhaps, because the first part is a guessing game—once we spot the fallacy in the arguments against the forms, we can see that they survive the attack.

[15] Cf. Owen, "Ryle's Plato," p. 86.

not imply that the forms are the topic of the second part. Rather, it stipulates an abstract discussion, such as *might* lead to the postulation of the forms. The first part of the dialogue has an explicit ontological commitment to the contrast between forms and particulars. Here Parmenides explicitly eschews any interest in the particulars, as would be appropriate to an abstract discussion. And while someone could still take the forms to be the appropriate focus of rational discussion, Father Parmenides himself did not suppose that a necessary condition of rationality or of abstraction. So while the forms might be a postulate, they need not be; the ontological commitment of Socrates' original theory is avoided. We are to have, then, a different type of investigation from physics, which concerns itself with real sensible objects, and from the discussion of the forms, where the ontological content is already determined. Rather, this part of the dialogue is an abstract thought-experiment, free of ontological commitment (hence, for example, the repeated suggestion that we should take the one "itself by itself in thought," e.g., at 143b7; cf. 158c2, 165a).

If the topic of *Parmenides* II, then, is not the form One, how are we to understand both the terminology Parmenides uses, and the topic itself? Think here about the meaning of the expression "the one" (*to hen*). Like "(the) white,"[16] this suffers from multiple ambiguity in Greek.[17] If I say, "The white has landed in the pocket," I use "the white" as a singular referring term for an individual particular. If I say, "The orange is a solecism in this elegant room," I may be describing an individual property. "Blue is a lovely color," on the other hand, speaks quite generally of a color, while "Black is beautiful" uses "black" to classify individual particulars. So "the one" may be a particular one or a group of ones; or it may be the unity of some particular or the unity of a collection of particulars. In the special case of Plato, we may be dealing with the character of unity, or the form that explains the character (and in this case, of course, it may be treated either as a universal or as a particular).

Consider a slightly different ambiguity—this time, perhaps, an ambivalence of purpose. "The one," if it is a class term, could describe a class whose members are already determinate ("these ones"); or it could be a variable ("any one"). In the former case, the conditions for being a one must be already decided; but if those conditions are still unclear, or disputed, then we should expect the indeterminate reading, "any one." Now the first part of the dialogue, I suggested, challenged two different conceptions of individual— whether a one might be many, and an individual generously conceived; or whether it might be simply one, and austere. But if that challenge remains unanswered, then the conditions for individuation remain undecided. If the hypotheses are about individuals, they will be about any individual, whatever turns out to count as an individual. Then we should understand the hypotheses in a quite general and abstract way. Thus, "if one is" cashes out as

[16] Cf., e.g., Aristotle, *Categories*.

[17] As does any term that uses the neuter definite article and an adjective or a participle.

"suppose any individual." That is, the "one" that is the subject of all the arguments may be understood to be any individual, abstractly conceived. The arguments that follow then consider what will follow from supposing any individual. This allows two different treatments, according to the two views of individuation already outlined: the generous view, whereby the individual is defined in terms of its properties; and the austere view, whereby the individual is seen to be what it is in isolation from any properties it might have. This contrast (I shall suggest) is the basis of the alternating movements within each hypothesis. And thus the characterization of the subject as "the one" or as "the one by itself" should be read as a variable, whose values are all the individuals there are or might be. But then the conduct of the arguments themselves amounts to an examination of what it is to be an individual, just because the hypothesis simply postulates individuals as such.

Recall, however, that the expression "(the) one" may designate *both* some putative individual *and* the condition of being an individual, just as "the white" can designate both a white object and the whiteness that it has—if (as I have argued) Plato understands both formal and material aspects of things to be properties equally. There is a risk, then, that Plato might conflate or confuse an individual with *being* an individual, especially if the discussion as a whole both postulates individuals and then examines the conditions of their individuation. We might expect Plato to keep rigorously separate the individuals he postulates from the property of being an individual; and yet the conduct of the argument seems to disappoint these expectations.

This point could be put a different way by reflecting on the problems Plato already has with "the one." First of all, the contrast between the generous and the austere conceptions of the individual could also be understood as a puzzle about priority.

Austerely: the individual per se is prior to the specification of its properties and can be specified as such. Take a trivial example. This blackbird before me has a grubby beak. Having a grubby beak happened to the blackbird, which was already digging holes in the lawn. The blackbird came first. And once we see the same blackbird among a flock, we would readily assume that this blackbird was an individual before it became one among the twenty-four for the pie. The individual (as Aristotle would agree) comes before its accidents— before its various and changing properties, affections, and relations. ("Comes before," of course, means, to Aristotle at least, that it antedates any particular accident, not all of them;[18] nonetheless, generally understood, the individual blackbird comes first.) Now suppose that this principle is generalized, in the austere manner. If what is one (an individual) comes first, is basic, then we should be able to understand it as one on its own, and not in terms of its properties, affections, or relations (including the property of being an individual). To reach what is basic (by this reasoning), we have to grasp what is *just one*—an austere individual.

---

[18] Cf. ch. 1, sec. 5.

Generously: all there is to being an individual is the having of properties, so that the having of properties comes first. After all, the blackbird cannot even be thought of without some properties, even if it seems to antedate this particular change (from digging up the lawn to appearing in a pie). Perhaps, then, the individual blackbird is some collection of properties (whether they be essential or accidental is a further, and later, question). In that case, there should be no question of some "just one," since any one is a collection of features. This generous view supposes that understanding one is understanding it in terms of the properties it has (including, presumably, the property of being one).

These approaches to "being one" are quite different; and they seem to be incompatible, since the austere view denies any appeal to the properties of what is one, while the generous view supposes that there is nothing but properties. Moreover, the austere view treats the individual as primary, while the generous view must explain the individual by virtue of the property of being an individual that it has. But once "some individual" is postulated, a further issue of priority arises: what is the relation between "some individual" and "what it is to be an individual"? Thus, suppose we have some individual: is it just an individual, *from which* we can grasp what it is to be an individual (so that the individual has priority), or is it an individual because it is *characterized by* "what it is to be individual"? In that case, how are we to understand that character? Is it a property, like any other? If it is, the property is prior, and we are committed to a generous view of individuation, with its attendant paradoxes. If not, then we must retain the austere view, and the individual and "what it is to be an individual" are one and the same; this view, too, brings paradox along. Dialectic seems to be in worse trouble than before.

Plato's two-world thesis emerged from the first part of the dialogue in disarray. It did so most of all, as I have suggested, because it turned out to be a theory about individuals (particulars or forms), but to lack a satisfactory account of what it is to be an individual. As a consequence, I suggest, the second part of the dialogue turns from the treatment of specified entities, forms, or particulars, to the discussion of individuals per se. The premise, that is, of *Parmenides* II is that we "take any individual"; the sequels then investigate the assumptions that we must and do make about such individuals, and conclude with the unsatisfactory state of affairs that no individual may be specified without absurd consequences.

3. Ones and Parts

The first movement claims that if something is one, it cannot be many. So it has no parts, but is itself one. So it has no beginning, middle, or end; it is indefinite, formless, in no place, and neither moving nor at rest.

These inferences rest upon the thesis that the one is "just" one, whose unity is unimpeachable. Hence, for example, the immediate inference "if one is, the one cannot at all be many" (*Parm.* 137c4), the claim that it is "one itself" (d2), and the closing condition "if the one is one"(d3). The argument begins, then, with reflection upon the one itself, not upon any properties[19] the one might have in addition to its being one.[20] And this strategy is justified by the assumption that any property of the one would, by adding to it, impair its being just one.

The second movement amplifies a similiar assumption to a different conclusion: "The being of the one is not the same as the one, or else this would not be the being of that, nor would that, the one, share in this; instead it would be the same thing to say 'one is' as to say 'one one.' But the hypothesis is not 'if one one' nor its consequences, but 'if one is.' So 'is' signifies something different from 'one.' "

If the one is said to be, as well as being one, then it has more than one part (the part that is one and the part that is being). While the first movement disallowed any talk of parts of the one (on austere principles that this would impair its being one), the second movement accepts that there are such parts, and uses that to generate the hopelessly generous one of the conclusion.

The hypothesis is about "one"; and so the focus of attack in both movements is *individual* entities—*any* individual entities. So the first movement hypothesizes what is "just one" and considers how its nature as "just one" precludes its partition.[21] So if it is, it cannot be one (because that will be an additional property), nor can it be whole; so it is indefinite. Such an item cannot even be said to be one at all; no individual, defined in this austere way, can be a definite individual, and so such an individual is no individual at all. Contrariwise, in the second movement, the one that is allowed to be turns out not to be one at all, but any number, and indeed anything you like and its opposite as well. Such an item is no more definite (no easier to mention, describe, or know) than the austere one of the first movement.

What exactly is the assumption on which all this depends? One account of what has gone wrong here is that Plato has muddled identity and predication.[22] When we say "one is one," we are using "is" in a different sense than when we say "one is half-witted." In the first case, the "is" gives us the equation of identity, so that the items mentioned are governed by Leibniz' law[23]—they are indiscernible, the same item, just one entity after all. Thus, if "this chapter is the one I was thinking about last week" is true, then if this chapter is about the *Parmenides*, so will the chapter I was thinking about last week be about the *Parmenides*. In the second case, we have the "is" of predication, which connects, for example, an object and a property in such a way that

---

[19] As before, this term will be used to cover all sorts of possible properties, especially relational ones.

[20] Compare with this the argument of the *Sophist* against Eleatic monism (*Soph.* 244e–245d), see ch. 7, sec. 2.

[21] Recall the argument that particulars can participate in neither the whole, nor the part of a form at *Parm.* 131a ff.

[22] Cf. Owen, "Ryle's Plato," p. 90.

[23] Intersubstitutable *salva veritate*—except, of course, in contexts where the law is modified by the context; e.g., modal contexts, or the various devices of direct and indirect speech.

Leibniz' law does not hold: even if one is half-witted, one does not exhaust all the half-wittedness there is. Thus, if this chapter is half-witted, that does not prevent several other chapters from being so too; nor, if they are half-witted too, will this imply that they are the same chapter as this one. I cannot say "half-witted" when I mean "this chapter," nor vice versa, and come up with the same truths.

This contrast—between identity and predication—is a tricky one to see, let alone to manipulate. The problem may lurk in "is" (which may, it could be argued, be ambiguous between the "is" of identity and the "is" of predication);[24] and it is exacerbated by the oddity of Greek expressions such as "the white" or "the one" that may signify both an object (on either side of an identity equation) or a property (on one side of a predication). Has Plato fallen into the trap of confusing the two—or failing to employ them differently in appropriate circumstances?

Suppose there is just one item to consider,[25] then maybe its being one constitutes exactly what it is; so to say "what is is one" or "the one is one" is not to attribute a property to what is, but to state its identity. To think about this from the grammatical point of view, the "is" of "what is *is* one" is an "is" of identity, not predication. Plato's mistake, then, is to treat identity statements as predications. For if being one is what it is for this one to be, then what is is identical with what is one, and not more than one. The first movement misses this point by supposing that "one" must be denied even identity claims (because they seem to be predications and to import extra entities). The second movement supposes that the one's being one attributes a property to the one, and so turns it into many.

Or perhaps Plato thought all "is" statements were identity statements. Then the first movement rightly denies anything but austere unity to what is one (and ends up not being able to talk about it—talk needs predication). The second movement, conversely, claims that the multiplicity of identity statements we can make about the one gives us a multiplicity of objects. Suppose we take the two statements "*x* is *x*" (identity) and "*x* is *y*" (predication). If no difference between the "is" of identity and the "is" of predication is discerned, then by Leibniz' law, *x* will not only be *x*, but also *y*; indeed *x* will be identical with any of its properties or predicates, and so it will be many, not one as it was originally postulated to be. (This, of course, looks like a further mistake —identity statements do not relate two items that are numerically distinct.) There lies here, then, a clear fallacy of equivocation, since predication statements are not subject to Leibniz' law.

So perhaps Plato did not understand "is."[26] He had not grasped that the identity relation is reflexive, and he associates one item with itself, not with something else. Nor had he understood that predication is not subject to the stringencies of Liebniz' law, but relates objects and properties, relations, affec-

---

[24] But cf., e.g., Mates, "Identity and Prediction," who denies any such ambiguity.

[25] This is clearer, perhaps, in the monistic passage of the *Sophist*; but the assumption itself is plausible in this Eleatic context.

[26] This, as we shall see, is a rich source of faultfinding. Cf., e.g., Ackrill on the *Sophist*.

tions in multifarious ways without impairing the original object's identity at all. (He may have been, quite generally, in a muddle about "is" and used both senses indiscriminately.)

But the difficulty may lie deeper than this. Identity statements themselves require some grip on the notions of singularity and individuation. Consider the following sentences:

1. "Hetty is fat."
2. "Hetty is a hippopotamus."
3. "Henry is the world's largest hippopotamus."

The first sentence gives us a predication (and is not subject to Leibniz' law). The second sentence may sort Hetty into the correct natural kind, and it may allow us to infer that

4. "Some hippopotamus is fat."

But it will not allow us to conclude that

5. "Henry is fat," or
6. "Henry is Hetty," or
7. "Hetty is the world's largest hippopotamus."

For while sentences connecting singular descriptions (such as 3) may be subject to Leibniz' law, sentences expressing essence (like 2), while more fruitful[27] than ordinary predications (such as 1) in inferential content, are nonetheless not full-blown identity statements and are not subject to Leibniz' law. For that establishes the identity of indiscernibles by trading on our existing intuitions about what counts as an individual; it is for that reason that the law connects singular descriptions, and not any old subject/predicate pair connected by "is." In short, this problem (about identity and predication) assumes that the problem of individuation is solved. But by this stage in the *Parmenides*, individuation is still a puzzle—as indeed it may be still.

So perhaps Plato's trouble was not "is" but what came after it. Plato may be making some assumption about the metaphysics of properties and their possessors, and not about the grammar of the verb "to be." Recall, first of all, the thesis of natural inherence. When, in earlier dialogues, Plato spoke of any properties of particulars, he supposed those properties (including relations and values) to be features of the particular in such a way as to make them composite (plural) entities. And when, earlier in this dialogue, Socrates faced difficulties with the theory of forms, his demand that they resist interpredication —any predication at all—seems to have been based on the assumption that they are simple entities with no plural properties at all. So there is a choice between something with properties (whose properties are *parts* of it) and something without properties (which may then be a simple entity). Both alternatives suppose that properties are parts in such a way that the thing that

---

[27] Provided, of course, that they make any sense at all. But are there essences?

has them is pluralized by them. "Plural characters pluralise a thing."[28] What has properties may be (nothing over and above) the sum of its properties; contrariwise, for something to be simple and one, it must have no properties at all. Once again, lacking some independent account of what makes something one, we cannot *deny* that it is the sum of its properties, nor that it is devoid of properties altogether. But the pluralizing assumption is threatening in two quite different ways, as the first and second movements of the first stage show.

1. The *negative* movement. Consider the statement "x is x." This represents, if anything, the self-identity of x. But what is that? If we consider it from the austere point of view, that is from the point of view of x separate from its properties, then x's self-identity cannot be explained in terms of its properties (ex hypothesi). But then how can x's self-identity be expressed or explained? Just *as* self-identity? But how does that differ from a property of x? Why is "self-identity" not a property?[29] So far, we have no grounds for a formal distinction between the self-identity of x and x's yellowness. Moreover, from the austere perspective, each will be excluded from mention on the grounds that it is a mere property. Consequently, only identity statements of the type "x is x" will have any claim to legitimacy, and predications will be ruled out, because, if you like, they violate Leibniz' law. So as far as x's ontological status is concerned, x will be represented by the statement "x is x" bare of identity, individuation, existence, or comprehensibility. Even "x is x" is otiose; indeed, even mentioning "x" turns out to be impossible.[30]

Here, plural characters pluralize, certainly; but that is problematic just because we are considering *individuals per se*. If we ask "What is an individual?" we are looking for some account of how any individual might be one. This objective is bound to be confounded if we are working also with the assumption that any properties (in the widest possible sense) that something might have will make it more than one. Lacking, at the very least, some restriction on the claim that plural properties pluralize (for example, a formal distinction between the properties that explain individuation and identity and those that may be attributed to individuals extra), all properties must be held on a par; and all must be excluded from austere individuals.

2. The *positive* movement. For generous individuals, the case is quite different. Here Parmenides asserts that since there is a semantic difference (*Parm.* 142c2) between "one" and "is" in the proposition "one is," then these must be different aspects of the one. The argument focuses clearly from the outset upon the "properties" of the one, not on the one itself. For example, at 142b7 Parmenides points out that being, the "property" (subsequently, "part") of the one, is not the same as the one, else they would collapse into each other. Thus, being is *said of* the one, and one of being (142d1); he infers that the one

---

[28] Owen, "Ryle's Plato," p. 90.

[29] Cf. here, e.g., Kripke, "Identity and Necessity," who treats self-identity (and its modality) as a property of things.

[30] Cf. a similar argument at *Cratylus* 432ff.

has parts. For since each aspect will have the property "is," it too will be divisible into two aspects or parts, and so on until an infinite (or indefinite) number of parts is conceded.

The strategy of this argument, then, is to press both the pluralizing assumption and the claim that the one and its being are *nonidentical*. For if being is something the one has—(and the one is understood *separately* from its being, hence: "The one itself, which we say partakes in being—if we think about it just itself by itself without that in which it partakes—is just one and not many"; 143a)—then they are not the same but different. So there must be two of them (because they are nonidentical), and thereafter an indefinite number.

> So its being must be different from it, and it must be different, since the one is not being, but as one it partakes in being. So if being is different and one is different, then the one is not different from being by virtue of being one, nor is being different from the one by virtue of being; instead they are different from each other by virtue of the different. So the different in not the same as either the one or being. [There follows the generation of all numbers from the one, *Parm.* 143c–144a; the division of one by being, 144b–e; that the one is both limited and unlimited, in itself and in something else, in motion and at rest, 144e–146a.]

The second movement, then, complements the first, since both employ the pluralizing assumption and another assumption about identity: in the case of the first movement, the assumption is that the one is just self-identical (and consequently not even mentionable); in the second, the assumption is that the one and its properties are nonidentical, so that there are any number of things.

In the first movement, the analysis of the individual *per se* has foundered; and this might encourage us to believe (as we embark on the second) that there is then no individual core to which the properties of some possible individual may attach themselves. So we might look for the individual in those very properties: all there is, on that account, to being one is being a collection of properties. Two consequences may follow:

1. Any property (of the one) whatsoever will be a member of the collection in the same way, since we lack any distinction between one sort of property and another (being self-identical and being yellow will be properties on a par). Thus, if any property represents a part of this one, then even formal statements (like "the one is the same as itself" or even "the one is") will bring along a new part of the original item under consideration (from this assumption Parmenides generates all the numbers). So the properties that might be thought to explain identity will be no more and no less than the accidental features of it, in the collection that makes up the one.

2. If the one just is a collection of properties, and if all its properties are on an equal footing, there will be no means of distinguishing formally between it and its properties (nor, in speech, between the subject of a sentence and its predicate). So while in the austere movement all we were allowed were the simple identity statements of the type "x is x" (only the subjects of sentences even stood a chance to be considered), now any term in a proposition (includ-

ing the term that in a different logic would be described as the subject) may be thought to represent a property. So this movement is based upon the semantic claim, that "is" and "one" differ; and this claim derives directly from the method of investigation of individuals that is being pursued here.

Consider the argument to generate all the numbers:[31] It gets off the ground by treating being and one as separate entities, occurring both in our original "one" and in its derived parts. Some complex arithmetic gives Parmenides the conclusion that he can derive any number in this way (*Parm.* 144a). Then just as the original one partakes in being, so do all the other numbers—being is "parceled out" among all the things that are. In each case, there will be a part of being (in each number); and each of those parts will be one (being one is basic).[32] So one will be divided up into parts and not a whole: and it will be just as many as its parts, and equal in number to being. Both one and being will be parceled out in the same way, and the one itself will turn out to be divided into many by being (144b–e).

What is it to be an individual? According to this positive movement, it is to have the property of being one. But that property is itself a pluralizing feature: so any individual, just by having that property, will turn out to be many after all. But while this (unlike the austere approach) still allows us to talk about the one, it renders the one contradictory. And (once again if this is an answer to the question "what makes something one?") the contradiction is not an innocuous one. For it is the very feature that makes something one that makes it many: the contradiction is built into the supposition that individuation is a property. If it is, then there are no individuals after all.

A Rylean complaint might help here.[33] Surely, Plato has made the mistake of failing to distinguish between different sorts of property (or concept or predicate), between the entirely general features of the world and the specific features that are limited to particular classifications? That is, Plato should contrast predicates (and their corresponding properties) like "exists," "same," "single"[34] with predicates like "is yellow" or "flies." In particular, he is wrong to ignore the asymmetry between objects and properties; and wrong again to suppose that any property (such as being one or being the same) is just like any other (such as being purple or being heavy). But does not that complaint beg the question? Unless we already know what constitutes a proper distinction between the properties that identify and individuate (that should not pluralize and cannot be parceled out) and those that are accidents, extra features of some objects, and might properly be thought to be real parts

---

[31] Plato foreshadows the argument of Aristotle (e.g., at *Met.* 1052b18ff.) by treating the individual as the measure of number.

[32] Cf. Owen's diagnosis of the assumptions here: "We cannot 'abstract from' the unity or existence of a subject because unity and existence must always be reimported in talking of whatever parts or members are left"; Owen, "Ryle's Plato," p. 92.

[33] Ryle, "Plato's *Parmenides*," p. 130ff.

[34] Ryle's list is longer, p. 131; in what follows I argue (especially in ch. 8, sec. 2) that Plato has a specific and limited list of formal properties in mind.

of whatever it is, then we cannot deploy that distinction to effect an account of individuation.[35]

4. SAMENESS AND DIFFERENCE

The first arguments of both movements turn on questions of identity, as we have seen. It is hardly surprising, then, that each movement also contains paradoxical treatments of sameness and difference. Compare this from the first, negative movement—

> The one is neither the same as anything else, nor as itself, nor different from itself nor anything else. If the one is different from itself, it would be different from the one and so not one. If the one is the same as the different, it would be the different, and not itself. But then it would no longer be what it is to be one,[36] but other than one. So it cannot be the same as the different nor different from itself. And so long as it is one, it cannot be different from the different; for it is not appropriate for one to be different from anything, but only appropriate for the different, and nothing else, to be different. So by virtue of being one, it will not be different. But if it is not different by virtue of being one, then it is not different by virtue of being itself, and if not by virtue of itself, then it will not be different. While it is different in no way, then it is different from nothing. Then again, nor will it be the same as itself. For the nature of being one is not the nature of being the same. After all, if something becomes the same as something, it does not thereby become one; when it becomes the same as many, it must become many, not one. But if the one and the same were no different, whenever something became same, it would always become one, and whenever one, then same. So if the one were the same as itself, it would not be one with itself; and thus while it is one it would not be one. So it is impossible for the one to be either different from the different nor the same as itself. So the one is neither different nor the same, whether in relation to itself or to anything else. (*Parm.* 139b–e)[37]

with its counterpart in the second, positive movement:

> It must, therefore, be the same as itself and different from itself, and likewise the same and different from the others. For everything is either the same as or different from anything else, unless one is a part of the other. But the one is not a part of itself, nor is it the whole of which itself is a part. Nor is the one different from the one, nor is it different from itself. So since it is neither different from itself nor related to itself as part to whole, it must be the same as itself. But if it is in a different place from itself, while itself is in the same place as it [this was shown earlier], then it must be different from itself. . . . But if something is different from something else, it will be different from something different. Whatever is not

---

[35] Indeed, as I understand Ryle's point, Plato's strategy is to generate paradox by ignoring these contrasts just so that we come to understand them. This seems to be the right way to read Plato's paradox-mongering; cf. ch. 1, sec. 7.

[36] I delete the comma after ἔστιν at c1.

[37] See Schofield, "Antinomies," on the text and the argument here.

one is different from the one and the one from those which are not one. So the one is different from the others. But same and different are opposites, and the same cannot ever be in the different or the different in the same. Then if the different is never in the same, then at no time will the different be in any of the things that are, for if ever it were, then the different would be in the same. So the different can never be in any of the things that are. So it will not be in either the things that are not one nor in the one. (*Parm.* 146b–147b)

The First, Negative Movement

The first, negative movement concludes that the one is not the same as itself or another, nor different from itself or another. The paradox, evidently enough, lies in the denial of self-identity and of difference from others; and the force of that paradox is felt particularly for an individual subject. If the nature of the one is one (vide, e.g., "otherwise it would not be that which is one," *Parm.* 139c1; "by virtue of being one it will not be different," 139c6), its nature is different from the nature of either same or different; so that the nature of one can neither explain nor cause the sameness of the one to itself or its difference from others. So, if it is just one, it is not the same as itself or different from the others.

Here, as in the denial of parts, Parmenides denies properties to the austere subject. But his strategy now seems rather different. For there he simply considered what is true of the one as such. Here he considers the nature of the one, and the consequences for the one of its having that nature. But it could be argued that Parmenides makes a mistake. Innocuously, some one might be identical with its (individual) nature. The Cheshire cat disappears grinning, because that is its (particular) nature—its nature just is its tendency to fade and to grin; its nature is not some other entity over and above the Cheshire cat that dictates its irritating behavior. Not so innocent, however, would be the claim that because Gerald is a giraffe, then he is identical with the (universal) nature of giraffe, and so is identical with (or possessed by, or the explanation of) any other giraffe we might find galloping across the veldt. So has Parmenides here slid from the nature of an individual to universal natures—and back again (as Plato caricatures at *Euthydemus* 301)? Consider the sequence of the argument:

"If the one is different from itself, it will be different from the one and no longer one." If the one is considered *as such*, as just what is one, then "itself" and "one" are intersubstitutable; the inference to "it will be different from the one" is sound. But if it just is one, then its being different from itself could result in nothing other than its no longer being one. This argument, which produces the truism that the one (or indeed anything else) cannot be different from itself, is the model for what follows.

"If the one is the same as the different,[38] it would be the different, and not

---

[38] The translation is tricky here: "the different" could mean "something different" or "what it is to be different."

itself." If the one is identical with something other than itself, it will be other than itself (and that is absurd). This will be true whether "the different" means merely some different item (which will be different as such) or "what it is to be different," which, if we are considering the one as such, will not be identical with the one. On the assumption that we are considering the one as such, the argument once again is sound, indifferent to the slide between something and its nature. And the conclusion, "So it cannot be the same as the different nor different from itself," is unexceptionable.

"And so long as it is one, it cannot be different from the different; for it is not appropriate for one to be different from anything, but only appropriate for the different, and nothing else, to be different. So by virtue of being one, it will not be different. But if it is not different by virtue of being one, then it is not different by virtue of being itself, and if not by virtue of itself, then it will not be different. While it is different in no way, then it is different from nothing." Here the same assumption seems to be in play. The *one as such* is not different from anything (not, that is, *qua* one, only *qua* different). But this one we are talking about is just one, and not (by virtue of being just one, or by virtue of itself) different from anything. Why not? Because (as before) Parmenides treats "being different" as an additional property of this one; and because on the austere hypothesis, the one has no such properties. The problem here, then, is not that the one is assumed to be "what it is to be one," nor that Plato conflates a particular with a universal; rather, he produces the paradox by relying on the assumption that relations (especially the relations governing identity like sameness and difference) are real features of the relata, and thus pluralize. But the one, as such, cannot be pluralized; and so it is precluded from all the relations of identity.

The one as such, then, is not different (from anything), nor is it what it is to be different, nor does it have the nature of what it is to be different. That follows from the austere hypothesis. But then the one, by parity of reasoning, cannot be the same (as anything), nor is it what it is to be the same, nor does it have the nature of what it is to be the same. "Then again, nor will it be the same as itself. For the nature of being one is not the nature of being the same. After all, if something becomes the same as something, it does not thereby become one; when it becomes the same as many, it must become many, not one. But if the one and the same were no different, whenever something became same, it would always become one, and whenever one, then same. So if the one were the same as itself, it will not be one with itself; and thus while it is one it will not be one." This argument works, again, without falling foul of the particular/universal fallacy. Suppose something is *just one*; and suppose further that for anything else (other than "one") to be true of this one would pluralize it, and make it not one at all. In that case, the only way in which the one could be the same as anything would be if to be one were the same thing as to be the same. But that is not so (some manies are the same as something). So we cannot substitute "same" for "one"; nor can we attribute sameness to the one (without pluralizing it). So the one is not the same as anything, either. "So it is impossible for the one to be either different from the different nor the same as itself. So the one is neither different nor the same, whether in relation to itself or to anything else."

Two connected points about properties might matter here.

First, if "yellow" means something different from "noisome," then we might argue that yellow is different from noisome and furthermore that being yellow does not explain, nor does it cause something to be, noisome. So this yellow thing is not by its nature (that is *by being yellow*) noisome. But that might be because yellow and noisome are ordinary physical and separable properties. Properties that could be formal (nonphysical) might interrelate in different ways. So some properties—such as one—might in fact bring other properties along with them—or even explain them. For example, it could be argued that if something is self-identical it is different from other things *just because* it is self-identical. So some properties might be interconnected (some may explain others) and not radically separable from each other, as Parmenides suggests they must be.

Second, there is something rather queer about relational properties, in just this respect. Relations are often reciprocal or correlative: for example, if Rotherham is north of Cambridge, then Cambridge is south of Rotherham. So "x is north of y" implies "y is south of x," just as, more simply, "x is different from y" implies that "y is different from x." And, as I have argued that Plato stresses in earlier dialogues, relations may bring their opposites along too: if x is equal to y, then there is some z that is not equal to x (just as if x is beautiful for a, there is some b for whom x is not beautiful: this has figured before as the compresence of opposites). So relations are not separable from each other as other properties (such as "yellow" or "smelly") might be. Now Plato may reach some way toward seeing this, if he insists that relational properties suffer from the compresence of opposites. If, nevertheless, he continues to view relations as common or garden properties like any other, then, despite their compresence, they may still be thought to be separable from each other (as common or garden properties are). In that case, they add something to (pluralize) whatever has them; and so the one cannot, in itself, be either the same or different.

One way of putting the point might be this. I have suggested that Plato's account of the objects in the world—as it figured in the *Phaedo* and the *Republic*—was dominated by two principles about relational properties: natural inherence and the compresence of opposites. Both principles together, I argued, generated a view of sensible particulars as composite entities, liable to change and destruction. Now, however, the tension between natural inherence and the compresence of opposites begins to appear, as relations (such as "same" or "different") start to cause trouble if they are the plural parts of some one thing. In these arguments of the *Parmenides*, Parmenides presses the paradox that even the relations that explain something's being one pluralize it. So no austere one is either the same or different (to anything, from anything); and, contrariwise, anything that has the properties of sameness and difference cannot be austerely one.

Return to the paradigmatic statement allowed by the austere position: "x is *x*." If this proposition is read as a predication, then there may indeed be a failure to distinguish "*x*" when it functions as a subject from "*x*" when it functions as a predicate; and this might correspond to a failure to contrast an object with its properties (or having a property with being a property). However, the austere view allows no such logical distinction, since, as we have seen, the attribution of properties of any kind to *x* is thought to be illicit; and this will apply no less to the property "being *x*" than to any other. That is not, of course, to muddle identity and predication, but to adopt a special stance toward the consideration of identity, as we have seen. Moreover, the refusal to distinguish formally between the one and the nature of the one has a great deal of point in terms of the methodological stance that is being adopted here. If, as I have suggested, these maneuvers take place in order to explain "the individual" by considering individuals in the abstract, then the nature of the individual will be just what is under consideration, and inseparable from the individual hypothesized. So either "the one has the nature of the one" is a licit identity statement, so that there is no difference between the one and its nature, or there is such a difference; and "the one has the nature of the one" will turn out to attribute a property to the one, and be illegitimate. For, from the denial of parts argument, any attribution of self-identity or difference from others to the one will result in a violation of its austerity, and must be disallowed.

This, then, will allow only the austere identity statement "the one is one," which may be thought to correspond to some individual in the external world. Since, however, the original hypothesis is a universal quantification (what I have called a "general truth"), then its instances will be "elephant is elephant" or "man is man" (not to confuse the issue by the addition of articles, definite or otherwise). We know from elsewhere that Plato was interested in both the logic and the metaphysics of such propositions: compare the position of the late-learners at *Sophist* 251 and the view that Socrates finds himself saddled with at *Euthydemus* 300. If we restrict our discourse to such propositions, as the *Sophist* will make clear, we deny any "communion" of terms and thereby any sentential complexity.[39] Consequently, in particular the terms "separate" (*chōris*), "from the others" (*tōn allōn*), and "in itself" (*kath'auto*) will be eliminated. These terms[40] will be disallowed for any austere individual, with the result that such individuals cannot be mentioned, and all discourse will come to a full stop. That, as the *Sophist* will point out (252c), is self-refuting. So, at the close of the first movement, Parmenides may conclude that austere individuals are unmentionable and ungraspable by the mind; and in saying so he reduces the original hypothesis, in its austere interpretation, to absurdity.

The Second, Positive Movement

The first movement works on the assumption that the one is just one. As before, the second, positive movement makes the opposite assumption, that

---

[39] Recall the way in which the forms were not allowed to interpredicate; *Parm.* 129e.

[40] This caused difficulties for the austere status of the forms.

the one is generously endowed with properties—indeed that the one just is its properties, multifarious though they turn out to be (hence, for example, the initial moves consider the relations between the one and the others, *Parm.* 146b2). And that is what produces both truism and paradox: the one "must, therefore, be the same as itself and different from itself, and likewise the same and different from the others."

Consider the truism and the paradox that the one is the same and different from the others. The truism comes first: "But if something is different from something else, it will be different from something different." Applause—some relations are symmetrical. So "whatever is not one is different from the one and the one from those which are not one." Fair enough—the negative marks the difference. "So the one is different from the others." Is that true, too? That depends, now, on what these others are. The others may be items that are not (are not identical to) this one we are discussing; or they may be items that do not have the character of one (and are for that reason nonidentical with the one we are discussing). "Difference," that is, may mean nonidentity or it may mean unlikeness (especially of quality). The argument might be harmless (although the premises may be false): if x is F and y is not-F, then $x \neq y$. So if the one has the character of one, and the others have the character of not-one, then one and the others will not be identical. Or the argument could be dangerous: if $x \neq y$, then any character that x has, y does not have. So if the others are other than (this) one, and the one is thus (e.g.) different, then the others cannot be different, because they cannot share characters with the one. Or the argument could be trivial: if $x \neq y$, then $x \neq y$. So if we take the one and some nonidentical others, the one and the others are nonidentical. The conclusion is taken as true (which suggests either the trivial or the harmless readings). Is the dangerous reading implied in the paradox that follows?

"Same and different are opposites, and the same cannot ever be in the different or the different in the same" (*Parm.* 146d).[41] Here sameness and difference are properties, which may inhere in something else, but which exclude each other. "And the different cannot be in anything for any length of time, or else it would be the same; so the different is never in anything, whether it be one or not." It turns out that difference is so extreme that it cannot even inhere in something else, at the risk of becoming its opposite. Why not? Why should difference be different (instead of making its object different)? "So it is not by virtue of the different that what is one is different from what is not one." If the one is to be different from something else, that must be explained by some character that it has. But the character is so slippery that it cannot do that explaining. "However, the one and the others are not different by virtue of themselves either, if they don't share in difference." So they cannot be different at all.

Suppose, as the generous hypothesis does, that anything just is its properties; and further, that the collection of properties includes the relations of

---

[41] Compare the argument in the first movement that suggested that to be one is not, *eo ipso*, to be the same.

identity. On this view, the identity of something is determined by (some of) its properties. How, on that account, are we to understand what makes $x \neq y$? Only by virtue of its character; in particular (why else?) by virtue of the character that determines its identity. Conversely, the nonidentity of something to something else can only be explained by some character that it has; indeed (once again on the generous hypothesis), the character that it has will be all there is to its difference from other things. But that character just is what it is to be different; and so the character itself cannot stay fixed, but slips away in constant flux.[42] In that case, there is nothing stable about the nonidentity of the one and the others—indeed, it collapses altogether.

This conclusion goes through if we concede the generous hypothesis in all its complexity. The claim (to recapitulate) of the generous hypothesis is that being "this" or "it" just is being a collection of properties; and that those properties account for the identification of the "it" in question. Indeed (as Plato saw), the "it" is an illusion, a mere way of speaking about this collection; properties are all there is. Nothing "has" a property; instead, the property occurs in a collection. But on that view, it is hardly surprising that the property displays its own character; for the appearance of the character is all there is to the property. And in that case, the identity of the collection of properties will depend on the properties themselves—but not on difference (which keeps slipping away).

What then is the relation between the one and the others? "What is not one cannot be one at all. So it can have no number, no parts, it cannot be a whole. But then it must, by elimination, be the same as the one" (*Parm*. 147a–b). The hypothesis suggests that there are the one and the others (which are not identical with it). This phase of the argument claims that the others do not have the character of the one; and concludes from that that they must be identical. Once again there seems to be a horrid fallacy here (what is not this one is not therefore completely devoid of unity);[43] but it is a fallacy that loses its grip in the face of the generous assumption. For there the nonidentity of the one and the others must be a matter of the properties they have; and that—if nonidentity is to be assumed from the beginning—must be a matter of the one having the character of one, while the others do not. But Parmenides then argues that this precludes the others having any numerical character at all; it follows from this, by elimination, that they cannot stand in any relation but identity with the one.

All of this, obviously enough, is paradoxical. But the real question is whether the paradox is to be resolved by finding a flaw in the argument, or by

[42] Perhaps we should balk at the claim that the character of difference is constantly becoming different. The generous hypothesis, however, makes it plausible. There is no central object to have this character; for a putative object to be different is just for the property of difference to occur in some collection of properties. But then there is no difference between being different and having the property of difference; and it might be thought to follow from that that the property of difference is different (if, indeed, the expression "different" can be syntactically complete).

[43] Cf. Owen "Ryle's Plato," p. 93; the I/P confusion once more.

disputing the premises on which the argument is based. Perhaps there is a Zenonian sophism—a failure to treat "same" and "different" with proper regard for their qualifiers[44]—but that looks trivial after Socrates' early dismissal of such puzzles. Perhaps, instead, there is here a careful exploration of an untenable assumption about identity; the assumption ends in paradox, as does its austere counterpart. The task of the reader, or the philosophical gymnast, is to steer a safe course between generosity and austerity, and rescue all these ones.

Think about it this way. The opening moves of the present argument make it clear that we do suppose that individuals are the same as themselves (*Parm.* 146c). So it is clearly paradoxical to say that they are not the same as themselves, as the argument concludes, let alone to claim that they both are and are not the same as themselves (147b). Likewise, while it is a matter of common sense to say that the one is different from the others (than it; cf. 147a, *ta mē hen*), it outrages common sense to assert, at the same time, that it is not different from them. Nonetheless we lack the apparatus to explain *why* we can confidently claim that *x* is different from others, and the same as itself, just as we lack a defense against the argument to show that the ever-changing nature of difference constantly slips away from the objects that might have it. That is, the argument does not suppress the qualifiers, but rather exploits our awareness that they are present to reach a paradoxical conclusion. The paradox is then the challenge to produce some kind of metaphysical underpinning for our conviction that individuals are the same as themselves, not different, and different from the others, not the same.[45] In particular, the challenge is to show how predicates such as same and different do not obey the same rules as ordinary predications. If not, how are the rules to be formulated?

5. THE ONE IN TIME

The first stage has a coda (c) (*Parm.* 155e–157b) on the one in time. In the first movement, the austere conception of the individual disallowed the individual's existence in time (*Parm.* 140e–141d). For it cannot be older or the same age or younger than anything else; nor, indeed, can it become older, simpliciter, since this would involve its becoming older than itself, and so would impair its self-identity (if, indeed, by this time it has any left; 141a7ff.). Now it could be argued that this conclusion can be warded off by observing that growing older does not imply growing older than oneself, and so does not entail the proliferation of the self. This defense is only available when we already have some sense of the identity of the individual over time, and some notion of how the individual per se can be implicated in any relations at all, let

---

[44] Cf. Owen, "Ryle's Plato," p. 93, "a flagrant fallacy of relations."

[45] On the way paradox works, cf. Quine,*Ways of Paradox*; Sainsbury, *Paradoxes*; Mackenzie, "Paradox in the *Phaedrus*," and "Heraclitus and the Art of Paradox."

alone relations with itself. The preceding arguments, however, have denied any such foundation to the individual; so that the present argument has nothing to fall back upon. Rather, the paradox about age and time is presented as flowing directly from the previous moves; its removal requires the solution to the earlier problems of the identity of the individual per se.

The second movement also confronts the issue of growing older (*Parm.* 151e–155d). Once again, "growing older" seems to imply "growing older than oneself." While the austere movement dismissed this as an impossible consequence for the one per se, the generous movement allows the conclusion that the one can be both older, younger, and the same age as itself in the now (152e). This inference is drawn from considerations of the properties of the one (see, e.g., the analysis of "older" at 152a) and completely ignores anything that may be true of the individual per se; consequently, it arrives at a conclusion that violates the very notion of an individual per se by implicating "it" in absurd relations with "itself." We find it absurd because of our (inchoate, incoherent, and inexplicit) intuitions about the integrity of "itself"; yet without the explicit statement and justification of those intuitions, the argument seems entitled to proceed as it does.

The paradox of the generous movement is derived from the properties of the one *now*. If, however, we consider what we may say of the individual that changes over time, further paradoxes are forthcoming; and these are exploited in the coda. When an individual changes, how can it survive through the change? What if the change is described as generation and destruction (*Parm.* 156b)? And, at the instant of change, what property can the individual be said to have? Surely at that point it cannot have no properties at all (156c6)—the austere view is ruled out. But equally, it cannot have both (opposite) properties at once—the generous view is ruled out, too. So there must be a "suddenly" between the two states that is the moment of change, and at that point the changing object is not in time at all (156e6); and it has, we may suppose, neither no properties nor both. This argument apparently mediates between the individual's having no properties at a time and its having both of a pair of opposites. The solution is "this absurd thing" (156d1), the "suddenly." Once again, both the austere view (the individual, at some time, has no properties at all) and the generous one (the individual, at some time, has both) are seen to be paradoxical. But then the argument offers a solution that is itself conceded to be absurd, and Pelion is piled upon Ossa.

The coda, then, considers the individual over time in both the generous and the austere manner; in retreat from either, the coda generates a higher level of absurdity, the "suddenly." So the coda is a separate movement in its own right; and it serves, first, to emphasize the contrast between its generous and austere predecessors; and second, to show how either is absurd. Both together are absurd; and so is neither. This complicates[46] and emphasizes the paradox.

---

[46] If the austere arm denies the law of the excluded middle (LEM), and the generous arm denies the law of noncontradiction (LNC) (and if LEM and LNC are converses of each other)—but the

One might say that the problem here is a linguistic one. The difference between the negative and the positive movements might be explained in terms of different completions of "*x* is becoming . . ." In some cases, the completion is a "threshold" expression (such as "forty years old" or "an astronaut"), where the process does not imply the end. However grimly my fortieth birthday may loom, I am still not forty until it is reached; I may be training to be an astronaut, but I cannot claim to be one until the rocket lifts off the launchpad. In such cases, becoming excludes being (as the austere movement claims). In other, sometimes vaguer, and certainly gradual cases, the end is part of the process—such as "older" or "fatter" or perhaps "blue." Here, my becoming fatter implies that I am fatter now (not, sadly, that I am not yet fat at all). This movie is getting blue—it may get bluer yet, but it is also blue right now. This allows the generous conclusion that becoming includes being.[47] Two kinds of mistake are possible. We might treat all expressions as threshold words—then the difficulties of the first movement ensue; or we might treat all expressions as gradual words—then the difficulties of the second movement are upon us. Or we might deny both—and find ourselves saddled with the "suddenly." The obvious solution here might be to tidy up our terminology, and to be sure to observe the different behavior of different sorts of words. Language is the clue to solving the problem.

Or is it? Return to the puzzle of the first movement. The one cannot be older or younger than anything, because it is just one (141a2; "how could it be older or younger than something, or the same age, *by virtue of being such as it is?*"). This appeals not to some accidents of language, but to the status of the hypothesis about this one; namely, that it is an austere individual. That assumption is pressed in the argument that follows, to show that the one, *such as it is*, cannot exist in time (and not that process, such as it is described, is indescribable). This one, such as it is, cannot be determined by any properties or predicates. If, however, it were to grow older, then it would be growing older than itself. But for that process to be even remotely plausible, both it now and its former self must have the properties of "older than itself" or "younger than itself"; but the one, such as it is, has no properties—so it cannot exist in time. The fallacy of relations that seems to be lurking here— ("older than itself" and "younger than itself" are both incomplete; read instead "older than itself at time *t* " and "younger than itself at time *t* + *1*")— is both irrelevant[48] and question-begging. It is irrelevant to the central paradox because that precludes attributing any property at all, however specified,

---

coda denies both—how can it be characterized? Owen, "Ryle's Plato," p. 95, suggests that the coda continues to deny LEM; this seems only half true. What the coda does, I think, is to deny that LEM and LNC are converses; it thus violates LEM by suggesting that both LEM and LNC are false at once. This allows the possibility that what goes on in "the suddenly" is nothing at all.

[47] This, of course, is grist to Aristotle's mill; cf. *Met.* 1048b18ff.; Owen, "Ryle's Plato," p. 95, suggests that Plato plays off these two approaches to arrive at his paradox—in order that we may see the difference.

[48] As Owen acknowledges, "Ryle's Plato," p. 95.

to this one. It is question-begging because it assumes that we can characterize the one in time (at t and at $t + 1$) when the argument suggests that this is impossible anyway.

The second movement, likewise, resists the solution that we should tidy up our language—and demands that we tidy up our metaphysics instead. Here, the one is allowed properties, as many properties as we like. So we can say that it is older or that it is younger. Is it then older than itself? Once again, the argument trades not on a fallacy of relations, but on the failure to specify what would count as "itself." If this one becomes older, then it must (of course we can get this relation completed, see Parmenides' insistence at 152d6) be older than something; and the something likewise will become younger than it.[49] But what something is this? Itself, or something else? So far we have no terms to mark off something else from this; in a generous world, there is no property the individual does not have. But then any individual may (as this argument suggests) collapse into any other; in particular, it may collapse into all its former selves, if we lack the weapons to cut it off from itself at time t.

The coda allows the one to change in temporal hiccups. But then what is one and becomes many will, inside the intervening hiccup, be nothing at all. Can we avoid this by linguistic reform? Once again, the answer must be no. The metaphysics of time (is it real or unreal, continuous or staccato?) is not just a matter of the·way we talk—or at least, to suppose that it is begs the question whether time is merely an abstraction. But the problem here lies deeper. Suppose that individuals are basic in the structure of the world. Then suppose that these individuals must have properties and be allowed to change. Both the having of properties and the possibility of change must be encompassed (if individuals are basic) without at the same time doing away with the individual that has the properties or undergoes the change. The puzzle of the coda is this: even if we take steps (postulating the "suddenly") to allow individuals to change, the exigencies of process demand that the subject of change go out of existence altogether as the change occurs.[50] That Zenonian conclusion demands from us a proper account of the subject of change—and not just a better grammar.

6. The Unity of the First Stage

The first stage contains two canonical arguments that hold the remaining sequences of inference together:

1. *What one* are we dealing with? This may be answered in the austere or the generous mode. Negatively or austerely, the one we are dealing with is just

---

[49] Why not? We can only tidy this one up if we differentiate *sorts* of becoming: we might want some real becoming for what grows older, but only allow the something it grows older than, some Cambridge becoming. That, too, demands that we see what counts as *it*, or as *it now*, or as *itself* now, as opposed to its *former self*.

[50] Recall the problems of Theseus's ship; see ch. 1, sec. 2.

one; so it has no parts. Positively or generously, the one we are dealing with is a collection of properties; that allows a collection to contain any property at all.

2. *What is it for that one to be one?* The identity of the one, or its nature, may consist in its being (austerely) just one; in that case it is nothing but itself (which implies in the end that it is not even that). Or the one may be one because it has the property of unity (generously distributed over all ones); in that case it is anything at all.

The first movement develops thus:
The one is

i. partless, etc.;

ii. in no place (*Parm.* 138b; via denial of parts, 138a6);

iii. neither moving nor at rest (139b; via denial of parts, 138d1);

iv. neither the same as itself nor different from itself, neither the same as anything else nor different from anything else (139e; via austere identity, 139c1);

v. neither like itself nor unlike itself, nor like/unlike anything else (140b; via austere identity, 139e9);

vi. neither equal nor unequal neither to itself nor to anything else (140d; via austere identity, 140c4; via denial of parts, 140c9);

vii. denial of existence in time (141d; indirectly, via v and vi);

viii. denial of being and reference (142a; indirectly via vii, and then by exhaustion of all the possibilities in i–vii).

The foundational arguments for this sequence exploit the austere account of individuation; from the inadequacy of that account all the other paradoxes flow, concluding with the denial of being. The puzzles here, then, are not about existence, but about being one, being an individual. If an individual has the austere nature of this one, then it cannot enter any relations at all with anything, whether itself or anything else. And from this conclusion flows another—that such an individual has no affections (*pathēmata*; 141d4) at all, and therefore no contact with being.[51] Being an individual is basic; being related to individuals (whether itself or others) requires the individual to be properly specifiable; having other properties can only follow from that.

Compare the sequence in the second movement:

i. The one has an infinity of parts, is infinite in number (*Parm.* 144a);

ii. so the one and being are divided up in just the same way (144e).

This sequence again betrays two dominant assumptions: first, that the one has parts, and, second, that being one, and being, are universal properties of whatever is one ("never lacking," 144b2; "distributed," 144b1; "parceled

---

[51] With *existence* or with *being something or other?* The argument shows that the one is not anything at all; from that, if we must, we can argue that the one does not exist, but for Parmenides to show that it is not anything at all (ie., has no contact with being or becoming) is enough. It ought to be enough for us, too. I shall return to this theme.

out," (144b5).[52] From these (premises of the generous account of individuation), the remaining arguments are drawn. The one

    iii. is limited and indefinite in number, has any shape (145b; via parts, 144e8),

    iv. in itself and in anything else (via universal properties, e.g., at 145d1);

    v. is both moving and at rest (146a; via iv);

    vi. is both the same as itself and different from itself, both the same as anything else and different from anything else (147b; via universal properties, analyzed above);

    vii. like itself and unlike itself, like and unlike anything else (148d; via vi, 147c; via universal properties, 147e5).

This last sequence of argument (like *g* and *h* in the first movement) derives secondary properties from the primary relations asserted of the one. If something is different from something else, then they are alike in being different. Further, the one is

    xi. both in contact and not in contact both with itself and anything else (149d; via parts, 148d7; via universal properties, 148d8);

    x. both equal and unequal to itself and to anything else (151e; via universal properties? 149e4; via parts, 150a1)

    xi. aged and existent in time (153b; via universal properties, 151e7; indirectly, via the generation of number, 153a5);

    xii. generated (155c; via parts, 153c5);

    xiii. knowable and mentionable, etc. (155d; this is self-verifying, 155d).

The arguments of the second movement are more complex than the first, but they echo the strategy of the first movement. They begin from the generous hypothesis that individuation is a matter of properties, and identification a matter of ascribing predicates, and its assumption that we can understand "one" and "being" as properties, universally spread out. From this are derived (as we saw, explicitly in vii) secondary relations between the one and anything else, and thereafter other affections, both at a time and over time. The conclusion is grossly paradoxical: this one is, was, will be, became, becomes, and will become anything at all; and we can know it as such because we can say it to be such.

Both movements, then, treat the discussion of individuation as foundational. So the first stage is, taken all together, about the problems of individuation. This has three consequences.

1. This is not a ragbag of philosophical puzzles (as some have supposed), but a connected whole. Doing dialectic, on this account, is not the uncovering of various fallacies piecemeal, but rather the pursuit of a single sequence of argument, where one hypothesis is investigated according to two exclusive and exhaustive interpretations, to an aporematic end.

---

[52] This assumption will appear again as a slice; see below, ch. 6, sec. 3. Compare, for κατακερμάτισται, *Meno* 79c2, *Rep.* 395b, and, importantly, *Soph.* 225b, 257c, 258e.

2. The subject of these puzzles is not existence, but individuation. The hypothesis is not, in the first place, about the *being* of the one, but rather about the *being one* of the one. Indeed, the paradoxes would fail to bite without the assumption of a *one*.

3. It then becomes clear that Plato treats being one, being an individual, as basic. He could understand the basicness of individuals in three rather different ways.

a. He could suppose that out there in the world, being one comes first, being many afterwards. This might be an assumption about the *natural world*; but it is not, in the *Parmenides*, an assumption he seems at all interested in, except insofar as Zeno's insistence on the priority of what is naturally and absolutely one is a claim that Socrates must reject.

b. He could make the sort of claim about *epistemological* priority that lies behind the theory of forms: if we are looking for explanations, then what is one comes before what is many. This is the focus of interest in the early arguments of the *Parmenides*, but not in the gymnastic session.

c. He could, instead, be looking to *metaphysical* priority. If we seek to understand what there is in abstract or theoretical terms (without, that is, the ontological commitment of (a) or (b)), we must look to individuals first, as the foundations of everything else. It is this metaphysical account of basic individuals that the second part of the *Parmenides* attempts; dialectic is what must persuade us to find a way out of the terminal impasse.

Think again about how the argument of this gymnastic session works. Moving away from the problems of forms and particulars, I have argued, Parmenides advances to a general consideration of the question of individuation, "being one" in *Parmenides* II. But (conforming to the original contrast between forms and particulars) he conducts this argument on the assumption that there is a contrast between two possible ways of understanding individuals: either they are austere or they are generous. Plato then shows how both accounts are paradoxical. We are challenged, therefore, to uncover their assumptions and to rethink What is an individual?

7. THE OTHER STAGES

Then how far will this interpretation serve to explain the remaining stages of *Parmenides* II?[53]

Stage II: If One Is, What Is True of the Others?

The positive movement (*Parm.* 157b–159b) argues that while the others are not the one, they partake in the one because they are wholes with parts (as

---

[53] That we should look for unity here is a desideratum of any interpretation of the antinomies; cf. Schofield, "Antinomies."

anything other than the one must be). The parts of these wholes, likewise, are each one by virtue of participating in one (but not by being the one). So the others, which participate in the one, will be many and indefinite (in contradistinction to the one); and thereafter prone to all opposite affections.

The trick is turned here by two different moves. First, Parmenides assumes that for something (some individual, emphasized at 158a) to be one, it must have the property of unity. Being one (as in the second movement of the first hypothesis) is spread out and divided up over all individuals. Second, he supposes that without such a property these others will be indeterminate and indefinite and will have no features of their own apart from their indistinct plurality. Even if they are hypothesized as individuals, their individual nature can only be explained by their having the property of unity. For something is either one, or many (partaking in one)—or it is nothing at all (158b4).

The negative movement, conversely, starts by assuming that the one and the others are totally distinct and separate; and that they exhaust all there is (159b). The one is completely one (as in the first movement of the first hypothesis). The others, then, can have no share in this one; nor can they be many (otherwise they would share in the one). So there is no number among the others, no likeness nor unlikeness (for possessing both qualities would make them two, not indefinite); indeed, they turn out to be unqualifiable and unmentionable, just as the one was in the negative movement of the first stage.

This argument exploits its positive predecessor by making the point that the one, austerely conceived, is not (after all) a property spread all about, but just one. If the others are defined as other than any such one (here the use of "one" as a variable starts to matter), then they cannot have any plurality either; and on that count they, like the one, turn out to be absurd. The conclusion insists once again that a proper account of individuation (not existence or anything else, but *individuation*) is vital for any attempt at dialectic, or any talk at all, to get off the ground. And yet the clear contrast between this treatment of the one, and the treatment of one as a property in the preceding positive movement, makes discourse impossible. The dilemma is complete.

Stage III: If the One Is Not, What Is True of It?

The first movement of this stage is positive (*Parm.* 160b–163b). It anticipates the discussion of the *Sophist* about not-being[54] and argues that despite the negative "not," this one (that is not) is knowable and identifiable—in particular, identifiable as what is not the others.[55] That allows sameness and difference to be attributed to it, as well as all sorts of other relations to all sorts of

[54] Compare the suggestion at 160c4 that "not" signifies difference. It is noticeable that here the one that is not, unlike "what in no way is" at *Soph.* 236e ff., *is* mentionable and describable; here, consequently, anything is true of it. I shall take up the sequence of thought between this passage and the paradoxes of the *Sophist* below, ch. 7, secs. 1, 2.

[55] Note the way that here "is not" is treated as incomplete—"is not something else." I shall return to this issue in ch. 7, sec. 3.

things. For if it is thought to be different from the others, it is different because of *its* difference from them, and not just *their* difference from it. So difference must be a property of this one; and it is determinate in other ways (it is "that," "something," related to "these," etc., 160e), if it is to be mentionable at all. So it has likeness and unlikeness, equality, largeness, and smallness; and even thus a share in being, motion, rest, and change.

This argument works, again, on generous assumptions (for example, the insistence that difference, or being, is a property that this one, which is not, has) to a generous conclusion. As in earlier stages, moreover, here Parmenides continues to suppose that being an individual is basic; it is this assumption that allows him to designate the one as a "this" or a "something."

Take the sentence "if one is not" and focus on the predicate, "is not." This seems to say something *about* the subject (namely, that it is different from something). But saying that begins to characterize the subject, to endow it with properties, to turn it into a mentionable individual. So once the term "one" is enmeshed with a predicate, even so unpromising a predicate as "is not," the subject becomes a collection of properties, and a viable subject for speech (even if it does turn out to have a hopelessly generous endowment of properties after all).

Take the sentence "if one is not" and focus on the subject term, however, and the result is quite different. The negative movement (*Parm.* 163b–164b) supposes that the negative deprives the one of any character at all; it cannot partake in being, nor in change, motion, size, likeness, sameness, or difference. In that case, there can be no knowledge or perception or opinion of it; it has no character at all. This reverses the moves of the positive movement and, by stripping all the possible properties of the one away (courtesy of the negative "is not"), reduces this one to nothing. The negative here fences off the subject from any predication; and such an austere subject is not mentionable at all.

These discussions of negation will bear fruit in later dialogues. Here they conform to the strategy found in the earlier stages; namely, the alternate treatment of generous and austere individuals—here particularly in the context of whether they are mentionable as the subject of sentences. If, as the generous treatment supposes, the subject term is merely a placeholder in the sentence, then all sorts of properties are allowed in—at the price of producing an absurdly multiform one. If, on the other hand, the subject term is treated as referential, but predicates are denied it, then nothing can be said of it at all, and the sentence becomes redundant or meaningless.

Stage IV: If the One Is Not, What Is True of the Others?

First of all (*Parm.* 164b–e), the others are shown to be other (how else would they be the others?) and different—from each other. Their difference, if the one is not, is multiform, or indefinite in number (even for the smallest of them); and then, while they cannot be one, they must appear one, and numbered, and even and odd, in their relations with each other. Notice how this depends on treating the one that is not as a uniform property (165b), which things that are one would have; since these others cannot have that property, they can only have a phantasm of it. On that basis, these others have the appearance of any property at all, like scene paintings, depending on our perspective.

Alternatively (165e–166b), if the one is not, there is no many either. For none of the many can be one; and then each is nothing, and there is no many at all, neither in reality nor in appearance. Anything must be an individual before it is anything else; but if the one is not, nothing is an individual. Why not? The conclusion would not follow, of course, if "the one is not" meant that some particular one is not; and indeed it might not be thought to follow if there is no form of one. It would, however, follow if "the one is not" is true *for any one*. For that implies that there are no ones; and that in turn implies that no member of a plurality can be a one. Parmenides concludes that without ones, there is nothing.

8. THE VERB "TO BE"

Is the *Parmenides* about individuals? Or is it rather about existence, and the misbehavior of the verb "to be"? Manifestly, the arguments do have some concern with existence, but not as such; and in particular, in this part of the dialogue, they lack any existential commitment. Existence will be attributable to any individual, if there are any; at present, however, we still do not know what the individual is, let alone whether there are any. Parmenides proceeds by examining the consequences of both there being individuals and there not being individuals—and finds neither tenable.

Is the *Parmenides*, instead, about the logic of formal terms? The general logic of formal terms is, of course, an issue here; but in fact the arguments concern not any old formal terms, as opposed to their material counterparts, but rather a clustered set of terms, centering upon the self-identity and difference from others of the hypothesized individual. And that is because, despite the interest of analytic philosophers, this dialogue is about things, not words; in particular, it is about the individuation of things. The terms that allow us to individuate must therefore be central.

So the issue of self-identity, for example, is of particular concern in the austere movement of the first stage, where it transpires that the individual per se cannot even have that attribute. The same is true of the austere movements of the remaining stages. Stage II movement b, thus, starts from the assumption that the one is separate from (*chōris*) the others, and the others are separate from (*chōris*) the one.[56] The one and the others are individuals.[57] This turns out to be lethal for both the one and the others. For their separation implies

---

[56] We should recall, here, the assumptions of the first part, 130b.
[57] If my earlier interpretation of χωρίς is correct; cf. ch. 3, sec. 4.

their total exclusion from each other (159c3); and the one, being truly such, cannot have parts (see 137c ff.). But then the others can have no share in the one; so they will not even be many, nor like and unlike, nor moving or at rest.

Once again it could be said that Plato here muddles the individual with being an individual. On the interpretation I offer, however, the move makes better sense. If "the one" is any individual, then it is no different, as such, from any of the separate others. But then they, *on the austere treatment*, will be as remote as any one; and all individuals, not just the hypothesized individual, will collapse and become unmentionable. This argument shows how the one is conceived as the value of a variable—or conversely how the others are themselves individuals of the same austere type. Likewise in Stage III movement b, if there is no one, then [it] can have no predicates or properties, including knowability; and Stage VI movement b infers from this that the others will lack being and knowability also. This results in nihilism.

The "positive" stream of argument develops in a parallel way, to reach the paradox of *Parmenides* 166c. Now just as the negative arguments, on the schema I offer, are to be characterized as austere—that is, as arguments that focus upon the individual sans attributes—so the positive arguments all operate with the generous emphasis upon the properties at the expense of the individual. So Stage II movement a has a generous conception of the others: they are not seen as other individuals, but rather they possess the attribute "other," that is in their relation to the one. But this "being other than one" implies that they are wholes with parts, limited by each other (158d) yet indefinite in number(158c), like and unlike to each other and themselves, and so forth (158e). In short, they will have all the opposite properties that were originally attributed to the one in Stage I movement b (159a). Likewise, Stage III movement a, if the one is not, it will change, become, perish—and it will not (163b) . And Stage IV movement a, the others will give the appearance of ones (164d) and will also suffer all the properties we can think of, and none of them(165d).

The paradox derives from Plato's focus upon the properties of things, not the things themselves. Is that legitimate? On the generous treatment, it is. For while austere individuals, if they can be described as different at all, can only be numerically distinct, generous individuals differ from each other precisely in their possession of properties (again, if they can be said to differ at all). The austere movement allows only identity (or nonidentity?) statements. But the generous movement, to labor the point, does not allow identitative distinctions, but only predicative ones, supposing that only predications are significant for individuation. Now this might look like a point about language (about the failure of ordinary—Greek—language to distinguish between formal predications and material ones); but it can be justified only in terms of a claim about the world—that the world is made up of individuals of this generous type.

The conclusion must be that neither the generous nor the austere approach accounts for the shape and structure of the world, since neither will give us a proper account of the individuals that are basic. In the first hypothesis, the first movement gave us a one per se, so naked as to be unmentionable. In the second movement, by contrast, the one is clothed with "one and being." This makes it mentionable, even knowable; but all there is of "it" are the opposing properties, so that "it itself" disintegrates. Both views of individuation come to grief on the notion of the absolute priority of the individual. If that is complete, then individuals are austere. But then the world in which they occur cannot be structured, since they cannot be interrelated; it turns out not to be a world at all, and certainly not one we can talk about. If, on the other hand, the individual is just a collection of properties, then it has no priority, and everything collapses into a muddle of properties all at once; in which case discourse becomes so disparate and contradictory that talk becomes impossible.

The puzzle is about the world, and the individuals in it—not in the first place about the way we talk. But the puzzle is made into a paradox by the way it affects our talk. Hence the first movement of the first stage appears to violate the law of the excluded middle; and the second, to violate the law of noncontradiction. In both cases, discourse is seen to be impossible, just as it is when, on a specific ontological commitment, we postulate complex particulars and austere forms. Neither account worked, neither admits the possibility of discourse; yet discourse happens, for here it is. The depth of this paradox echoes the closing stages of *Parmenides* I . Neither postulating austere individuals nor denying them seems to leave us with the possibility of dialectic; yet that very claim is dialectically made. How can we explain the dialectic that we do?

Parmenides II challenges us to explain "what is an individual?" By this stage, I suggest, Plato has abandoned the hope that forms alone will explain the nature of the world before us; we need, in addition or instead, some formal metaphysical analysis of the individuals that compose this world—or any other. In particular—the focus of *Parmenides* II suggests—we need proper analysis of the terms of individuation and identity. So it is that Parmenides' arguments turn on "one"—for this determines what can be counted and what can be unified—and on "same" and "different"—for these determine what is identifiable both at a time and over time. And yet no plausible acccount of the individual is forthcoming, not least because Parmenides offers us only two extreme characterizations of "the one": either it is austere, just one, or it is generous and pluralized. In the first case, its unity is pure simplicity, but as a consequence it can participate in none of the relations that would allow it to be counted (if, that is, relations are understood as pluralizing parts of something). In the second case, the generous individual turns out to have no unity at all; since anything is true of it, nothing makes it cohere as one, and no sense can be made of its identity at a time nor of its persistence over time. It fails to qualify as an "it" at all.

The *Republic* told us that "one" is basic; the *Parmenides* worries about how "one" can be made comprehensible, either as a unit or as a unity. Next, the *Theaetetus* and the *Timaeus* elaborate both the generous/austere contrast and the paradox, and they do so, I shall argue, by means of the same pairing of arguments as the *Parmenides* offers. The dialectical gymnastics continue.

Bundles and Lumps

"EVERYTHING FLOWS," Heraclitus may have said. The phenomenal world is changing, all the time, in every respect, Heraclitus may have meant. After him Plato, notoriously, was worried about flux.[1] Does everything change all the time? And if it does, can we ever know anything about it? And is this (total flux) something that troubles Plato?

Constant change was not a troubling feature of the particulars of the *Phaedo*; as we have seen, the problem of identity over time there is one of the long-term survival of particulars, not one of their persistence through any time at all.[2] But in the dialogues after the *Parmenides*, the problem of flux begins to dominate Plato's discussions of the physical world.[3]

Look, first of all, at the arguments of the *Theaetetus*—a dialogue that tries, and fails, to define knowledge. The attempt falls into three parts: the long discussion of the views of Theaetetus, Protagoras and Heraclitus; the partly unsuccessful account of false belief or judgment; and the final attempt to define knowledge as "true belief with an account."[4] The arguments are about knowledge; but they are also about the nature of what may be known and about the nature of the people who know them. I shall postpone discussion of people; consider first the *Theaetetus*'s analysis of things.[5]

1. KNOWLEDGE AND PERCEPTION

In the first section of the dialogue, Socrates takes on three opponents at once—Theaetetus, Protagoras, and Heraclitus. Theaetetus has come up with the hypothesis that knowledge is perception. To support such a claim, Socrates suggests, he might appeal to the famous dictum of Protagoras, that man is the measure of all things; on this basis, Protagoras defends his sophistic profession by arguing that everything is true. But Protagoras also holds the flux doctrine of Heraclitus—this is his "secret doctrine": "Nothing is one itself by itself, nor could you correctly call it something or something of such and such a sort. But if you call it large, it will also appear small and if heavy then light and everything likewise, since nothing is one or something or

---

[1] Cf., e.g., here *Crat.* 411; *Soph.* 249; and Irwin, "Plato's Heracliteanism."

[2] Cf. ch. 2, sec. 4.

[3] Cf. Appendix A on the dating of the dialogues; I take the *Theaetetus*, the *Cratylus*, and the *Timaeus* (the subject of the next chapter) all to be later than the *Parmenides*.

[4] See throughout now Burnyeat's excellent discussion, *The Theaetetus of Plato*.

[5] For people, see ch. 9.

suchlike. For everything that we say is, we describe wrongly, since it comes into being through motion and change and mutual mixture; nothing ever is, but always becomes" (*Tht.* 152d2–e1).

So the claim that knowledge is perception is connected to an epistemological or logical thesis—"man is the measure"—and a separate ontological thesis—Heraclitean flux. All three hypotheses—that knowledge is perception, that man is the measure of all things, and Heraclitean flux—are, however, said to "come to the same thing"(160d). Do they?

Theaetetus offers the claim that knowledge is perception without making it clear what he wants to say. He could be offering a straightforward empiricist view: that knowledge is always based on data from the senses. Or he could be saying that only sensation qualifies as knowledge, or that only perceptual judgments qualify as knowledge. Or perhaps both: all perceptions produce knowledge, and knowledge only derives from perception. Socrates handles this indeterminacy by *interpreting* Theaetetus's hypothesis as Protagoras' dictum,[6] on the grounds that both require individual perceptions to be veridical and incorrigible (cf. *Tht.* 152c5). And this implicates Theaetetus in Protagoras's inference, that what everyone thinks to be true, is true (true-for-them).[7]

But this implies, further, that "perception," as Theaetetus originally spoke of it, is wide enough in scope to cover the content of all judgments. When Theaetetus says, "What seems to me is true for me," he may mean merely that what appears to my perception is true for me, whatever subsequent (mistaken) judgments I may make about it; the "seeming" is perceptual. But once Protagoras is involved, "What seems to me is true for me" implies "Everything is true"; so it must be glossed as "What seems to me to be the case *is* the case (for me)," and the "seeming" is judgmental.

The target in all this is truth. Both Theaetetus (insofar as he goes along with Socrates' interpretation) and Protagoras want to show how "it seems to me" gives us a privileged access to the truth. Why should it? The canonical case of "it seems to me . . ." is taken to be a case of perception; and we might argue that perceptions are veridical because they occur to me willy-nilly—they just happen, without scope for error; and because they are private to me (you do not see my perceptions, nor I yours). There are, that is, two grounds for allowing perceptions to be true: *causal* grounds and grounds of *privilege*. However, once "perception" is taken to include "judgment," perhaps those grounds disappear. My *judgments* may not be merely caused by the perceptual world (what, for example would be the cause of my judgment that optimism is the best policy?); and they may not be privileged or private, either (we may, for example, share the opinion that Beethoven wrote good music). So in

---

[6] This is controversial; cf., e.g., Burnyeat, *Theaetetus*, p. 10ff.; Bostock, *Theaetetus*, p. 41ff. If Protagoras's thesis is an interpretation of Theaetetus's hypothesis, then they can be treated as logically equivalent, while allowing Theaetetus's thesis still to stand, under some other interpretation, when Protagoras's has been refuted (*Tht.* 170ff.).

[7] Cf. the discussions of Protagoras's thesis at *Crat.* 385e ff, or at *Euthyd.* 286.

order for Protagoras's doctrine to be plausible, he needs to develop some grounds for showing that judgments are, after all, like perceptions—caused and privileged. My judgments, no less than my perceptions, that is, are true for me because they occur to me (they just happen; I cannot stop this judgment from popping into my head any more than I can prevent the rabbit from impinging on my visual field as it hops across the clearing before me); and my judgments, no less than my perceptions, occur to me (they are in my head, not yours, they are incurably relative to me).

Socrates starts by defending the Protagorean position. First of all, it may be understood in terms of a theory of perception that insists that each perception is private or relative to the perceiver (154b). The perception of a quality occurs exactly when the perceived object and the perceiver interact:

> [Sophisticated theorists claim that] everything is motion, and there is nothing else; but there are two forms of motion, each infinite in number, one of which has the capacity to act, the other to be acted upon. From the association and the rubbing together of these two with each other offspring are born, again infinite in number, but in twins—the perceptible and the perception which always turns up and is born along with the perception. (*Tht.* 156a–b)

> Did we not take them to suppose that any generation of heat or whiteness or any such took place at the same time as the perception between the agent and the patient, and that the patient became perceiving but not perception, while the agent became qualified but not a quality? Perhaps "quality" seems a newfangled word and you do not understand its general meaning; listen to some examples. The agent does not become heat or whiteness but hot and white, and everything else likewise; for you remember perhaps that we agreed earlier that nothing is one itself by itself, neither the agent nor the patient, but from the relations between both they give birth to the perceptions and the perceived; the latter become such somethings, the former perceive. (*Tht.* 182a–b)

This is a mechanical account of perception. Perception occurs when the movement of the "object" and the movement of the perceiving subject interact. Imagine an active stream coming from the white stone out there, and a reactive stream coming from me as I am in a position to see it. When the two streams meet, I see the stone; then and *only then* does the perception take place.

Now this account of perception has several conditions:

1. Any perception is relative to some perceiver. So each perception is private to that perceiver, and disconnected from any other perceiver. My perception of the white stone has nothing to do with your perception of the white stone.

It will follow that any perception of mine (or, more generously, any perceptual judgment of mine)[8] will be true-for-me and not in competition with some

---

[8] That begs the question that perceptual judgments are informed exclusively by the perception. More below and at ch.9, secs. 3–7.

perception of yours that is true-for-you. So when I say, "The wind is cold," and you say, "The wind is hot," each statement is relative to each perceiver; they do not contradict each other, and both, on this theory of perception, count as true.

2. Each perceptual event is momentary (each perceptual episode is the "off-spring" of the two movements). This allows individual perceptions to be discon-nected from any other perception of the same perceiver; thus, it is not only private to the perceiver, but private to the moment it is perceived.

On this account, not only is every perception of mine true-for-me, whatever you think, but also any perception of mine is true-for-me at the time it is perceived, regardless of what I may have perceived before, or may come to perceive later. Not only can you not contradict me, but I cannot contradict myself;[9] all my perceptions are true when they are true.

Now if "perception" is taken to include "judgment," and if this theory of perception is designed to show that not only all perceptions, *stricto sensu*, but also all judgments are true, then it must be possible to tell the same story about anything that might figure in a judgment, as well as just in a perception. If judgments, no less than perceptions, are to be caused and privileged, then the objects of judgment need to be like the objects of perception in the appro-priate ways. So not only sensible properties of things are at issue here (such as hot, or sweet), but also values (at 166d Protagoras takes "good" to be gov-erned by the measure doctrine) and other more abstract matters (notably, "truth" itself at 170e ff. and "being" in the original formula). This suggests a further condition of the perception theory:

3. All the properties of things (including relations and values) are "perceiv-able" in this way.

But the story does not end there. For the theory of perception forges a link between Protagoras's thesis and the Heraclitean doctrine of flux (153d ff.). If Protagoras were to hold both the theory of "man is the measure" and the theory of perception, he then has reason also to hold the secret doctrine. After all, the theory of perception is itself a theory of some kind of flux, insofar as it claims that our perception is dependent on change and motion; namely, the interaction of perceiver and perceived. Everything that is perceived is, as such, moving. Furthermore, if the theory of perception is to ground the "measure" doctrine, it cannot tolerate any objective reality beyond what is perceived when it is perceived; and this will be true for all the properties of things that figure in our judgments. So although the theory of perception begins by postulating an objective perceiver and an object of perception, by the end of Socrates' account of the theory he will only concede that they exist in the momentary interaction itself (157a). Hence:

4. What is perceived and what perceives are constituted solely by the moment of their interaction.

[9] Compare a similar strategy used by the sophists at *Euthyd.* 287b.

So this theory of perception, like the secret doctrine, will not tolerate the view that such things as "white" are fixed, outside of our perceiving them; and it insists that our perceiving them is momentary. But if knowledge is perception, all there is to know is what is perceived; and everything *moves as it is perceived*. Granted the theory of perception, then, the three hypotheses under scrutiny—knowledge is perception, "man is the measure," and flux—do "come to the same thing."[10]

2. PROTAGOREAN THINGS

In this world of Theaetetus, Protagoras, and Heraclitus, what is there? The theory of perception gives us two different ways[11] of understanding Protagoras's "man is the measure": (1) as a theory about what we know and (2) as a theory about what there is:

1. The refutation of Protagoras later in the dialogue (*Tht.* 170c ff.) takes him to be offering a theory of truth that is thoroughly relativist. So here, the theory of perception shows that any appearance is *incurably relative*[12] to the perceiver and therefore true for that perceiver. This, generalized for anything that can be known, implies that everything is true.

2. But if, as the theory of perception implies, Protagoras also holds the secret doctrine of Heraclitus, he has a view also about the way things are, a view that is even more radical than his theory of knowledge. If any perceptual event is a momentary and self-contained episode, and if this is to "come to the same thing as" the measure doctrine, then there cannot be some further, objective reality beyond those moments of perception. So these episodes are all there is to perceive; they are not some real features of some (other) real object. So, if perception (judgment) is just the momentary interaction between perceiver and perceived, then it will be episodic and private; and so too will be the perceiver and what is perceived ("there is no agent [sc. of perception; i.e., the object] before it comes together with the patient [sc. of perception; i.e., the perceiver], nor a patient before there is an agent"; 157a4–6).

How would Protagoras explain what there is? If there are no objects independent of our perception, what sort of objects are there? And if he supposes that perception is momentary, how does anything persist over time?

Take Plato's own example. Suppose that you feel the wind as cold, and (at the same time) I feel the wind as hot. This suggests, first of all, that the wind has two properties (at that moment)—cold-for-you and hot-for-me. But what

[10] Cf. here Burnyeat, "Plato on the Grammar of Perceiving."

[11] Or perhaps more than two; Protagoras also has some philosophy of mind (see ch. 9, sec. 3), this will be (3), a theory about who does the knowing. Bostock, *Plato's Theaetetus*, p. 51ff., suggests that we have to choose between interpretations; Burnyeat, *The Theaetetus of Plato*, more subtly suggests that we do not. Instead, Plato invites us to do the interpreting, to "make the theory and see." In what follows in this chapter, I shall be considering the effect Protagoras's theory has on his conception of the world and the things in it. I shall adopt a different approach in Chapter 9.

[12] Cf., e.g., "everything becomes *in relation to something*," 157b1.

about the wind itself? That, too, must be relative to my perception of it (suppose I say, "Thank goodness, the wind has risen," while you persist in thinking us still becalmed?). What, then, is the wind? Only a collection of these perceptions (if it is anything at all). The wind—cold, hot, or lukewarm—just is the perceptions there are; the perceptions are not (in the final version of the theory of perception)[13] *of* some wind out there in the real world; they just occur, and they are all there is to the wind. How things seem to us just is how (and what) they actually are ("man is the measure of all things, of the things that are, how they are, of the things that are not, how they are not").

How about the persistence of the wind over time? Suppose that I feel the wind as warm now, and then as freezing in five minutes' time. Has the wind persisted over that five minutes? Or if not, is there anything here we can say has changed, and how?

Remember that Protagoras's dictum requires my judgment now to be a separate episode from my judgment in five minutes' time—otherwise I might find myself contradicting what I say, and one of my statements will turn out to be false. So the episode, "wind warm now," is separate from the episode, "wind freezing now," and each is true for me at its own moment. For this to justify the claim that everything is true, however, Protagoras should insist that the separation between episodes is absolute. After all, if episode *a* overlaps somehow with episode *b*, the perception of the overlap will itself be an episode (veridical and private); namely, the judgment passed on the two episodes (*a* and *b*) that they overlap. But this "superepisode" is reflective on other episodes; and as such it seems to reflect on past episodes, episodes that have already taken place. Yet the reliability of past truths is unreliable—hence, Protagoras's constant attention to my judgments now. So perhaps there can be no "superepisodes."

Now someone might take a succession of episodes (e.g., "wind warm now" followed by "wind freezing now") to show that something (perhaps the wind) has changed. Then on Protagoras's account, we shall be able to determine what it is that has changed (we must be the measures of the change). If there has been a change between t and $t + 5$ minutes, it must be possible for us to compare the two moments for continuity, gradual change, or total difference. Now think about how any episode (any property) might be related to any other in our judgment. Protagoras's claim that everything is true is supported by the assumption that the moments of perception are momentary, caused, and thus incorrigible. Because they are like that, there is no room *within* them for correcting the impression I have—I just have it. Moreover, for each episode to be veridical, there can be, as I have suggested, no superepisode in

---

[13] It may, of course, be objected to the interpretation that I offer, that when he formulates the theory of perception, Socrates speaks of the object and of the perceiver (the agent and the patient of perception) without any of the difficulties I suggest. To that, I reply that it is not until the theory of perception is fully developed that Socrates kicks away its ladder and denies that there is even an object or a perceiver (156e ff.). It is only later (on my interpretation, from 181d for things, from 170e for persons) that this consequence of the theory is seen to bring disaster.

which I might compare subordinate ones. For not only will this admit past truths, but a synoptic view might admit error as well, or it might allow the subordinate judgments to contradict each other, instead of being thoroughly relativized.[14] Perception provides truth only if we interpret each episode as strictly separate, numerically nonidentical each from its successors and predecessors, and from perceptual episodes occurring to other perceivers.

Perhaps I could still have a synoptic view of the episodes, an awareness that this episode succeeded that one, without supposing that this awareness is in itself veridical, or a case of measuring. But now consider four different episodes: at t, "wind warm now"; at $t + 1$, "wind freezing now"; at $t + 2$, "rabbit runs across clearing now"; at $t + 3$, "Empire State Building large now." If each episode is separate and veridical, how is my awareness of their succession going to help my understanding that something has changed? I have to be able to judge, somehow, that the first two episodes are relevant to each other, while the second two are not. But judgments like that are both corrigible and reliant upon some independent criteria of persistence (there really is a wind; rabbits really are not Empire State Buildings) for their truth. But since Protagoras cannot maintain his grip on "everything is true" and admit such criteria, then all four episodes will be separate from each other, disconnected equally from each other and from any other.

Consider, then, some putative object (the wind) and its claims to persist over time. The history of the wind, on the present account, is a series of episodes. But then it is difficult to see how we could determine which episodes would be the history of the wind, and which the history of the Empire State Building. Lacking a synoptic view, we cannot separate out the histories of things; and thus it seems impossible to say that something in particular persists over time.

But Socrates' account of the secret doctrine looks more positive than this. The claim that each episode is distinct from its predecessors and its successors might give us the conclusion that nothing is continuous (nothing actually persists). But the flux doctrine is stronger; not only are things moving all the time, but they alter in quality as well. From the nonidentity of the Protagorean episodes, it seems, Socrates infers that each episode must be qualitatively different from its predecessors and successors. So all the properties (of things, if there are any things—or just the properties themselves) are constantly becoming different, and thus changing. Therefore, flux is true. Surely this is an outrageous inference? Numerical difference does not imply qualitative difference, as many a commentator has wailed,[15] and Socrates has just made a mistake (connected, maybe, with the failure to distinguish identity from predication elsewhere).

Not quite. The theory of perception suggests that the properties of things are episodic. But the judgment that they persist is the judgment that they are

[14] Compare Protagoras's trouble with judgments about judgments; 170d.
[15] Cf. Macdowell, *Plato: Theaetetus*, p. 180ff.

the same (item), or alike (the same quality). What purchase does such a judgment have within this theory? None. If knowledge is just perception, and everything is true when it is true, there is no room for those comparative judgments. And in that case, the distinction between statements of identity and statements of similarity is irrelevant. All there is is the perceptual episode. Whatever information that contains is self-contained, noncomparative, and itself episodic; this makes the world out there (that is, the collection of episodes) indeterminate.

But then think about how we might deny a theory of flux. Flux is false, we might say, because some objects persist over time. But that defense against flux is not available to Protagoras (even were he to want to use it), for he has left himself no terms in which to describe something persisting over time. Thus, it is indifferent to him whether "The wind is warm now" is followed in five minutes by "The wind is freezing now" or by "The Empire State Building is in the distance." Each episode is irrelevant to the others; and nothing they contain can be said to persist at all. So, for Protagoras (if his theory of perception is as Socrates supposes it to be), flux must be true.

So not only is the world indeterminate, it is also in flux. The secret doctrine turns out true. Consider its three rather different claims:

1. Nothing is "itself by itself."
2. Nothing is "one something."
3. Nothing is "such a something."

What does this mean? The focus of attention is the "something." The Heracliteans say that there are *no "somethings."* Nothing is "itself by itself" or "one," so there is nothing that is capable of being qualified. All relations are properties, but not properties of something, for there is nothing underlying the properties to possess them; the "properties" are all there is. This might be thought to be true for two different reasons.

First, if everything is changing, then there can be no fixity in anything. This means that everything becomes, nothing is—so we are not justified therefore in describing anything as "something," only in referring to "suches." We may ask whether that is reasonable, or why suches should be permitted to shift while somethings must remain still.

Second, the theory of perception, combined with the claim that knowledge is perception, shows that what we know is confined to perceptual episodes. But then there is nothing to persist or to underlie those episodes; there are only the momentary appearings, and those are merely the momentary appearings of properties, not of basic entities beneath. There are only (changing) properties, no *things* to have the properties. Insofar as we could think of "things" at all, they (apparent things in the physical world) are just bundles of properties—and flux-ridden at that.

> As we said at the beginning, nothing is one itself by itself but everything and all
> sorts always become in relation to each other as a result of motion, and being
> must be removed from everywhere, and we should not allow ourselves to use that

expression over and over as we did just now out of habit and ignorance. We must not do that, so the view of the wise tells us, nor must we allow "something" or "someone's" or "of me"[16] or "this" or "that" or any other name at all that makes things stand still, but by nature they are uttered as they come into being and are acted upon and perish and change. So if someone allows the talk to stand still at all he will be easy to refute. Thus must we talk of things both piecemeal and when many things are bundled together, when people talk of the bundle as a "man" or a "stone" or any animal or form. (*Tht.* 157a–c)

How does Protagoras/Heraclitus become committed to the extreme view that there are no somethings? The problem lies in Theaetetus's hypothesis that knowledge is perception.

If "knowledge is perception" means that knowledge and perception are identical, or at least coextensive, then anything we may say about something (and know about it) comes from perception. So all the properties or attributes of things are discovered by means of perception. But directly perceptible properties are explained, by the theory of perception, as momentary episodes. So (for knowledge to be equivalent to perception) all the items that appear in our language are knowable, and "same" or "valuable" or "one" must be explained in the same way as "white" or "bitter," and will be momentary episodes, likewise. But (since perception, ex hypothesi, actually does put us in touch with the world as it is, or as it becomes) then any putative object in the real world will be *just* a collection of such episodes—a bundle of properties.[17] Any expression that may be thought to convey the object, one object, itself by itself, will correspond not to some fixed feature of the object itself, but to just another property in the bundle. Consequently, we cannot say that anything is a something, only such.[18]

3. PLATONIC BUNDLES

So here Socrates saddles his opponents with an extreme theory of knowledge and, correspondingly, with an extreme theory about the world. What has any of this got to do with Plato, or with his worries about flux? How far can anything the sophist offers be plausible or compelling to him?

Just after the exposition of the theory of perception, there is an odd episode.

[16] Cf. Burnyeat, "Grammar," p. 32, n. 16, on the text here.

[17] The Protagorean's point here is that individuals (as the vulgar herd perceives them to be) are at best collections or bundles—and thus no less flux-ridden than piecemeal episodes. Burnyeat, "Grammar," p. 32, makes this point against Sayre, *Analytic Method*, p. 78. So the Protagorean—as Plato represents him—understands the puzzling nature of bundles; and that, on my account, is exactly Plato's point.

[18] Compare M. Frede, "Being and Becoming," on the sense of "becoming" as "displaying the character F but not having the nature F." Plato wants to say, I think, that no Protagorean object qualifies as something (Frede's "qualifies as really being"?), but only as such (Frede's "displaying the character"). The same account goes for the *Timaeus*; cf. ch. 6, sec. 5.

Socrates offers a puzzle (the dice): "Consider a small example, and you will understand everything I mean" (*Tht.* 154c1). But now the dramatic situation has changed: Protagoras is on the offensive, challenging Socrates and Theaetetus about what they believe. Socrates urges Theaetetus, then, to look to their own position: "Like ordinary people, we shall consider our thoughts themselves, and what they mean—whether they are in agreement with each other or not at all" (154e). The puzzle that follows, Socrates suggests, has a wider application than the oddities of Protagoras's measure.

Suppose you have six dice, and you compare them with four dice—the six is larger than the four by half as much again. Then compare the six with twelve dice—the six is smaller than the twelve by half. So the six, which were large, have become smaller, apparently without anything happening to them. How can that be? Becoming larger (or smaller) is surely a matter of change. If I become larger, I grow; smaller, I shrink. So when I compare the six dice to twelve, and they have become smaller, they must have shrunk. And yet nothing has happened to them at all—they are still six dice.

How can this account be correct? It is based, apparently, on three assumptions (*Tht.* 155a–b):

1. Nothing becomes larger or smaller in size or in bulk so long as it remains equal to itself; becoming larger or smaller is growing or wasting away.

2. Nothing grows or wastes away without having something added or removed; instead it remains equal to itself.

3. Whatever was not thus-and-so before cannot be thus-and-so later without having changed.

For the case of the dice, these three assumptions seem to imply that the six dice, while remaining the same, have both grown (become larger vis-à-vis four) and wasted away (become smaller vis-à-vis twelve). And this—that the dice both remain the same *and* grow or diminish—appears to be a contradiction.

Why should Protagoras offer this challenge to common sense? Protagoras wants to construe all change as real change (hence, his Heraclitean leanings), so that anything which was not-F and is later F (assumption 3) has changed in a radical way (assumptions 1 and 2). This can be generalized to the thesis that everything really changes constantly if Protagoras can also maintain that at any moment anything is F where it was not-F before. Now there are two moves that Protagoras might make to allow him to deny (against common sense) that anything remains "equal to itself."

First, he might offer a relativist stance.[19] After all, the measure doctrine advocated a relativist account of judgment and a relativist account of the world. If man is the measure of all things, then the things are just as they are measured. It follows from this that when we compare the six dice and the four and the twelve so that they stand in different relations to each other, then they will actually be characterized first by one relation (larger than) and then by its

---

[19] Cf. Bostock, *Plato's Theaetetus*, p. 45ff.

opposite (smaller than) as we make the different comparisons. On a Protagorean view, then, they have changed; so they are subject to Heraclitean flux from moment to moment of our perceptions.

Second, Protagoras might claim that "Cambridge change is real change." An objector could argue that relative change (e.g., change in relation to different perceivers) is not the sort of change that we could call growth or wasting away. Instead, such changes are mere "Cambridge changes," and do not affect the real constitution of the object itself. Protagoras, on the other hand, would argue that this distinction is a meaningless one; if any change, whether it is relative or absolute, figures in an episode, it counts not merely as Cambridge but also as real.

Try some examples. The pink roses are painted white; the roses have lost one property and gained another—they have changed in a perfectly standard way.[20] The way we talk about them ("the roses are white when they were pink") mirrors the actual change in the real world, the successive colors of the roses. Or suppose that two ships pass each other in the night, one on its way to New York, the other to Southampton. Both ships have changed location; and, further, they have changed in relation to each other (the *QE II*, which was west of the *Cutty Sark*, is now east of the *Cutty Sark*, and vice versa). So "The *QE II* is now east of the *Cutty Sark*" records some real change in the real world (at least, the motion of the two ships). But suppose the *Cutty Sark* is becalmed while the *QE II* steams past. Both ships still change in relation to each other; but now the *Cutty Sark* seems not to have changed in any real way, even if its relation to the *QE II* is now the opposite of what it was. Has the *Cutty Sark* changed? Has it changed in any way like the way the roses changed? Is a mere Cambridge change anything like a real one?

For Protagoras, any change must be a real change. After all, his epistemological relativism has an ontological counterpart. All the properties of things are relative to the perceivers, and are only *real in that way*. So for Protagoras the problem is a serious one, sufficient to send him into the arms of the Heracliteans. Socrates and Theaetetus, on the other hand, represent common sense, and they want to insist that things do have stability. They need, at least, to modify assumption (3) in order to claim that some relative changes are not classified as real. Nonetheless, they appear here on the defensive—and for Plato, too, such a modification may not be so easy as it appears to us. For Plato has already suggested that, for example, relative size is a real feature of the relata, or that value is a real property belonging to what is valued. So for Plato the problem of Cambridge change is no less urgent than it is for Protagoras, if for the opposite reasons. For Protagoras, that is, all change is real

---

[20] A common way of putting this is to point to the way in which the truth-value of the statement "The roses are pink" has altered (from true to false), exactly corresponding to the way in which the properties of the object out there in the world have changed, too. Whenever the truth value of such a descriptive sentence changes, that is a Cambridge change; whenever the logical change corresponds to some real change in the world, the change is real *and* Cambridge. Cf. Geach, *God and the Soul*, p. 71ff.

because all properties are relative to their perceivers. For Plato all change is real (a) because all relations are independent of the observer or the perceiver or the valuer, even if they are qualified in relation to some observer,[21] and (b) because relations are real properties of each of the relata.

So for the *Cutty Sark* to remain becalmed while the *QE II* steams past is a change no less real for the *Cutty Sark* than for the *QE II*; for six dice to be first smaller than twelve, then larger than four is a real change for the dice, and not just part of the Cambridge effect.

But then maybe there is no problem for Plato. First, since all these relations are properly qualified, there is no lurking contradiction when we say that six dice are larger than four, smaller than twelve. Second, there are no dangers of change; in the case of the dice, the change occurs because we consider the dice first vis-à-vis the twelve and then vis-à-vis the four. Surely, nothing in that time has happened to the dice at all; have we not just considered the real relations of the dice one at a time? So even if Plato is committed to the natural inherence of relational and evaluative properties, that does not commit him to flux here, or change—the change is illusory, since the properties of the dice hold all along.

These rebuttals, however, may not be enough to allow Socrates and Theaetetus out of the grip of the puzzle of the dice. Recall, first of all, that in this confrontation between Protagoras and Socrates/Theaetetus, the thought that objects might stay the same as themselves conflicted with the Protagorean conclusion that objects constantly change. Protagoras welcomes this and resolves the contradiction by jettisoning any claims about identity (the assumption that things stay equal to themselves). But that assumption is one that the common view needs to retain. Recall, secondly, that the original Protagorean/Heraclitean thesis made a claim not only about change over time, but also about what things are at a time; like the dice, anything is both large and small, heavy and light, and so on. That consequence, unqualified, is what the common view needs to reject. So the common view is committed to the claim that things do have a stable identity at a time; they are not contradictory nor episodic nor discontinuous over time. But in that case, the challenge that the dice pose for the common view is to show exactly *how* this can be true, exactly how the identity of a thing is constituted.

If Protagoras and Heraclitus are right, things are just collections of properties. But those properties include relational properties that are treated on a par with other, more ordinary properties. In particular, the relational properties that determine identity are no less episodic, for Protagoras, than any others. This has three consequences.

1. The object just is the sum of its properties: none of its properties seems privileged or formal or able to explain how the other properties are assembled. So, at any time, something just is its properties, a collection of suches.

2. If the object is a collection of suches, what happens when one such is replaced by another? We seem to have a new object because we have a different

[21] Cf. ch. 2, secs. 2, 3.

collection. And, on Protagoras's account, this will happen constantly—every episode is followed by another, so that the collection changes all the time and the object (which is no object at all) never persists.

3. In any case, we have no persisting objects of perception in which the persistence of some object could be noted. Because every episode is momentary, persistence is an empty notion.

So if the story of the dice gives us a true account of the way things are, we are in trouble. For this account of relations and relational change, Socrates claims, entails the secret doctrine, that nothing is itself by itself but is, instead, a bundle of all its properties. The challenge offered by Protagoras's puzzle to Plato is to show, given his account of the natural inherence of relational properties, that the identity of things can be explained and defended against the Heraclitean view. This challenge is one that Plato must take seriously.

4. FLUX ATTACKED

Socrates attacks the complex doctrine of Protagoras-Heraclitus-Theaetetus one limb at a time, in that order; and these refutations, like the original doctrines, contain both epistemological and ontological strands. Leaving the discussion of knowledge to one side,[22] consider Socrates' objections to his opponents' view of what there is.

The secret doctrine, of course, is an extreme view of the way the world is—there are no things, and there are not even properties[23]—there are only "suches," which come into being and perish in a stream, just as they are perceived. But then they change even as such, so that you can never grasp what they are, you can never even get hold of "some color"—even as you speak, they slip out from under; and even as you perceive, your perception itself changes. Nothing is what it is any more than it is not. In the end, then, it is impossible even to state the theory—nothing is any more true than its opposite, and you end up contradicting yourself to infinity (*Tht.* 183b). The secret doctrine turns out to be self-refuting:

> Socrates: For it appears—or so it seems—that if everything is in motion then every answer, about anything, is equally correct, so that we should say that this is so and that it is not so—or becomes, if you wish, so that we should not come to rest in the argument.
> Theodorus: You are right.
> Socrates: Except, Theodorus, that I said "so" and "not so"; for we must not even say this "so"—for then the "so" would not be moving, nor the "not so"— for that would not be motion either; but those who offer this thesis must find

---

[22] I shall return to Protagoras's measures in a later discussion; see ch. 9, sec. 3.

[23] This point denies any fixity at all; maybe even universals may be thought to suffer change; 182a.

some other language, since now they have no words for their hypothesis, unless indeed "not even so" best suits them, since it is an indefinite expression.
(*Tht.* 183a–b).

A shorthand version of the same argument turns up at *Cratylus* 439d, to much the same effect—if the world is in flux, then it cannot be known or even mentioned: "But would it be possible to talk about it [something in flux] correctly, if it always slipped out from under, saying first that it is 'that' and secondly that it is 'such'? Instead, surely it must become something else even as we speak, and slip out from under and no longer be thus?"

Discourse collapses, on these arguments, because there is no stable object of reference. And on reflection, this will be a problem both over time (because everything keeps changing) and at a time (because there is no way of determining what the bundle is at any time). That is, in a world where everything is changing, we can find no fixed point even to start to talk about the world; each successive moment is different from its predecessor. But in an even more viciously Heraclitean world—a world that is indeterminate, where "so" and "not so" are both true at once—we are worse off still; for each moment is incoherent as it occurs (Is it? It is if the bundle theory persists).

What exactly is the problem here? Socrates' objection could work in two different ways, for he could be attacking the theory, or the world it postulates. His argument, on the one hand, could claim that however the world actually is constituted (whether or not it is in flux), any theory about a flux-ridden world is self-defeating. Or he could be complaining that any world such as this is an impossible world—witness the fact that we cannot even talk about it. That we cannot mention the theory, that is, may be the disease, or it may be the symptom of the disease that afflicts the secret doctrine. Which?

Socrates' refutation works in stages. First, the secret doctrine itself disallows objects in favor of properties (*Tht.* 153e; 182b); then properties are disallowed (for they too constitute a "something" [182a–b] disallowed by flux); then even the changing suches slip away, for they too refuse to stay still long enough to be "something" (182c–d). In just the same way, the means we have of getting at the objects of the world refuse to be anything: "you couldn't call something seeing any more than not-seeing" (182e3); nor, when we ask "What is knowledge?" can we say that it is knowledge any more than it is not (183a). There are no "somethings" for our talk to get a grip on; and so our talk fails to mean anything at all.

The coup de grace is delivered when the Heraclitean realizes that he cannot even formulate his position. But still the focus of Socrates' attack is the failure of the secret doctrine to allow us any things. Now this is not just a problem about talk (not just the problem of reference)—although Socrates assumes that talk, to work, must be able to refer. The trouble lies deeper, in a conception of the world that has no somethings but only suches (*Tht.* 182a–b). The suches, Socrates suggests, fail to get a purchase on our speech, either because they have no somethings to hang on to, or because they themselves cannot be construed as a something (182d; "that what flows flows white" is a substantive to which, because it never remains still, we cannot refer; here the property is a quasi-thing). The argument rests on the assumption, therefore, that referring *to something* is basic for all speech. But the secret doctrine disallows both somethings as the core of a bundle of properties and properties as quasi-somethings. But then the world full of suches is full of nothing at all—the theory is meaningless, because such a world is not a world at all. First things first—the problem with the secret doctrine is that it gives us an impossible world; the symptom of its failure (and not the disease itself) is the fact that we cannot even talk about a world like that. Why not? Because in any possible world, things must come first; somethings are basic for the world to hang together at all. If Heraclitus's world does not hang together like that, it fails altogether to be a world; and as a consequence the theory is absurd. And Heraclitus's world *cannot* hang together like that because in its primary formulation there are no principles to show how *at a time* any given collection of suches is a proper bundle. There is no principle of bundling, no way of allocating different suches to different bundles. But without such a principle, contradictions cannot be held apart; so we shall have "thus" and "not thus" all at once, and then our discourse becomes altogether impossible.

If Heraclitus is wrong, we must have some things in the world that are *stable* and *coherent* enough to be called "something." But this requirement on our ontology recalls a series of questions that have been asked in the earlier arguments with Protagoras.

First of all, it was the consequence of the secret doctrine that there are no somethings, only bundles of properties. That thesis ended in incoherence; but Plato now needs urgently to find some way of specifying what a something might be, other than just a collection of suches.

Second, the association of Protagoras with Theaetetus suggested that all the terms that figure in our judgments correspond to properties accessible to perception. What terms, then, are left to explain a "something" other than those that express a "such"? What, if you like, is the difference between a something and a such?

Third, the puzzle of the dice implied that relational properties, no less than common or garden ones, are subject to the secret doctrine (indeed, this reemphasizes the wide scope of "property" both for Protagorean measures and for Plato). All suches, that is, are on a par, all are bits of the bundle, all are real pieces of the world (albeit a world in flux). But then once again, what features of a thing are left to explain its being a something?

Heraclitus and Protagoras are not the only ones to feel the sting of these difficulties: Plato, too, as the puzzle of the dice makes clear, needs to be able to explain not only the problems of relational change, but also how he would specify the somethings that have relational properties, and that remain stable within a changing world. So far, when we are considering an object, anything we say of that object is a piece of it; so then the object just is those pieces—it is a (real) bundle of properties. In that case, there is no account to be given of the individuation of something that has properties, other than its having of properties. It is impossible, therefore, to specify *what* has the properties, for it is the properties that provide the specification. The challenge, now, is quite general. If the world is not composed of bundles of properties, what else is there? And what means do we have of specifying these basic "somethings" in order to escape the absurdities of Heracliteanism, or worse?

Heraclitus's theory is unstateable; and it is unstateable because it fails to allow for the way in which talk mirrors the world. For the secret doctrine begins by rejecting stable objects in the real world, and admitting only their properties as real. So the Heraclitean only uses the terms corresponding to the predicate in a simple sentence, while he disallows the subject term. But that, Socrates argued, is lethal to his case, since all meaningful talk requires our sentences to have subjects as well as predicates, just as all proper ontology needs things as well as their properties. Thus the argument against Heraclitus displayed the *grammatical prejudice*—the view that the structure of reality matches the grammatical structure of simple sentences, and that the contrast between subject and predicate is representative of a real contrast between object and property[24] In order to understand that contrast, we need to be able to specify subject or predicate independently of each other—if, that is, the grammatical prejudice is to sway us. Suppose that the object just is what has properties. If anything we say about an object represents a property of the object, including its relations with everything else, then we are left with no means of discriminating the object itself from its properties. Consequently, there will be no object apart from its properties; the object will be just a bundle.

Perhaps that is all right, and there is nothing wrong with bundles. If we read the dialogue as a whole, however, we may come to doubt that.[25] The "bundle" theory gives us a generous account of what it is to be something or other, whose largesse is lethal. Bundles are so generous as to be impossible to mention or to understand; as such they fail to allow a satisfactory account of individuation. Suppose we ask, "What makes this bundle this one bundle?" Within the limitations of the secret doctrine, the question might be understood in two different ways. Consider the individual either as the possessor of properties, comprehensible as such independently of the properties or as merely a collection of properties. The bundle could be this one bundle because the properties cluster around, and attach themselves to a central core—so the

---

[24] Cf. ch. 1, sec. 3.

[25] Compare the restrictions on mentioning the "objects" of the secret doctrine, 157a–b, with the way in which we can only mention the elements at 202a. Lest it be objected that this is to read the dialogue backwards, consider how *reading* a Platonic dialogue works: it is a complex and circular process, not merely linear, so that we are encouraged to reflect later on what has gone before, and (when we reread) to anticipate what comes later in earlier arguments. Compare the advice Plato offers his readers at *Phaedrus* 266b, and Burnyeat's discussions, *Theaetetus* passim, of how to read the dialogue.

bundle is a collection of properties hung on a hatstand. In that case, we need some means of specifying the hatstand independently of the bundle, and we need to understand the thing independently of its properties. But if the bundle exhausts all we can say of the thing, there is nothing left for explaining the hatstand. Hence, there are no somethings. Or the bundle could be this one bundle because the properties are tied together with a piece of string; that is, there is some extra principle to explain the coherence of the bundle. This extra principle, however, must be one of the properties, on the story so far. So a similar difficulty obtrudes. If all the specifications of the thing are already items in the bundle, what is left for the piece of string? What, of all the properties in a bundle, is the property that bundles them all together?

5. PERCEPTION ATTACKED

If knowledge is perception, then perception gives us access to all sorts of features of the world out there. Theaetetus's thesis, that is, fails to distinguish between common or garden properties available to perception directly and the other features of something that might allow us to determine what it is and how it is held together. The trouble is that "knowledge is perception" is too general; and this feature of it is brought out clearly by its association with Protagoras's "measure" doctrine and Heraclitean flux. The same point is emphasized in Socrates' final refutation of Theaetetus's thesis at *Theaetetus*184b ff.[26]

Socrates' first objective here is to show how perception is inadequate to supply all the content of knowledge. His attack on perception is on two different fronts: first, he objects that the faculty of perception is inadequate to explain fully the content of our judgments, and second, he argues that some features of the world are not themselves directly perceptible. His second objective, to establish a full account of the judging mind, is discussed further later.[27] It shows, I think, how fertile are the arguments of the *Theaetetus* that the same sequence of argument can give us two quite different perspectives on "knowledge is perception"—the first a difficulty with its objects, the second a deficiency in the psychology implicit in the "knowledge is perception" thesis.[28]

Socrates proffers an argument to show that perception cannot be knowledge because perception fails to "grasp being" (*Tht.* 186e). Why? The argument has three phases.[29]

[26] This is discussed further below; ch. 9, sec. 4.

[27] See ch. 9, secs. 3–7.

[28] Compare Burnyeat's maxim "make the theory and see," Burnyeat, *Theaetetus*, p. 7ff.

[29] This is disputed; three stages or two? Plato marks two breaks in the argument, at *Tht.* 184e3–5 and 185e3; and the argument itself, I suggest, makes three separate moves. But cf. Cooper's detailed analysis, "Sense-Perception." On the passage as a whole, cf. also Burnyeat, "Grammar," Holland, "Plato's *Theaetetus*"; D. Frede, "Silent Dialogue".

1. The senses are the instruments of the soul, through which the soul perceives "white" or "bitter" (184b–e).

2. The senses are inadequate, however, to deliver a judgment about both a sound and a color:[30] judgments of "what is common" are made, instead, by the soul (185a–186a).

3. The senses are useless, moreover, when it comes to comparing, or to thinking about, these common terms themselves. Instead it is the soul that reasons—so the soul, not the senses, aims at the truth, and the soul, not the senses, may aspire to knowledge (186a–e).

What exactly is Socrates' complaint against perception here? Is he arguing, as some have suggested,[31] that perception can give us some exiguous judgments (e.g., "this is pungent"), but that it fails to tell us anything about the way things really are?[32] Or is Socrates contrasting the raw feels of perception ("pungent" to the nose) with the propositional content of even the most elementary judgment?[33] Why is it that perception fails to grasp being? Because it cannot say "is" (there is no propositional content), or because it cannot determine how things really are?

One of Socrates' complaints against the combined theory of Protagoras and Heraclitus was that it cannot give us any account of the basic objects of the world—for, in a Heraclitean world, there are no objects, only events. His complaint against perception (on either interpretation) seems to echo the same point. Even if perception does deliver exiguous judgments, it is inadequate to tell us—what the arguments against Heraclitus demand that we know—whether we have here a "this," a "something," or just a "such." That is (and this is a familiar complaint against perception), it tells us nothing beyond the phenomena, nothing about the things behind what we see or taste, nothing about what there is in the world at all. So, first of all (as at 1), sweet or heavy must be felt by the soul (and not just afflict the sense organ itself).[34] Second, the soul must be able to think about these sweet or heavy things.[35]

[30] Socrates expresses this as "how do we come to think about them both that they are both?"; *Tht.* 185a9.

[31] E.g., Cooper, "Sense-Perception."

[32] What is actually said by the perceiver at this stage? Is he labeling the sensation, and thus is involved even from the beginning in an exiguous judgment: do "red," "sky-blue," "bitter," really mean "this is red," "this is sky-blue," etc.? Cooper argues that this makes better sense; and perhaps, from a philosophical point of view, it does. I suspect, however, that at this stage in the argument Plato is simply recording the limitations of perception of a special sensible, rather than making a point about the propositional content of perception of this basic kind. It is in the next two stages of his argument that he elaborates propositional content. Cf. D. Frede, "Silent Dialogue."

[33] Cf. Burnyeat, "Grammar."

[34] The importance of this point will appear in ch. 9, sec. 7.

[35] The interpretation of the passage hinges on the neuter plurals at *Tht.* 184e. If (as Cooper does) we take them to be sweet or heavy things as they appear, then the second phase involves the judgment that these things are one or both, and so on. If, on the other hand, we take them to be raw feels, then the second phase should compare feels (e.g., a sound compared to a color). But the

Suppose we are thinking about a sound (a sounding thing) and a color (a colored thing). First, we suppose that they both are; then, that they are different from each other, the same as themselves; and then, that both are two, each is one. Thereafter we can consider their other relations to each other (the catchall "how alike they are"). Third, the soul engages independently in reflection on these ideas—being, sameness, difference, and number, and the other relations. Only then, Socrates argues, can the soul attain truth.

Suspending judgment, for the moment, on the theory of truth that Socrates offers here, and on the philosophy of mind that underlies it, reflect on the second phase of the argument. Socrates insists that a proper account of judgment, let alone knowledge, demands a closer look and a richer account of the world than is given by the immediate perceptions of the original Protagorean theory. But it seems that the sine qua non of such a rich account of the world is to be able to judge *being, identity, and number* (*Tht.* 185a–b); in short, to be able to individuate the objects that populate the world. Socrates' thesis, offset as it is against Heraclitus's, insists once again that a grip on individuals is fundamental for any judgment, and therefore for knowledge.

But how are these judgments to be made? How can the soul individuate the objects of the world? How are we to understand the concepts involved in individuation (the concepts involved in this argument itself)? The third phase of the argument offers a promissory note. Theaetetus suggests to Socrates that the soul makes its own calculations of being, of identity, and of value "making a calculation within itself of past and present compared to the future" (*Tht.* 186b1). So—on this view—some features of the outside world come to the soul from perception, while others come from the judgments of the soul itself. But foremost of the judgments made by the soul are judgments about truth and about being; and these, most of all, are remote from the immediate affections of perception. So perception is not knowledge, since it does not give us truth.

Socrates encourages Theaetetus to come up with a different account of truth than Protagoras's insistence that it be caused and privileged. Instead, he offers a thoroughly intellectual account of truth; and on the back of that a new look at the structure of the world. If truth is caused, then the objects of true judgments must be such as to do the causing; they must be real and perceptible features of the world out there. But if, by contrast, truth is discovered by reasoning, then the elements in our judgments may have a different status from the objects of perception. Such a complex account of truth will escape

---

second phase seems to have a wider brief (that is, this seems to be about the objects we perceive, not the data themselves), so there is either propositional content all the way through the argument; or there has been a shift from phase (1), raw feels, to phase (2), propositions about the objects provoking the feels. I incline to the second view (despite some doubts about the sense of "sound" and "color" at 185a—are these sounds or sounding things?); certainly by 185e1 Plato is talking quite generally about everything, not just sounds and colors. In any case, the crucial point will be the failure of perception to get beyond the data received by the organs—we need the soul to do that.

the gross view of reality that characterized Protagoras's and Heraclitus's theories; and it will revise Plato's own view, too.[36]

Theaetetus and company had supposed that all the features of a thing that figure in our judgments are equally properties of the thing; so any thing is just a bundle of properties. From this followed Heraclitus's claim that there are "no somethings." But look a little harder at the scope of the refutation. What "no somethings" boils down to is the claim that there are no basic entities because there are *no individuals*. For all the terms that might be used to determine whether something is a something (counting, being, same/different), the terms—that is, *for individuating*—are preempted for the "such" category. On that view, then, all we have are the suches, with no prior account to be given—or indeed any account at all—of the something to which the suches belong. Heraclitus's ontological view, then, is not merely a thesis about existence ("being" denied, "becoming" asserted); instead, the claim is directly and centrally a claim about individuation. Now, on the other hand, Socrates suggests that *just those terms* may be arrived at by the soul "itself by itself" and not by perception.

The refutation of Heraclitus argued that we need to get hold of "somethings" before we can attribute properties or qualities to them. Now Socrates reinforces the point. The terms for individuation come first for knowledge; and they may—if Theaetetus has got the right end of the stick—be discovered by the soul itself by itself, rather than being properties of the objects themselves that affect us through sensation.

Perhaps, consequently, Plato will rethink the assumption of natural inherence—but not yet. This passage offers some suggestions, but no detailed account of how the problem of "somethings" may be solved. So far, all we have is a promissory note and, as we move into the next two sections of the dialogue, a different puzzle.

6. The Objects of Thought

Theaetetus's claim that knowledge is perception seemed to fail because it prevents us from referring to anything; there are no somethings, only bundles. But, Plato consistently supposes,[37] all significant speech must have some referential component. Any account of knowledge or dialectic or even just chat must incorporate some direct contact between what is said and what is out there in the world (Plato is thus some kind of naive realist, as well as suffering from the grammatical prejudice).

---

[36] See below (ch. 8, sec. 9, and ch. 9, sec. 9) on the question whether this claim would turn Plato into some kind of idealist, by supposing that these criteria of identity are mind-dependent. My contention will be that they are not, but that they have a different ontological status from the objects of perception.

[37] Compare *Crat.* passim and *Soph.* 262e; Owen, "Not-Being."

Protagoras's claim that man is the measure of all things failed because it implied that every judgment, made by anyone, is true. The measuring man creates his world; and so he cannot be wrong. For him, all significant speech represents the world as it is (for him); so all significant speech is true. Protagoras must be wrong about truth—because if everything is true, the notion of truth becomes vacuous. So—once he is refuted—we still need to understand what falsehood is, and how it can occur. In particular, if truth is about the world out there, and significant speech is also about the world out there, how can falsehoods ever be significant? Or, conversely, if truth is caused by the world out there, what causes falsehood?

Falsehood, surely, must be possible. We can come up with all sorts of examples, of mistakes that occur over and over again in our ordinary lives. For example, we can make a mistake about the figure approaching us down the street, and say "Magwich," when in fact it is Quasimodo. Or we may say, "Quasimodo is pretty," when in fact he is nothing of the kind. Or we might find ourselves committing mathematical solecisms—Socrates' example is "7 + 5 = 11"; surely, we often make simple mistakes of that sort?

Falsehood occurs, all right—but how? It seems, paradoxically, that it should be impossible—on the basis of two different arguments.[38]

A. First Argument: 188a–c

1. Either I know something or not.

2. So if I make a judgment, it must be either about something I know, or something I do not know.

3. It is impossible to know and not to know the same thing.

4. It is impossible for me in making a false judgment to think that one of the things I know is another one of the things I know.

5. It is impossible for me in making a false judgment to think that one of the things I do not know is another one of the things I do not know.

6. It is impossible for me in making a false judgment to think that one of the things I know is one of the things I do not know, or vice versa.

7. So false judgment is impossible.

Perhaps, Socrates suggests, we can get at false judgment by thinking about what is and what is not, rather than what we know and do not know; after all, falsehood seems to be when someone judges what is not about something or other. But can we judge what is not, whether about something that is or absolutely?

B. Second Argument: 188d–189b

1. It is impossible that when I see something, I am seeing nothing.

2. So if I see one something, I see something of the things that are.

3. So if I see one something, I see something that is.

4. Likewise for hearing and touch.

---

[38] Among the many contributions, see, e.g., Ackrill, "False Belief"; Fine, "False Belief"; and especially Burnyeat, *Theaetetus*, p. 65ff.

5. If I judge something, I judge one something.
6. So if I judge one something, I judge something that is.
7. So someone who judges what is not judges nothing.
8. But then, that person does not have a judgment at all.
9. So false judgment is impossible.

These arguments look pretty suspect. The first seems to equivocate on "know" (recall the problems of Meno's paradox, where the same trick seemed to be turned by conflating "know completely" with "have in mind").[39] The second seems to slide between "judging what is not" and "not judging at all" (the equivocation here, perhaps, is in the use of the verb "to be").[40] Are these arguments mere sophistries?

I think not. Recall that the first long section of the dialogue attacked an account of truth and the world that lacked "somethings." Now "something" is replaced with a vengeance. Suppose (again, taking our lesson from the refutation of Protagoras and Heraclitus) we insist that truth and speech must contain reference to a something; *and* that the something to which we refer is basic both to a well-conducted grammar and to a well-structured world. We must—when we think about the world—start with the basic individuals that ground everything else.

But if those individuals are basic, they must—you might suppose—be simple, the sort of things you grasp all by themselves, at once. Suppose, for example, I want to deal with the sort of something prohibited by the secret doctrine—a something *before* it is such. Now how can I specify the something? Not by saying how it is such and such (for that would be to put the such before the something). Any characterization I give it will be precluded thus; and that will include my understanding it as a complex something. For then it will fail to be basic. So if "somethings" are basic, we may suppose them to be simple units.

And that assumption is at work in Socrates' opening puzzles about false judgment. Take any simple item. Either I know that item, or I do not know it at all. So long as the original item genuinely is simple, it figures in my judgment as a whole, or not at all. But of such an item, Socrates' first puzzle holds good: either I know it (completely), or I do not know it at all. In that case, there is no scope for muddling it up with anything else, or thinking that it is something else. So long as I continue to understand it as a simple item, it can figure in my judgment, or it can be absent altogether. In neither case is it easy to see how it can constitute a false judgment, nor, failing more complex psychological or linguistic apparatus, how it could be muddled up with any other (equally simple) item.

Part of the problem, undoubtedly, is the thin account of "having in mind" that Socrates is working with here.[41] But another part of the problem is

---

[39] Cf. ch. 3, sec. 1.

[40] See more below, ch. 7, sec. 3.

[41] As some have put it, it is an "all or nothing" affair; either you have something in mind or not;

inherited from the earlier arguments, which forced Socrates into the assumption that judgments must start with "somethings" and that those somethings must be basic and simple. But in that case we can make no mistakes about them; and we seem to be back with the paradox that "everything is true."

The problem, it may be said, lies in the original assumption made by Protagoras that truth is caused. Now that is all very well for truth—it can easily be explained by the causal relation between a believer and the object of belief. But in the case of falsehood, it is not so obvious what could count as the object of belief, nor how such an object could be responsible for the mistaken state of mind. Socrates tackles this from the psychological end.[42] To explain how false belief or judgment might occur, he offers two models of the mind— the wax tablet and the aviary. (191b–195a; 196d–199d).

Imagine that we have a wax tablet in our minds that contains the imprints of all the things we "have in mind." When we perceive something, the image enters our minds, to fit into one of the existing imprints; that gives a truth. When, however, the imprint fails to fit, we have a falsehood. The wax tablet succeeds just insofar as it allows the object presented to sensation to be mismatched to the expression or the concept in the mind; thus, the judgment comes out wrong. This will apply in cases when "Theaetetus" is uttered but Theodorus is present; or "burnt umber" is uttered when yellow ocher is present.[43] What happens, then, when a mistake is made? The mistakes are simple ones, mismatches of one simple item with another. The object of the false judgment is atomic (Theodorus), and the utterance is equally simple ("Theaetetus"). There is no room in this account for either sentential complexity (not even for "That is Theaetetus") or any complexity in the object (burnt umber is a single color, not a mixture of some burnt and some umber). The mistake, instead, is a mechanical one, where the causal mechanism (the image of Theodorus coming in to my eye) fails to match what is already in my head (etched on my wax tablet, the image of Theaetetus); since the incoming image settles into the wrong slot (Theaetetus), it triggers the wrong utterance ("Theaetetus").

These atomic mistakes can occur when perception is present, but not otherwise (for example, we never say "the beautiful is ugly" because we cannot make the mismatch at the conceptual level, at least as far as the wax-tablet image goes). This is because the mistake is, if you like, a causal hiccup, a

---

cf. Fine, "False Belief"; Annas, "Knowledge." Socrates has explicitly ruled out any of the psychological mechanisms that might introduce some vagueness, such as forgetting or remembering; cf. 188a; and see further discussion below, chs. 9, secs. 3, 4, and 8.

[42] Contrast the attempt to deal with the logical account of falsehood in the *Sophist*.

[43] What does not happen, as the preceding argument makes clear and as some of Socrates' examples of false judgments that do not occur attest, is the utterance: "Burnt umber is yellow ochre." Rather, we have the situation where I say, in the presence of yellow ocher, "burnt umber"; the inappropriateness of my remark is its claim to falsehood. Compare Cooper, "Sense-Perception"; Fine, "False Belief."

failure of the mechanism, rather than some more complex piece of psychological error. The only way in which such a mistake can be explained is if the object and the concept in the mind of the perceiver are in different locations, so that the move from one location to the other (from outside the mind to within it) allows for a place in which the mismatch can occur.

But then what of "7 + 5 = 11"? Here, first of all, the mistake is a conceptual one, not one that is triggered by perception, so there is no difference of location. Then how can we escape the original puzzle that here we are absurdly muddling two items that we already know, have fully in mind? A priori mistakes do occur. How? Second, is a mistake like this a muddle of two items? Surely this example, unlike the "Theaetetus"-Theodorus case, is irretrievably complex. Suppose that we try to think just what is the object that is being mistaken here. We may say that "7 + 5 = 11" is being mistaken for "7 + 5 = 12"—and convert what seems complex into a simple whole. But that seems to miss the point of arithmetical mistakes, where we do in fact get to grips with some of the conceptual apparatus, even although we come up with the wrong answer.[44] There is a difference, we might say, between the mistake "7 + 5 = 11" and the mistake "7 + 5 = 359." Can we explain these degrees of error? We can do so, I suspect, only if we acknowledge the complexity of the proposition we are talking about. The sentence "7 + 5 = 11" is structurally complicated, different in character from "11" on its own.

But then how, on the mismatch account of mistake, are we to explain the mistake here? Socrates offers a new model for the mind—the aviary.[45] Suppose we have a birdcage in our minds, full of birds representing pieces of knowledge. When we want to know the answer to a question, we reach inside the aviary and catch a bird; having the answer is having the bird in hand. Mistakes, then, will occur where there is a mismatch between the bird we are looking for (the question—"7 + 5 = ?") and the answer ("11"). Here, then, the mismatch takes place within the mind (thus breaking Socrates' first paradox) by allowing the mind to be complex, so that there are different locations within it, and a place available where the mismatch may occur.

So the aviary is more sophisticated than the wax tablet. But it is still hopelessly naive. One of the many difficulties it faces is to diagnose what is mismatched with what. Theaetetus tries to suggest that what has in fact happened is that 11 and 12 have got themselves muddled up. Socrates ridicules that; but can he do any better?

The aviary continues the assumptions of the earlier passages by supposing that mistakes are one-by-one, exchanges of simple entities with each other. But then, does that take into account at all the complexity of the proposition "7 + 5 = 11"?

If mistakes are one-by-one, perhaps complex mistakes are collections of one-by-one simple mistakes? But then, where is the mistake in "7 + 5 = 11"?

---

[44] Cf. Burnyeat, *Theaetetus*, p. 101ff.
[45] Again, more on this below, ch. 9, sec. 7.

How many of the bits of the proposition have gone awry?[46] And then think about a pair of different sentences:

Paris is south of London.
London is south of Paris.

One is false, the other true; but they have the same component parts. Suppose that sentences are simply their semantic components, and the difference in truth value between these two sentences will vanish.

We need, then, an explanation of a priori mistakes that will accommodate more than the one-by-one mismatch of simple perceptual items and that will avoid the dangers of a causal account of truth. What is more, we need to do more than suppose that complex items are merely strings of simple ones (for propositions *and* for objects). And we need to do all that without falling foul of the problem faced by Protagoras: if a complex is a collection of bits, what makes the bits stick together?

So Plato presents a difficulty with falsehood; but this arises because of some assumptions we might make about the way our language fits the world. Consider three maxims, two of which are by now familiar:

1. The thesis of *natural inherence*. Anything we say does, or may, correspond to something or other in the world. That is, all the significant elements in our speech have their counterparts in the real world. In particular, values and relations are real features of real objects.

2. The *grammatical prejudice*. The structure of language reflects the structure of the world. Thus, the distinction between subject and predicate is the correlate of a real distinction between object and properties. This requires that the object be specified independently of its properties (hence the trouble with Protagoras's bundles).

3. The hypothesis of *logical or semantic atomism*.[47] If (1) and (2) are true, perhaps words mean what they mean by corresponding to real items in the real world. But in that case, perhaps truth may also be understood atomistically: thus, sentences are true because their component parts correspond to the parts of what is being discussed. This thesis is, of course, rather at odds with the grammatical prejudice, because it supposes that sentences are just strings of semantic atoms, whose ordering, or syntax, is insignificant. Nonetheless, without a deep analysis of the difference between semantics and syntax, it is easy to see why Plato might be governed by the grammatical prejudice at the same time as he held semantic atomism to be true.

But if Plato supposes all these theses to be true, can he specify the things that furnish the world any better than Protagoras can?

[46] Compare the argument at *Crat.* 385. On the principles enunciated there, all the words in a complex true sentence must be true, i.e., in "7 + 5 = 12" each part, "7," "+," "5," "=," and "12" will correspond exactly to what is out there. Out where? we may ask. And how many parts of a false sentence need to be false? All or just one?

[47] Cf. Ryle, "Letters" and "Atomism." But n.b., Burnyeat's discussion, *Theaetetus*, p. 149ff., where the priority of objects over their semantic counterparts is emphasized.

7. SOCRATES' DREAM

The final section of the *Theaetetus* reiterates this difficulty. It also, however, takes a different direction in the attempt to understand how something can be a something—this is the thesis that somethings are *lumps*.[48]

Once again, the topic is knowledge (not the furniture of the world); and yet the realist assumptions throughout mean, first, that what is said about knowledge has a consequence for (our understanding of) the furniture of the world; and second, the arguments about the nature and structure of knowledge can be applied, *mutatis mutandis*, to the discussion of the objects in the real world.

The initial hypothesis reinforces that claim: "[He said that] true belief with an account is knowledge, but what is without an account is outside knowledge; and the things of which there is no account are unknowable (he coined the phrase), while the things that have an account are knowable," (201c–d).

To interpret this distinction between what is knowable and what is not, Socrates recounts his dream. Suppose that *everything* (here we are firmly in the ontological, rather than the logical, realm; cf. 201e2) is composed of elements that can only be mentioned, not described any further. For, being elements, "it is only possible to name each one itself by itself, and no other predicate can be attached to the name, neither that it is, nor that it is not: for that would already be to attribute being or not being to it, which we must not do, since someone could only mention it itself. So we must not say 'it' or 'that' or 'each' or 'only' or 'this' or anything else in addition; for all those things run around and are attributed to everything, although they are different from the things to which they are attributed, but this, if it were possible to mention it and it had its own account, should be said without all these attributes" (*Tht.* 201e2–202a8).

So the elements are indescribable and unknowable, though perceptible; they are "themselves by themselves" and single-formed (notice the language of the forms here). They cannot be said to be "it," or "each," just because attributing anything else to the elements is attaching something different to the element in question. If, that is, the elements are to be considered themselves by themselves, they cannot have any properties, and cannot be described, only mentioned. They are just lumps.

The compounds of the elements, on the other hand, are knowable and utterable, and can be the objects of true belief. For the weaving together of the elementary names makes a sentence; and that is the essence of an account, a weaving together of names. Thus, while the elements are perceptible, the complex items are knowable and susceptible to true belief.

That is Socrates' dream; but it fades under scrutiny, as the interlocutors

---

[48] I use this expression rather than, for example, "atoms" or Wittgenstein's "simples," to emphasize that Plato's first interest is in things, and so to detach this view from its modern descendants.

examine further the claim that knowledge is true belief with an account. Either the compound (of unknowable items) is the sum of those items (and thus as unknowable as they), or it is a whole over and above its elements (in which case the elements do not help us to understand it). If—as any rationalist hypothesis supposes—explanation is possible, then how can appeal to such indeterminate and indescribable items help us at all?[49]

Socrates starts his attack with a familiar analogy—with letters and syllables (we shall see later that this analogy is crucial for understanding Plato's final solution to the problems we face here). The letters are like the elements of the dream, indescribable or unaccountable, while the syllables have an account. That is, as Socrates' example of the syllable *SO* shows, the syllable's account just is the collection of the elements—while the elements cannot be accounted for further, but only mentioned.

But that, of course, will not do, for two separate reasons:

1. *The syllable.* On this account, what it is to be a syllable is to be a collection of its elements. But if the syllable *just is* such a collection, then a syllable is a bundle of bits. But in that case, there is no organizing principle to explain the order or the coherence of the bundle over and above the bits themselves—unless the organizing principle is itself another bit in the bundle (cf. *Tht.* 204a). (So, for example, this theory cannot distinguish between *SO* and *OS*, or between dog and god.) But if the ordering principle is a bit of the bundle, how is it ordered within the bundle? Is there a further bit that orders both the bits and the ordering bit? And then another bit that orders all those bits? And so on . . . The principle of complex items made from simple elements falls into the trap set by the bundle argument: how is a collection *unified* when its unity can only be a member of the collection? This is a trap that will continue to threaten Plato's ontology until he can show that the organizing principle might not be one of the ordered items themselves. But he cannot do that until he cleans up his theory of relations and abandons his wholehearted commitment to the thesis of natural inherence.

Alternatively, the syllable may be held to be a single indivisible entity (*Tht.* 205c). But in that case, the syllables and the elements are similarly unknowable (205e).

2. *The element.* Supposing, however, that we charitably grant that there can be a complex syllable. This is what it is just because of its component parts—so its nature and its coherence are transmitted from the nature and coherence of those parts. But the parts have no nature (and no proper account, no *oikeios logos*) and no coherence—they are not even an "it." So the parts cannot contribute to the coherence of the whole, lacking coherence themselves. So the whole, by virtue of its parts, can have no coherence or unity at all.

Consider how this characterization of the elements of a complex echoes or

---

[49] Cf. here Fine, "False Belief"; Annas, "Knowledge"; and Aristotle's wrestling with the problems of foundationalism, *An.Po.* A.3.

complements the original Protagorean view that there are no somethings. An element is thought to be unknowable because it is the basic, primary building block from which a complex is formed. The contrast between element and syllable is produced by eliminating all the characterizations that might generate complexity (cf. *Tht.* 205c9), and by imagining the element to be "itself by itself." But there looms the paradox. Here is something that is "itself by itself" (201e2) and that cannot be called "itself" (202a3). The element is so elementary that it is indescribable, indescribable even as elementary. Here, we may suppose, is the something that underlies the bundle, the element that forms the complex; but it is a something without individuation or description. None of these somethings is "a something" at all, since they are devoid of individuation (counting) and identity (being, same, and different).[50]

Once again, we may ask why that account of being something is at all tempting. Once again, the answer lies in the thesis of natural inherence and the grammatical prejudice. If we want to understand the subject of a sentence and its corresponding object without appealing to (prior to) its predicates or properties, then we need to think about the object just by itself. But then how can we explain what it is? Any attempt to individuate this object will attribute properties to it at the very least by enmeshing it in relations. In that case, to say that it (itself by itself) is just one is to attribute unity to it; to give it identity is to attribute sameness to it; to discriminate it from other lumps is to allow it to have the property of difference. If the lump is a lump and nothing else, lacking parts or properties or attributes or even relations, it cannot be individuated. Thus, the atomic, bare subject of sentences, or the object that underlies properties, cannot be known or understood or specified or even made the object of reference. How then can it be a basic individual?

Reflect now on the structure of the *Theaetetus*'s argument, in terms of Socrates' discussion of "somethings." The beginning of the dialogue is concerned with elaborating the thesis that there are no somethings, only bundles of suches. The close of the dialogue advances—and shows to be incomprehensible—the hypothesis that there could be bare somethings, unspecifiable in any way, maybe even unmentionable in any serious sense. Now consider the connection between the two hypotheses provided by what I have called the grammatical prejudice. The "bundle" view of individuals emphasizes the importance of the predicate in understanding what there is—and it does so at the expense of the subject term. The "lump" view, contrariwise, looks at the subject naked of predicates—and it does so at the expense of being able to say anything at all about that subject. The grammatical prejudice, perhaps, engenders this contrast between subject and predicate; and yet that prejudice also may encourage us to believe that the structure of the sentence is somehow significant in a way that is not granted by exclusive focus on either subject or

---

[50] Cf. Burnyeat, *Theaetetus*, p. 134ff., who emphasizes the proviso that the elements are perceptible.

predicate. Somehow, Plato needs to meet the grammatical prejudice without explaining individuation either by bundles or lumps.

The explicit subject of the *Theaetetus* is knowledge, so that epistemological and logical concerns are paramount. But there is an underlying thread—an ontological thread—of argument about what there is out there in the world. It is, of course, reasonable for Plato to connect epistemological with ontological arguments, since he supposes that what we say somehow or other matches what there is. However, his interest in "what there is" is not primarily an interest in "existence," since he is worried instead about what we say about what there is. So he thinks about *being* in terms of *being something or other*. Then (once again, correlating semantic and ontological ideas) he obeys the grammatical prejudice in supposing that "being something or other" can be understood either as the subject term ("being something") or as the predicate term ("being such"). However, if we think about what something is exclusively in terms of the subject (as atomism—semantic, logical, or ontological—persuades us to do), we end up with a view of individuation where the individuals are so austere as to be impossible to mention; nothing is even "itself by itself" or "one." On the other hand, if we think of something exclusively in terms of the predicate, it ends up hopelessly generous—a bundle of properties, and no something at all.

So we appear to have a choice—individuals are either austere or generous; in neither case is it possible to understand what it is to be an individual at all. The choice is foisted upon us by the grammatical prejudice, and by the thesis of natural inherence. The grammatical prejudice urges the contrast between the subject/object and the predicate/properties of the object. Suppose that individuals (unities or units) are basic. Natural inherence then suggests that the properties of something pluralize it. So to understand an object, we need to think of it as austere, prior to its properties. Then it seems indescribable (a lump). Conversely, if we think of it in terms of its properties, it is a plurality with no unifying principle—a generous bundle. In order to escape this dilemma, Plato needs to suggest a different account either of the structure of what there is (objects versus properties) or of the nature of properties, relations, and values. Without such a revision of his views, he cannot account for basic entities, for individuals, for being "something or other" at all.

Slices and Stuffs

1. READING THE TIMAEUS

The reader must take the *Timaeus* with several pinches of salt.[1] For here is a dialogue whose central section is a myth, presented to a Socrates, hilarious at completing the *Republic*, by Timaeus, the "expert" in cosmology. Just that short description should be enough to make us worry about how to read the dialogue. After all, Plato is the writer who warns us against the deceptions of storytelling; and Socrates was the gadfly who never accepted the expertise of others. So we should be wary of the myth and its setting; and attentive to the explicit epistemological background to Timaeus's disquisition.

What is a myth doing in a philosophical text? Myths are stories, particular accounts of particular mythical or legendary events, handed down from generation to generation. So a myth does not present itself as a literal truth; nor as a general theory; nor as something directly arrived at by observation or intellectual means. Consequently, a myth seems remarkably out of place in the austere generalities of philosophical reasoning; and hard to construe as a stage in a theoretical argument. What, then, are we to say of the truth value of a myth, of its theoretical status, and of its transmission or provenance within the context of a philosophical argument?

Consider one aspect of myth in particular—what a philosopher would call its existential commitment.[2] Myths are extravagant stories, full of monsters and incredible creatures.[3] If I tell you a story about Jack and the beanstalk, and you take what I say to be a myth, you abrogate skepticism ("Surely there are no giants like that in a land above a magic beanstalk?") and accept the story as it is told. If, on the other hand, I represent Jack and the beanstalk to you as a scientific theory, you are entitled to object to its absurd proliferation of entities ("What beanstalk?" "There are no giants!"). Myths, that is, are free from the considerations of economy demanded by Ockham's razor; scientific theories, on the other hand, must be tightfisted in their ontology.

The myths of the *Timaeus* are many-headed beasts. The setting itself is a fictional world (the day after the *Republic*, Socrates and his friends meet again—to replace the *Republic* with someone else's story). And then two

---

[1] Interpretations differ widely; cf., e.g., Cornford, *Cosmology*; Vlastos, *Universe*; Keyt, "Mad Craftsman"; Osborne, "Topography," and the debate between Owen, "Place of the *Timaeus*," and Cherniss, "Relation of the *Timaeus*."

[2] Cf. McCabe, "Myth."

[3] Thus, for example, the *Phaedrus* both represents Socrates as a monster and suggests that the dialogue itself is alive.

different myths are offset against one another: Critias's myth of Atlantis, which tells a sad story of the consequences of human ignorance; and Timaeus's myth of the cosmos, an account of the splendid creation of divine omniscience. And these in turn are set against the background of a philosophical claim—that the contrast between knowledge and belief, like the contrast between being and becoming, is absolute and cannot be bridged. So the myth is embedded in theory: how then are we to read the myth? Is it the truth about the divine, inaccesible to us in any other way? Or is it a story to be scrutinized with a critical eye? In particular, are we to believe that there are the things in the cosmos that Timaeus says there are? Or should we be urging tightfistedness?

A different question may produce the same answers. Philosophy is about argument, not storytelling. How can these stories, then, be construed as arguments? How are we to read the tale of Timaeus?

Timaeus's account of the world is divided into three sections, carefully signposted. The first describes the work of reason and the construction of the soul of the world by the Demiurge, god (30c–47e); the second explains the role of necessity (48a–68e); and the third attempts to explain the reconciliation of reason and necessity in the objects and persons of the phenomenal world (69a–92c). This exegetical structure turns out, I shall suggest, to be an argument.

2. The Universe Is One and Whole

How did the Demiurge set about constructing the cosmos? Since he is a craftsman, then like any craftsman he does his work by *imitation* (after all, there is a difference between a craftsman and a mad inventor).[4] And since craftsmen do not (as such) bother to make useless or footling things, the product of his craft will be beautiful, fine, for the best, as will be the original from which it was copied. So the cosmos can be explained teleologically.

In order to understand the copy (the visible world), we must think about its original, the intelligible universe. Timaeus's myth suggests that the world is alive, it is an animal that in turn includes all visible animals. But its original, which contains all intelligible animals, cannot be a part of some other animal, it must be a whole; after all, the parts of animals are not teleologically arranged (*Tim.* 30c4–5).[5] Why not? Perhaps because taken separately they are not *arranged* at all—excellence turns up when we are talking about wholes, not about parts.[6] So the original cosmos must be what includes all the parts. Hence the intelligible universe contains all the intelligible animals as parts,

---

[4] Cf. Keyt, "Mad Craftsman."

[5] Aristotle would be appalled, I suppose, at this claim; it is worth keeping in mind that Plato's teleology is structured, not piecemeal. But see now Sedley, "Aristotle's Teleology," for an account of Aristotle's teleology as an anthropocentric structure.

[6] This may be the point of the relative clause at *Tim.* 30c5–7.

and the visible universe contains all visible animals as parts (*Tim.* 30c6ff.). The intelligible universe is the complete and most beautiful whole. The visible universe is also a complex whole, including all the animals interrelated to each other (31a1), arranged by the Demiurge to approximate as closely as possible the perfection of its model.

How many visible universes are there? Just one—because there is just one intelligible universe. After all, if the intelligible universe were not one, it would be part of some other whole, and so would not include the other animals. But, ex hypothesi, it does include all the animals, so that it is just a whole, and not a part of something else (*Tim.* 31a4ff.) So it is just one. And the visible universe, in order best to imitate the properties of its original, will also be just one (31a4).

This conclusion—that there is just one cosmos—is reechoed (with a touch of skepticism) at *Timaeus* 55d and then in the closing remarks, at 92c. What grounds does Timaeus have for claiming that there is just one cosmos? What are the criteria for being "just one"?

As the argument develops—and as a little reflection will show—this last question is in fact two quite different questions, when we come to think of the number of universes (either at once, or over time).

One is a counting question: why is there just one universe and not any more? This question is concerned with the exhaustiveness of the universe, with the universe considered in the context of other possible worlds.[7] In that case, we are thinking of the universe as it were *from the outside, contextually.* So the counting question can be understood as a question about something being *one among others* (the universe as a unit). As such, of course, arguments about the unity of the cosmos can readily be transferred to arguments about other individual items; and indeed Timaeus stresses the connection between the living world as a whole and the living beings within it, or between the whole body of the universe and the bodies that are its constituent parts (e.g., *Tim.* 30c; 33a; 34b).

But then the second question, which arises as soon as we think of the universe as a whole *with parts,* can be understood neither contextually nor externally, but only *internally,* as a question about the coherence of a complex whole. What makes this item itself one (and not two or an indefinite many)? Once again, the question of the internal unity and coherence of an individual is one that applies no less to the many individuals that inhabit a universe than to the universe itself. The arguments about the cosmos are of quite general application.

But Timaeus's arguments to show that both universes are wholes, and ones, trade on a particular use of "whole" and "one." Consider, first of all, the inference that if the intelligible universe is to include all the parts, there can be no other. This rests on the assumption that "whole" means "exhaustive, all-inclusive." That assumption relies on treating "whole" as a complete expres-

---

[7] This notion should be taken in the sense of ancient cosmological speculation, not modern problems in modal logic. On the different approaches of ancient cosmology, see Furley, *The Greek Cosmologists.*

sion. We cannot say, for example, of this universe that it is a whole *cosmos*, all right, but not a whole *galaxy*. Once it is a whole (constructed of parts), it cannot also be a part of some other whole. It is just whole. But then it exhausts everything (intelligible) there is (on the hypothesis that everything is interconnected). So it must be one. Its being one, therefore, like its being whole, is absolute, and the expression "one" is complete. It is not one something or other—one universe but not one galaxy—it is just one, exhaustive and complete. So its unity, like its wholeness, is a property that the visible universe can imitate. Just as the intelligible universe is spherical, so is the visible; just as the intelligible universe is one, so the visible universe is one.

For Timaeus, then, the sentence "the universe is one and whole" is not elliptical.[8] Now to treat either "one" or "whole" in this fashion—as complete expressions—is a tricky business. Aristotle, after all, could plausibly maintain that both "one" and "whole" are syncategorematic expressions, incomplete without some qualifier: "one armadillo," "one tooth," "a whole loaf." What is more, Aristotle would complain, something is whole not merely because it has exhausted all the possible parts, but because the parts are arranged to fulfill their proper functions. That supposes parts and wholes to be incurably relative to whatever function accounts for the whole—and the same whole, for one function, may be a part for some other.[9]

We might make a similar complaint about "one." If my rabbit is one, is it unique? Timaeus's argument suggests that if the cosmos is one and whole, then it is singular, we can count no more. We, on the other hand, suppose that he has made a mistake in shifting from "one" to "only one" (a mistake that becomes clear if we run the same account for any object within the cosmos— if this is one rabbit, is it the only one?) Has Timaeus made a mistake? We await some account of "being one."

From 31b, Timaeus's discussion focuses on the visible cosmos, and thus on its material constitution. Since it is visible it must be fiery; since it is tangible it must be earthy; since it is three-dimensional it must have at least three components. But component parts of a whole must be held together by something else: so the cosmos is composed of earth and fire held together in three dimensions by air and water. Its interconnection is a stable proportion that "comes together into the same as itself" and is indestructible save by its creator.

Once again the world is supposed to be one and whole. It has these properties for two reasons: first, because it is ordered from within (its material parts are well proportioned, *Tim.* 31b–32c), and second, because it exhausts all the material there is (33a). So the world is complete, ageless, and virtually indestructible, fitting the teleological pattern of its intelligible original.

I suggested that arguments about something being one could be charac-

---

[8] Compare *Tht.* 204a ff., discussed at ch. 5, sec. 7, or *Parm.* 137c and 142b, discussed in ch. 4, sec. 3.

[9] The most notable Aristotelian example here is the contrast between the man of virtue, who functions as a whole person, and the virtuous citizen, who functions as a part of a larger political whole; *Politics* III.2.

terized as arguments about a thing's internal constitution ("What makes it one?") or about its external context ("How many are there?"). Timaeus's discussion of the material nature of the world has the same two aspects.

First, the cosmos is a unity *from within*, by virtue of the internal order of its parts. This account of an individual is markedly Eleatic (cf., e.g., spherical, *sphairoeides*, *Tim*. 33b4, single-generated, *mounogenes*, *Tim*. 92c9). After all, Parmenides claims that his one is one and the same as itself because of its internal consistency and coherence (DK28B8.22–30, 42–49); and he infers from that account of his individual entity that it is the only individual there is.[10] And Parmenides, of course, provides Plato with a target elsewhere when he is discussing the question of how many things there are, and how each counts as one (cf. *Parm*. 137ff.; *Soph*. 244ff.). If we understand "being one" this way, we treat individuation *absolutely*.

Second, we might think of the unity of something *from without*. In the *Timaeus*, the argument for unity by exhaustion of all the material looks at individuation from without, by exhausting the "without," unity is ensured. Context matters for individuation. From a common-sense point of view, for example, one could argue that this mass of water is individuated by the bucket that contains it; take the bucket away, and the water joins the puddle on the ground—it is no longer the same identifiable mass. That approach to something's being one may be quite general. Suppose I am searching for the villain among the crowd; I find him when I can *mark him off* from all the other upright citizens milling around. But if, on the other hand, I am a physiognomist, searching for a particular skull formation, I may shout, "Oh, there's one," when I spot the forehead of the same miscreant, ignoring its connection to its owner. This kind of individuating could be understood in two quite different ways. On the one hand, picking out the miscreant may be a matter of sorting (persons in a crowd, villains, characters wearing a sinister mask) and counting as we sort. Or, on the other hand, individuation might happen just when we differentiate one item from another. Something's being an individual, on this account, would be a matter of its difference from (nonidentity with) all other things, no matter how they are sorted. This, for example, might be a matter of grasping how one atom ends just where another begins, or of understanding that this is one person just because this person is distinct from the surroundings through which he moves. From this I might argue that any individuation is *relative* (relative in the first case to which one—"one what?"—that I am looking for), down to, and including, the bare cases where an individual is specified by its spatiotemporal coordinates; that, too, is relative (to the space and time around).[11] Timaeus's argument that the cosmos is

[10] This is, but it should not be, controversial; compare Barnes, *The Presocratic Philosophers*; Mackenzie, "Parmenides' Dilemma."

[11] Perhaps, if I am a pluralist, I could believe that all individuation is relative—but not if I am a monist. For in that case there is no "without" to measure the one against, or to contextualize it within. So the one absorbs all the context and exhausts all there is (cf. the argument for the impassivity of the cosmos from without, 33a4). Thus, the Eleatic Melissus argued from the

one because it exhausts all there is around it is, in spirit, an argument for context-relative individuation. For he suggests not that we can count the universe by sorting universes, but that we can count it by looking at the context in which it exists and by considering its possible differences from everything else. Consequently, since the context is exhausted, there is only one universe after all.

There are, on this account, two different perspectives for individuation—one internal and absolute, the other external and context-relative. We might think about this as a contrast between deciding the internal *unity* of something and counting it as a *unit* by determining its identity vis-à-vis other individuals. The first possibility might be a matter of coherence or wholeness, of self-identity at a time: this hedgehog is a complete and coherent organism —and so trivially the same as itself now. The second fits the individual into a context of both time and space: this hedgehog is different from that one, but the same as the hedgehog I came across last week; these are the identity conditions for this hedgehog, and it is by virtue of them (sameness and difference) that it can be individuated.

Why is this universe one and the same? And further, why is anything in it one and the same? It seems obvious that questions about internal unity and questions about identity in context are complementary. After all, take either question alone and it produces absurdity. Suppose, on the one hand, that the individual is understood as merely contextual so that it gets its identity merely from the context that surrounds it. Then the individual is nothing but the space, as it were, between other individuals (and, of course, they too are individuated by the same criteria); and such individuals are characteristically austere—they have no features in and of themselves (at least so long as the relations in which they stand are thought of as features of the relata—a view Plato is tempted to take). Conversely, if we focus upon the internal constitution of some "one," then we may allow it to have parts; at that stage we need to supply some cohesive principle to hold the parts together and to individuate the whole. But here the problem confronted by Protagoras's bundles starts to loom; if this individual is held together by a cohesive factor, is that factor itself a part? In that case, surely must not that part also be made coherent with the whole? Is the individual that results a unity at all—or a hopelessly generous plurality?

3. SLICES

The physical material of Timaeus's universe includes the bond that ties the other components together. If parts are parts of a whole, then their interrela-

---

infinity of what is to its unity: "if it (what is) were not one, it would be bounded by something else" (DK30B5). "For if it is infinite, it must be one; for if there were two (things that are) they could not be infinite, but would be bounded by each other" (DK30B6).

tion itself is seen as a part of the whole. This naturalist, not to say physicalist, assumption pervades the account of the universe and the living things within it. Despite the mathematical approach of Timaeus's account (the teleological slant of the proportions of the universe), Plato is still working with a view that relations (connections, tyings together) are real items in the world, to be understood as elements in their own right gluing other elements together.

Of course this physicalist emphasis may just be the consequence of Timaeus's treating the body of the universe before its soul. However, the naturalist assumption looms even larger in the account of the composition of world soul.

The soul of the world is created by the Demiurge as a piece of cosmic pastry: "From the indivisible and unchangeable being and then from the being which becomes divisible in bodies he mixed a third intermediate form of being out of both, and likewise from the nature of the same and the different and on the same principles he established [third types] intermediate between their indivisible type and the divisible physical one; and once there were these three things, he mixed them all into one form fitting the nature of the different, which is hard to mix, to the same by force and mixing them with being. And making this one whole from three he then distributed the appropriate portions, mixing each from sameness and difference and being" (*Tim.* 35a1–b1).[12]

The Demiurge has a difficult task. To create soul he makes a mixture of intermediate being, sameness, and difference, and then he divides his mixture up and meshes it together in strips, thus totally enveloping the universe in strands of world soul. This explains both the unity and the teleology of the world; and, since the world has a soul, the combination of being, same, and different explains the cognitive capacities of the universe: "Whenever world soul encounters something that has divided being, or something indivisible, moved through all of herself, she tells what (the something) is the same as and what it is different from, and in what relation, place, manner or time each changing thing is related to others, and each changeless thing likewise" (*Tim.* 37a5–b3).[13]

What now makes this cosmos one and the same? Timaeus earlier argued that it is one both by virtue of its internal constitution and by its exhaustion of what could have been outside it. Now he offers an equivalent account of its self-identity—it is *one and the same* because it has the appropriate layers of the right sort of sameness, difference, and being. It is same and different: and therefore it is one and itself.

---

[12] I have tried to avoid the contortions of Archer-Hind's interpretation here (which supposes that sameness is the proper description of the indivisible being, and difference the proper characteristic of divisible being, and adds a further epistemological dimension to this account) by retaining αὖ περὶ in 35a2, and punctuating, with Cornford, . . . συναρμόττων βίᾳ μειγνὺς δὲ μετὰ τῆς οὐσίας. καὶ ἐκ . . . at 35a8–b1. The text confirms at several points (35a5–7, 35b1, 35b3) that Timaeus envisages a cosmic mixture made of three intermediate stuffs: intermediate being, intermediate same, and intermediate different. Each stuff is intermediate between the indivisible and divisible types of (respectively) being, sameness, and difference.

[13] Cf. Cornford, *Cosmology*, p. 94, n. 4.

How can any of this explain the individuation of the cosmos? Think again about what our commonplace assumptions might be when we try to answer. The hedgehog needs to be an organic whole, sure enough, and not just a collection of hedgehog-bits or animal-stages. But (reconnoitering the snail population in the garden) we might wonder whether this hedgehog is the same as the hungry beast from last week: then to ask whether it is the same is to inquire about its identity over time. Or (again with the growing snail population in mind) we might want to know how many hedgehogs there are in the garden at once. Is this one the same as that one? This question is not so much about identity over time as difference at a time: and determining that is crucial for counting. In both cases, identifying something is capturing its difference from other somethings; so difference is treated as the basic relation between individuals. But these questions about difference and sameness invite us to consider the context in which the individuals appear, for they ask about this hedgehog's being the same as last week's (here the context is temporal), different from the one over there (here the context is spatial). Considered in this way, identity is fundamentally context-relative, and perhaps necessarily so, because it treats difference from others as the primitive, irreducible relation identifying individuals.

But Timaeus approaches sameness and difference otherwise. If the Demiurge can mix world soul, then his ingredients must be real; the naturalist assumption persists. That is, Timaeus supposes that it is reasonable to treat being, sameness, and difference on a par, as extended, quasi-material entities. If we think about being, sameness, and difference as qualifying *things* (in this world or some other), then Timaeus's supposition turns out to have two parts:

1. These are properties of things, on a par with colors or textures (this I have already decribed as the naturalist assumption).

2. The expressions to which they correspond are to be understood as complete, at least in their primary, cosmic manifestations. That is, the intermediate sameness and difference that are parts of the cosmic psyche are not relative (same as one thing, different from another) but absolute—just sameness, difference simpliciter.

What is more, being, sameness, and difference are seen no less as primary features of things in the world as of the world itself. The world soul is constituted of these ingredients, not some others; and the world soul's thought processes are first and foremost determined by discerning those features in the things it observes.[14] So the account of the constitution of the identity of the world may be understood as quite general, a view of the identity of any thing we care to think about. Timaeus emphasizes over and over again that the things in the world are analogous to the world itself;[15] and consequently, the assumptions and the argumentative framework that he uses to explain the individuation and identity of the world may also be applied to the objects in the world. Once again, his assumptions seem perfectly general.

[14] Cf. D. Frede, "Rationality and Common Concepts in the *Timaeus*."

[15] Cf., e.g., *Tim.* 30c6; 32d1; 33a7; 34b2; and look at the way the question of the number of worlds is revisited at 55d.

Recapitulate, therefore, the salient points:

1. The account of the unity of the world can be understood both in terms of its context and in terms of its constitution (as I have expressed it, from the outside or from within). This offers two differing accounts of individuation—*context-relative and absolute.*

2. But questions of individuation and identity are thought to focus upon a series of central features of a something: unity and wholeness; being, sameness, and difference. All these features are assumed to be *natural features* of the thing in question (and are not understood as mere relations, or as merely conceptual).

3. Perhaps as a consequence of this naturalist assumption, the expressions "one," "whole," "being," "same," "different" are treated as *complete expressions*, not as incomplete or syncategorematic. Thus, identity is absolute, not relative.

4. While all these expressions represent real pieces of the world's furniture, they turn up together in a *mesh* of inextricable ideas—cosmic pastry. For they are mutually determined, at least insofar as questions of individuation involve both unity and wholeness; questions of identity require some understanding not of being alone, but of sameness and difference, too.

Try this model of "a something." Imagine that properties occur as extended layers—grey, for example, would be a layer of a particular color—and that properties are layered on top of one another, resulting in a dense three-dimensional pile of different layers, like a gateau. A particular object, on this model, would be a slice of the pile, or the cake; and the properties of the object would be just those properties that appear in the slice. Or perhaps an object might be more complex than a slice, outlined by a template to give it shape—an elephant-shaped slice, or an armadillo. So instead of being bundled together, perhaps the properties of a thing are just piled up on top of each other by virtue of the original structure of layered properties. So there need be no principle of coherence (of the properties into just this bundle) because the properties cohere by being layered in the first place, before (if you like) the slice is cut.

The "slice" analogy suggests, as the "bundle" one does too, that a thing *just is* its properties. There is no object underlying my slice of gateau; the slice just is whatever the layers are, in the order they occur. So the cosmic gateau of ordered properties—we might suppose—already gives sufficient material (just the properties) for there to be objects, without supposing there to be something else (on top, or underneath) that constitutes the object in contradistinction to its properties.

A moment's reflection may suffice to show that the slice is as tricky as the bundle. If I am cutting my cake into slices, I need some kind of principle to determine both the size and the shape of the slices I cut (whether that principle be one of distributive justice, or an aesthetic one—symmetry perhaps—or a gastronomic one—that each slice should have just the right proportion of crust to undercooked middle). But it is that principle, or the template, that determines what each individual slice shall be. The slice of properties, no less than the bundle of properties, fails to give us a principle of individuation for the slice, even if it does succeed in telling us what the relation between the properties (e.g., next to each other in the pile) might be. Moreover, it fails to tell us why any slice might have different properties from any other slice. If, that is, properties are layered throughout the cosmos in this way, why is one animal grey and another brown, or one smelly and the other immensely easy on the nose? Or, worse, if the elephant and the armadillo both have the properties of sameness and difference, how do they differ from each other, how are they the same as themselves? How are the relations between different things to be explained at all?

Plato might, nonetheless, have found congenial the idea that properties are spread out in layers. In general, remember, he supposes that properties are real features of the world—not merely those properties that are directly perceptible but also those that seem not to be so. Thus not only "pink" or "smelly" but also "same as," "larger than," and even "nice" represent real properties, inherent in the thing they qualify. Now think about a particular color, say this purple. It might be argued that this (piece of) purple in this pair of socks is an individual, separate and distinct from any other occurrences of the same shade of purple in another pair of socks or in a tulip or in a motorcar. On the other hand, one might be forgiven for supposing that the particular purple is an individual extended over those items—both pairs of socks and the tulip and the motorcar share in the same individual color, this purple. But then it might seem easy to conclude that this is a layer of purple, spread out over the objects that have it. In that case, if all properties and all relations and all values operate in the same way, then surely the world is a layering of properties, all piled on top of each other. A thing, then, will just be a slice of those properties, since "property" includes everything that we might say about the thing in the first place.

Several passages in Plato's later dialogues present the view that properties are spread out in this way; or that their presence in a particular is to be explained by their being cut out of the original layer.

Of the former, perhaps the most famous is "the sail":

> "You think, as you say," said Parmenides, "that the forms are somethings, by participating in which these other things get their names—e.g. like things become so by participating in likeness, large things in largeness, and beautiful and just things in beauty and justice?" "Certainly," said Socrates. "Does each thing that participates participate in the whole of the form or a part? Or could there be any other participation than those?" "How could there be?" he said. "Do you think, then, that the whole form, being one, is in each of the many—or how does it happen?" "What prevents it from being in them,[16] Parmenides?" said Socrates. "Therefore the whole, being one and the same will at the same time be in the many which are separate, and so it would be separate from itself." "It wouldn't,"

---

[16] Following Schleiermacher's emendation ἐνεῖναι at *Parm.* 131a10.

Socrates said, "if it were one and the same like day, and were in many places at once and nonetheless not separate from itself—perhaps that is how each of the forms is one and still the same in all." "That's a good idea, Socrates," he said, "you make it one and the same and yet in many places at once as if you spread a sail over many men and said that this was one whole over many. Is that the sort of thing you mean?" "Perhaps," he said. "Would the whole sail be over each man, or one part over one, another over another?" "A part." "So then the forms will have parts, Socrates, and what participates in them will share in a part, and there will no longer be the whole in each, but a part for each." (*Parm.* 130e–131c)

The naturalist assumption is here expressed in an extreme form (and put into the mouth of Socrates' opponent, Parmenides) as the idea that properties are layers; and it is embellished by a treatment of "whole" and "part" as complete, absolute expressions.

The sail has its sophistic counterpart at *Euthydemus* 300e–301c:

"Have you ever seen a beautiful thing, Socrates?" said Dionysodorus. "Certainly," said I, "indeed I have seen many, Dionysodorus." "Are they different from the beautiful or the same as the beautiful?" he asked. And I was completely covered in confusion, and reckoned that I had paid the penalty for grousing; but still I said "They are different from the beautiful; however some beauty is present to each of them." "So if an ox is present to you, you are an ox; and since I am present to you, you are Dionysodorus?" "Don't blaspheme," I said. "But then how could one thing which is different from another make the other the same as it?" "Does this confuse you?" I said. I was already trying to copy their wisdom, insofar as I desired it. "How could not I—or anyone else—be confused at something that is not ?" "What are you saying, Dionysodorus?" I said. "Surely the beautiful is beautiful and the ugly is ugly? " "If it seems so to me," he said. "And does it seem so?" "Certainly," he said. "And so the same will be same, and the different different? For it is not the case, I suppose, that the different is same, nor would even a child be puzzled by the claim that the different is different."

Once again Socrates' opponents adopt the same assumptions: first, that properties, including the identifying properties of sameness and difference, are to be understood as physically present in their objects; and second, that words such as "same" and "different" are already complete expressions, with no need for further qualification or relativizing.

In both these passages, the point about the nature of properties is made in a negative, adversarial way. In the first passage, Parmenides is interpreting Socrates' view by suggesting that the form is like a sail (and not like a day). For throughout the argument between Socrates and Parmenides the realist hypothesis is maintained (that forms, and what they explain, are real items) and even overemphasised as a physicalist view, that forms are physical objects. But of course the view that the properties (explained by forms) are, first, not the same as the forms that explain them and, second, real features of the real objects, is standard in middle Plato. The elaboration offered by Parmenides wrongly conflates form and property; but then it makes a plausible (for Plato) suggestion that the property is itself just a single item, spread out over its instances.

If that conclusion (for properties) is denied, two difficulties follow. First, it is unclear how else the property is present to the object (that is, being spread over the instances may be a useful image for inherence); and second, if each property is individual to each individual in which it inheres, it is unclear how there can be any explanation of the property in general (such as the theory of forms attempts). The view that a property is spread out allows the possibility of explaining both the instances of the property (parts of it) and its universality (this is just one property over all the instances). If, that is, we resist the conflation of form and property, we could easily imagine that the sail would be a good analogue for a property for Plato.

The same conclusion may be derived from the *Euthydemus* argument (which may, indeed, be interesting in several ways when it comes to thinking about individuals and their properties). Here, the theory of transcendent forms is not explicitly under attack, although we may find it irresistible to conclude that it lurks in the background of this passage. Socrates, defending himself from sophistic attack, argues that beautiful things have the beautiful in them. He is talking, at this stage, then, exclusively about the "property" of beauty, which he supposes to inhere in the beautiful objects. But what can be meant by such inherence ("being present to")? Dionysodorus parodies Socrates' hypothesis by suggesting that having a cow implies being a cow, or that being in Dionysodorus's presence implies being Dionysodorus. Once again—as in the *Parmenides* passage—Socrates' opponent appears to have committed a category mistake. A property (even a queer property, like beautiful) is not an individual item like a cow any more than it is an individual like a form; so having a property is not like having a cow. Aside from the category mistake, having a cow exhausts the cow (possession is nine points of the law), while having a property allows others to share in the property, too (vide Socrates' original contention that there are many beautiful things). The property of beauty is spread out, then, among the beautiful things in which it inheres, and is not used up by any single instance.

We might express the contrast between the *Parmenides* passage and the *Euthydemus* passage in terms of the *Parmenides'* argument about parts and wholes. This assimilates properties and forms; and supposes that (since properties are distributed over their instances) the form will be partitioned. The *Euthydemus* assimilates properties and individuals; and supposes that (since individuals are not distributed over instances) properties must be restricted to a particular instance (the consequence will be that the individual will be identical to its property or properties). In the *Parmenides*, what must be one (the form) is found intolerably many; in the *Euthydemus*, what must be many (the property) is found intolerably one. Both arguments appear paradoxical precisely because they appear to deny the assumption that properties are spread out over their many instances—like a sail.

"And so being is distributed over all the things that are and is not absent from any of the things that are, neither the smallest nor the biggest. Or is it absurd even to ask that? For how could being be absent from any of the things which are?" "In no way." "So it is parcelled out over things that are, both the smallest possible and the largest possible and in every way, and it is partitioned most of all, and there are an infinite number of parts of being." (*Parm.* 144b)

This passage comes from the paradox mongering of Parmenides in the second part of the eponymous dialogue. Here, Parmenides' account of being has exactly the same characteristics as his sail; and what is more, the layer of being covers everything. This "property," that is, is a seamless and universal layer, a part of which is in every slice.

The *Sophist*, too, exploits the "layer" image (although as we shall see, not wholeheartedly). The job of the dialectician is to show how "kinds" combine —to show how discourse can be made possible by allowing some kinds to combine universally, and some not. Such a person "is able adequately to distinguish one form spread out over many distinct items, and many forms different from each other embraced from without by a single form, and a single form, again, collected together into one through many wholes, and many separated altogether apart." (*Soph.* 253d).

Now recall the Demiurge's skills as a pastry cook. He rolls out and cuts up sameness and difference, and then folds them together to make world soul. But the sameness and difference that he uses is of an intermediate type— between the sameness and difference of the intelligible world and the sameness and difference that turn up down here, among the phenomena. So there is an analogue between cosmic sameness and the sameness in us; so, it seems irresistible to conclude, the sameness in us is a layer, too. We, like world soul, are a slice of our properties.

The properties themselves—sameness and difference—will be spread out across the objects that have them, just as both the sophists and Father Parmenides himself suppose. But then, if we compare Timaeus's account with these other similar passages, we may readily see that the Demiurge's cosmic haute cuisine is a contentious activity, even a paradoxical one. How far should we see this as Platonic doctrine?

If individuals are bundles of properties, it is difficult to explain how they cohere. If individuals are slices of properties, the difficulty is the same—it is difficult to explain why they are cut just so. Both bundles and slices lack a principle of individuation. The *Theaetetus* makes it clear that Plato saw the problem for Protagoras's bundles; and Plato himself is vulnerable to the problem with slices, as perhaps the puzzles about the limits and determination of things at *Parmenides* 144b ff. make clear. Is the purpose of Timaeus's account to offer us some cosmic templates (the eternal forms) to individuate particular items? Even if that is the implication here, Plato still needs to explain how—without dangerous pluralizing—anything can be just one, a single, unified individual, whose identity conditions do not impair its individuation.

4. THE WORK OF NECESSITY

Bundles turned up as models of individuation in the context of Protagoras's secret doctrine of flux. Protagoras's difficulty was that, in a world of flux, there are no somethings. But this failure to specify definite individuals is lethal to the *Theaetetus*'s secret doctrine. In order for discourse to survive, we need to be able to *count* "somethings" and to explain their being and their sameness and their difference. But discourse obviously does survive, so a proper account of individuation and identity must be given. The *Timaeus* version of the argument from change, perhaps, meets this challenge. For Timaeus's theory gives him a something to meet our demand for definite individuation.

After concluding the account of the work of reason, Timaeus makes a new start (*Tim.* 48a) to explain the work of necessity in the cosmos. What is going on here? Commentators have often suggested that the analysis of the behavior of the elements is merely an account of the primordial chaos (cf. "We must consider both the nature and the affections of fire, water, air and earth *before the generation of the heavens*," 48b3) and has no bearing on the metaphysics of the physical world now. Is this passage a cosmogony? Or does it provide a deeper insight into the problems of analyzing the present?[17]

Two preliminary considerations tell against the view that this passage is "mere" cosmogony:

First, think about the teleological aspect of the work of reason. Timaeus wants to argue that the sensible world aims at the best. In comparison to the eternal world of the forms, of course, it always falls short; but nonetheless it is persistently teleological. But what explains the failure to reach perfection? This, of course, foreshadows the problem of evil faced by later teleologists: against what background of fall short, of deficiency and sheer badness can we set the teleological drive? Timaeus's answer to that question is his introduction of necessity: that is, what pulls against pure reason and provides the tension against which the aspiration to the best must be understood. Hence, the need for reason and necessity to be reconciled: "For the generation of this universe took place from a mixture of necessity and the arrangements of reason. Since reason rules necessity by persuading it to lead most of the things that become to the best, in this way and for these reasons this whole was composed thus from the beginning because necessity is overruled by reasoned persuasion. So if one would say how the whole really came to be on these conditions, one must include the form of the wandering cause, by which it naturally moves" (*Tim.* 47e5–48a7).[18]

Second, we should recall the chronological setting of the work of reason. The Demiurge created a world that is eternal, and he created time to measure the eternity of that world in contrast with the timelessness of the intelligible. That looks paradoxical already. How, as Aristotle might remark, could we

---

[17] Compare, eg., Sorabji, *Matter*, p. 32ff., here. There is a similar problem with the analysis of the cosmos at *Pol.* 273b6.

[18] Cf. Cornford, *Cosmology*, p. 160, n. 2.

talk about the generation of time without that process itself being within time? If time measures the before and the after, surely there can be no generation of time, any more than a generation of something that lasts throughout time? The paradox of time invites interpretation. But Timaeus's point, surely, is to be made about the world now. This world is a mere copy of the intelligible world because it exists in a different chronological dimension ("when Abraham was, I am"); that difference persists now, since this world incorporates change and thus time, while the other excludes any variation—so it is outside time. But if that is the center of Timaeus's point, the account of the generation of the world by reason can be understood as metaphor, a compelling image to demonstrate the radical difference between being and becoming. His interest lies there, not in the generation of time. Likewise, the discussion of necessity is couched in the metaphor of cosmogony; but its point is a serious and present metaphysical one about the nature of things within the changing world.

Indeed, the text suggests that we can move freely between the cosmogonical talk and the discussion of a continuing state of affairs. At *Timaeus* 52d, for example, Timaeus says that he has given an account of being and space and becoming, which was true *even before* the heavens were created; the implication is that this analysis applies both to the primitive state and in the present.[19] This passage then describes present change, not primitive flux; it goes on to suggest that change was once strictly mechanistic, and thus chaotic (53a2), while now order has been imposed on it (53b). However, the underlying mechanisms (the wanderings of necessity) persist, and explanations must look to both aspects (cf. 68e, on the actual mechanisms of perception). Timaeus's argument allows us two points of view—one of reason and the other of necessity—and invites us to consider whether they can indeed work together.

5. Something basic

We may, then, take the cosmological talk both literally and as a metaphor for the constitution of the world and its contents now, as Timaeus takes us back to "first principles" (*Tim.* 48e).[20] In the earlier discussion, Timaeus reminds us, there were two "forms"—the paradigm and its copy. The relation between the two is described as the contrast between being and becoming, where the latter is parasitic on the permanence and knowability of the former; because the things in the phenomenal world are just copies of the intelligible world, they are inferior and subject to change (28a ff.). Now Timaeus undertakes to elaborate his account of becoming by showing us a third "form." The third

[19] Note the continuous verbs, *Tim.* 52d4ff., and the prevalent use of φαίνεσθαι, e1.

[20] Cf. Cornford, *Cosmology*, p. 161ff., on the ambiguity of ἀρχή; for my purposes the important contrast is between ἀρχή as a beginning in time—hence the cosmogony—and ἀρχή as a constitutive element of things. In the event, thinking about things "from the beginning" allows us to see them "from the bottom up." In both ways, we are thinking about ἀρχαί.

form is necessitated (*sic*) by the account (49a3); but it is, nonetheless, difficult to understand. What follows, then, is an *argument* for the third form, the "receptacle of becoming," whose obscurity is signposted from the start.

> We must first puzzle about fire and its companions. For it is difficult to say for any of these [1] which sort should be called water rather than fire; and [2] which is any particular one rather than them all, or severally—in such a way as to offer a credible and fixed account. So [3] since we are reasonably puzzled about them, how can we speak of them and what can we say? (*Tim.* 49b1–7; my enumeration)

Timaeus suggests three puzzles about "fire and its companions":

1. How is each really (whatever it is)?[21]
2. How is each different from the others?
3. Thence, how can we sensibly talk about them?

But the puzzles themselves are puzzling. Why should we find ourselves in any such difficulty about fire or water?

> First, what we now call water apparently freezes and becomes stone and earth, and then the same thing melts and separating out becomes breath and air; and the air burning becomes fire; and then coming together and being quenched the fire goes away again into the form of air, and then air coming together and thickening becomes cloud and mist and then when these condense still further, flowing water; and from water earth and stone again, thus reciprocating round in a circle they have their generation, it appears, into each other. So since each of these things *never appears the same*, of *which of them rather than another* would one not be embarrassed to claim firmly that it was *this particular one*, and not another? It is impossible . . . (49b7–d3; my emphasis)

The first difficulty here seems to be about change. All the four elements change into each other, as we can (readily?) see. But then each of them is never the same. The same as what? And why not? Suppose that fire does *change into* air, air into water, and so forth, and suppose that we get a patch of fire now (over some period of time). Even if this patch of fire came from a patch of air, and will turn into a patch of water, there seems no reason to deny that it is the same (as itself) now. Timaeus's puzzle seems to rest on a mistake: he has supposed that because the elements change into each other, they are in a state of total flux, constantly slipping away and never *remaining the same*. But that conclusion just does not follow from elemental change, which could be moderate, well ordered and periodic, perfectly suitable to be "the same."[22]

Perhaps the problem of flux is not what Timaeus is worried about. Perhaps his argument is not predicated on the idea that the primordial state of things is chaotic and flux-ridden. Instead, maybe his appeal to cosmogony allows him

---

[21] In this sentence "fire" appears in predicate position; the verb is a copula, not an existential.

[22] Compare the elaborate way in which the problem of total flux is set up at *Tht.* 181c ff.

to consider whether what there is can be understood without the benefit of the apparatus of reason—forms and the Demiurge. If what necessity provides is amenable to explanation at all, then—as Plato's predecessors had urged—it must be analyzed into its basic constituents. And those, the discussion of reason had assumed, are the elemental masses: earth, air, fire, and water.[23] And then Timaeus's problem turns away from flux into a puzzle about the nature of substantial change.

Suppose we ask of this element—fire, say—"What is it, really?" Our first response may be "fire"; but we may be tempted to recant when we see it turning into air. What is this really? It is not fire, because that has gone; nor is it air, for that has just arrived—so it is not really either. So what is it really? The question searches for *what is basic*, where fire and air turn out to be transitory. It searches, we might say, for what came first in time (what underlies cosmogony); it also asks about what comes first in constitution (what underlies what is here and now). In the quest for what is basic, the origins of the universe and its present constitution may be thought to coalesce.

The second difficulty here seems to be about speech. Even if I attend to this patch of fire, followed by this patch of air, I may find it hard to differentiate them. Why? This difficulty follows from the first. If (because none of them really is what it is) I cannot say of each of them that it is *this*, then I cannot differentiate it from the others. This is a problem for the world and its composition from elements (fire is never elementary enough to be this and not that); and it is a problem for me, since I can never confidently say, "This is fire," without risk of contradiction. So we cannot say, of any of the elements, (1) that it really is (whatever it is), nor (2) that it is different from the others. This is not so much a problem of flux as one of indeterminacy. We can never say which element is which—because one keeps changing into the next one; we cannot tell whether they might not all be each other, nor whether any one might be any other.

If the elements are indeterminate in this way, why are we in trouble? There are three different difficulties.

The first is directly about the indeterminacy of fire and company. Fire, by virtue of its liability to change, is not "the same" (sc. as itself?); nor is it different from the other elements. Fire, that is, fails to be basic, fails to be permanently *this*. But—the argument suggests—there must be something basic, something continuously the same as itself and different from anything else. If fire fails the test, it is not reasonable to call fire an element, since there must always be something else with a better claim: for to be an element is just to be basic in this way.

The second difficulty follows from the first, and it is anticipated by Timaeus's opening salvo: "as if we were speaking to people who know what fire is, or each of the other beginnings, we posit them to be the elements of the whole—although it is not at all appropriate for someone who has even

---

[23] Cf. *Tim.* 40a2, or the analysis of sight, 45a ff.

thought about the thing a little to liken them to the elements of a syllable" (48b).

If fire and company fail to be *basic elements*, then they cannot explain as elements are supposed to do. If elements explain by being the basic components of the world (as any dull reductionist might claim), then they must be more basic than their explananda. But these items are not basic (they are not even items at all), so they do not explain.

The third difficulty faced Heraclitus, too (*Tht.* 183a–b). For the world to be arranged properly (or even to be susceptible to arrangement), it needs to be based on fixed elements. Likewise, if speech is to be organized properly, it needs to refer to some "this."[24] Proper speech needs a proper subject; and the so-called elements fail to supply one.

Can we, then, avoid the conclusion (3) that we cannot sensibly talk about the elements? Can we rescue ourselves from the dangers faced by Protagoras's secret doctrine, that all talk becomes meaningless? At this stage in the discussion, disaster looms. If we cannot even talk about the elemental masses, how can we talk at all? We must, Timaeus suggests, have recourse to a "safe" explanation.[25] Since fire and company change all the time, we cannot call them "this" or "that." But, of course, we do talk about them; how can our talk be saved? We can say "such," or "such as fire," or "such and such always recurring." We must call each of them not "this or that," but only "such":

> Far safer to adopt the following theory about them: whatever we always see becoming different now at one time, now in one way, now otherwise, as for example fire, we should not call fire "this," each time, but "such";[26] or water never "this" but "such," nor anything else as if it had some fixity as in cases where by the expressions "this" and "that" we think we show a something. For it escapes and does not stay behind for "this" or "that"[27] or any expression that points these things out as being stable. We must not use each of those terms, but must call them "such-like which keeps recurring" in each and every case; so fire is "what is such throughout," and likewise for everything which has generation. (*Tim.* 49d3–e7)

How is this safe answer an improvement on the total indeterminacy that has gone before? Has Timaeus answered his own puzzle, or merely slid out from

---

[24] Compare the insistence at *Soph.* 262e that all speech must be "of something."

[25] Compare *Phd.* 102ff.

[26] The interpretation of this sentence determines how we understand Timaeus's argument as a whole. For a start there is some trouble with the text. If πῦϱ at 49d6 is correct—as symmetry with what follows suggests—then this should be the referent of "this" or "such," and not part of the referring phrase; thus, Cornford, *Cosmology*, p. 179 ff., but compare Cherniss, "Relation of the *Timaeus*," p. 358. Timaeus envisages some fire appearing before us and wonders how, commensurate with its changing status, we are able to speak of it. His problem seems to be with whether fire ever properly deserves a pronoun, rather than with whether there is ever any proper fire; this argument is an argument for the receptacle, not for the form of Fire. Contrast M. L. Gill, "Plato's *Timaeus*," pp. 34–53.

[27] With the majority of scholars, I delete ϰαὶ τῆν τόδε.

under its coils? His argument has three parts (and a sting in the tail). First, he rescues fire, air, earth, and water from the unspeakable. Second, he shows how there is still a basic subject for discourse, an element in the cosmos. Third, he gives a complex physical account of how the two fit together. But there remains a sting in the tail.

If fire changes, it does not qualify as "this." But we can speak of it as "such" and treat it as a quality or a property (of some "this"). Then, we might say, what seemed intolerable as the substantial change of the cosmic elements is made bearable—for now cosmic change is just change in property. This safe answer then supposes that qualities ("suches") may change, constantly if necessary, without endangering discourse altogether.

So fire and company are no longer to be treated as elements. But the collapse of discourse—according to this argument—can only be avoided if there are things we can mention that do not suffer from indeterminacy and change. Qualities can only be treated as nonbasic if there is something else basic in which they may inhere. If the question What is it really? is sensible, then there must be something that qualifies as really being (whatever it is): "But that in which each of them repeatedly appears to comes to be and into which they perish—only that can be mentioned by 'this' or 'that'; and no 'such'—hot or white or any other of the opposites and everything else made from them—should be described by any of these expressions" (*Tim.* 49e7–50a4).

Thus Timaeus concludes his argument to establish what underlies all change—the substrate, space, the receptacle of becoming, the nurse of change. This substrate alone deserves the title "this." Since this alone underlies change and alteration, this alone is basic. In the receptacle come to be the imitations of the intelligible forms, which change and perish, while the substrate remains throughout changeless because it itself has no qualities or properties save indeterminacy alone. Like the liquid base of perfume, like gold that can be molded into shapes, like wax that can be imprinted by a seal, the receptacle provides the vehicle for change and difference while itself remaining just "this" and nothing else at all. This is a theory of *stuff*.

Obviously, this postulate meets some of the difficulties of the puzzle. The receptacle is basic because it underlies everything else, nothing underlies it; and it is free from the dangers of change or even flux because it is the place where change occurs, and is not itself changing. To that extent the receptacle is explanatory (and to that extent alone).

Recall that this argument turns up in the context of a cosmogony. I suggested that the cosmogonical talk may be metaphorical, a means of expressing some thesis about the constitution of the world now. Timaeus was puzzled about two things—change and talk about what changes. The problem of change may well apply to primordial chaos, but the talk about what changes seems to be about what is changing now (and there are no speakers in the primordial chaos). His argument for the receptacle of becoming applies, therefore, both then and now; and it is an argument strictly limited, so far, to the workings of necessity. The argument is designed, that is, not to show that there are fixed forms, but to show that there is a receptacle underneath phenomenal change.

What is safe about this answer? There are, I think, two reasons for suggesting this contrast between the "this," the receptacle, and the "suches," the affections of the receptacle, from the elements up. The first is cosmological; the second, grammatical and ontological.

The cosmological reason would be that any change must have some underlying substrate in order to avoid the dangers of not-being—a rationale for a theory of matter that is common in Greek theorizing about the cosmos. Something must persist, but if everything seems to be changing, the something that persists cannot be like any of the things we see change; so it must be indeterminate by definition—stuff.

It does not, however, follow directly from this that we should deny that the affections of stuff are mere "suches," while only stuff counts as a "this." For that move, Timaeus needs a further premise, that the substrate always (or fundamentally) appears in the subject position, while its affections always appear in the predicate position in a sentence. Here is the grammatical prejudice, apparently, underlying the semantic claims that Timaeus makes here. But then this grammatical prejudice has an ontological counterpart. The items in the world that correspond to the subject/predicate distinction (object/property) differ from each other in their ontological status. Only the object counts as a something, as an individual; the others all count as properties, whose status is dependent on the object (but not vice versa).[28]

Think now about the combination of these two reasons. The grammatical prejudice generates the thesis that only objects count as somethings; while the cosmological argument requires that the only something there is is utterly indeterminate, has no properties, is just stuff. To be a something, on this view, is to be nothing but a something; nothing else can be attributed to the something as such—all its attributes are accounted for in terms of its affections, which are distinct from its being a "this" and posterior to it. But in that case— for the reductionist account of the workings of necessity—the attributes or properties of "this" cannot explain *what it is to be* this, this is just itself, not qualified in itself by any such at all.

How good is this solution to the original problem of elemental change? In one sense Timaeus has lit on the perfect reductive account of identity—as a later move in the argument makes clear (after a fashion): "On the one hand, since not even that on condition of which the image exists belongs to the image, but the image is always carried around as a phantasm of something else, the image must therefore come to be in something else clinging somehow or other to existence (or else it would be nothing at all). But on the other hand

[28] Cf. M. Frede, "Becoming," and ch. 5, sec. 2.

the truth comes to the rescue of what really is, so that so long as one is one and the other the other, neither will come to be the other, nor will they become thus one and two at the same time" (*Tim.* 52c).[29]

Since the "this" and the "suches" are different categories of being, they cannot be confused with one another. This will remain true even if, as here, one category is parasitic upon another. Moreover, the conditions of identity for the receptacle are based on the absoluteness of that category distinction. So long as an object and its properties are in different categories, they must be non-identical; but so long as the receptacle has no properties, it must just be itself. By elimination, the receptacle is self-identical and nonidentical with anything else; it is, in fact, an individual of the austere type—just itself and no more.

Now Timaeus goes on to elaborate an account of the cosmos that incorporates this metaphysical analysis. Throughout he maintains the assumption that *analysis* is the right approach to cosmology (*Tim.* 53c–d). In particular, fire and company, even if they are bodies, can be further analyzed into plane figures (53d4–6). This is how they are able to change into one another (within some limits, 54c–d) while maintaining their status as affections of the underlying stuff. Think, for example, of the analogy between figures in gold and the affections of the receptacle (50b: notably these are *plane* geometrical figures). If some gold has a triangle in it, the triangle is an affection of the gold, not some new substance—not least because the triangle describes a single plane of the gold mass. Or if the phenomena are like the images in a mirror, again we are dealing with two-dimensional affections of a three-dimensional substance. If those plane figures are the basic components of the world, then the appearances of the world will be affections of stuff (the gold analogy) or epiphenomena (the mirror analogy), never impugning the basic substance itself.

Now of course even if the relation between the receptacle and the triangles gives the basic physical analysis of the world (*Tim.* 53–61), it still cannot tell us what makes this collection of planes or this appearance, fire (and not water). But reason, of course, has already told us what fire is: the form of fire—and so on for any of the paradigms available to the Demiurge. So the affections of stuff are *what* they are by virtue of the form; they are *where* they are by virtue of the receptacle—and discourse is restored once again.

So the receptacle of becoming performs several functions in Timaeus's account. First, it allows there to be something that persists through change; and by the same token it provides a place for change to occur. So the changing properties are held together by the stuff in which they inhere; the receptacle is what there is, really. Second, the receptacle is the referent for sensible

---

[29] Cf. here Cornford, *Cosmology* Appendix, p. 370. Timaeus makes two separate points about images: that they are parasitic on their original ("that on condition of which the image exists") and that they are dependent on the medium in which they appear. They "cling somehow or other to existence" by being instantiated in the receptacle; and neither they nor the forms can be collapsed into it (hence "so long as one remains one," etc.).

speech—the "this" without which sentences cannot be constructed. Third, the receptacle is what is most basic of all (because it is entirely unqualified); thus it provides the bottom level of analysis, an ultimate explanation. All three of these considerations came to influence Aristotle; and Aristotle saw, as Plato did before him, the sting in the tail (*Met.* 1029a17ff.).

How are we to get hold of what is basic, in the way these arguments demand? The arguments postulate, it seems, a contrast between an object and its properties; and they assume that the contrast is readily understood. But is it? Is there—as the receptacle arguments require—an absolute contrast between an object and its properties?

The argument about change might allow us to make a preliminary move. Suppose that the philosopher Soriticus, who was thin, becomes stout. Soriticus's thinness has been replaced by his stoutness (this is the process envisaged at *Phaedo* 102ff.), and Soriticus is said to have changed. So he underlies the change; he is the object, stoutness and thinness the properties. But that contrast is only relative (to some object persisting through some change). Suppose we try to make it absolute, and allow the title "object" only to what persists under any change whatsoever—Soriticus's perishing and turning to dust or vanishing into thin air. Only something that must always persist (on such a train of thought) is entitled to be called "this." But if it must persist under any possible change of property, then surely it has no properties at all in itself. It is *just* "this," never "such."

> The third type is the permanent space which does not admit decay but presents a place for whatever has generation itself, grasped by the lack of perception, by some bastard reasoning, scarcely credible. We look to it as if in dreams, and we say that everything that is must be in some place and to have some space—for that which is neither on earth or in the sky is nothing. Since we are at the mercy of this dream, we are unable to discriminate and speak the truth, either about these things and what is akin to them, or about the sleepless and true nature. (*Tim.* 52a8–c1)

Timaeus's theory is an explanation of the phenomenal world. He postulates forms, the receptacle, and the affections of the receptacle. The forms explain the affections; and the receptacle gives them somewhere to be. Phenomenal particulars, therefore, are doubly parasitic—on the forms for their explanation and on the receptacle for their instantiation.[30] They cannot be said to be, but only to become. More accurately, the receptacle becomes such, and then such, and then such—becoming is defined by the properties of the receptacle that can change into one another (and this, of course, is a far more subtle problem than the dangers of Heraclitean flux). Being, on the other hand, is constituted by the Demiurge, the forms—which are always just what they are—and also the receptacle itself, which, underlying its affections, is permanently "this." But, that being said, the contrast between the receptacle and the

---

[30] Cf. Lee, "Image," p. 352ff.

forms is a telling one. For while the forms are essentially determinate, the receptacle (like the liquid in which perfume is made) characteristically has no character, and is only to be understood by means of some sort of thought-experiment (imagine something, then strip it of all determinate qualities or properties or affections). And then the danger becomes apparent. Fire and company failed as elements because they lacked permanence: so they were disqualified as the ultimate components of an explanation. The receptacle, contrariwise, has permanence alright, so that it is perfectly suitable as an element; but it is so indeterminate as to be ineligible as an explanation. It is something we can scarcely believe, something we grasp by illegitimate reasoning, something we see only in dreams. Is it, then, a sensible component in Timaeus's likely story?

6. REREADING THE *TIMAEUS*

The *Timaeus* is a myth about what things there are and how they are to be understood. In particular, it is a myth about how we can understand the unity and identity of the things that are in a cosmos ordered by reason in balance with necessity. But why is this account put in a myth? Myth is readily profligate with its entities, whereas science and philosophy are parsimonious. So then the philosopher, reading a myth, maybe inclined to be skeptical about its claims and to rethink the assumptions it makes and the ontology it proposes. In particular, a myth about ontology, and about the conditions for considering anything to be something, is immediately vulnerable to the philosophical reader, who asks, "Are all these entities necessary?"

If the mythological setting calls into question the content of Timaeus's theory, so do the details of the theory itself. First of all, the *Timaeus* resounds with the work of earlier cosmologists. Indeed, Timaeus appears explicitly to take on the claims of his predecessors and reject them; hence his repudiation of the elements as constituent principles of the cosmos (*Tim.* 48b). Yet his earlier analysis of the material structure of the world suggested that earth, air, fire, and water are indeed elemental masses, holding each other together (31b ff.). These positions appear to be inconsistent. Likewise, he attempts an analysis of the whole world and its (living) parts as if they were made of slices of extended properties (30c ff.); yet he argues later in the work that these properties are impressions inhering in some underlying stuff, mere "suches" (48a ff.). In the earlier passage, he implies that his analysis has reached what is; but his later analysis denies that the elements are basic at all—so much so that he refuses to grant them the primary name "this."

So throughout Timaeus's physics runs a discordant metaphysical theme. If we were to ask him what makes something one something, he has two kinds of answer.

In the earlier discussion of the work of reason, he first explains the unity and the identity of individuals by claiming that they are composite wholes, hammered together with difficulty by the Demiurge. They may, perhaps, be held together by metaphysical glue, by a further feature or property of themselves that does the holding together, just as the identity of the world is explained by the (identifying) properties that it has. This account, however, looks tricky, just so long as the glue is itself a part of the composite whole. What makes the glue stick to the other features of the thing? And what detaches this thing from the other things around it? Can "being individual" be just a property of the things that are individuals?

Second, when he comes to discuss the receptacle of becoming, Timaeus seems to insist that there is (in the phenomenal world) only one individual, only one "this"; namely, the receptacle itself. The receptacle is an individual because it is indeterminate; it is nothing but "this," just one. He arrives at this conclusion by stripping all its properties from it and producing a bare entity, an austere individual. But can this individual ever be understood, or even mentioned? Can any sensible theory postulate such a something?

It seems that the *Timaeus* contains at the same time both a generous and an austere account of individuation. But if the arguments of the receptacle passage are to be taken seriously, then the earlier composite wholes are not "somethings" at all; and if the arguments of the earlier sections are taken seriously, the theory of the receptacle suffers from serious indeterminacy to the point of being unmentionable and hostile to reason. The two accounts are in counterpoise. Why?

This might just be a mistake—carelessness on Timaeus's part. Perhaps Timaeus does not mind that he gives an account of the constitution of the perceptible world by virtue of something that has no account. Perhaps Timaeus thinks this does get us further forward, even if the Plato of the *Theaetetus* might not. We have, I suppose, two options. *Either* we can take the *Timaeus* at face value—as the best available account of the constitution of the cosmos— and argue that it is pushing the text too hard to ask for consistency either with itself or with other, possibly later (or possibly earlier) dialogues; *or* we might say that the theory put into Timaeus's mouth is not dogma, but a challenge, a puzzle designed to set us thinking about the relations between a substrate and its attributes, between object and property, between subject and predicate. The counterpoise between the two accounts of individuation constitutes a dilemma. In the *Theaetetus* we saw how bundles and lumps were antithetically posed to raise a question about two contrasting accounts of individuation. In the *Parmenides*, likewise, the argument was explicitly dilemmatic, and it also focused upon the contrast between the generous and the austere versions of "being one." The same effect can now be seen in the *Timaeus*—the dilemma of slices and stuffs.

One way of tackling this issue is to look at its logical underpinnings. Suppose, first, that the cosmology of reason is, as I have suggested, inconsistent with the cosmology of necessity. That inconsistency may be dealt with in three different ways. The first is tolerant; at 29c Timaeus disavows consistency, so perhaps, on his own principles, the clash between reason and necessity is benign. But are those principles ones that either Plato or we can tolerate? Even if they do not make Timaeus uneasy, surely they should trouble us? Second, perhaps we can explain the tension between reason and necessity charitably by suggesting that the earlier account is supplanted by the later—reason is overruled by necessity. How congenial, though, is that characterization of a scientific explanation? Or third, we might think of the counterpoise as deliberate—disjunctive not conjunctive; a dilemma, not a contradiction. Either we understand the world according to the canons of reason (so that the objects of the world are slices, with no principle of coherence) or according to the demands of necessity (in this world, what there is really is stuff). The dilemma offers a challenge to our criteria for establishing *any something* in the world.

In general, it seems plausible to suppose that the *Timaeus* is a challenge. Even at a cursory look there is an immediate clash between the cosmological theories offered here and the Socratic attack on primitive cosmologies in the *Phaedo*. That, of course, could also be explained developmentally (Socrates was not up to cosmology; Timaeus is). But then, think again about the *Timaeus* itself. Here we have a dialogue (to be generous) that undercuts itself. It begins with a recapitulation of the *Republic* that is wildly off the mark,[31] continues to some rude remarks about myth; and then offers a grand cosmological myth, founded on principles of likelihood—principles that Timaeus's epistemology rejects as second-rate. The "dialogue" is highly self-referential, not to say explosive. How then are we to read a passage in the middle where the force of reason persuades necessity (reason and persuasion are already divorced by decree absolute) to undergo change; and where the substrate that undergoes that change is, *eo ipso*, indescribable except by virtue of some bastard reasoning (look how bastard reason is offset against the legitimate? family it produces)? The contrast between stuff and its affections creates a gulf between the indescribable and the only descriptions it could have. And is this to be an explanation?

Compare two dreams: Socrates' dream in the *Theaetetus* and Timaeus's dreamlike reasoning about the receptacle of becoming.

The *Theaetetus*'s analysis of the physical world is compared to the relation between letters and syllables, words and sentences. But at *Timaeus* 48b5ff. Timaeus is talking about the generation of fire and other things—that is, about their real nature—and he rejects comparison with the letters of a syllable "as if we were speaking to people who know what fire is, or each of the other beginnings, we posit them to be the elements of the whole—although it is not at all appropriate for someone who has even thought about the thing a little to liken them to the elements of a syllable."

Why this repudiation of Plato's favourite analogy with letters and sylla-

---

[31] Off the mark in the sense that it omits the cornerstone of the arguments in the *Republic*—the metaphysics and epistemology of the central books.

bles?[32] Perhaps because fire and company are here being considered as elements, and are not at all like letters in a syllable, since they fail to be primary and are not "this," but only "such." The receptacle of becoming, on the other hand, *is* analogous to the elements of the *Theaetetus*, since it too is unknowable and indescribable, just what it is, and not in itself having any properties. But then, perhaps the conclusions that are explicitly drawn for the elements/lumps of the *Theaetetus* should be carried over to the receptacle of the *Timaeus*.

If lumps and stuffs are the objects underlying properties, and correspond to the subjects of sentences, neither lumps nor stuffs will do. For they are ultimately insusceptible to reason. So to argue that change requires an indeterminate substrate as subject, as Timaeus does, is an absurdity: it is absurd from the point of view of explanation (for explanations must be scrutable), and thus—for Plato—it is absurd from the ontological point of view. Indeterminate items neither explain nor can they be explained. How could such items be items at all?

Timaeus's dream and Socrates' dream both turn out to be nightmares; and the *Theaetetus* makes explicit the problem that the *Timaeus* implies. In the *Timaeus*, as in the *Theaetetus*, Plato offers a contrast between bare subjects (austerely conceived) and individuals as collections of properties. The *Theaetetus* offers the contrast between bundles and lumps; the *Timaeus*, the contrast between slices and stuffs. The contrast itself, I suggest, is dictated by the grammatical prejudice, which suggests that the world is ordered as sentences are ordered. If that is the case, then perhaps we should be able to specify subjects independently of their properties; or otherwise, subjects just as collections of properties. The contrast between subject and predicate underlies the contrast between lumps and bundles and between stuffs and slices. None of these accounts of individuation is tolerable.

All right, suppose the dilemma of slices and stuffs is puzzling. That, of course, is nothing like enough to explain the complexity of the argument. But suppose, further, that the mythological setting is designed to turn the puzzle into a challenge—a challenge to the reader to find the way out of the absurdity.

Think, first of all, about how dilemmas work. Suppose that a dilemma is a good one (that is, not easy to escape, not obviously flawed), and that it is apparently complete (exhausts all the possible options). Then, I suppose, it will be compelling (at least to those who accept that arguments are compelling at all), and consequently alarming. What happens next?

There are, at that stage, three strategies open to the victim of the dilemma. First, you might attack the premises of either horn (or both). In order to do that, those premises must be uncovered and investigated. Or second, you

---

[32] Compare *Politicus* 277e ff., and cf. Ryle, "Letters and Syllables," Owen, "Undepictable"; Skemp, *Plato's Statesman*, ad loc.

might deny the completeness of the dilemma; that is, the relation between the premises of both horns should be scrutinized. Or third, you might just walk away—either denying that argument is significant, or denying that the argumentative assumptions of dilemmas in general are correct. In the last case, you are just refusing the philosophical bait; in the first and second, perhaps, you might suggest a radical review of logical assumptions, such as the universal application of the law of noncontradiction.

Now of course, such a radical review was proposed by the sophists portrayed in the Platonic dialogues. They will readily deny the need for consistency; so no dilemma can compel them, even if they exploit others' commitment to noncontradiction themselves (look here at the exchange at *Euthydemus* 284ff.). But the dilemmas about individuals that I have suggested appear in the Platonic dialogues are not aimed at some interlocutor within the dialogue; rather, they remain as a challenge to the reader. What is the reader to do with them? Options one and two remain: scrutiny of the premises of the dilemmas, and of their interrelation.

Now think about the dilemma-monger. What is he doing with his dilemmas? Plato could, of course, be offering a closed argument for some kind of skepticism or nihilism; by being strung up by these arguments we are forced to deny the effectiveness or validity of any argument about any thing. Or he could be offering a dialectical challenge—a challenge (to us and to himself) to solve the dilemmas and restore the discourse in which they are framed. My analysis of the *Parmenides*, the *Theaetetus*, and the *Timaeus* has suggested that these large-scale dilemmas recur; and that, I take it, is evidence that Plato knew they were there. Supposing that he had dialectical (not skeptical) intentions; we then need a clear focus on what constitutes the premises and their interconnections.

Consider, for the moment, three premises that are apparent in the *Timaeus*:

1. *The grammatical prejudice.* This, as we have seen most clearly in the receptacle argument, is the supposition that there is some real difference out in the world corresponding to the grammatical contrast between subject and predicate. Plato explains this difference not only in terms of the contrast between "this" and "such," but also in terms of the contrast between "being" and "becoming"; those expressions themselves are explained in terms of individuation (being one, being whole—or not) and identity (being same, being different).

2. *The naturalist assumption.* I have argued that this assumption pervades Plato's work from the early period; and we might by now suppose it to be the villain of the piece. The naturalist assumption—to recapitulate—supposes that every predicate represents a property that appears naturally in the real world. This assumption is manifest in Timaeus's account of world soul, where a mixture is made of being, same, and different, producing some stuff that can then be divided up and parceled out. Being, sameness, and difference, that is, are treated as quasi-physical entities, as natural items (even if not material items) in the real world. Such an assumption (as earlier chapters have at-

tempted to make clear) is consistent with the assumption that such terms are relative; thus, "same as Socrates" might express some natural property no less that the bare "same." But it denies either that relations between things are not naturally occurring or that relations cannot be reduced to the properties of the relata. So the naturalist assumption does not consider whether relations might be aspects of the contexts in which natural individuals occur (aspects, perhaps, that supervene on the objects themselves), or coordinates (points in a spatiotemporal continuum that are not constitutive parts of that continuum), or in some other way not parts of the relata. At present, although this assumption causes Plato difficulties, he is not ready to offer a different account of how something might reflect what is said of it.

3. *The mesh of identity.* Consider, once again, the contrasting approaches of reason and necessity to the question, What makes this one and the same? Necessity offers a minimalist view—this can only be a something insofar as nothing whatever can be said of it. But then (taking the lessons of the *Theaetetus* to heart), this cannot even be said to be "it" or "this." It has a minimal unity (it exhausts all the stuff) but no identity, no claim at all on sameness and difference. And that is why we cannot even mention it; like the objects of Heraclitean flux, to have no identity over time or at a time means nothing to be said at all.

Reason, on the other hand, gives us a rich account of identity. "Being the same" means "having the property of sameness"; "being different" means "having the property of difference." Identity is not relative but absolute—a matter still of the internal constitution of a thing. Consequently, six expressions are notably treated as complete expressions in the *Timaeus*: "one," "whole," "is," "becomes," "same," and "different." Aristotle might argue that only sentences such as the following are well formed:

Arnie is one armadillo.
This is a whole sentence.
Rudolf is a reindeer.
Alexander becomes arrogant.
Lewis Carroll is the same as Charles Dodgson.
Bush is different from Gorbachev.

Plato, on the contrary, suggests that I can successfully say:

The form of beauty is one.
The sensible cosmos is whole.
The Demiurge is.
Fire becomes.
Supremacy belongs to the motion of the same.
The orbit of the sun is the different.

All of these expressions represent properties of things, not relations nor qualifications of properties (this, of course, is the naturalist assumption at work), so that the terms turn out to be complete. But Plato uses the expressions this way, as the *Timaeus* makes clear, not by sheer carelessness but by virtue of arguments to establish conditions for one, whole, being, becoming, sameness, and difference. Those arguments suggest, moreover, that while these expressions may be grammatically or linguistically complete, they cannot be understood each one on its own. On the contrary, the six notions in this list are mutually explicatory. For the cosmos to be one, it must be understood in terms of its constitution; and that constitution is only understood when we see that it involves being, sameness, and difference (and becoming as well); and then it is a whole. Likewise, being is thought to be a property of the things that are, but a property that is "made" of being, sameness, and difference in a mixture. Identity, then, is treated absolutely, but as a congeries of properties, nonetheless. I shall call this congeries the *mesh of identity*.

Plato draws a distinction between what appears in the subject position in a sentence and what appears in the predicate position; and he suggests further that what appears in the subject position represents something that is ontologically basic. In that case, however, the object/subject cannot be explained in terms of its common or garden properties/predicates, because that would vitiate the assumption that it is basic after all. But then how can it be explicated? There are, between the work of reason and necessity, two options:

1. Basic somethings merely exist and cannot be qualified in themselves. But in that case—as the receptacle shows and as Aristotle later understood—they cannot be explained. And then, perhaps, they fail to be basic after all. If individuals are stuffs, are they still proper individuals? Or

2. Something can be understood in terms of its unity and its identity (on the model of the rational cosmos). Plenty then can be said of it (after all, the cosmos is multiform). In particular, its basic character (its self-identity) can be explained in terms of properties that it has, the interconnected properties of the mesh of identity. But even if such a thing is self-identical, has its unity been properly explained? The difficult task of the Demiurge (*Tim.* 35a8) leaves this question unanswered; the problem of generous individuals, slices, remains unresolved.

The antithesis of reason and necessity poses a dilemma that may be explained once again in terms of its grammar. Start with the two basic parts of a sentence, subject and predicate, and their corresponding object and property. Suppose that we focus on what makes something "a something." If we want to think about the something as a bare something (subject of sentence, object that has properties), then we must think of it as devoid of properties, austere (this will be a lump in the *Theaetetus* or stuff in the *Timaeus*). But then, can we think of it at all? Conversely, if we want to think of something in terms of any of its properties (including such properties as make it a something, the properties appearing in the mesh of identity), it must be not just a something, but a (generous) collection of things (the bundles of the *Theaetetus*, the slices of the *Timaeus*). What, without hopelessly adding to the collection, makes such a thing one thing? And if both horns of the dilemma are unbearable, is there a way through the middle?

To individuate, I argued, you need to establish three things: that your individuals are basic; that they are unified, and that they are countable units. The *Timaeus*, I have argued in this chapter, is involved in this question, and it makes some vital contributions to the debate Plato is staging.

1. The argument to establish the receptacle of becoming presents a reductive account (hence it is the work of necessity) for a *basic* individual: the "this" is what underlies all properties, underlies any "such."

2. *Unity*, by contrast, is understood in terms of reason, not necessity. Here, first of all, being one is treated as a property of the cosmos and the things in it.

3. The cosmos is also composed of the properties of identity: sameness and difference. Here again, formal properties are no different from any others; naturalism still prevails, and with it are the difficulties in finding a middle course between the generous and the austere accounts of individuation.

4. But nonetheless, the properties that might explain identity are both isolated and interconnected (being, sameness, and difference are the materials from which world soul is constructed). This is the mesh of identity.

5. Finally, the discussions of the unity of the cosmos counterpose two different analyses of its unity and its identity. While much of Timaeus's account treats unity and identity as properties, so that individuation is absolute, the argument from exhaustion betrays a different account. For here, individuation is context-relative. Here, as I shall suggest in Chapter 8, lies Plato's way out.

Being and Talking

PLATO APPEARS now to be faced with a complex difficulty about the nature of individuals. He needs to explain how there can be individuals—rather than either indeterminate stuffs or mere bundles of properties. And further, he must give a consistent explanation of how something's being an individual is related to its having properties. Is "being an individual" just another of the properties that it has? In that case, can we distinguish between the individual that has the properties and the properties that it has? If individuals are to have properties at all, can they be fixed individuals underneath—in particular, underneath properties that are liable both to change and compresence? If we cannot, perhaps the individual is no more than a bundle. If we must distinguish the individual from its properties, what criteria can we adopt that do not themselves impair the unity of the individual they determine?

Suppose that we are trying to understand just what it is to be an individual. We might, on the one hand, argue that the individual (which has the properties) is somehow or other prior to those properties, so that it can be specified or understood independently of them. Or we might argue that the individual is just a collection of properties, so that the properties define the individual. In either case, any property will be conceived as somehow a part of the individual—on the austere conception, as a *posterior* part; on the generous conception, as a *constitutive* part (recall the contrast between the hatstand and the piece of string). On the one hand, no property must then be found to be constitutive of the austere individual, for that would violate its priority. On the other hand, if properties merely collect to form an individual, there is no individual core to determine which properties collect where, since there is no rank-ordering of properties, and no determination of their logical connections. This generates the generous view, wherein no property is posterior, and no formal distinction is available between a thing and its properties. Each view ends up with an indescribable individual, the first for reasons of austerity, the second for reasons of hopeless generosity.

One way out of this difficulty would be for Plato to distinguish between those properties (or relations or attributes, etc.) that establish the nature of the individual as such, and those that may be attributed to it on top of its individual nature; such a distinction might constitute a contrast between formal and "proper" properties.[1] Certainly a part of such a project must be to contrast relations and properties (since some of the problems of hopeless generosity

---

[1] Cf. Ryle, "Plato's *Parmenides*"; or second-order versus first-order properties—cf. Schofield, "Likeness," on the *Parmenides*, or Keyt, "Mad Craftsman."

arise because relations are conceived as properties). But more comprehensively, Plato needs to come up with an analysis of those properties that constitute the essential features of an individual as such; and to show how they do not run foul of the contrast urged in the *Parmenides*, the *Theaetetus*, and the *Timaeus*.

Plato answers the problems of the *Parmenides* explicitly in the *Sophist*; and his strategy is pure metaphysics, a proleptic repudiation, if you like, of the sortal approach to individuation.[2] Here he attempts an account not of being qua being, but of *being one as such*, which is designed to mediate the choice between the austere and the generous view of the individual.

But first, the puzzles of individuation are revisited. The *Sophist* challenges the sophist, the maker of semblances, the speaker of falsehoods, to defend his profession. The sophist retorts that the challenge itself is incoherent, on two grounds. First, he asks, What is a semblance? And second, What is a falsehood? Are semblances, or falsehoods, things that are, or things that are not? If they *are*, they cannot be explained as semblance or falsehood, both of which mention *what is not* (this is a decoy duck, is not a duck); if they are not, how can the sophist be charged with making them?

The first half of the *Sophist* (236e–251d) notoriously expatiates on the difficulties attached to "is" and "is not." The overriding assumption (what G.E.L. Owen has called the Parity Assumption)[3] is that "is" and "is not" should be understood together—light up the one and you illuminate the other (243c; 250e). The Eleatic Stranger, consequently, presents a series of puzzles about both being and not being; the two sections (237-243; 244-249) are interdependent; and, as we shall see, the argumentative structure of the first is mirrored in the second. Both, I shall argue, follow the pattern to be found in earlier dialogues—a contrast between individuals in themselves and individuals as collections of properties.

1. Not-Being

If we charge the sophist with tangling being and not-being, we must be able to explain what not-being is. Can we? Two Eleatic arguments suggest that we cannot. Worse still, what "in no way is" cannot even be mentioned (*Soph.* 237b7); for the name appears to be used for no "something" and no "such."[4]

> Eleatic Stranger: Tell me, do we dare to utter the expression "what in no way is"?
>
> Theaetetus: How could we not?
>
> Eleatic Stranger: Suppose that without being contentious or playing games, one of us had to answer thoughtfully and in earnest whither this name, what is

---

[2] Cf. here ch. 1, sec. 4.
[3] Owen, "Not-Being."
[4] I take this to be programmatic of what follows; see below, n. 20.

not, is to be applied, how do we think that he would answer? To what thing and of what kind would he apply the expression and show it to someone who wanted to know?

Theaetetus: This is a difficult question, and almost impossible for someone like me to answer.

Eleatic Stranger: Well, then, [A] this at least is clear, that what is not is not applied to something[5] of the things that are[6]. . . . And if one could not apply it correctly to what is, then one could not apply it to a (the) something . . . And this, I suppose, is obvious to us that when we say this "something" we mention what is, each time. For to utter it ("something") alone, naked and deprived of all the things that are, is impossible. . . . Then would you agree that the person who mentions something mentions one something? (Yes) For indeed the "something" is the mark of one, the "somethings" of two or more. . . . So it is absolutely necessary, then, that he who mentions what is not says nothing at all—or so it seems. . . . So we must not concede that this person, who attempts to utter "what is not," speaks, but says nothing—he must not be said to speak at all.

Theaetetus: The argument would otherwise reach a complete impasse.

Eleatic Stranger: Don't boast. For there is still the greatest and first of these impasses to come; it turns up at the very beginning of the argument. . . . [B] I suppose that something else of what is can be added to what is. . . . But surely something of what is could not be added to what is not. . . . We posit number as being one of the things that are. . . . So we must not try to add number—singular or plural—to what is not. . . . So then how could someone either utter or even conceive what is not, or the things that are not, without number? When we say "the things that are not," surely we try to attribute plurality of number; and when we say "what is not," we attribute singularity. . . . Indeed, we say that it is improper to fit what is to what is not. . . . Do you realise then that it is not possible to utter what is not correctly, or to mention it, or to think of it itself by itself, but it is unthinkable and unspeakable and unutterable and indescribable.

(*Soph*. 237b–238c; my lettering)

The ES claims that his argument has two separate phases ("there is still the greatest and first of these impasses to come," *Soph*. 238a2); they must be kept distinct (I have marked them in the passages above and below as A and B).

A. "What is not" cannot be "applied to" any of the things that are. But if so, it cannot be applied to any something, a fortiori, since all "somethings" must be things that are. The expression "a something"[7] cannot be used alone, naked, divorced from what is. But to say "a something" implies "one something"—or in the plural, "two or more somethings." So when someone says "not something," he is saying nothing; and saying nothing is not saying anything at all.

---

[5] Reading τῶν ὄντων ἐπί τι τὸ μὴ ὄν . . . as in Burnet.

[6] I omit most of Theaetetus's answers, for brevity.

[7] Notice that αὐτὸ at 237d2 refers back to "τι" and not to τὸ ὄν. So αὐτὸ refers to what is said, "something," rather than to what is, to which we apply the expression "something."

B. We can "add" one of the things that are to another of the things that are. But something of the things that are cannot be added to what is not. After all, number—singularity and plurality—is among the things that are; and number (as argument A showed) is not to be ascribed to what is not. But number is primary; we cannot understand anything without ascribing number to it, whether we speak of "not-beings" or of "what is not." Therefore, what is cannot be fitted to what is not.

In conclusion, we can neither mention nor say nor conceive of what is not itself by itself, but it is unthinkable and unmentionable and unutterable and irrational.

How have these arguments worked? Notice, first of all, what they have *not* done. They have not merely claimed that to associate "being" and "not-being" generates a contradiction; instead, they take a roundabout route to show that "being" and "not-being" do not fit together. Nor, on that route, do they exploit an equivocation on "is"; instead, the arguments turn on "something" and "one." Nor do they produce their absurd conclusion by sliding from "not-being" to "nothing" (as in "The Mad Hatter mentions the Dormouse; so the Mad Hatter mentions what does not exist; so the Mad Hatter mentions nothing; so the Mad Hatter does not talk at all"—or in the Prodican variant:[8] "Socrates says what is false; Socrates says what is not; Socrates says nothing").[9] Instead, argument A *grounds* the conclusion that what is not is unmentionable; argument B, the claim that it is indescribable.

Think again about the development of argument A:

1. What is not cannot be applied to something of what is.

Theaetetus takes this to be obvious; that, presumably, is because it would be contradictory. Is it? Only if "applying" is taken to be utterly simple. To make his point, the ES must rule out, for example, cases where I "apply" the expression "Mr. Micawber" to the stout person standing before me. So to "apply" what is not to something that is must be taken in its most transparent sense: what is not cannot be applied to something qua something that is.[10] Suppose that I have in front of me something that just is (that is all there is to be said of it); then, to *refer to it* as "what is not" is an immediate howler.

2. Therefore, what is not cannot be applied to a something.

---

[8] See the Binder/ Liesenborghs fragment of Prodicus, discussed in Mackenzie, "*Cratylus*"; cf. Macdowell, "Falsehood."

[9] Amid the plethora of discussions of this, note especially Owen, "Not-Being"; Mates, "Identity"; Bostock, "Is Not"; Brown, "Being"; Heinaman, "Self-Predication"; M. Frede, *Prädikation*; Wiggins, "Sentence Meaning."

[10] Transparency: I mean here that the referring relation is direct, not to be turned aside by its intentional context, or under different descriptions. I may say "here is Tully" when confronted by Cicero and fail to realize that here is Cicero (because I don't know that Tully is the same senator as Cicero). Here, direct reference is interfered with by its intentional context. But on Plato's view, "a something" cannot be deflected or qualified: it must always refer to something that is. This, I suspect, is because Plato supposes that somethings are basic.

(This seems to follow a fortiori from 1.) So all somethings are taken to be things that are, even if not everything that is is a something. Being a something, on this account, may be a rather more specialized matter than just being.

> 3. The expression "a something" cannot be used on its own; instead it must refer to something that is.

"A something" always refers; and, the ES implies, it always refers successfully.[11] "A something" always hits the mark of something that is. Once again, the referring relation is understood transparently; there is a simple correspondence between the utterance "a something" and something out there in the world. What is more, the something out in the world (via 2) is determinately a something (not just being, but something that is).

> 4. To mention something is to mention one something.[12] The ES insists that being something and being one something amount to the same thing; (4) is a central assumption in his argument.

> 5. So "something" signifies one, "somethings" signifies more than one.

"Something," therefore, is both a referring and a *counting* expression; and it has, built into it, the assumption that in the singular, it corresponds to a singular thing out there.

> 6. So someone who utters the expression "no something" mentions nothing.

Why? This move turns on the earlier point about counting (again, clearer in Greek).[13] If "something" signifies one (or in the plural, many), "not something" signifies not (one or many) (via 4 and 5). So "not something" mentions neither one nor many; it gives us no count at all. How are we to express that? Perhaps by using the expression "not one" (*mēden*) as shorthand for "not any countable item or items," no individual at all. "Nothing," in (6), is a thoroughly healthy negative existential quantifier *over individuals*. No sleight of hand here.

> 7. But someone who mentions "nothing" says nothing at all, fails to make sense.

This is the dangerous move in the argument. Why should uttering "nothing" be senseless? Suppose I am trying to say "nothing is law that is not reason." Is my attempt always doomed? Or suppose I want to conduct a logic lesson:

---

[11] This, at any rate, is the way Plato might express it. He might be more sympathetic to a modern view of "something" as a quantifier if he claimed that all reference is reference to a something. My thanks to Keith Hossack here.

[12] This point and its sequel are clearer in an inflected language. Contrast Cornford's emendation of *Soph.* 239a3, *Plato's Theory of Knowledge*, p. 207, and see M. Frede's remarks, "Bemerkungen."

[13] It is worth comparing here the pun made by Democritus (fr. 155), who was as aware as the ES of the etymology of οὐδὲν/μηδέν. Democritus glosses as "not-thing," the ES as "not-one."

"There is nothing such that it comes out of nothing." Must I give up and go home? Does the ES prohibit my use of the expression "nothing" altogether?

Surely not. The argument so far has turned on the assumptions made at (3) and (4) that we are dealing not with any old being out there in the world, but specifically with *somethings*, and in particular with the sort of somethings that can be directly mentioned in the way outlined in the opening move (1). We might imagine the ES making his point in this way: "All speech, to get off the ground, must start with a something (or some somethings). Reference, that is, is fundamental to successful speech; speech that fails of reference is failed speech.[14] But reference is a tricky business. To refer, you simply must get hold of a countable something (one or many). To refer, first catch an individual. Any expression that tries to refer without corresponding to an individual is simple nonsense." What this amounts to is a strong claim about a necessary condition for successful talk—that it must contain successful reference. To talk, begin with *basic individuals*.

Now argument B:

1. Something that is can be added to something that is.

The ES seems to be talking about the attribution of a property[15] to something. This is legitimate, he suggests, when both object and property are things that are. But

2. Something of the things that are cannot be attributed to what is not.

Why not? Perhaps, as at the beginning of argument A, the ES is suggesting that to attribute something that is to what is not is a contradiction? But the solution to the puzzle suggests a more complex reason. For the final analysis of falsehood shows that what is not can sensibly be attributed to what is; but it still insists that what is cannot be attributed to what is not (*Soph.* 262e ff.).[16] If the problem here were merely a contradiction, then the solution should allow *both* what is not to be attributed to what is and what is to be attributed to what is not. What happens here, I suspect, is that at (2) the ES makes a superficial point about the appearance of contradiction in mixing being with not-being (and echoes the first move of argument A), while the real work of the argument is done in what follows. As in A, the ES denies that there can be a meaningful sentence that has "what is not" in the subject position, because "what is not" refers to no basic individual and because every meaningful sentence must in the first place refer to some basic individual. Sentences that attribute what is not to what is (false judgments on the analysis of *Soph.* 262e ff.) are not, on this account, ruled out.

[14] That this is his point is confirmed by the solution to these puzzles at 262e.

[15] See ch. 8, sec. 5 on the scope of this discussion; the property that is being ascribed is called "something" (where the preceding argument had used "something" of the object to which the property is ascribed). This, I think, does not affect the reading I am offering; the question whether properties are individuals remains open.

[16] See Macdowell, "Falsehood," on the asymmetry of the solution.

But then a better analysis of (2) is available. What is cannot be attributed to what is not for the reasons stated in A—"what is not" cannot licitly appear in the subject position in a sentence. And then further consequences will follow.

> 3. If anything, number is of the things that are.

> 4. But number (unity or plurality) cannot be attributed to what is not.

This is, of course, a conclusion reached at A. But it is formulated here in a rather different way. At A, the claim about number was that any basic item to which we can refer must, *eo ipso*, be a countable individual. Now, by contrast, number is understood as something attributed to the basic object of reference, a property, albeit a fundamental property, attributed to an object:

> 5. It is impossible to utter or to conceive "what is not" or "what are not" without number.

After all, we can distinguish between singular, "what is not," and plural, "what are not"; those expressions bring number along with them.

> 6. For when we say "what are not," we try to imply plurality.

Notice the difference between this claim, that to use the expression "what are not" is to attempt to add the property of number to our subject, and A4, that something is one something.

> 7. When we say "what is not," we try to imply singularity.
> 8. So[17] what cannot be fitted to what is not.

The argument has shown, then, that when "what is not" appears in the subject position in some putative sentence, the sentence starts meaninglessly and ends up saying nothing about its absent subject. When what is not is considered in itself, it cannot be mentioned, thought or described.

Arguments A and B are connected; but they are not the same argument.[18] Argument B is presented as the greater problem (perhaps because it generates the self-refutation that follows at *Soph*. 238d ff.);[19] but it uses the argument of A to reach its conclusion. Yet it may be difficult to see how the arguments differ at all; in both cases, the ES appears to be arguing directly to the unmentionability of what is not from its failure to be one.

The ES opened his discussion with some programmatic remarks (*Soph*. 237c1–4):[20] "Suppose that without being contentious or playing games, one

---

[17] I take καὶ μὴν at *Soph*. 238c5 to introduce a strong assertion at the end of the argument. It picks up the opening gambit, (2), but reasserts it, now properly grounded.

[18] On Owen's reading of the first puzzles, "Not-Being," the first (about "what is not" as subject) collapses into the second (about how we can predicate anything of what is not), despite the clear change of tack at 238a2.

[19] Arguments A and B conclude by attributing properties to what is not, namely the properties of unmentionability and indescribability. But that very operation is ruled out by [B].

[20] Programmatic I take them to be, since they anticipate the complex structure of the argument—reflecting (1) the problem of reference (ποῖ χρὴ ἐπιφέρειν); (2) the problem of

of us had to answer thoughtfully and in earnest whither this name, what is not, is to be applied, how do we think that he would answer? *To what thing and of what kind* would he apply the expression and show it to someone who wanted to know?" (my emphasis).

There will turn out to be a difference between considering *to what thing* the expression "what is not" refers (argument A) and worrying about *what kind* it is (argument B). So from the beginning the argument was set up to investigate both "something" and "such" (*Soph.* 237c2); and that is just what happens. The first argument looks at how what is not can figure as a *something*. The second shows how, if it fails to be a something, it can have any "*such*" said of it, even the most basic of all (that is, number); so it itself fails to be such-and-such. The central claim is the thesis that being a something entails being, in the primary case, *one something*; and it is the failure of what is not to meet this basic requirement that makes it unsuitable either to be the referent of a name or to be expressed as the subject of a predication.

Now consider the way in which the notion of "one something" is deployed here. In both arguments, being one something is basic. But in the first argument, being one something is basic to reference (one something is *just one*); while in the second, being one, albeit still primary, is treated as the fundamental *property* of something that is anything at all. Thus, the contrast betwen the two arguments corresponds to a contrast between an object (in itself) and a property (held by the object), and further to a contrast in speech between subject and predicate terms. The argument concludes that what is not cannot figure just as subject; nor can it figure as subject with predicates. Both possibilities are ruled out by the failure of "what is not" to be an individuating expression, and the impossibility of a nonbeing to be an individual at all.

This failure of "what is not" to figure in discourse at all is, of course, founded on the denial of being to what is not. But the argument turns, not on being, nor yet on questions of existence, but on questions of individuation. Being an individual is what is basic for speech, discourse, and understanding because the interesting thing about being is being an individual. "Being is being something or other"[21] all right, but in the primary and basic sense *being is being one something*. This assumption is the driving force of the rest of the dialogue.

2. BEING

The two-stage argument about not-being has a companion piece in the discussion of being. The project is to investigate the early thinkers to discover "how

---

predication (ἐπὶ ποῖον); and (3) the problem of communication, of talking about what is not. This is compounded in the sequel where the ES points out that the puzzles are themselves self-refuting. Argument [A] does not begin until *Soph.* 237c7: "well, then, this at least is clear . . ."

[21] Owen's famous slogan; cf. Owen, "Not-Being," "Snares of Ontology."

many and of what sort are the things that are" (*posa kai poia ta onta esti*, *Soph.* 242c5–6). As with the puzzles about what is not, there is a dual view of the problem: we need to be able to *count* the things that are (compare argument A) and to *say what they are like* (compare argument B). The ontologies, as I shall call them, cover monism, pluralism, materialism, and idealism (244b–249d). The discussions of particular ontological views can be understood quite generally as a collection of arguments about being in general— "what do you mean when you utter the word 'is'? (244a5). But, as we shall see, "being" always means "being something or other."

MONISM

In the first place, the problem is *counting* what is (*Soph.* 243d–e)—how many things are there? We start with the limiting case, "there is just one"—monism.

1. If monism is true, there is just one.[22] If monism is true, there is something that is. What is the relation between "is" and "one"? Are they two names for the same thing? Can there be two names, in a monistic system? Worse still, it looks as if monism will not allow even one name. For the name and what it names must either be different from each other or the same as each other. If they are different, there are two things, not one. If they are the same, then the name either names nothing, or it is the name of a name, and nothing else.[23] And "one," which is the name of one, will itself be one being (the one being of the name).[24]

Consider the similarity between this and argument A about not-being. The problem is how anything that *is one something* can be understood or mentioned, if being one is basic or fundamental or even—as the monists affirm— exhaustive. If being one is basic, then such a one must appear in subject position as one. But if it is one, and is represented as the subject of a sentence, then how is it related to the name that represents it in the sentence? To name it results in one of two things: either naming multiplies it, by superadding the

[22] Notice here again the complete use of "one"—the monist's one is just one. Compare the monism of the *Timaeus*; see ch. 6, sec. 2.

[23] Cf. Owen, "Eleatic Questions," p. 74.

[24] See *Soph.* 244b–d. There is a huge problem with the text here. Cornford, *Plato's Theory of Knowledge*, p. 222, notes that the closing difficulty, 244d11–12, is textually tricky, and deletes it, on the grounds that the final remark is otiose: "The dilemma stated in the Stranger's last two speeches is complete. It has been shown that the very existence of a name is inexplicable, whether it be distinct from the thing or identical with it. This argument applies equally to the name 'real' and to the name 'one,' and there is no need for any special application of it to the name 'one.'" Of course it is precisely the assumption that being, rather than individuation, is basic that I question here. Instead, I argue that the final speech of the argument is rightly about one rather than the name, because being one is treated as basic. After all, such an argument turns up elsewhere in Plato (*Parm.* 137c ff.), and its point is successful here against a monist who might claim that a name is not anything after all. On the contrary, argues the ES, a name must be something—and if so, then one something . . . and the argument can start up all over again. Of the textual variants, I prefer the following: καὶ τὸ ἕν γε, ἑνὸς ὄνομα ὄν καὶ τοῦτο ὀνόματος αὖ τὸ ἓν ὄν—translated as "and as for 'one,' which is the name of one, this too is the one being of the name."

name to the one it names, or, if that is forbidden, naming fails to mention it altogether. This problem arises most clearly for monists, but it is a quite general problem for anyone who wants to give *a something* primacy. Monists may want to mention their one; pluralists may suppose that one something can be signified as the subject of a sentence. But if either party wants to understand *one something as basic*, then naming it will either be secondary to it (so that its name will not represent it as basic) or irrelevant to it (the name will fail to mention this something altogether). Neither way (the argument supposes) can something basic figure in sentences as subject.

2. The whole (all there is) must be either the same as the one, or different. Suppose, as perhaps a monist must, that the whole and the one are the same (that is, the one exhausts all there is).[25] A whole has parts, and so it will have the property of divisibility throughout. But what is just one (*auto to hen*—a monist's one) cannot have such a property, since it must be partless in order to be truly one. And yet if the one is (just) one, and so not the same as the whole, then it cannot be the one of the monistic hypothesis, which exhausts all there is. So the one is thus not whole (because it has the property of being "just one"); but yet it is the whole (via the monistic thesis). Then what is (the one) will fall short of itself. So what is will be something that is not, and everything will be more than the one, since what is and the whole are distinct. And even if we simply deny that there is a whole, what is is still enmeshed in not being, and it is even denied becoming. For becoming implies becoming a whole, and that is ruled out. But we cannot even claim that anything is not a whole, since anything must have some quantity, and thus be a whole. These and many other similar difficulties arise, whether we postulate being to be two some-things or one something (*Soph.* 244d–245d).

The ES's tactic here echoes the second argument, B, against not-being in discussing the properties of the subject, so that the pair of arguments against monism is a companion piece to the earlier arguments against not-being.[26] Moreoever, the ES's closing remark emphasizes the generality of the paired arguments; once again the attack on a specific thesis can be seen to have universal application. This argument, like the second puzzle about not-being, reinstates the target of the first argument (in this case, an austere one) in order to show that it can have no properties, and nothing can be said of it. The austere unity of the monistic one precludes its having complex properties; but something like that cannot be the sole object in a monistic cosmology, because it is incompatible with any cosmological ideas (the whole, all there is, every-thing). But even without explicit monistic assumptions, something that is austerely one cannot have attributes, since they would pluralize it, or involve it in being what it is not (hence, the suggestion that what is just one will fall

[25] It is worth comparing here Timaeus's argument about the exhaustive unity of the cosmos, discussed above, in ch. 6, sec. 2. If I am right in thinking that this argument is meant to pose a metaphysical puzzle, its echo of the *Timaeus* might encourage us to believe that the *Timaeus* was supposed to be metaphysically puzzling, too—and not cosmological dogma. Cf. ch. 6, sec. 6.
[26] Consider, for example, the emphasis on the πάθη of what is one, 245a1, b4, b7, c1.

short of itself by failing to be a whole, *Soph.* 245c). Nor could it coexist with something else (so that there are two), because the being implicit in its unity will thus be contradicted by all the things which it is not (cf. 245c8–9). Nor indeed, could such a thing come into being, since that too would involve it in having properties such as being a whole (245d). Such an item, that is, cannot be even considered in relation to anything else or as having any properties at all; such an austere individual is so austere as to be impossible.

If, then, we postulate something as one, on the austere model of the monistic hypothesis, it can neither be named, nor have anything said of it. The monistic hypothesis is itself unstateable; and it is an object lesson in the difficulties of postulating basic, austere individuals.

PLURALISM

Pluralism, however, fares no better. The ES next stages a battle of the gods and the giants, the idealists and the materialists. Both parties reject monism. The materialists deny that there are any but material entities—"being is being body." The idealists are the friends of the forms, who distinguish, as Plato himself did in the middle period, between the changeable and the changeless, the perceptible and what is accessible to reason. For them, only the changeless forms are real, and everything else merely becomes—"being is being itself by itself." The argument forces a compromise between the contestants.

Against the materialists the ES urges a counterexample: must they not agree that animate creatures have souls, and that souls are real, even if they are not physical entities? What criterion, then, can the materialists offer for "being" that will accommodate both physical objects and souls, and yet retain their original intuition that what there is *is what we can touch and what touches us* (*Soph.* 246a10)? This intuition is cashed out, not so much as the view that everything is made of physical stuff, nor yet as the view that everything is perceptible, but rather as the view that we can only say that something is when it acts or is affected. So the mark of being, on that view, is power—power to act or to be acted upon.

The conduct of this argument, if it is understood to be against gross materialists, is unexpected, to say the least. First of all, it seems wildly improbable that any gross materialist would concede that there are souls, since that concession is lethal to his insistence on physicality. Second, it is hard to see why the ES does not move from the concession about soul to a direct refutation of the materialist premise, that whatever there is can be squeezed between our hands (*Soph.* 247c6). Why take the indirect route of arguing that "power" is the mark of being? The solution to this interpretative puzzle lies in the nature of the materialists' assumption. Their argument rests not so much on the assumption that all there is is physical, but on the prior claim, that being must make a difference to what surrounds it:[27] "They [sc. the earthborn

---

[27] This assumption, after all, is shared, at least dialectically, by Zeno, DK29B2.

giants] drag everything down to earth from the heavens and from what is invisible, grasping stones and trees simply, with their hands. For touching all such things as these, they affirm that there is only whatever presents any resistance or contact,[28] defining the same thing as body and being" (*Soph.* 246a7–b1).

So being must either be something that we can affect or that can affect us.[29] This is construed by the giants as an argument for the sole existence of physical body.[30] However, as soon as they concede the contrast between animate and inanimate things, they must widen the scope of their criterion, to include the actions and the passions of animate things. But what that means, of course, is that they must grant (as obvious) that animate things *do* things. To accommodate that obvious fact, they need to focus, for being, not so much on body, but on power—the power to act and suffer.

If we construe the argument that way, its sequence begins to make sense; and so does its connection with the argument against the idealists. The materialists have been brought to admit that what we say about the things in the material world is not limited to their strictly material aspects, since they can be seen to act and to suffer. Put this another way: sentences that describe the physical world describe not only the physical affections of bodies ("water is wet," "porridge is lumpy") but also the less obviously material actions of animate bodies ("owls hoot," "philosophers wander"). In grammar, we need verbs as well as adjectives to modify the subjects of sentences. Of course to make that admission is not to give up materialism altogether (the grosser giants have still not admitted justice or intelligence to their ontology, *Soph.* 247c5) but to allow for a sophisticated materialism that fits the observable data of the interactions of the physical world. That materialism focuses on the affections of things, and identifies the things by means of their affections; hence, the conclusion of the argument, that anything that has any power to act or be affected is—"being is being able."

The ES uses a similar strategy against the idealists, again by challenging the qualifications they apply or deny to the things that are. In the case of the idealists, they say that things that are are limited to the things that are *not* affected, but just are as they are, themselves by themselves. Whatever is affected, they argue, is changeable or even in flux, and can only be said to become (whatever it becomes). The materialists are wrong, therefore, to allow "the power of acting and being acted upon" to be the criterion of being, since in fact that is a criterion of becoming, and must be excluded from being altogether, in order that being should not become ridden with flux.

---

[28] The Greek has προσβολὴ καὶ ἐπαφή. προσβολὴ (LSJ gives "means of approaching," but the original sense is "attack") suggests that the object acts upon whatever comes up against it, ἐπαφή suggests that it can be touched, is passive to whatever comes up against it.

[29] The point of "touching and being touched" is not about perception but about affecting and being affected; despite Cornford's "the real is tangible body," *Plato's Theory of Knowledge*, p. 251.

[30] Note the inferential γὰρ at *Soph.* 246a9.

Against this view, the ES urges the conclusion that nothing, even austere intelligible bodies understood in the idealists' way, remains unaffected. Even becoming known, he suggests, affects what is known;[31] if we postulate austere objects of knowledge, they cannot function as objects of knowledge without sacrificing some of their austerity to become qualified.

Once again, the focus of this argument needs examination. It can be construed as a crude attack on the airy-fairy notions of any idealist—"surely any idea is so remote as to be incomprehensible." However, the ES's strategy is better constructed than that. He ties his attack on the idealists to the concession he won from the materialists, by showing how the idealists reject the criterion of being—that it is the power to act or be acted upon. They reject the criterion because they think it conflicts with the claim that being is "always in the same respects at the same time" (*Soph.* 248a12). From this they are forced to infer that "what absolutely is" has no share in motion, life, soul, or intelligence—so that it is "austere and holy"—and impossibly inaccessible (248e). But then, of course, the idealists' position amounts to a denial of what is wrung from the materialists—they deny that "being is being able," and stick instead to "just being." The charge that their entities are austere is the charge that they cannot be qualified in any way at all; they can only, therefore, be the subjects of sentences with no predicate. The extreme version of idealism turns out to be absurd. In the end, then, giants and gods must make peace and allow that what is must be qualifiable, but not so qualifiable as to be in impossible flux. If being must be determinable, then "being both moves and is at rest" (249d). Being is being something or other.

The ontologies conclude with a challenge. The ES has mounted a comprehensive attack against monism and pluralism, which contemplates the different answers to how something can be something or other. Theories that suggest that something is just one (occupies the subject position in a sentence) fail to explain how the something can be one. Theories that tackle "being something," from the perspective of the properties that something can have, run the risk of failing sensibly or comprehensibly to limit the properties themselves. How can we compromise—the closing dilemma asks—between total flux and hopeless austerity? How can what is be something or other without being either flux-ridden or so austere as to be unmentionable? If we allow something to have some properties, not all, can we restrict the proper-   'n order to preserve its identity) without producing an entity too austere .nention? S meho· · must show th ·t ·hings are both fixed (so as to be individuals) and changir (so as to have ·r ,perties). Things must both move and rest.

Motion and rest, however, are not to be understood in a crude or simplistic manner; the ES is not merely insisting that the objects in the world must change, but in a moderate way. On the contrary, motion and rest have been defined by the battle of the gods and giants in a thoroughly technical sense.

---

[31] I have discussed this argument, and a similar one at *Crat.* 439–40, in Mackenzie, "*Cratylus.*"

Motion matters to the giants because it expresses the "power to act and be acted upon"; but that power represents the way in which the objects of their world interact, are related to each other, make up a connected collection of entities. Motion should matter to the idealists for the same reason; without it the objects of their world are hopelessly remote from any relationship with us (and that, as the *Parmenides* pointed out, makes senseless the theory of forms). Rest, on the other hand, matters to the idealists because it suggests that there is stability in the objects of their world, so that those objects can be considered in themselves. Likewise, rest should matter to the giants, for without it their world collapses into flux, and nothing remains itself by itself (and that, as the *Theaetetus* pointed out, means that nothing is anything at all, and discourse disappears).

The contrast between motion and rest turns out to have little to do with locomotion and everything to do with identity.

Motion is a catchall for the affections of things. The affections of things, and their properties, are determined, as the materialists show, by their relations with other things. On such an account, "motion" identifies objects in a context of other objects; motion is *difference and relative identification*. I have called this individuation from *without*.[32] Thus, for example, we might try to count our individuals by marking them off from others: the counting, therefore, will depend on our understanding their difference from others, and so on their relations to others. So here, objects seem to be determined by their properties and affections.

Rest, on the other hand, identifies objects in themselves. The idealists' insistence on the austere nature of the forms depended on the forms remaining unaffected in themselves. So rest is *sameness and absolute identification*. I have called this individuation from *within*,[33] whereby we may identify something by looking to its internal coherence or unity, its identity with itself. But these "objects in themselves" seem thus to be entirely separate from any properties they might be thought to have. So there must be a compromise between rest and motion, a reconciliation of objects in themselves and their properties. Moreover, the final demand of the ontologies will be that the ES should show that the entities in anyone's world are *both self-identical and different from others*; that any individual is one from without and from within. Only then will individuation, which is basic for any discourse, be possible.

3. "To Be" Or

All the arguments of the first part of the *Sophist* display certain common assumptions that we have seen before in Plato's arguments about "being something." First of all, there is a pairing of arguments (or sequences of

[32] Cf. ch. 6, sec. 2.
[33] Cf. ch. 6, sec. 2.

arguments) according to how they treat "something" (or "nothing") as just whatever it is, or as the possessor of properties. This may be understood, epistemologically, as the difference between trying to understand a something before we tackle an understanding of its properties, and trying to understand it as determined by its properties. Or it can be understood grammatically—as the contrast between looking at the subject of the sentence before the predicate (can the subject be understood without the predicates?) and looking at the subject of the sentence as specified by its predicates (is there then anything to which the predicates apply?).

The close connection between ontological and linguistic issues in Plato's account of the problem has urged commentators to find a solution in the semantic or logical assumptions of the dialogue. Perhaps the problems of the sophist can be dissolved by observing an ambiguity in the verb "to be"; or perhaps the dangers of turning negations into nothings can be prevented by distinguishing between the negative *mēdamōs*, "not in any way," which expresses a contrary, and the more innocuous negation *mē*, "not" (something or other), which merely points to the contradictory of the negated term.[34]

Consider first of all the suggestion that the dialogue uncovers, as a means to solving the initial puzzles, the ambiguity between two, or perhaps three, senses of the Greek verb "to be."[35] This may involve a semantic contrast between sentences where the verb "to be" expresses.[36]

1. existence—"Pheidippides is";
2. predication—"The runner is fast";
3. identity—"Pheidippides is the first marathon runner."

Or it may involve a syntactic contrast, between complete and incomplete uses of the verb to be:

1. complete—"Socrates (just) is";
2. incomplete—"Socrates is (something or other)."

The complete use of the verb may be thought to express existence (or perhaps truth); and the incomplete use may be thought to span the predicative and the identitative uses. But the various distinctions overlap uncomfortably. First of all, the syntactic contrast may not represent an ambiguity at all, merely an elliptical way of talking.[37] It may be, that is, that the expression "Socrates is" is shorthand for "Socrates is something or other," so that the complete use turns out to be an incomplete one in disguise. So the mere appearance of a complete usage may not of itself constitute evidence for the semantically

---

[34] Owen, "Not-Being."

[35] On the viability of this approach to εἶναι, see Kahn's exhaustive survey of its use, *The Verb "to Be,"* and compare M. Frede, *Prädikation*.

[36] There is a further complication here that the expression τὰ ὄντα may signify "truths," τὰ μὴ ὄντα "falsehoods"; on the veridical use of εἶναι, and its tendency to bridge various ambiguous expressions, see Kahn, *The Verb "to Be."*

[37] Compare here Brown's discussion, "Being in the *Sophist*."

complete claim of "existence."[38] Furthermore, the ambiguity that may be thought to lurk within the incomplete use (semantically, between the "is" of predication and the "is" of identity) may in fact be an illusion; perhaps, on general grounds, it could be argued that any clear distinction between having a property (such as yellow) and having an identity (Cicero's being Tully) is unwarranted and heavily loaded with metaphysical assumptions.[39] In short, there is nothing canonical about the claim that there is any such ambiguity; it must be seen to appear in the text before we can be reassured that these contrasts have any significance in our understanding of the Greek verb "to be."

So does Plato get the verb "to be" muddled up? Are the puzzles of the *Sophist* vitiated by ambiguity and equivocation?

Owen argued that they are not—for two important reasons.[40] First, the Parity Assumption demands that we explain being in the same way as not-being. But if the puzzle about not-being takes "not-being" to mean nonexistence, then not-being remains irredeemable (even if we can explain being as existence). The parity assumption is then broken. So the opening puzzle cannot just be about nonentities. Second, the solution must solve the puzzles, without trivializing them. But the solution definitely treats "is" as the "is" of predication (and perhaps it sorts out identity as well).[41] So (if all this is about interpreting "is"), the puzzles must also be about the "is" of predication. But if they are, they simply look silly. (Why should anyone, even Theaetetus, deny that confronted with Kiri te Kanawa I may say "not my mother," and tell the truth? Or that, confronted with a patch of purple, I may say "not puce" and be both right and sensible?) So all this is not about interpreting "is," but about "not." The initial puzzles work, Owen argued, by treating the sentence "*x* is not" as denying any properties to *x*.[42] The "not" inhibits any predication, or any completing of "is," because the "not" should be understood as "not at all." Thus, when I say "*x* is not," I mean "*x* is not anything at all"; but then I can neither mention *x* nor predicate anything of it—and my discourse collapses. Similarly, and with parity, my claims about "*x* is" cannot be understood either, because I cannot understand how to complete the "is"—since I cannot prohibit any completion, negation being denied me. The puzzles (wrongly) treat "not" as an expression that introduces the contrary and not the contradictory of its complement; and the solution sorts all that out by distinguishing between contraries and contradictories (*Soph.* 257b). This brings with it, of course, a better understanding of predication; but predication is not the villain of the argument in the puzzles.

Owen's interpretation is both telling and plausible. "Not" is undoubtedly a

---

[38] Perhaps the senses are somehow "fused"; cf., e.g., Furth, "Eleatic Ontology."

[39] Cf. Mates, "Identity and Predication in Plato."

[40] Owen, "Not-Being"; although Owen is rather keen on the identity/predication confusion.

[41] Cf. here the entire argument of *Soph.* 257–58, and the discussion of the ἀντίθεσις of being to being.

[42] Cf. τὸ μηδαμῶς ὄν at *Soph.* 237b7.

tricky customer, and one that Plato will now serve (*Soph.* 257b, 256e).[43] But does Owen's interpretation make enough of the complexity of the puzzles? Why offer two different arguments about not-being (the arguments I have characterized as A and B) if both will claim that something of which nothing can be said is unmentionable? Why emphasize the problem of being *one*? There still seems to be a lack of fit between the solution as a whole and the puzzles as a whole, for the puzzles include the ontologies. Why (apart from philosophical joie de vivre) does the ES embark on these complex puzzles, when his real difficulty is "not"? And the long discussion of the "great kinds" (the *megista genē*) seems unnecessarily tortuous if all that needs to be established is the difference between "opposite" and "other," asserted at 257b. "Not" is not enough.

Owen's objection to locating the problem in the ambiguity of "is" seems well founded. His further claim, that the "is" throughout is incomplete, is borne out by the arguments themselves. After all, the first two puzzles work not by examining the contradiction of saying that is not (simpliciter) is, but in analyzing how impossible it is to understand *what* the thing that is not is said to be or not to be. In other words, as we have seen, the problem concerns the difficulty in understanding "being something or other (or not)." But the arguments themselves show that the main force of Plato's difficulty is neither "is," nor "not," but "something or other."

This account of what is going on in the first half of the dialogue implies that the syntactic ambiguity is missing from the text; since, in fact, all the uses of the verb "to be" are, overtly or covertly, incomplete—being is *always* being something or other. What then of the semantic ambiguity that is compatible with the incomplete "is"—namely, the contrast between the "is" of predication and the "is" of identity?

4. IDENTITY AND UNITY

The ES advances a further problem about being at *Soph.* 251a–c: the challenge of the late-learners. How do we apply many names to one thing?[44] After all, we attribute colors and shapes and sizes and values to individual men:

> Eleatic Stranger: In all of these cases, and a myriad others, we do not merely say that he is a man, but that he is good and countless other things; and so on for everything else by the same reasoning we posit each thing to be one and yet say that it is many and the subject of many names.
>
> Theaetus: True.
>
> Eleatic Stranger: Hence, I think, we have prepared a feast for the young and for the latelearners among the old.[45] For they immediately insist that it is impossible

---

[43] Cf. Macdowell's elaboration of Owen; Macdowell, "Falsehood."

[44] This problem has appeared before in the dialogue, in the confrontation with Parmenides, 244a ff.

[45] Notice here the recurring theme of the young and their interest in puzzles; cf. *Phdr.* passim on the relation between jokes, youth, and education; *Phil.* 15d ff.; and *Pol.* 269d.

for many to be one or one to be many; and thus they enjoy themselves by not allowing us to say that man is good, but (only) the good is good, man is man. (*Soph.* 251a10–c2)

What is the late-learners' objection to ordinary ways of speaking? There are, I think, three different possibilities:

1. *The identity/predication (I/P) confusion.* They complain that there is only one legitimate use of the verb "to be" (namely the identitative) and rule out the pluralistic consequences of predication.

2. *Sentential complexity.* They do not allow us to do more than label what we have in front of us. Confronted with a man, all we may say is "man," and never "good."

3. *One/many.* The prohibition is not so much on the legitimacy of certain expressions as it is on treating items posited to be "each one" as also many.

The text suggests clearly enough that the late-learners are worried about ones and manies; there is no suggestion that they are attacking the verb "to be" (conspicuously inconspicuous here), and little to allow us to conclude that they disliked sentential complexity. But then, perhaps their complaint is just silly. Why should not one man have many parts, a myriad properties, a host of colors and shapes (at least in different places or at different times)? After all, in parallel passages elsewhere,[46] Plato appears to dismiss as a pseudoproblem the claim that no individual in particular can have many properties. How then could this one/many problem be taken seriously here—seriously enough to provoke the complex solution that is to follow? Perhaps the problem can only be worrisome if it is connected to a further thesis that the verb "to be" only identifies, or that words can only label. Accordingly, it has been argued, both the issue of syntactic complexity (*Soph.* 251d ff.) and the I/P difficulty (255e ff.) emerge resolved in what follows.

Let us, however, reconsider the seriousness of the one/many problem. It appears here at the end of a long discussion of the nature of reference and predication and of the status of individual objects and their properties. It is indeed obvious (what the late-learners and the mischievous children of the *Philebus* deny, but the young Socrates of the *Parmenides* allows) that there are individual particulars in the world that are both one and many. Such items will be "each one" and at the same time many. But by this stage in the dialogue we have no way of understanding how this might be so. The complex puzzles about being and not-being have attacked both our identification of a subject and the attribution of properties to it. This attack did not take the form of a play on the difference between the "is" of identity and the "is" of predication. Instead, we were asked two connected questions.

1. How can we refer to something without, by the very act of reference, multiplying our somethings? If we name it, do we add the name to it? Then is there still only one? If we ascribe a property to it, is the property a part of it, so that it has as many parts as properties, and is itself many?

[46] Notably *Parm.* 129, *Phil.* 14d ff.

2. In the *Parmenides*, Plato suggested that "plural properties pluralize." How can properties be attributed to a subject unless we already have some understanding of the unity of the subject to which we are granting the properties?

Consider the problem this way. Any sentence, we might argue, has to start with a subject; and that subject—we might further suppose—must be, in the most common scenario, an individual particular (like a man). How do we determine that the particular is an individual? By claiming that it is "a one." But then how is that claim compatible either with naming it at all—(the historical Parmenides' problem) or with attributing properties to it? Granted that we must attribute properties to individual particulars, how can the operation be done and still allow that they are indeed individuals?

This, consistent with the preceding arguments, is the real nub of the one/many problem. However, it has obvious links with the other interpretations of the late-learners' difficulty. First of all, the problem of the individual particular could be interpreted as a difficulty about understanding how we may identify something, and then predicate other expressions of it. In that case, the problem is about being—about being something or other. But the difficulty as I have formulated it arises not with *being* but rather with *something or other*. "Something or other" may represent what something is in the sense that this is what individuates it; or it may mention what it has—in the sense that this is some property it possesses. The contrast between these two aspects of "something or other" could be understood as an ambiguity in the verb "to be"; but disambiguating the verb will not solve the problem. For the problem is not about muddling one sentence with another, nor about prohibiting some kinds of speech in order to prevent such a muddle (as the late-learners may be thought to do). The problem is about how we may individuate any particular item; and how, having done so, we may further attribute properties to it. The problem is neither semantic, in the first instance, nor syntactic; it is a problem about our understanding of what there is, and only thereafter about how to express truths about what there is.

Some passages in the *Parmenides* appeared to conflate identity and predication. Reflection on the *Sophist* might confirm my different view.[47] Recall the *Parmenides*' discussions of sameness and difference: (a) *Parmenides* 139b4–139e6 and (b) *Parmenides* 146a9—147b8.

The first (a) assumes that the one is "just one." In that case it cannot be either other than itself or the same as anything else, since then it would not be "just one." But for the same reasons (that it is just one), it cannot be other than another, or the same as itself, in case it risks being not one, but many. For something is not the same by virtue of being one, but it is one by virtue of being one. Something that is just one, then, is nothing but one.

The opening move of this argument depends on our understanding what

---

[47] See ch. 4, sec. 3. And the connection between the late-learners and the *Parmenides* arguments might be warranted by the echo of the late-learners' position and the problem of sameness and difference at *Euthyd.* 301b–c.

the one is (namely, just one), not on understanding what being is for it. If just one is what the one is, then it cannot be many. But then it cannot be understood to have any identity at all—all it is, is "just one." This, indeed, looks like the conclusion of the late-learners, expressed in terms of what more one might say about (what more might be true of) what is just one than its being one. Without some way of expressing its being something or other without pluralizing it, we cannot identify it at all.

The second argument (b) begins instead from common-sense assumptions about the relations of identity: that everything is either the same as, or different from, anything else—unless they are related as part to whole. Since the one is neither a part of itself, nor different from itself, it must be the same as itself. But if (from a previous argument) it is in itself and in something else, then it will be different in some respect from itself; and then itself will be different from it. Whatever is not one is different from the one, and the one is different from whatever is not one. But difference implies change; and so it cannot be a property of the things that are (since that would be for difference to remain in the same place and cease to change). So difference is a property of neither the one nor what is not one. So they are not different by virtue of difference, nor by virtue of themselves. But then they cannot be different (but must be the same).

Once again, this argument does not turn on the sense of the verb "to be," but on the consequences of saying that something is something or other— even in terms of the basic, universal relations of identity. To identify something, we say that it is same (as itself) or different (from something else). But how are those relations to be understood? If they are treated as properties of the something, then it becomes a hopeless collection of conflicting properties, none of which succeeed in identifying it at all. This conclusion does not follow from an I/P confusion, but from a failure to be able to account for the identity of a one. Either we give it no identity, as in (a), or all identities and any nonidentity, as in (b). Why should we be tempted to treat basic entities only in extreme ways either with intolerable restrictions or absurd license? We do so not because we have made a semantic mistake, but because we fail to understand the nature of the relations crucial to identity. Relations are here conceived as properties. Consequently, they both pluralize and confuse the relata—and that confusion may be the consequence of seeing relations as natural features of the real world.

So are these arguments just manifestations of the I/P confusion? Think about their logical structure. Both are reductiones ad absurdum; but these work dialectically by focusing attention on their premises. In both arguments, the premises are about the nature of identity claims: (a) offers an identity claim by virtue of the sheer austerity of the subject; and does so (b) by virtue of what can be attributed to the subject. Since both claims are about identity, the arguments should not merely reflect a contrast betwen identity statements and predications; instead, as we may now easily see, they offer a challenge. How can we individuate, or identify, individuals?

"Being is being something or other." But that slogan itself needs explaining.

Plato's fundamental problem lies in the question of how to understand the "something or other." He displays the prejudice that somethings or other may be hierarchically arranged; that is, some somethings are more basic than others. Then he needs to know what makes any of those somethings *a something*.

The passages I have discussed so far make it clear that he understood that puzzle in two different ways. First, he wants to understand how to *count* somethings, and to that end he supposes that the unit—one something—is basic (you start with one and work up to two; starting with none is abortive). That assumption about counting individuals clearly underlies both the *Sophist's* puzzles about not-being and the ontologies, since both display the prejudice that counting starts with a one. Second, he explores the *unity* or coherence of his basic individuals. But the expression "one," unlike the expression "is," appears to be semantically complete.[48] Plato is not, at least in these passages, allowing the Aristotelian possibility that "one" might be syncategorematic, a term that allows us to count only when it is further determined by the proper kind of count noun.[49] Nor, in these passages, does he suggest that the form or essence of a thing might provide the criteria for its individuation.[50] Rather, the unity of something is irreducibly basic, the primary feature of any something as such.

But this approach to the unity of basic entities risks incoherence, for two reasons:

1. Plato needs to explain how the *unity* that something has does not impair its being a unit. He needs to explode the pluralizing hypothesis that lurks in the assumption that unity, among other features, is a real property of a something.

2. He needs to be able to explain how such a something might have an *identity*, how we can understand this one as opposed to that one. The late-learners construed entities as austere units (and have been thought to be talking about identity as a consequence), and prohibited any analysis of their identity but a reiteration of their names. They disallow "being"; and they prohibit "separate," "from the others," and even "by itself" (*Soph.* 252c2–5). In insisting, that is, on an austere account of any one, they force us to have an austere account of its identity. And at that stage, as the ES points out in the discussion of the "communion of kinds" (the *koinōnia genōn*), they end up not being able to talk at all.

5. TALKING ABOUT SOMETHING OR OTHER

The claim that being is always being something or other is confirmed when we turn to Plato's parallel treatment of grammar and speech. The *Sophist*, after

---

[48] Cf. ch. 6, sec. 2.

[49] Cf. ch. 1, sec. 4.

[50] The template theory suggested at ch. 6, sec. 3.

all, is about the possibilities of discourse. If words correspond to things, then the word always mentions the "something or other" (whether in the subject or the predicate position). Do words always correspond to things?[51]

That certainly is the assumption of the *Sophist* until the confrontation with the late-learners. Thus, the puzzles about not-being turn on the claim that the expression "not-being" names something that just is not (I described this as a "transparent correspondence" between word and object). The ontologies confronted Parmenides with the impossibility of naming a monist's one, and the late-learners hinted that sentential complexity might be a dead duck. This seems to involve two separate claims:

1. Words correspond to things, so that all words function as names.

2. Meaning is exhausted by the naming process. Words *mean* just because they correspond to the things they name, and there are no other units of meaning than words; complexes of meaning are collections of units.

Semantic atomism of this type is a common-enough hypothesis in the late Platonic dialogues. It figures, after all, in the discussions of falsehood in the *Theaetetus.*[52] In that dialogue, Socrates was able to explain simple falsehoods as mismatches of the name with the nominatum,[53] but he was unable to explain complex mistakes ("7 + 5 = 11") for the reason, among others, that no account could be given of the ordering factor in the mistake. The *Cratylus*, likewise, assumes that meaning is piecemeal, as naming is (e.g., at *Crat.* 385a ff.).[54]

This view—that semantic atomism is true—has two consequences for present purposes. First of all, it confronts the monist's problem of just how the name (which picks out the thing for us, identifies it for us) can be said to correspond to the thing. Plato's argument against the monist suggested that the name either collapses into the thing (in that case, is it a name?) or else it is other than the thing (in which case, he argues, it has a dubious claim to identify the thing at all). Second, it confronts the problem, of the late-learners, of how anything more than the name of something could be used to establish the identity of the thing itself. The name is what names it properly. All else that is said of it (the late-learners aver) is improper and illicit. If, that is, there are problems about the relation of one thing and its name, there are many more problems about the relation between a thing and an indefinite number of descriptions.

Plato could have thought about this thus. There is a relation between names and things. But that relation is a real feature of the world (as are all relations on the naturalist view), and the relata are really characterized by that relation. If the nominatum is to remain what it was before it was named, it must remain

---

[51] Compare Nehamas's stronger, and stranger, suggestion that words correspond to forms; Nehamas, "Self-Predication." Cf. also Fine, "Naming," and Bestor, "Semantics."

[52] Cf. ch. 5, sec. 6; despite Cooper, "Sense-Perception," Fine, "Naming."

[53] Cf. Mackenzie, "*Cratylus*," but contrast Fine, "Naming."

[54] Cf. Ryle, "Atomism."

unaffected by the naming.[55] But it is not unaffected, if the name/nominatum relation is a real relation. How, then, can anything be named and still stay one something? Can we talk about ones at all?

In the *Cratylus*, Plato once again argues by dilemma. He approaches the question of how we are to communicate (name things, talk, teach others by naming and talking) by considering both the names and the nominata ("things," *pragmata*). "Things," Socrates eventually suggests (*Crat.* 439c ff.), are incommunicable because they are either in hopeless flux or so remote as to be unknowable. This is the familiar contrast between items that are characterized with extreme generosity and those that are utterly austere. But names are as troublesome as things. Compare two complementary arguments, the first against Hermogenes' Humpty-Dumpty conventionalism (*Crat.* 385a ff.), the second against Cratylus's crashing naturalism (*Crat.* 431a ff.).

Hermogenes has advanced the thesis that any name goes, for anyone who wants that name to name something. Socrates' counterargument is designed to show that this gross conventionalist account of naming will not do, because it results in the same sort of dialectical collapse as Protagoras's account of truth. To avoid such collapse, we must have some kind of natural connection between the name and what it names. In order to prevent everything being indeterminate, or hopelessly private, "it is clear that the things themselves have some kind of fixed being of their own, not relative to us, nor dragged upside down by us as we perceive them, but some being relative to themselves in themselves, as they are by nature" (*Crat.* 386d9–e4).

This insistence on the natural origin of a name carries two further assumptions with it. The first is that names have not only a meaning but also a truth value. Thus, Socrates can argue[56] that a sentence is true just if the words in it are true; likewise, a sentence is false just if the words in it are false. This produces the unpalatable conclusion that if we cannot show how words/names can be false, then we are robbed of falsehood altogether. The second assumption lurking here, of course, is the view that sentences are just strings of semantic atoms. In Socrates' modification of Hermogenes' view, these semantic atoms display the real nature of the nominata (whether they be nouns, which represent things, or verbs, which represent actions, *Crat.* 386e); and thus, on both sides of the semantic fence we have items that are conceived as simple elements, connected by a one-to-one correspondence. In that case, we may ask ourselves, are they communicable? If all there is to communication is semantic atomism, we may be stuck with a language that fails to account for sentential complexity at all. We are forced, perhaps, to live in the land of the late-learners.

The argument against Cratylus explores the relation between name and nominatum further, this time attacking the naturalist assumption. Cratylus

---

[55] Compare the argument about knowing forms; see above sec. 2, and ch. 3, sec. 7.

[56] See Schofield's argument, in "A Displacement in the Text of the *Cratylus*," that the text has been displaced here. This leaves my point unaffected.

has claimed that only the right names are true—and only those names are names at all, since every other attempt at naming is just banging on a brass pot, vain and useless (*Crat.* 430a). Just as paintings imitate their subjects, names are imitations of what they name. But the extreme naturalist claims further that only the right imitations count as the names of the things they name; otherwise, the name fails altogether. Then Socrates raises the objection the ES will bring against Father Parmenides. If names correctly imitate what they name, and otherwise do not name at all, then falsehood will be impossible (since names are the component parts of sentences). But how correct docs the imitation have to be? If there is room for some inaccuracy, then strong naturalism will have to give way, and some kind of error can be accommodated. If, on the other hand, there is no room for inaccuracy, then the name will become just another one of the things named ("Cratylus," if a sufficiently good imitation of Cratylus, will become another Cratylus, and we shall have two naturalist nuisances, not one). How then, can the name, conceived in a strict correspondence with the nominatum, tell us anything at all that the thing itself did not already communicate?

The underlying difficulty seems to be this. If something is an atom or a lump (whether it is an atom in the real world or a semantic atom), it is not susceptible to further description. Any relation it may be in (and names are necessarily in some relation to the nominata) is indescribable, just because the relata are themselves austerely conceived, as atoms. The problem of the lumps, that is, extends to the world of grammar. Worse still, the world of grammar shows up the problem of understanding things as atoms in their relation to other things of the same kind. If all words are semantic atoms, then sentences are strings of atoms, themselves not governed by any principle of order over and above the atoms themselves. This entails that the truth value of sentences is merely a result of the truth value of the component parts. In that case, unless truth and falsehood can be accounted for piecemeal (by allowing for false names or words), falsehood will collapse. If falsehood collapses, truth goes with it, and that is the end of dialectic.

If words are bits of sentences, are the wholes anything over and above a string of words? Suppose that sentences are made up of words—and even suppose that we see that it matters how they are ordered.[57] Is the ordering principle another bit of the sentence? In that case, that itself needs to be ordered—and so on. If on the other hand the ordering principle is not a part of the sentence, then what is it? Sentences need ordering relations; but can we understand the ordering relations of a sentence if we do not understand any other relations?

This then turns full circle. The problem about whether the syntax of a sentence is merely another part of the sentence is a direct echo of the problem about the pluralizing of an individual by its individuating characteristics. Suppose that a given sentence has a string of semantic atoms, and is made into

[57] N.B. This is a different issue in an inflected language.

a whole by a further syntactic principle ("wholeness"). If that syntactic principle is treated as being of the same order as the semantic ones (that is, as itself another semantic atom), how can this collection of parts of the sentence actually form a whole? Likewise, if an individual is a collection of properties, how are the properties collected? If the collecting principle ("wholeness," "unity") is itself another property of the individual, how then is the collection made whole?

6. The Unanswered Questions

Grammar and reality seem to march hand in hand. Plato has assumed that there is some ready connection between what we say and what there is. But the dialogues of the late period launched a severe attack on the coherence of what there is; and the same goes for grammar too. We must not ignore the seriousness of the challenge. It seems obvious (and many of Plato's arguments trade on this obviousness) that there *is a determinate reality out there in the world.* Likewise, it seems obvious that we can talk about whatever there is out there, even if our talk is itself only skeptical. After all, here we are arguing, doing dialectic, thinking—all of these intellectual operations seem to be self-verifying. And yet we seem, if Plato's arguments are correct, to be unable to *explain* what we are doing when we talk, any better than we are able to explain what there is out there. In order to relieve ourselves of the paradox that argues that we cannot argue at all, we must be able to solve the puzzles Plato has offered us. What is more, Plato himself, who poses these puzzles in their paradoxical context (in a dialogue), urgently needs to solve his dilemmas.

To recapitulate, I have suggested that the core of the difficulty lies in the challenge to explain how anything can be a something. This problem is not, as I have argued, a problem in the first place about existence, but rather a problem of being something or other. Plato suggests—at the mercy of the grammatical prejudice—that entities can be arranged, and that some are more basic than others, just as the subjects of sentences are prior to the predicates. If there are to be basic entities (real or linguistic somethings or other), Plato must be able to explain the following:

1. The individuation of his basic entities. How are they one and countable? How are they unified and coherent?
2. The self-identity of the basic entities. How are they the same as themselves and different from others?

He must do so without reducing his entities either to indescribable austere lumps or to hopelessly generous bundles. That is, he must be able to determine basic entities without saying either too little about them or too much.

Part—perhaps a major part—of his problem seems to be in explaining how one item may be related to another, without this relation itself affecting the relata in such a way as to pluralize them. To put this another way, Plato must show how something could be an individual (just one) at the same time that it may have an identity (be the same as itself and different from others). How is individuation to be done?

PART THREE

Two Answers

Resolving Relations

1. Communing Kinds

The challenge is taken up in the second part of the *Sophist*, and here at last the answer to the problem is forthcoming. Dialectic may be understood in terms of the "communion of kinds" (*Soph.* 251d ff.). What is it for kinds to commune? The ES starts by explaining how they do not.

1. The late-learners allow no communion at all: "We cannot add being to motion or to rest, nor anything else to anything else; but we must treat them in our speech as being incapable of mixing and unable to share in each other" (*Soph.* 251d5–8).

This claim works for both words and the world. Motion and rest do not share in being; so neither of them "are." But then none of the ontologies will work; flux theorists, monists, and idealists alike attach being to motion or rest; but if there is no communion of kinds, they will do so no more. Without communion, being is divorced from everything else, so that nothing is. And without communion, there is no accounting for what there is; no scientific theory *about* what is can sensibly be explained or even expressed.

Mercifully, this theory turns out to be self-refuting, anyway. After all, the late-learners end up with such austerity that there cannot even be *separate* objects *in their world*. For, on their account, no predicate can be added to a subject, nor any property to an object; so they cannot say that anything is, or is different from anything else, or that it is the same as itself (*Soph.* 252c). They rule out expressions for identity at the same time that they suppose that there is no identity out there; yet talk about identity and difference itself breaks the prohibition on communion. Such a theory cannot even be formulated; as the early arguments allow us to see, the objects in the late-learners' world fail to be individuals at all, so that reality and speech have no basis. That theory is self-refuting.

2. Contrariwise, we might go for total interrelation. "Shall we collect everything together as capable of communing with each other?" (*Soph.* 251d8). But that generates a contradiction: motion will rest, and rest will move—and that is impossible.

3. So (since we can talk), we must compromise. This allows us to have our cake and eat the fruits of dialectic. They ripen in the next passage, where the ES explains how the kinds commune.

Consider, first of all, the letters of the alphabet: "Some of them somehow do not fit with each other, while others do fit. . . . The vowels, especially, run through them all like a bond so that none of the consonants are able to fit with any other consonant without some vowel (*Soph.* 253a).

To understand this, of course, is a matter of some skill: for letters, we need the grammarian, as we need a musician to understand the combinations of musical sounds. Likewise, in order to understand the communion of kinds, we need an expert—the dialectician—who can explain how things are collected together and divided. For, "surely we shall say that it is the task of the science of dialectic to divide by kinds, and not to think that one form is the same as another, nor another the same as it. . . . Therefore the person who is able adequately to distinguish a single form[1] spread out over many distinct items, and many forms different from each other embraced from without by a single form, and a single form, again, collected together into one through many wholes, and many separated altogether apart" (*Soph.* 253d).

The dialectician will collect and divide. Why should that be useful?[2] And what exactly does collection and division have to do with the problems thrown up by the discussion of being and not-being? After all, most of the actual collections and divisions Plato gives us are comical analyses of absurd skills (weaving or angling), with little claim, some might suppose, to philosophical significance. How can the dialectician come to our rescue here?

This passage says nothing about weaving or angling; instead the terms are thoroughly abstract and still fairly programmatic. Plato began with his favourite analogies—letters and music.[3] But notice how his discussion of the alphabet differs from Socrates' dream in the *Theaetetus*. In the earlier work Socrates made two assumptions that were lethal to the success of his theory. First, he supposed that his elements (the letters) were atomic, simple, and austere—they were not just unknowable but indescribable as well. They could have, thus, no attributes that would explain their capacity to combine together into syllables or even words. Unfortunately, Socrates next assumed that a collection of letters was just that, a clump of letters lacking a principle of coherence. The words and syllables, then, turned out to be as unknowable as the letters (unless the letters are somehow loaded with information; in which case the foundationalist enterprise of the *Theaetetus* comes to a sticky end anyway).

Now, however, things are quite the other way about. Instead of supposing that the elements of the alphabet, or of the musical scale, or of the dialectician's science, are just elements and nothing else, the ES now suggests that the important thing about them is the principles according to which they combine. Combination, however, is now suggested to be not a matter of some feature of the combining element, but rather a relation between all the ele-

---

[1] The Greek here is ἰδέα; perhaps "character" would be a better translation; but note, at any rate, that there is no warrant for taking this to be a transcendent form such as we find in earlier dialogues; despite Cornford's "Form," in *Knowledge*, p. 262.

[2] Note, for example, Ryle's comment on the *Politicus*—which is all about collection and division—that it is a "weary" dialogue; Ryle, *Plato's Progress*.

[3] The same analogies turn up again in the *Philebus*; cf. below, secs. 6–8.

ments; in collection and division, that is, the context, no less than the individual items within it, is fundamental to understanding.

What is more, the relations between the items that are to be collected and divided is conceived (as a legacy of the refutation of the late-learners) in terms of identity, difference, and individuation. For while both the late-learners and the "total combination" merchants were attacked on the basis that their cosmologies were impossible, the dialectician is interested not in being as such, but in *being one*; in *difference* and in *identity*. Consider the different relations between forms or kinds that he must be able to grasp: "[1] A single form spread out everywhere through many, where [2] each of the many is separate each from the other, and [3] many which are different from each other embraced from without under a single form, and [4] a single form, again, connected in a one through many wholes, and [5] many separated altogether apart" (*Soph.* 253d; my enumeration).

1. One (form) over many.
2. Many (wholes) quite separate from each other.
3. Many separate from each other *but still embraced by* one.
4. One over many and *still retaining its coherence*.
5. Many completely separate.

These relations are just what has been causing the trouble. For hitherto Plato has been unable to show how some individual could be spread out (say over many instances, like the sail) and still retain its identity (1 and 4); and he has been unable to explain how individuals are "quite separate" and yet have various attributes (properties, aspects, 3 and 4); nor yet again how something might be just separate, and otherwise unqualified (2 and 5). So if the dialectician is interested in weaving or in angling or in kingship or in love, he cannot get on with his job until he understands the fundamental rules—and those rules require him to grasp the principles for individuating and contextualizing any of the items in his division. Individuation, once again, is basic; but it is complemented by the skill of understanding the system, the context in which the individuals may appear, so that both individuals and context are susceptible to understanding.

So far so good; but so far still schematic. Plato badly needs to give a proper account of how individuation can escape the difficulties he himself has put before it. In the extensive argument that follows he must show three things:

1. How can I *count* individuals? Collection and division work by counting (ones, divisions into two or three; cf., e.g., *Politicus* 262a ff.). I must, for a start, be able to resist gross divisions, such as "Greek/barbarian" or "redheads/the rest." But even before I can do that I must understand the principles of counting, I must know what a one is.[4] How, for example, can I tell when I have a single unit in my division, and not an undifferentiated mass of stuff?

---

[4] Notice how, for Plato, understanding the principles of counting and counting itself are two different issues, whereas for Aristotle individuation would be implicit in making the right divi-

2. How can I say anything about individuals, as such? "Being an individual" must be understood in such a way as not to violate the priority of the individual over its properties, and yet in such a way that I do not sup at the late-learners table. It must be comprehensible and expressible that being is being *a something*. (This will dispose of the *austere* approach).

3. If I start attributing properties to something, how can I stop without attributing everything to it? What limits are there on the properties an individual may have? Can I show, in particular, that something might have one property but not thereby its opposite? Can I show that the total communion of kinds is wrong? If being is being something, something can be such or somehow, without danger of contradiction. (This will dispose of the *generous* approach.)

To answer these questions, Plato must make one important concession. He must abandon the view that relations are pluralizing properties of things. Only so can individuals be specifiable.

2. THE MESH OF IDENTITY

The "great kinds" (*megista genē*) passage is commonly thought to fall into two parts (*Soph*. 254c–257c and 257c–258e), with some commentators finding difficulty with the apparently redundant repetition of the arguments in the second stage. However, the arguments fall not into two parts but, like Gaul, into three. This is explicit in the introductory passage: "Choosing beforehand some particular ones of those kinds which are said to be the greatest, first [to consider] what each one is like; and then how they have the power of combining with each other" (*Soph*. 254c).

This gives three stages: first, the enumeration of the kinds ("choosing beforehand", *Soph*. 254d–255e); second, the attribution of properties to each of the kinds ("first [to consider]"; 255e–257c); third, the analysis of their connections with each other ("and then . . ."; 257c–258e). The first two sections correspond exactly to the pattern we have found elsewhere—the contrast between the countable individual and the properties it has. This contrast is now explained and justified, and supplemented (crucially) by an analysis of the logic of contradictories in the third section, which puts to rest the dangers of hopeless generosity.

The first phase of the Eleatic Stranger's argument runs from *Sophist* 254d to 255e (the enumeration is mine):[5]

[1] Now the greatest of the kinds we mentioned just now are being itself and motion and rest. And indeed we say that two of them are incompatible with each other. But what is is compatible with both, for both in some way are. So they are three. . . . (254d4–12)

---

sion. I hope that it is by now clear how utterly different are Plato's assumptions from Aristotle's essentialism.

[5] Omitting Theaetetus's answers to the ES's questions.

[2] Therefore each one of them is different from the other two and the same as itself. But what do we mean by "same" and the "different"? Are these two individual kinds (themselves somethings) other than the other three, but always necessarily mixing with those, so that our inquiry now is about five, not three, things that are? Or do we in fact use the terms sameness and difference to refer to some one of the other three, and not notice that we are doing so? . . . (254d14–255a2)

[3] But surely motion and rest are neither the same nor the different, for whatever term we use in common for both, cannot be either—otherwise motion would rest and rest would move. For in both cases, each one [e.g., motion], if it became one of these [e.g., same], it would force the other [i.e., rest] to change to the opposite of its own nature, insofar as it partakes of the opposite [from motion].[6] So both of them share in the same and different, but we should not say that motion is sameness or difference; nor rest. . . . (255a4–b6)

[4] But perhaps we should concede that being and same are a single something? Yet if being and the same signified nothing different (from each other), then when we say that motion and rest both are, we should imply that each of them, eo ipso, were the same (which is impossible). So it is impossible for sameness and being to be one, and let us posit sameness as a fourth in addition to the three forms. . . . (255b8–c6)

[5] Should we then say that difference is a fifth? Or should we recognise that difference and being are two names for one kind? I suppose that you would admit that some of the things that are are themselves by themselves; and some are always said in relation to others. Now different is always said in relation to something different. This would not be so if being and difference were not altogether distinct. But if difference shared in both these characters [i.e., itself by itself vs. in relation to others] as being does, then at some point there would be something different which was not different from anything—yet now we categorically assert that whatever is different turns out to be just what it is in relation to something else. So the nature of the different should be posited as a fifth among our forms, in addition to the ones we have already chosen. And we shall say that difference runs through them all; for each single one of them is different from the others not through its own nature, but by partaking in the form of different. (255c8–e6)

We end up with five kinds; and the argument has five stages:

1. *Compatibility and incompatibility.*
   a. Being, motion, and rest are all "great kinds."

This premise comes both from ordinary speech and from the ontologies: recall that motion and rest are now terms of art (representing the contrast between the properties an object has—its affections and actions—and the object considered in itself).

   b. Motion is incompatible with rest.

---

[6] The Greek here is horribly compressed. See below for an analysis of the argument.

Why? The ES makes great play with this incompatibility, so it had better be a good one. He cannot mean that motion (a transcendent form, or an idea) is not at rest—for that might well be false. His point must be more banal: "motion" and "rest" are contraries, since what moves is not at rest.[7] So he is simply trading on the common or garden truth that what moves (when and in the respects in which it is moving) is not at rest—he is talking about the ordinary world.[8]

    c. Both motion and rest *are* in some way.

This could mean that "there are things that move and are at rest,"[9] or it could be a straight claim that motion itself (the form, the idea, the property?) "is in some way." How guilty is the ES of shifting his ground between what is said of instances of a universal and what is said of the universal itself? And how much does it matter to this argument if he does?

    d. So, being is compatible with motion and with rest.

So far as the phenomenal world goes, earlier arguments have assumed that anything that moves, in some way is, and anything that rests in some way is, too. But that does not explain the idea that being is "able to mix with," is *compatible with* motion and rest. The ES is no longer (if ever he was) talking about the necessary features of the particulars in the world (*anything* that moves is etc.); instead, he is describing the logical relations between the predicates that represent that world ("is," "moves," "rests") and the great kinds that pervade it (being, motion, and rest). Hence, being is *compatible* with either motion or rest, or both (cf. 2c below).

    e. So there are three—being, motion, and rest.

If a–d are generalizations about the world, how successfully do they generate the conclusion that we are dealing with three items, whose identity the ES will go on to discuss? Three different interpretations seem to be available to us:

    (1) Being, motion, and rest are considered here merely as universals; in that case the rest of the argument is thoroughly question-begging (speaking, as it does, of the nature of each).

    (2) Being, Motion, and Rest are Platonic forms—separate, transcendent entities that are interrelated in the ways the ES explains; in that case, the evidence he uses from the phenomenal world may well be beside the point, if not actually false for forms.

---

[7] Compare a similar point about the "communion of kinds" at 252a5, and note the use of the now technical term ἀμείκτω at 254d7; cf. 251d6.

[8] Compare the discussion of the communion of kinds, 252a ff., where the counterexamples to "total communion" and "no communion at all" are taken from the everyday world. Thus here ἀμείκτω and μεικτὸν have almost technical impact; cf., e.g., σύμμειξις at 252b6.

[9] It would be a case of Pauline predication, where the abstract noun is in fact a collective noun: "motion" = "all the movers"; cf. Vlastos, "Unity of the Virtues in the *Protagoras*."

(3) Being, motion, and rest in this section are just understood in a minimal way, as features of speech (predicates) corresponding to features of the world (kinds); they will later be elaborated as full and countable individuals, whether those be forms or not.[10]

Charity is on the side of the last interpretation (3), which allows three "items" in a very loose and undetermined sense of "item." The topic here, then, is the compatibility or otherwise of the three predicates—"being," "motion," and "rest"—and thence the relations between the corresponding features of reality. What is more, the charitable view fits well with the strategy of the dialogue so far, which has been thoroughly critical of anyone's ontological claims, while insisting on the importance of well-managed grammar. And, finally, the charitable view—if I am right about the emphasis throughout the critical phase of the dialogue on the problems of individuation—provides us with three candidates for individuation without preempting how their individuation might be achieved; the rest of the argument is designed to do that.

2. *Sameness and difference.*
   a. (From 1) Each one of the three is different from the other two.
   b. Each one of the three is the same as itself.

These conclusions are offered as obvious inferences from the counting of the kinds at 1. Are the inferences obvious? On one view, being must be self-identical and different from motion and rest just if the three predicates/properties are incompatible. However, we should notice the importation of larger assumptions when the ES starts to speak of being, motion, and rest as individuals ("self," "others"), not just properties or predicates. From here, the argument can turn not only on questions of how the predicates feature in the phenomenal world, but also on what can be said of those kinds *in themselves*.[11] The mention of sameness and difference has done the trick here; it remains to be seen whether here the ES can avoid the traps of the *Parmenides*, which suggest that to attribute sameness and difference to something, so far from making it a something, makes it a collection of indeterminate things—or else nothing at all. Hence the ES's next question: "But what do we mean by 'same' and the 'different'?"

   c. Sameness and difference necessarily and always mix with being, motion and rest.

Point *c* is taken to follow from *a* and *b*, and thus from the "count" conclusion of 1. In that case, the mixing that sameness and difference do with being, motion, and rest is not at the level of the phenomenal world, but at the level of the kinds in themselves; and the grounds for concluding *c* are not taken (as

---

[10] Compare ch. 4, sec. 1, on "the one" as a variable for anything that may turn out to be an individual.

[11] Recall the assumption that the words we use correspond to reality, somehow or other; the kinds are not just expressions of speech, but parts of the world (some world).

they must have been at *1b*) from the phenomenal world, but rather from formal considerations (hence "necessarily, always" at *Soph.* 254e4) about the three kinds themselves. However, it should be noticed that those considerations will apply to anything that can be counted in the way that the three kinds were—so that these formal moves will be available for any talk about any individuals at all.

    d. Either sameness and difference are two further kinds; or
    e. Sameness and difference are names for some of the first three.

Here the counting operation clearly turns on questions of identity: is sameness (or difference) identical with some one of the other kinds, or not? Either we can count two more kinds, or we should allow that some kind can have two different descriptions without violating its identity. Hitherto the late-learners have been influential; perhaps there are just as many things as there are descriptions of them. Now the ES concedes formally that something may have two different descriptions and still be the same something. (But notice that while I may perfectly plausibly say that this star has two different descriptions without degenerating into two different stars, I may not be able to do the same for kinds.)

    3. *Incompatibility and coextension.*

Now the ES exploits the conclusions about compatibility of 1 and the identity and nonidentity claims of 2.

    a. (Examining *2e*) If one kind is coextensive with another, then where one term applies, so does the other.[12]
    b. If one of a pair of coextensive terms for a kind is incompatible with some other kind, the other of the pair will also be incompatible with the third kind.
    c. Motion is incompatible with rest.
    d. Sameness and difference are said of both motion and rest.
    e. Neither sameness nor difference can be coextensive with either motion
or rest.

Thus, for example, if same were coextensive with motion, then whenever "motion" applied, so would "same"; whenever motion was excluded (i.e., when "rest" applies), so would same be excluded. This rule for extension works at the level of the phenomenal world. And it suffices for the argument to show that it holds in the phenomenal world, since both items that move and items that are at rest are both same as themselves and different from others, irrespective of their locomotive status. Does the rule for extension hold at the level of the kinds? That, it appears from *Sophist* 255a11, is what the ES intends, and that is what is needed at *3d* (since motion is the same as itself and different from the others qua kind, not qua instantiated in the phenomenal world; cf. 2). Here the differences in order become tricky, but not lethal. After

---

[12] This could only be true in referentially transparent contexts.

all, sameness and difference appear to be formal expressions for the interrelation of the three original kinds; and as such they apply to the kinds no less than to their instantiations. In that case, sameness cannot be coextensive with motion, since sameness is a necessary feature of rest and motion qua kinds, whereas motion is not. As I suggested above, the expressions the ES is dealing with are true for individuals in the phenomenal world and *for any other putative individual* (particular, form, bundle, lump, stuff, or kind). Now the differences of ontological level may matter for forms and particulars, but the kinds will apply to anything, including themselves, without prejudice. They individuate in a quite general way; and they are themselves individuated on the same principle.[13]

This argument thus rules out the option of 2*e*. Is 2*d* therefore true? Are sameness and difference two further kinds?

4. *Difference of meaning and nonidentity.*

Argument 3 exploited the extreme case where same might be coextensive with motion, to show at least that sameness is wider in scope than motion. Now the ES takes on the possibility that sameness and being might be synonyms, coextensive as they may be thought to be (particularly by an Eleatic).The argument is concerned to distinguish, formally, items that may be extensionally equivalent, and it does so by getting to grips with the relational nature of "same."[14] The argument is a reductio.

> a. If being and sameness were identical, then "being" and "same" would have the same meaning.
> b. Motion and rest both are.
> c. If "being" and "same" had the same meaning, then motion and rest would be same.
> d. But motion and rest are not same.
> e. So being and sameness are not identical.
> f. So sameness is a fourth kind in addition to the first three.

This argument could be thought to turn on an equivocation, between "same as itself" (which might plausibly be thought coextensive with "being" at *a*) and "same as something else," which is the sense of "same" in the consequent

---

[13] This may, I think, solve the issue in the literature about the status of the argument at *Soph.* 255a10, that motion would otherwise rest, and rest move. This is only straightforwardly absurd in the phenomenal world, but at the formal level if either motion or rest were synonymous with sameness or difference, contradictions would arise: suppose R = S; then if M is same, M rests, just as R is same and so rests. But if R = S, then surely M = D; in that case, insofar as M is different, it moves just as much as it rests—and that will be absurd. The argument at the formal level is more complex than the argument about the phenomenal world, but it still exploits a contradiction for its absurdity. It also, interestingly, looks forward to the distinction between relative and καθ' αὐτό predicates at 255c12.

[14] This should not, of course, lead us to suppose that "is" here is used existentially, if it is used nonrelationally. N.B. M. Frede, *Prädikation*, here.

of *c* and in *d*.[15] It could also be thought to rely far too heavily on an equivalence between words and things, between meanings and individuals, between what we say and what there is. The last charge, however, seems wrong; although the ES does shift from "same" to sameness throughout the argument, that shift is an express part of the argument, not a surreptitious import. Once again (as I have suggested), the ES builds up a formal account of what individuation (counting, first of all) might be like when I have only what I say to go on in determining which items enter the competition. Unless (implausibly) we suppose that speech is mere babble, then speech is a useful source of candidates for the individuation game. In that case, evidence from speech and meaning is licit, not sneaky.

The charge of equivocation here, however, is more serious. We should notice, first of all, that what does *not* happen is a shift between this use or abuse of "same" and the conclusion (at 3*e*) that same and being are nonidentical—this is expressed as a denial of their being *one* (compare the original question, "Are they one something?"). In that case, the argument might be constructed thus, without an equivocation: Being and sameness are coextensive, but different in intension, because the first connects a subject and a predicate, while the second brings in a relation between the subject and other subjects. Thus, while I can say sensibly, if elliptically, "motion is" (meaning, e.g., there are things that move, or there is such a thing as motion or motion is good for your health) in just the same way as I can say "rest is" (warranting the generalisation "motion and rest are"), when I use the term "same" in the same sort of sentence I end up with an ellipse, a confusion, or a lie. "Motion is the same" could be read, as "motion is the same as itself" (the ellipse). "Motion is the same as rest" would be the confusion (how is motion the same as rest?). "Motion and rest are the same thing" would be the lie. These semantic contrasts come, perhaps, from a syntactic point; for example, "same" is, where "is" may not be, an incurably relative expression ("same as something or other"). Perhaps, likewise, if sameness is a feature of things then—unlike being—it is an incurably relative one (*x* is the same as *y*). Thus sameness, considered in itself, is not the same item as being.

5. *Ways of being.*

That this contrast is the focus in 4 is suggested by its being made explicit in 5.

    a. Some of the things that are, are themselves by themselves.
    b. Some of the things that are, are always said in relation to others.
    c. Different is always said in relation to something different.
    d. So "different" and "is" are not coextensive (via a).
    e. So different is some fifth kind.

Again this argument uses semantic considerations to draw a metaphysical conclusion. There are at least five kinds, which are not just expressions, but items that have their own nature.[16] They are each "one something" (individ-

---

[15] I have tried to mark this with a clumsy expression "is same."

[16] An objector might well ask what it is for something to "have its own nature." Is not that the

uals), countable. How—without running the gauntlet once again of the pluralizing feature of relations—could they be counted?

Conclusion

By the end of this section of argument, the counting principles have been put into practice five times: each item was counted by determining whether it was the same as any of the others, or different from it. That there turn out to be five (not less) is because each one was seen to be different from the others—hence the ES's conclusion:

> So the nature of the different should be posited as a fifth among our forms, in addition to the ones we have already chosen. And we shall say that difference runs through them all; for each single one of them is different from the others *not through its own nature, but by partaking in the form of different. (Soph.* 255e)

The language of the conclusion is reminiscent of earlier dialogues;[17] but the techniques for counting are not. Once each item is allowed to be anything at all, its individuation is determined contextually—against the background of, and in relation to, the other items that are also under consideration. Counting, then, is a matter of determining the relations between things, and individuation is thus relative to something's place among other somethings, over and above its nature. The significance of that contrast between something's nature and its difference from other things should not escape us. Now difference from others is not part of the something, but a feature of its context. In that case, there is no question of the difference impugning its unity (its being one something), since while unity may be something it has in itself, difference is not (but something that comes from its context). Hence, the ES's insistence, and Theaetetus's ready agreement, that there is an important contrast between things that are "in themselves" and things that are "relative to something else" (*Soph.* 255c–d).

   Think about that a little further. This conclusion does not make the difference of any individual from another accidental (where its nature is essential); instead, it makes it *contextual,* one individual among others. And that, of course, makes counting it reasonable, where an individual, thought of in terms of its internal nature, could not be readily understood as one among a series of others. Such a count does not require sortals; motion, rest, and so forth are individuated by each other and their differences from each other (from without), not by virtue, as I hope to have shown, of some further conception of what makes something a kind.

---

principle of individuation on which Plato relies? My response to that objection is that Plato does not, in what follows, expatiate on what it is to have a nature; and that if he did, his arguments themselves would require him to explain the natures of things in terms of their unity (and not, as Aristotle might, in terms of their natural kinds). Having a nature, on my view, is the analysand, not the analysis. I am grateful to my anonymous commentator at the Press for making me think again about this point.

   [17] For example, "runs through them all" may remind us of the physicalist accounts of properties, e.g., at *Parm.* 131 or at *Tim.* 35a.

Since the attacks on the forms in the *Parmenides*, Plato has been concerned, I have argued, with general theoretical questions. In particular, because forms and particulars fail to be individuals in any satisfactory way, the question has been, What is it to be an individual? But then it should not surprise us to find the treatment of the answer to be thoroughly theoretical, too. We may suppose that individuation cannot take place without a preemptive understanding of how to sort things into kinds. Plato, by contrast, supposes that we should be able to grasp what it is to be one first.

Plato supposes, then, that individuals are basic. *This* or *a something* or *one* comes first—in the structure of the world (*Theaetetus, Timaeus*), in our talk about the world (*Sophist, Cratylus*), and in the structure of our understanding (from the *Republic* on). But then, individuals must be understood as individuals, not according to their natural kinds.

Such an approach, however, confronts the common-sense objection: how can we specify *bare* individuals? All counting, the objector might say,[18] presumes that we have sorted first: kinds, not individuals, are basic. Plato might retort, of course, that we cannot sort until we know what items we are sorting: so we must be able to identify members of any putative kind before we grasp the kind itself. How then are the individuals to be identified?

Plato, as the counting of the kinds in the *Sophist* suggests, makes two moves:

1. He isolates the terms in which individuation is done.
2. He establishes the possibility of identifying individuals by virtue of their relation to each other, and *not* in terms of the kinds to which they may belong.

Take (1) first. Since Ryle's discussion of the *Parmenides*, commentators have been considering the possibility that Plato is contrasting two different features tures of things in general and, correspondingly, two different orders of predicate. There are, on the one hand, the specific things we say about something ("blue," "is a Georgian what-not," "fortifies the over-forties"). On the other hand, there are the general, all-pervasive terms: Ryle's examples are " 'not,' 'exists,' 'same,' 'other,' 'is an instance of,' 'is a species of,' 'single,' plural' and many others."[19] But the trouble now is (a) how can we explain or formalize the difference between first-order and second-order predicates? and (b) how do these general terms work?

I have argued that Plato's position is rather more determinate than Ryle makes it out to be. For Plato argues that individuals come first. In that case, the terms for individuating are the ones that matter most among the general, all-pervasive terms. And just those terms are marked off by the first three great kinds, "is," "is the same as," "is different from"—corresponding to being, sameness, and difference. For being, sameness, and difference determine whether something is one. Motion and rest, as the ontologies maintained,

---

18 Let us call this objector Gabriel Segal.
19 Ryle, "Plato's *Parmenides*," p.131.

affirm that something is a continuant and that it can also affect and be affected by the rest of reality. The five great kinds individuate and allow the individual to have properties without paradox: they are the mesh of identity.

But how does the mesh of identity work? Perhaps Plato's intuition began with Zeno: "If there are many, what is is infinite [sc. in number]. For between the things that are there are always other things, and again others between those. In this way, what is is infinite [in number]" (DK29B3).

Zeno's argument may have been something like this: Suppose we have two extended entities side by side. What separates them from each other, keeps them from coalescing? Surely there is something between them to keep them apart; and something further between each of them and what is between them, and so on. So plurality is infinitely many.

One response to this argument might be to block its first move. Any two items next door to each other are marked off from each other by being different from each other. The limit of A is its border with B, and there is no third entity C to come between them and keep them apart. So the separation of A from B is—one might respond to Zeno—mutual, and thus relative. A is separate from B just because A is not the same item as B, but it is the same item as itself; and the same goes for B. So A and B are marked off from each other by the facts that $A = A$ and that $A \neq B$. These identity relations are *primitive* and *irreducible*.

This opponent of Zeno shares some assumptions with Plato's Eleatic Stranger. To establish basic entities we need to identify: this can be done by applying the fundamental relations of sameness and difference that contextualize any item, among others. And it is a consequence (Plato may plausibly say) of this contextual view that when we have identity, we have entity;[20] and any identifiable entity will thus be one (among many). Now we have *this, it, a something*.

The Eleatic Stranger counts kinds by just this procedure. Suppose you try identifying any kind with any other (thus suppose, for any kind x, that $x = y$). For each attempt we can see that the identification is false except where $x = x$. So, the ES concludes, we are able to count five kinds—and we count without sortals, just by virtue of the all-pervasive kinds.

This conception I called the *mesh of identity* in the *Timaeus*. The *Sophist* presents it again, but in a new guise—for now the naturalism that beset Plato's account of relations has disappeared, allowing him a relative theory of individuation without hopeless generosity.

Being one (or a something), therefore, is determined in two different ways, made explicit here for the first time. The first is absolute (being the same as itself, being "itself by itself," *Soph.* 255b12);[21] the second is relative (being different from the others, being "with relation to something else," 255c13).

---

[20] I am grateful to Keith Hossack for suggesting this pithy way of putting it.

[21] Something that is the same as itself has, *eo ipso*, a nature; but its identification is not achieved by considering its nature as a specific feature of it.

So to be one/an individual/countable, each something is one in itself (by virtue of being the same as itself) and in the context of others (by virtue of being different from them). If *both* "same as itself" *and* "different from the others" are true of the item, then it is conceded to be a one.

This conclusion refutes the late-learners thesis by suggesting that something can be one without being completely cut off from anything else, and without being denied the condition of identity. So this short argument at last *denies the austere view*, that if something is a one, then it is *just one*. Instead, being one is now connected with the other formal characters, being itself in itself, being same and being different. If those characters are understood as part of the context (not as pieces or parts or features or properties) of the individual itself, the danger of pluralizing is past. So relations have been radically revised; they no longer inhere naturally in the relata; they are the context in which the relata appear, their place, the mesh of their identity.

3. SOMETHINGS ARE SUCH

The next stage of the argument builds on what has gone before (*Soph.* 255e–257c).[22] In this phase, and in the discussion of opposites of the third and last phase (see below sec. 4), the ES tackles the issue of how each of his chosen individuals can be characterized. He begins with an expansion of the formal characters of something, now legitimated.

> Eleatic Stranger: So let us take the five kinds one by one and speak of them as follows. Firstly motion is altogether different from rest. So it is not rest; but it is through partaking in being. Secondly, motion is different from the same. So it is not the same, but it is the same by virtue of everything partaking in same.[23] So we should agree without demur that motion is the same and not the same. For when we say that it is the same we do not speak in the same way as when we say it is not the same. Whenever we say it is the same, we do so by virtue of its partaking in the same in relation to itself; when we say it is not the same, we do so by virtue of its connection with different, whereby it is cut off from the same, and turns out to be not that but different, so that we can legitimately say that it is not the same.
>
> Theaetetus: Entirely legitimately—if we concede that some of the kinds mix with one another, and some not.[24]
>
> Eleatic Stranger: So if at all motion were to participate in rest, there would be nothing odd in saying that it is resting?
>
> Theaetetus: How not?

---

[22] Just, you will recall, as did the second of the puzzles about not being; and the second wave of the ontologies.

[23] Reading πῦ ταὐτοῦ with Madvig.

[24] There is some kind of lacuna in the text here; cf. Cornford, *Knowledge*, p.287. I suggest that Theaetetus's replies be reordered to preserve the sense: move b8–9 to b5, c4 to b7, and b5 to c4. My translation here takes Theaetetus's replies in that order.

Eleatic Stranger: This we demonstrated earlier, when we argued against the view that this is the case by nature.[25]

Theaetetus: Certainly.

Eleatic Stranger: To recapitulate: motion is different from the different just as it is other than the same and than rest.[26]

Theaetetus: Necessarily.

Eleatic Stranger: So according to this argument, it is in some way not different and in some way different.

Theaetetus: True.

Eleatic Stranger: Next, should we say that it is different from the three we have discussed, but not from the fourth, even though we agreed that there were five kinds which we are investigating? . . .For we cannot allow that they are less in number than appeared just now. So we should fearlessly assert that motion is different from being. . . . Therefore clearly motion really is something that is not and something that is, since it partakes in being. . . .

So then necessarily what is not is attributed to motion and to all the kinds. For the nature of the different by ensuring that each of them is different from what is, makes each not be; and we are correct to say of all of them in the same respects that thus they are not, and, in reverse, that because they partake in being, they are and are beings. So for each of the kinds, there is a great deal of what is and an indeterminate amount of what is not. (*Soph.* 255e-256e)

The arguments of the *Parmenides* had found intolerable both the idea that what is is indeterminately many and that it might be conflated with, or even connected with, what is not. The notion of "indeterminate in number" is associated with hopeless generosity (e.g., at *Parm.* 143a2, or at *Parm.* 132b2), with the impossibility of any individual being able to achieve proper unity.[27] In the *Parmenides*, in the *Philebus*, and here, the problem is not just about what is not, or not just about the dangers of contradiction or sheer nonsense brought along by "nothing"; rather, as the context of this passage makes clear, the danger the ES envisages is the danger that something, established laboriously to be one (among others), should nonetheless turn out to be many, hopelessly many, and thus not one at all. If the first stage of this argument was about how to count somethings without conceding that they are too austere to

[25] That is, at *Soph.* 255a—where again the counterfactual is stressed: if motion = sameness or difference, then it would swap natures with rest. This cannot happen; but the two opposed kinds can share a character, as here motion could be at rest . . .

[26] There are two different terms in play here for "different": ἕτερον/θάτερον, and ἄλλο. I have translated them as "different" and "other," respectively, although I am aware that the latter may suggest a non-identity claim, the former a predication (registering dissimilarity). But since this passage seems designed to analyze that contrast between identity claims and predications (although not, as I shall argue, lurking in an ambiguous "is," but rather in the complex metaphysics of individuation), there seems to be no serious danger of equivocation; the laboriousness of the ES's language makes it entirely clear when he means to assert nonidentity and when merely dissimilarity. See M. Frede, *Prädikation*, and Bostock "Is Not," here; and now Denyer, *Language*.

[27] Cf. ch. 4, sec. 3.

mention, the second stage is instead about how we may say anything about any counted individual without upsetting the count (and ending up with rather more than we bargained for). The second phase, then, in the argument about the great kinds, is not about somethings, but about how a something can be such. (Again, compare the two phases of the argument about nothing, *Soph.* 237a ff., and the two phases of the ontologies, *Soph.* 244ff.). So this is about predication—but incidentally; the ES's attack is in fact on the incomplete or paradoxical pictures of individuation given before (in the *Parmenides*, the *Theaetetus*, the *Timaeus*, and the first part of the *Sophist*, if I am right so far). This phase shows how some predication of a counted individual can occur; the third and final phase shows how predication is in fact limited, and not liable to generate hopeless generosity. The third phase puts somethings and suches into the context of a determinate, and determining, logical strucutre, which prevents the total absurdity of the close of the *Parmenides* from coming about.

There are five distinct kinds, established in the preceding section; this reappears as an important premise, e.g., at *Soph.* 256c11. For each kind, various different propositions may be seen to be true:

Motion is different from being: motion is not being.
Motion is:[28] motion partakes in being.
Motion is different from the same: motion is not the same.
Motion is the same as itself: motion is the same.
Motion is different from rest: motion is not rest.
Motion could partake in rest without being identified with rest.
Motion is different from the different: motion is not the different.
Motion is different.
So, in different ways, motion is and is not.

None of these propositions, the argument shows, is at all paradoxical; they merely represent different ways of understanding what we say about motion and its relations with other properties. (At this stage, of course, it becomes important for the thought experiment that the great kinds are properties; otherwise, the neat paradoxes would not be so readily available.)

Does the ES here trade on different senses of the verb "to be" (an identitative versus a predicative), or on different senses of "same" and "different"—that is, by making a semantic point at *Sophist* 256a? Or does he exploit different syntactic structures (a complete versus an incomplete use of "is"; a reflexive versus a nonreflexive use of "same"), for example, by his use of the *dia* construction from *Sophist* 256a1ff., and by looking back to the point made at 255b12? Is his point about language at all? No. What is going on here is an analysis of the way things are. This may have semantic or syntactic

---

[28] This is still obscure. Perhaps, "there is such a thing as motion"? or "things move"? or "motion is (a property of things)"?

consequences, of course (inevitably so, for someone whose account of language has such strong realist assumptions); but the real issue is the relations between things.

Once again, we may reflect on the nature of relations as the ES now presents them. He starts with a series of individual items, all of which are counted as one. So they are nonidentical with any of the other ones—they are implicated in the mesh of identity. But that contextualizing of the five kinds, as we saw, does not in itself pluralize each one of the kinds on its own, apparently because the context is not internal to their constitution.

Suppose, however, we think about the consequences for their internal constitution of their being one among five, in terms of their own nature. Then we can say more about them—that they are the same as themselves, that they are, that they share in difference. Now they have these characters by virtue of (because of their relation to) the other individuals in the mesh. What is more, their having such a character (e.g., motion is different from different) is explained by the fact that the character they have is represented among the kinds. Each *has* some character that it *is* not (and maybe also the character that it is; e.g., "being is") without collapsing into, or being identified with, what it is not. But now having such a character does not affect what each kind is, because now the characters they have are construed as relations and not as properties, no longer as natural *parts* of each kind. To understand the identity of each kind by virtue of its context is to see identity as fundamentally relational, and no longer to see relations as properties. So these nonidentity relations do not represent a material or natural feature of the relata. But the same seems to be true of the internal features of the kinds. For example, "same as itself" (*Soph.* 256b1) is a reflexive relation; if nonidentity is no longer conceived as a natural part of each, it is hardly likely that self-identity will be so (and thus liable to pluralize). Understood, then, as relations, these characters of the kinds will not be naturally inherent in them. On the contrary, these relations can be understood in a purely formal way, either in terms of the context in which they fit or in terms of each item in itself. On neither count is any individual an impossible plurality.

So, the characters of each kind are derived in this argument from purely formal considerations, true of each by virtue of its being just an individual, and not by virtue of its special nature. But then if the initial count of the five kinds does not pluralize each one, a fortiori the derivation of other formal features will not do so. Think about the collection of just these kinds. Why this five? Because, as the argument throughout has shown, these are characters of things in a strictly formal sense. What do we mean by that? That an individual is the same as itself, different from others, is true of that individual as such and is not a peculiar feature of its nature (of its being a giraffe, or a lightning bolt). This now is a formal, nonreductive account of basic individuals, as such. The mesh of identity allows us to have individuals, each just one something, and to talk about their individual character too, without interfering with the unity that is vital to their being individuals at all.

4. Opposites and Difference

The ES has still not solved the problem of hopeless generosity, though. He may now have basic individuals (somethings). But he has not yet shown how the individual may be protected against flux or indeterminacy, nor how it is that the individual does not possess all properties at once, so that it is a mess of contradiction. How can something be determinately such? Recall the challenge of Protagoras's secret doctrine: if something is light, it turns out also heavy; if large, then also small.[29] This claim has affinities with the problem of the compresence of opposites; for example, if Socrates is smaller than Cebes, then he is taller than someone else (say Simmias). And the problem of the compresence of opposites, I argued, caused difficulties especially when it turned up together with a thesis of natural inherence about relational properties.[30]

Now the first two phases of the final argument of the *Sophist*, as I have suggested, offered an account of the formal relations between individual items that is not conjoined with natural inherence; so part of the danger of the compresence of opposites—that the objects in which formal properties inhere are thereby pluralized—is past. Nonetheless, the Protagorean version still has some ammunition left. If any term predicated of some subject implies also its negation, then even if the objects of the world remain coherent, we shall be unable to talk about them sensibly (this would happen if all the kinds communed). Talk needs to be defended by a sensible account of negation and of the connection between "not" and the predicate it negates. The final phase of the interrelation of kinds sets out to find such a weapon, beginning, as the second phase ended, with the challenge of pluralizing predicates. "What is itself must be said to be different from the others; so as many as the others are, so many times being will not be; for not being those others it is itself one, while it is not the others, indefinite in number. But we should not demur at that, since it is the nature of the kinds to have communion with each other (*Soph.* 257a).

The conclusion of the previous phase, there expressed in terms of the indefiniteness of the predicate "is not," is now reemphasized in terms of the contrast between the coherent individual subject (in this case, being) and the indefinite number of its predicates (in this case, "different from some other"). How can the ES now avoid the dangers of incoherence? At *Sophist* 257b he makes a new start.

> Whenever we say "is not," it seems, we don't mean the opposite of being, but just something different. For example, when we say that something is not large, we don't thereby imply that it is small rather than equal. So we shall not concede that negation signifies an opposite—but merely that "not" signifies something other than the words that follow it—or rather other than the things to which the words after the negative refer.

[29] See ch. 5, sec. 2.
[30] See ch. 2, secs. 2, 3.

Let us think about this point: the nature of the different—it seems to me—is parcelled out just as knowledge is. For although knowledge is one, each part of it which is concerned with a particular area and thus marked off has some individual name of its own, with the result that there are many specifiable skills and sciences. The same thing happens in the case of the different and its parts, even although it is still one. Thus there is some part of the different which is contrasted with the beautiful, and has a name of its own—for whenever we say "not beautiful," we mean just what is different from the nature of the beautiful. Surely therefore in this way the not beautiful turns out to be a determinate part of some one kind of the things that are, set off in contrast to something of the things that are. So the not beautiful turns out to be an antithesis of something that is to something that is.[31] On that account, the beautiful is no more something that is than the not beautiful; likewise the same should be said of the not large and the large itself, or the not just and the just—neither should be posited to be any more than the other. The same holds for the rest, since the nature of the different turns out to be one of the things that are; and if that is, necessarily its parts should be said to be no less. So when the nature of a part of the different and of being are contrasted with each other that antithesis is being no less than being itself (if we may say so) signifying as it does, not something opposite to being, but something different. (*Soph.* 257b–258b)

This analysis of the relation between contradictories is supposed to solve the original Eleatic problem about "is not" posed at *Sophist* 236e ff. It does so by insisting on the legitimacy of expressions such as "not large" on the grounds that they correspond to some reality out there in the world (the property of not large, the things that are not large). But that insistence is based upon two insights expressed in the argument itself. First, the ES shows how the negative does not point—as he had originally suggested—to an empty class, but to the complement of the negated term; this is expressed in terms of the reality of the two connected kinds in a negation—difference ("not") and the negated kind ("large," "beautiful" etc.). Secondly, he shows how this can be understood in terms of a proper logic of negation, where the negative *excludes* what it negates. By expressing the relation between "large" and "not large" in terms of the reality of their corresponding classes, he shows just how the contradiction of "large and not large" is ruled out by the antithesis of the class of large and its complement.

Recall that the discussion of the communion of kinds invited us to choose between three options: (a) no kinds commune, or (b) all kinds commune, or (c) some do and some do not. The first option (a) is totally austere; if there is no communion, as the late-learners suggest, then there is nothing to be said. The first two phases of this argument have shown how we can sensibly have subjects of sentences (counting kinds) and how we can say things about them (showing how kinds can be such). The Heraclitean view turns up in the second option (b); if all kinds commune, then anything will be true of anything, all

---

[31] Cf. here Lee, "Negation." The interpretation of the following passage is vexed; in what follows I try to ride lightly over rough ground.

the time, and talk will collapse. The final phase of the ES's argument (c) shows how this is not so, since there are rules for communion, especially the rule that rules out contradictions by virtue of the antithesis of a positive and a negative expression and their corresponding kinds. For here he explains the logic of negation, and the corresponding metaphysics of a property and its complement (*Soph*. 257c–259a). In doing so, he establishes two things.

First, he shows how the negative works; that is, how the use of a negative does not commit us to talking about nothing. Second, he shows how the function of the negative is to exclude one of a pair of contradictories; and to indicate how an object has only a property, not its complement (or the complement, not the property). This move rules out the dangers that lurk in the *Parmenides* and the *Theaetetus*, that an object might be indescribable because it is held to have both the property and its complement at once. Correspondingly, he excludes Heraclitean sentences, which use predicate and contradictory at once; but does not thereby exclude all subject/predicate structures. This formal move is the crucial one to avoid the traps of hopeless generosity.

5. WHAT KINDS?

At this stage, of course, we might want to ask the $64,000 question. What are these entities/kinds? They could be forms, or classes, or properties. If they are forms, then they are clearly much modified—no longer austere, no longer strictly self-subsistent; they would be self-predicating and perhaps even inherent in their instances. If they are classes, how are we to understand their ontological status? If they are properties, how can they be easily taken as subjects or, worse still, as individuals? Once again, I suggest, the *Parmenides* gives us the clue. In that dialogue, the topic of the long piece of dialectical gymnastics was best understood hypothetically—as a variable.[32] "Take any individual, what will be true of it . . .?" Here, a similar kind of thought-experiment is going on. The ES takes a series of terms upon which the discussion has turned in earlier arguments and discusses what should be true of them as such. By a series of formal arguments, he concludes that they are, at least, countable individuals. Why should we object to that view? If we suppose that Plato has already decided on the scope of the expression "individual," then we might worry that properties are to be treated as such. But why make that assumption? If the present passage is designed as a piece of pure dialectic, then its formal conditions may be thought to apply without consideration of other theories—about the world, or about the forms—that Plato may or may not be thought to hold. It would be begging the question to complain, "But these are not proper individuals," if the argument's premises show that on formal grounds they are.

---

[32] Compare Macdowell's point, "Falsehood," p. 125, that forms are the only values of the ES's variable. Why should they be?

If we look at the way in which the problem of falsehood—the official difficulty for the whole dialogue—is solved, this interpretation of Plato's overall strategy may be confirmed. For in the concluding passages, the ES draws a distinction between the subject of a false statement and its predicate (*Soph.* 261c ff.). He finally claims that any sentence, to make sense, must refer successfully to some subject. The subject term refers to a something, formally accounted for at 254–5. Once we have a subject, we may then ascribe a predicate to it; this corresponds to the relation of participation between object (a something) and property (being such). Now it is a necessary condition for a successful sentence (on Plato's view) that the object be actually out there (and be a proper something). But it is not necessary that the predicate correspond to what is out there (at least not to what is actually true of this object; realism still rules insofar as Plato thinks that any of his predicates, positive or negative, must be instantiated somewhere).[33] When the predicate fails, thus, to correspond to the real state of affairs, then we have a false—but nonetheless meaningful—sentence.

This account of falsehood could only be offered if the subject could be specified as such without its predicates; and if the properties so attributed could fail to be features of the object out there. This feature of the relation between the object and its properties is ensured by the thesis that any property has a contradictory; if the object does not have this property, then it has its contradictory (and not both at once, as the excessively generous view maintained). So although objects must have properties, and subjects must have predicates (if any complex speech takes place at all), it remains contingent, and falsifiable, which property/predicate the object/subject has.

I said that to solve the problems about individuals offered by the *Parmenides* and by the first half of the *Sophist*, Plato needs:

1. A distinction between an object and its properties.
2. A distinction between properties and relations.
3. Some account of how criteria of individuation may be understood.
4. An account of how this has a semantic implication—namely, that speech and dialectic are possible.

Each of these requirements, as I have argued, has been met by the end of the dialogue. My interpretation says that this (connected as it is to the problems of the *Parmenides* and the *Theaetetus*) is the project of this dialogue.

How does that leave the question of the verb "to be"? Obviously, this semantic issue is not central. Questions such as Is the verb complete or incomplete? and Does Plato understand ambiguity? turn out to be red herrings, not to mention old chestnuts. Being, throughout, is being something or other, existence parasitic on being something or other. So the verb, if you must, is incomplete. But Plato's problem lay with the nature of the completion; and

---

[33] Cf. below, ch. 9, secs. 6, 7. Fiction and falsehood pose an interesting problem in the philosophy of mind that is hardly tackled in this dialogue but is confronted in the *Theaetetus*.

the ambiguity (again, if you must) lies in the notion of "being something or other"—"being a something" versus "being something or somehow." You might still want to put this question in terms of the contrast between identity and predication; or you might say (à la Bostock or Mates) that this contrast is not here at all. Six of one and half a dozen of the other, I say. The contrast between identity and predication is one way to see what is going on in this work; but this characterization of it is far too limited in scope.

Instead, the evidence suggests that Plato might have seen the crucial issue as a difference between different sorts of property, or perhaps in terms of the one/many contrast—what is the relation between this one something and the many properties that it has? He is coming to terms with the original puzzle posed first in the *Parmenides*; how can we reconcile the contrast between an individual in itself (austerely conceived) and an individual in terms of its properties (which it possesses generously)? Individuals are basic components of the world, and reference to them is a necessary condition of sensible discourse. So some way must be found to express the nature of the individual in which the properties inhere. That is, we need some grip of the identity of the individual as opposed to its predicates. This project, I submit, is in hand in the *Sophist*.

If I am right, Plato thinks that "being one" is not a syncategorematic expression (as Aristotle would claim)[34] or substantive-hungry (as Austin would have said)—for example, "one hippopotamus," "one igloo"—but rather a central and primary feature of the subjects of sentences. These refer to countable individuals that may be understood to be *one as such*, both in themselves and in the context of others. Only thereafter may they be considered in terms of their properties. That is, he suggests to us that being one is a fundamental and primary aspect of being; and that the properties of individuals (not as such) are posterior. The arguments of the *Sophist* are designed, that is, to offer a thesis of *ontological fundamentalism*, wherein we can discern the individuals underneath as such before their properties (qualities, relations, etc.). This view is to be understood, on the one hand, as the precursor to the assumptions of Aristotle's theory of the categories;[35] and Aristotle, like Plato, claims that there is an inextricable connection, both logical and metaphysical, between "being" and "one" (e.g., *Met.* 1053b9ff.). Yet the two philosophers differ radically in their explanation of individuation. Aristotle requires us to understand individuals in terms of sortal predicates, with a bias toward natural kinds ("one horse," "one armadillo"; cf. *Cat.* 2a13; *Met.* 1030a10ff.); and many modern accounts of individuation follow this Aristotelian assumption. Plato, by contrast, supposes that being one is what is formally true of the subjects of sentences; their sortal predicates, we may

---

[34] Were Aristotle to use the expression "syncategorematic," he would mean that the term in question needed modification by some category, and could not licitly turn up on its own. Ryle's use of "syncategorematic," in "Plato's *Parmenides*," p. 131, is rather different—he just means "all-pervasive" (although it could be argued that any all-pervasive term would have to be modified by some category, that is not immediately obvious).

[35] Aristotle also has an ontological fundamentalist premise, *Cat.* 2a11ff.; but his is different.

suppose, are applied afterward. This view of individuation is perhaps harder for us to grasp, Aristotelians as we tend to be. The question that thus remains is this, Is it correct to follow Aristotle's view? Or should we give some mileage to Plato's suggestions that "being a something" is fundamental?

6. LIMIT AND UNLIMITED

The trouble with individuals can be characterized as a puzzle about one and many. Any something needs to be one something; but individuation seems to implicate it in plurality. At the extreme, a something must either be austerely one or hopelessly many. How then can there be a something at all? The *Philebus*[36] returns to the problem of one and many that beset its predecessors (resonantly so—the echoes of earlier works are unmistakeable)[37] and, I shall argue, elaborates the mesh of identity in three stages.

Socrates, Philebus, and Protarchus are talking about the relative merits of pleasure and intelligence, and pleasure (if not intelligence) is getting into trouble: "For I know that pleasure is complex [*poikilos*] and, as I said, we must begin thinking about that and considering what its nature is. For, to hear it spoken of generally like that, it is one something—and yet it has all sorts of shapes which are somehow different from each other" (*Phil.* 12c).

The problem here appears to be that pleasure is a genus whose species are radically different from each other (in a way that is not true of the species of intelligence?). It is therefore puzzlingly both one and many. Now this is not the kind of "vulgar" (*Phil.* 14d4) one/many problem dismissed early in the *Parmenides*—that one Socrates is large and small, heavy and light, or that he has two legs, two arms, and at least three strands of hair. Such "monsters"[38] may be one and infinitely many, but they are still child's play. The real problem about one and many[39] is this:

> When someone posits one man, one ox, one beautiful and one good, great enthusiasm for making divisions makes for controversy among such monads[40] as these. . . . First of all, if we must suppose such things genuinely to be monads,[41]

[36] On dating, see Waterfield, "Place of the *Philebus*," and Mackenzie, "*Cratylus*."

[37] E.g., from *Phd.* 99d, the δευτεϱὸς πλοῦυ is echoed at *Phil.* 19c; the ox of *Euthyd.* 301 is echoed by the cow of *Phil.* 15a; Parmenides' monads are henads at *Phil.* 15a–b; from *Soph.* 253a the bond (δεσμός) connecting the letters is revised at *Phil.* 18c.

[38] Compare a similar description of two-faced explanations at *Phd.* 101b.

[39] It may be worth noticing that *Phil.* 15d ff. describes the "one-many" puzzles as the delight of the young and the old, who enjoy their Heraclitean dizziness; there is an echo, or a foreshadowing, here of several other passages, notably *Phd.* 90, *Tht.* 152ff., and *Soph.* 251c. This seems to connect, significantly for my purposes, the problem of compresence of opposites and its later revision into the secret doctrine, the puzzle of the late-learners, and the issue of collection and division. These connections have, I hope, become obvious in my discussions of Plato's arguments.

[40] Translating ἑνάδων, to pick up on what follows. Cf. Hackforth, *Pleasure*, ad loc. for a defense of Burnet's text.

[41] This translation takes there to be a comma (not a semicolon) after οὔσας at b2, εἶτα αὖ to register the apodosis of the conditional, so that the first problem runs right up to ταύτην at b4.

how [can we take] each of these, which is always one and the same and does not admit generation or destruction, nonetheless to be most securely that one [thing]?[42] And next, whether it must be supposed to be spread out in what becomes and in what is infinite and thus to be many, or whether it is a whole apart from itself, which appears to be the most absurd of all, [how can we suppose that] being one and the same it comes to be in one and in many? (*Phil.* 15a–b)

The urgent question is not whether there are monads,[43] but how they retain their character as such; do they persist as ones?[44] What is a monad? It is not a transcendent form—or else it would be neither spread out nor many; nor is it a sensible particular (those are not spread out either). Monads must at least be universals: we can identify some monad by name (man, ox, etc.); this monad seems to be instantiated in the manifold world, and seems still to be one. How can that be? How can we explain its unity? And how can we explain its having any plurality at all?[45] Worse still, monads appear to be just one (because they are monads) and to be hopelessly many (because they are spread out indefinitely). How can this (ancient) difficulty be assuaged?

The pair "one and many," Socrates suggests, can be explained by the pair "limit and unlimited." This will work both for what we say and for how things are arranged in the world. The first provides us with an analytic method, and the second with a cosmology: do the two explanations of one and many, limit and unlimited, cohere?

The ancients passed on this tradition that the things that are always[46] said to be are from (out of?)[47] one and many, having limit and unlimited *naturally* built into

---

Some might object that this is not a puzzle at all; the argument of my last three chapters is that it is—the problem of austere ones. This reading has the advantage of offering counterpoised puzzles (μὲν . . . δὲ) with the same grammatical structure of open conditionals: If we suppose there to be monads, how can they be just one? If we suppose them to be parceled out, how can they be one and the same as themselves?

[42] I take μονάδας ἀληθῶς οὔσας to be the complement of εἶναι, so that the verb to be is not existential, as many take it to be (see, e.g., Sayre, *Ontology*), but the copula. This makes not only better Greek (cf. Kahn, *The Verb "to Be"*), but better sense of the puzzles put forward here, which are, after all, represented as about one and many, or many and one. On this reading, we get puzzle one about ones, and puzzle two about manies.

[43] If after all Socrates has three problems, not two, the first would be about the existence of monads (rather than their characterization as such). But I have suggested that the background to these arguments ties existence to individuation, so that the issue of existence would not constitute a different question from the monads' being one. Instead, the first clause of the passage gives the hypothesis: shall we suppose these things are monads? If so, either we need to explain how they are strictly monads (puzzle one), or how they are related to the indefinite (puzzle two).

[44] Compare Gosling's treatment here, *Plato: Philebus*, p.145, which is sensible.

[45] Or, how can it count as a whole? Shiner, *Knowledge and Reality*, is surely wrong to disconnect this use of ὅλην from the opening arguments of the *Parmenides* or from the *Sophist*'s attack on monism.

[46] What does ἀεὶ qualify, and what does it mean? Vide 15d5, it qualifies λεγομένων, not εἶναι; and this might give us Gosling's "from time to time" or, I prefer, "at any time"—the sense is indefinite, "anything which is ever said to be . . ." I discuss ἀεὶ further in McCabe, "Persistent Fallacies."

[47] The first issue here might be what kind of physics underlies this account; is the point that

them.[48] Since things are arranged in this way, we must always investigate by positing a single idea in every case, each time—for we shall find one there—and then if we get it, after one then we should look perhaps for two, or else three or some other number; and each one of them again in the same way, until someone sees that the original one is not only one and many and unlimited in number, but exactly how many it is. The idea of the unlimited should not be applied to the plurality until someone sees the exact number of it, between the unlimited and the one; and then he can let each one of them go into the unlimited. For the gods, as I said, handed this down to us for investigating and learning and teaching each other; but wise men nowadays make the one, when they find it, and the many either faster or slower than they should, and offer the unlimited immediately after the one, while what is in the middle escapes them—and that is the difference, as far as we are concerned, between the dialectical and the eristic approach to words. (*Phil.* 16c8–17a5)

This account of the way we talk (of "things that are always said to be") looks like a repeat performance of the method of collection and division to be found elsewhere—dialectic is a matter of collecting a series of items under one heading, and then seeing how the one is divided into many.[49] But in other passages Plato describes this process in terms of "one and many"; here, "one and many" is glossed as "limit and unlimited." How does "limit and unlimited" illuminate "one and many"?

There is, first of all, a problem of interpretation: is Socrates either consistent or clear in his use of the expression *apeiron* (which I translate as "unlimited")?[50] At *Philebus* 16c10 it is a component of "the things that are said to be"; at 16d6 it describes the many, indeterminate before they have been counted; at 16d7 and 16e1 it is allowed to be a character of the many after we have counted them, and dismissed them from attention; and finally at 16e2 it seems to refer to the indefinite number of instances of some one of the many we have divided and counted.[51] "Unlimited," therefore, seems to mean either "indeterminate in character" (of some collection of items to be divided and understood) or "indefinite in number" (of an uncounted collection of particular instances of, at least, a universal). The latter, however, seems unproblematic; there is no sign here that the one/many problem is about counting the particular objects there are (sensible particulars, if you will). And yet the problem is one of counting: we start with some all-embracing one, which is

---

things are made out of the definite and the indefinite (thus Sayre, *Ontology*)? Surely not so much can be read into ἐξ at 16c9; vide Aristotle on this, *Metaphysics* 1023a26ff. "From" introduces the explanations of things, not their consituents; on this, more below.

[48] My emphasis. Second, what is the indefinite/infinite? Some suggest that the indefinite is the indefinite plurality of physical objects (cf. Hackforth, *Pleasure*, p. 23)—but that is surely precluded by the claim at 15a that we are not going to talk about physical objects as such. The problem, no doubt, is not the conflation of the universal with the particular but the failure to observe the proper interrelation between the one and its subsections (whatever they may be).

[49] More below; see sec. 9.

[50] Cf. Gosling, *Plato: Philebus*, Sayre, *Ontology*, on this.

[51] Gosling, *Plato: Philebus*.

also many—this is collection. But that one cannot be understood, nor can the many either, until we can count each of the ones in the many—by division. It is only when we have a grip on *each one* of this many that we can allow them to go away into the indefinite. That is, only when we have made determinate the interrelation of the overarching one and the many that fall under it can we afford to recognize that each one and each many may be instantiated in countless particulars. But then counting the instances will not give us a determination of the one and the many; instead, this must be done by analyzing the one and the many themselves. So the threat posed by "unlimited" is not that the original one we collected may have infinitely, or uncountably, many instances under it, but rather that the *many* that fall under it have not been properly determined, and so counted. The determination they need will allow us to say that each is one—that is, they need to be individuated, which the character of *apeiron* (now "indefinite," "indeterminate") pervading the many prohibits.

Next, Socrates tries to clarify his analysis of limit (*peras*) and unlimited (*apeiron*) by offering three examples:[52] articulate speech, musical notes, and the letters of the alphabet.

He begins with sound ("voice," *phōnē*). Sound comes out of our mouths as just "one" (*Phil.* 17b3); it is all noise. It is also indeterminate, *apeiros* (if we think of it just as noise); we only know what it is when we can determine how many and what sort the sounds are (17b7–8). Now the noise that comes out of our mouths[53] is not in fact indeterminate, but articulate. The issue is not how to change an inarticulate murmur into proper speech, but rather how to understand what may appear—when it is spoken—to be merely a mass of sound. We need to know how to pick out individual sounds from an apparently indeterminate mass (17b8), to differentiate and individuate the sounds as they are uttered (to determine how many they are and of what sort, *posa t'esti kai hopoia*, 17b8).

How does this account of sound explain "limit and unlimited"? Sound, as such, is unlimited, because (heard as such) its articulations are not picked out. Once we are able to count and differentiate the different sounds, however, we understand what is said, and may be called an expert. This is to bring limit to the unlimited. Two points are significant. First, there is no suggestion here that the articulate sounds are *produced from* a mixture of limit and unlimited; rather, they can be *understood in terms of* the limit/unlimited antithesis. That antithesis, to put it another way, is not the cause of sound, or its constituent parts, but rather its explanation, its rationale. Socrates is not suggesting that to get an articulate sound, we take some "sound-stuff" and make it precise or determinate with the application of some limit—and lo and behold, a sound is born; instead, he is thinking about the way in which we might understand

[52] Or possibly analogies??? 17a8 implies that they are examples; cf. Sayre, *Ontology*, on this point; and compare *Soph.* 253, discussed above.

[53] We are not talking about the babies beloved of linguistic philosophers, but of ourselves, 17b3.

the sounds that we hear and the ones that we articulate ourselves. Second, that understanding takes as its basic requirement that we can count the sounds, or individuate them. Their individuation is done *within a context* (indeterminate noise); they can be counted when *their place in that context* has been located (this is determinate). But this counting is not of particular sound events (this "s" I utter now), but rather of individual sound universals ("s" whenever uttered). Once again, determining the indeterminate is a matter not of counting the countless particulars of the world, but rather of articulating the hitherto inarticulate relations between all the determinate sounds (hence universal sounds) there are.

As for letters, so for musical sounds; someone only counts as musical who can determine each particular note. The expert must locate the note within the context of indeterminate sound—and that involves relating one note to another:

> When, my friend, you grasp the intervals in high and low pitch, how many they
> are and of what sort, and the limits of the intervals, and the systems that they
> make—things which our predecessors discovered and handed down to us to call
> scales; and again in the movements of the body there are equivalent affections
> which they say must be measured by numbers and called rhythms and measures;
> and at the same time to realize that we should investigate every one and many in
> the same way—when you have grasped these things thus, then you will have
> become wise, and whenever you capture any other one by investigating in this
> way, then you will be intelligent about that. But the indefinite number of each
> thing and in the plurality of each thing each time makes you indefinite in thinking
> and neither rational nor numerate insofar as you did not look at any number in
> anything. (*Phil.* 17c11–e6)

The discussion of musical terms of art is strikingly about the relations between notes. Music is structured, essentially, because music is about the relations between one note and another. Furthermore, each note only is the note it is because of its place on the scale, its position within the structure. With music, just as with articulate sound, understanding requires that we understand the whole structure and the determinate items within it. Music, like speech, is the context within which individual notes and sounds (middle C, D flat, "s," "b") find their determinate place.

The same story can be told for the next example, letters of the alphabet, where Socrates improves upon the atomistic account of the alphabet urged in the *Theaetetus* and the *Cratylus*.[54] Theuth—as Socrates' story goes—first recognized the alphabet.[55] He noticed the indeterminacy of sound, and real-

[54] Cf. ch. 5, sec. 7, and ch. 7, sec. 5.

[55] He did not invent it, but he saw it in the sounds he was presented with. Plato's use of myth here suggests that we should not be taking literally the notion that this was the origin of the letters (compare Socrates' complaints about the rationalization of myth at *Phdr.* 229); the point is rather a thought-experiment in the analysis of what letters actually are, not what they came from. This reflection on the status of myth should give us pause at 23ff., a passage that echoes the *Timaeus*'s

ized that in the indeterminate there are many (not just one) vowels, and likewise for the other sounds.[56] He proceeded in the proper fashion until he worked out the number of the letters, and grasped each one; then he called them all elements: "For he saw that none of us could grasp each one itself by itself without all of them; and then reasoning that this link between them was a single one which thus makes all these things in some way one, he declared there to be a single skill governing them all, grammar" (*Phil.* 18c).

Theuth's alphabet is an articulation of the context of sound into the science of writing. The identification of each letter is made within the context (the *apeiron*) and in relation to the other letters. Two things matter here.

First, here writ clear is the insistence that individuals, like letters or the elements of speech or music, cannot be known or grasped in isolation—but only in context (*Phil.* 18c7–8). We, like Philebus, understand these things *related to each other* (*auta ge pros allēla:* 18d3)—and their interrelation is what individualizes them.

Second, notice that the context in which they are individualized is, for the Theuth example, "grammar," the nexus of the relations between the letters. Grammar unifies the letters—but it is not some extra entity over and above them, any more than "indeterminate sound" is some stuff out of which these letters were "created." Instead, Theuth is credited with noticing how what seemed indeterminate can in fact be rendered determinate, and the object of science. Thus, there is a difference between the indeterminate (the mass of sound) and the one (the structure of letters that is the object of the grammarian's skill), since the one is ordered and the other is not; but neither is some extra thing—instead, they are versions of (or different descriptions of) the contexts within which the entities, the letters, are to be found.

So the individuation of each item in the complex is presented as a feature of its position in the whole—individuation is contextual. Thus, the significance of Socrates's use of musical notes as examples of the *peras* and the *apeiron* is that here the relative nature of each "one" is emphasized. Each note is what it is because it fits into what appears to be indeterminate; that is, because it fits into a context of other notes. The whole complex is a network of items that mutually define themselves. This is how the method defined earlier works—both working downward from the one, and upward from the indefinite (*Phil.* 18a–b).[57] If pitch is understood as a continuum, then individual notes on that continuum are what they are by virtue of the other notes on the continuum (the continuum itself, if I am right, does not have independent existence). For example, middle C is the note it is by virtue of its relation to B natural and D flat; and once we understand that, of course, we can readily see that any

---

mythical cosmology. Is the *Philebus*'s cosmology literal truth? Or does it need a more subtle interpretation than mere rationalization? Cf. ch. 6, secs. 1, 6.

[56] Cf. Waterfield, "Place of the *Philebus*."

[57] That, I suggest, makes it clear that the issue in the method is not one of relating determinate universals to indeterminate particulars, but instead one of making anything determinate—whether type or token. As in the *Parmenides*, a monad is whatever turns out to be an individual.

instance of middle C is likewise related to instances of B natural and D flat on either side. Once we understand what middle C is, we can " let it go into the indefinite." So pitch is thus understood relationally; and individual notes can be understood in terms of their relations to other notes, without, it seems, suffering the dangers of pluralization or becoming indefinite. Thus Socrates suggests that his method guards against the twin difficulties of focusing on the indeterminate instead of some determinate number; and of grasping the one in relation to the indeterminate instead of understanding how it has some particular number (*Phil.* 18a–b).

7. A DIVINE COSMOLOGY

Now Socrates offers a new division—of everything in the world, "all the things that are now" (*Phil.* 23c4). He proposes to give an explanation of the world in terms of the mixture of *peras* and *apeiron*, limit and unlimited, which forms individual somethings (23d1); and he promises a fourth item, the reason for their combining.

Limit and the unlimited[58] occupy similar positions in the cosmos; both are scattered and spread out in the world, and both can still be understood as one. So limit and unlimited are both one and many (*Phil.* 23e).

The unlimited (*Phil.* 24a–25a, 25c) can best be characterized as what admits the more and the less, and has no terminus; it has no definite quantity, no fixity. Instead it "always advances and never remains" (the same?)[59]. For example, "hotter" has no definite temperature so that it shifts around, and even could be said to be its opposite at the same time (24d).

Limit, on the other hand, stands still. This is what eliminates the "more and less" character of unlimited—it is responsible for the terminus, the quantity, or the number: "equal and equality, and after equal double and everything which relates number to number or measure to measure"[60] (*Phil.* 25a–b) and "the nature of the equal and of the double, and whatever (nature) prevents the opposites from being at odds with each other, but putting in symmetry and harmony, it makes number" (25d11–e2).

These two principles together are responsible for "some generations in each case" (*Phil.* 25e4), and, more especially, when the principles are joined in the right way, they produce good things—such as health, music, and good weather (26a–b). So Socrates has his third (enormous) category: "the unified class which is all the offspring of the previous two, the becoming into being[61] from measures crafted from limit" (26d).

---

[58] "The same items as we have been discussing before," *Phil.* 24a1–2.

[59] The echo of Heraclitus here allows, surely, this completion of οὐ μένει.

[60] Cf. Gosling, *Plato: Philebus,* p. 92.

[61] N.B. the oddity of the expression here, literally the "becoming into being," γένεσιν εἰς οὐσίαν. Does this make process and becoming respectable at last? Compare a similar oddity at *Pol.* 283d.

This "becoming into being" is explained (*Phil.* 26e)[62] by the fourth class, the class of what makes[63] and is responsible for the third, that which comes into being and is made.[64] So the third class is the class of "all the unlimiteds bound by a limit" (27d9); this is body, the composite of the first two classes—in universal terms, the body of the cosmos (29d). The fourth class, on the other hand, is mind; and this turns up in the rational ordering of the world (28d), so that the cosmos is itself intelligent (30a ff.).

Socrates' account, then, ends with a cosmology; and one which, moreover, is strongly reminiscent of the *Timaeus*; for example, the teleology is explained in terms of an intelligent craftsman, here conflated with the soul of the world. Is this discussion of limit and unlimited merely a rerun of the *Timaeus*'s argument about forms and stuff? Are *peras* and *apeiron* components of the world, constituent parts of the entities that form the third class, parts of the cosmic body? And if they are, does the discussion of cosmic body cohere with the investigation of limit and unlimited in the way we talk?[65]

Think first of all about the unlimited. In the earlier discussion, this represented the indeterminate nature of some "one" that had been collected, but not yet articulated by division. This process appeared to be a theoretical one—the collections and divisions were metaphorical, representing the conceptual analysis of a system of universals. But in the divine cosmology, the unlimited looks very much like stuff, the indeterminate material from which physical objects are made. In that case, there is no immediate connection between the cosmology (which is about actual entities and their actual components) and the method of collection and division, which is about abstractions. To make the two cohere would require a gross kind of physicalism—universals are made of stuff; dialectic is chopping stuff.

But can the unlimited be stuff? Consider the example of "hotter." This has two descriptions: it never stays still, and it is even characterized by its opposite. Suppose that hotter is some actual "temperature-stuff." What would it mean for that never to stay still? Is "it" always getting hotter or colder, never sticking to the same temperature? Suppose there is a chemical, Heracliteum, whose molecules constantly interact to make it hotter, until it reaches a critical temperature, or which it starts to get colder again—this stuff would be always moving in temperature, never staying still—but it would still, at any time, be some determinate temperature, even if only instantaneously. Moreover, it would not thereby have opposite characters *at the same time*. Yet

---

[62] αἰτία—this may be a cause or an explanation; but reflection on *Phd.* 96ff. should encourage us to take it as the latter.

[63] It "demiurges," 27b1—a reference to the *Timaeus*?

[64] N.B. the argument for the nonidentity of the third and fourth classes—one is the agent, the other the patient, 27a.

[65] Socrates suggests that in deciding whether pleasure or reason should win the second prize, they need another strategy, μηχανή (cf. 16a7). The reference back to the initial puzzles suggests that the "strategies" are connected if different. How different is "another"???? Perhaps not so much; hence, the next caveat, "some of them may be the same" (23b7–9); cf. Protarchus on repeating the same point, 24d9ff.

Socrates' *apeiron* does.[66] If it is stuff, how does it avoid the dangers of contradiction? Notice the difference between something's lacking character in itself (and therefore, as Timaeus points out, being indescribable) and something's actively having opposite properties. Either option may be intolerable—but they are not the same option. If something has opposite properties, it cannot be an individual particular entity[67] (and yet the *apeiron* is *one*); but it could be a universal (for example, individual members of the same class may possess opposite properties), and it could be a continuum (for example, a spectrum of the color red could be dark at one end and light at the other without suffering from intolerable contradiction). But neither the universal nor the continuum need be actual, real, or stuffy. Socrates' *apeiron* is neither completely indeterminate (since it does have specific characters) nor is it material stuff (otherwise it would be contradictory); instead, it seems to be a continuum—and thus a universal.

But it is a universal of a particular sort—a *relative universal*. The discussion of "hotter" and "colder," "more" and "less," is striking because it involves relations between two items ("hotter than what?"—"this bath is hotter than that cup of coffee"). The continuum, then, represents a series of possible relations between various items; those relations are realized when points on the continuum are actualized by limit, and a temperature, for example, is made determinate. When this happens, the hotter stops sliding away (because there is now an actual temperature), and there is no longer a contradiction (this is actually 43°C), although there may still, innocuously, be the compresence of opposites (43 degrees centigrade is hot in the shade, cold for a cup of coffee). But how does this imposition of the limit on the continuum occur?

There are two ways of answering that question. We might attempt an answer in terms of what this temperature is made of, or the conditions it came from (the coffee is hot because I boiled the kettle; the bath is hot because the thermostat is broken). Or instead of looking at causes, we might go for explanations. Forty-three degrees can be explained or understood in terms of a particular point on the temperature scale; middle C is a definite item on the musical scale; this brilliant scarlet here is a particular point on the spectrum of red. All of these explanations cite both the unlimited (the continua) and the limit (the particular points on the spectrum). But although the language of physical composition is overwhelming (this point *on* the scale; the colors *in* the spectrum, and so forth), the limit and the unlimited are not *components* of 43 degrees, or middle C, or this brilliant scarlet, for they are not real physical entities, actual parts of the items before us (43 degrees, middle C, this brilliant scarlet); instead, they are part of the conceptual apparatus we employ to explain them.

Is that what Socrates is offering us? If he is, the discussion of limit and unlimited as classes of things that are is of a piece with the discussion of *peras*

---

[66] Notice the difference between this characterization of the unlimited and the earlier problem of the compresence of opposites, which is not a problem of contradiction; cf. above, ch. 2, sec. 3.

[67] Plato, of course, recognizes that; cf., e.g., *Rep.* 436.

and *apeiron* in the way we talk. Consider the development of his argument in the following way. In the first stage of the analysis of limited and unlimited he showed that universals can be determined by the context articulated by dialectic. But the thought that the context in which something occurs explains its individuation is not restricted to universals, for in the second stage, the divine cosmology suggests that just as universals are understood contextually, so individual particulars are what they are by virtue of the context in which they occur. So *this* middle C is what it is because there is a B natural lower than it, and a D flat higher. Its context, no less than the context of the universal, detemines what it is. So the structured explanations of things are isomorphic with the things they explain.

Throughout, therefore, Socrates distinguishes between a universal of enormous scope, and its determination into individuals. In the first place we could collect the art of hunting and divide it into species, or we could collect temperature and articulate it into degrees; conversely, we could find out how sophistry fits into a wider scheme of things, or discover where brilliant scarlet comes on the spectrum. Each stage (the wide scope universal and the subordinate types) can be described as "one"; but only when the subordinate types have been determined does the feature of unlimited disappear from our account. Then, in the second place, we could find this particular temperature on a continuum, that particular color on a spectrum—the contextualizing method is the same.

Suppose, then, we ask how to understand the discussion of the "becoming into being" of the third class. Socrates could be interested in the fact that this class becomes, undergoes the process of generation, is affected by the limit and the unlimited. In that case, we should expect him to be talking about causes, conditions, and constituents. Or Socrates could be interested (hence the oddity of the phrase "becoming into being") in the fact that the third class is a class of things that are, of entities—and of entities, moreover, discussed under the general heading of "one and many." This, I suggest, is exactly what happens here. Socrates is concerned to show not how these items are generated, but what it is for them to be.[68] In that case, we should expect to find him worrying about how they are one (as the outset of the discussion predicts) and how they are determinate—"to be is to be something." Hence, perhaps, Protarchus's comment on Socrates' third class: "You seem to me to be saying that mixing these (sc. the first two classes) will result in certain generations in each case" (*eph' hekaston autōn*, 25e).

Return to the examples of *peras* and *apeiron* taken from music and speech. An articulate sound is what it is by virtue of its place in the spectrum of spoken sounds: the spectrum, the context, is the continuum of sound; the place in the context is determined by limit. But the same story could be told of concrete

---

[68] But then the final passage, which sums up the list, suggests that only the third category counts as one of ὄντα (26c6); this is the offspring of the other two, which has its γένεσιν εἰς οὐσίαν from the measures created by limit.

physical objects. They are what they are, it could be said, because of their place in their context. Being something or other is determined by the context in which the something occurs; that is, its relations to other items and their relation to it. It is, then, on a continuum; and it is (to be an individual) at a fixed place on that continuum. Imagine this in the most abstract terms—the continuum might be space/time; the limit on the continuum will be the coordinates that individuate a particular object. And the combination of the two (spatio-temporal coordinates) will allow us to identify and to count each individual particular thus determined.

8. NUMBERS OR WHAT?

Socrates' discussion of limit and unlimited is an answer to the problem of "one and many"; it is all about *counting*, as Socrates repeatedly asserts (*Phil.* 16d4, 8; 17c12, e5; 18b2, c1, c5; 19a1; and then again at 23d2; 25a7, e2). For until we can enumerate things, we cannot really understand them (17e); and counting them involves us in assessing their individuation and their identity (19b). We must be able to say "how much" something is, in order to be able to locate it among the one and the many and thus to understand it (cf. 24c ff.)—and that can only be done when we grasp the limit and the unlimited in things.

So numbers are obviously important in the scheme of this passage; and this has encouraged commentators[69] to connect what Socrates says here with Pythagorean mathematics, on the basis of Aristotle's evidence.

> Furthermore he [Plato] said that in addition to perceptible things and forms, mathematical objects were in between, although they differed from perceptible things in being eternal and immobile, from forms in being many items, all similar, while the form is itself one and unique. Since forms are the becauses[70] of the other things, he thought that the elements of them [the forms] would be the elements of all the things that are. And so for principles he posited the large and the small as the matter and the one as the being; for from these by participation in the one the forms are numbers[71]—however he took the one to be being, instead of something else which is being said to be one—and thus he said much the same thing as the Pythagoreans, agreeing with them in saying that numbers are responsible for the being of everything else. But instead of making the unlimited one, he made it a dyad, and made the unlimited out of large and small—and that claim is peculiar to him . . . (*Met.* 987b14–27)

[69] E.g., Sayre, *Ontology*.

[70] I translate αἰτιὸν as "because," not "cause," since "cause" looks like an efficient cause, rather than a reason or an explanation; cf. Vlastos, "Reasons and Causes"—it is obvious that Plato could not have meant transcendent, austere forms to be efficient causes, or constituents. The same should regularly be said for Aristotle, who can cite a because without making a strong ontological commitment.

[71] Following Stenzel's text here.

There are unmistakable references to the *Philebus* here; Aristotle seems to interpret Plato in a manner congenial to himself, by explaining the *peras/apeiron* analysis in terms of form (*ousia*) and matter, and it is a part of that interpretation that Plato offers a Pythagorean analysis of the constituent parts of forms. Now this account sits ill with a theory of transcendent forms, which are incomposite, and hardly to be better understood by deconstructing them into the one and the dyad. Furthermore, transcendent forms seem to be irrelevant to the ones and manies of the *Philebus*. What, then, is Aristotle's complaint against Plato here?

Consider the following passages:

> Since "one" is said like "is," and since the being of the one is itself one, and the things whose being is one in number are one in number, it is clear that neither one nor being can be the substance of things, either by virtue of being an element or a principle. (*Met.* 1040b16–19)

Here Aristotle complains that one cannot be a principle; that is, he enveighs against precisely the thesis he earlier attributed to Plato ("And so for principles he posited the large and the small as the matter and the one as the being"). Why? The answer, perhaps, lies in Aristotle's primary explanation of "being one": "being one something or other":

> Again "one" is said of those things whose account when it mentions the "what it is to be" is indivisible to someone else who indicates the thing. . . . In general when the intellection of something is indivisible, intellecting the what it is to be, and cannot be separated either in time or in place or in account, those things are most of all one, and of those, most of all those which are substances. . . . Most things are said to be one by virtue of doing something else, or having it or suffering it or in some relation, but things said in a primary way are one whose being is one, and they are one either by continuity or by form or by account. (*Met.* 1016a32–b9)

Aristotle's account of "being one" and thus his analysis of individuation is, as I have argued, dependent on his account of substance or essence.[72] Being one is understood in terms of the categories, so that the expresssion "one" is always parasitic on some predicate: "one something or other," "one somehow or other." In the primary cases, and those on which all other cases depend (both for their definition and their existence), "one" is parasitic on some form or essence term; thus, being one is dependent on sorted kinds. But Plato, in Aristotle's view, got this wrong, in two connected ways.

1. Plato sees "one" not as a predicate term, but as a subject term; and he makes the same mistake for "being." That is the objection against Plato launched at *Metaphysics* 987b22 ("however he took the one to be being, instead of something else which is being said to be one"). If one is a subject, it

---

[72] Cf. ch. 1, secs. 4, 5.

is then susceptible to further analysis into its elements. For that reason, perhaps, Plato can be assimilated to the Pythagoreans.[73]

2. Plato supposed "one" to be both a univocal term and a complete expression; this assumption, indeed, may be why he could treat "one" as a subject.[74] Consequently, "one" is a common term, and being one is a property common to all sorts of things. But in that case, argues Aristotle, it cannot be substance (*Met.* 1040b23); nor could it be an element or principle (*Met.* 1040b18); nor, since it is common to many things, could it be indivisible, and thus a suitable account for individuation (*Met.* 1016a32ff.). Plato misses the fact that terms like "one," "good," and "is" are multivocal because they are syncategorematic (cf. *E.N.* I.6). Plato's treatment of one as complete means that he misses the correct means of explaining what it is to be one.

Aristotle's account of Plato, interpreted thus, is true to Plato's insistence that being one is basic to being anything at all. I have argued that Plato understands being in terms of individuation; and Aristotle's remarks confirm that view. For Plato, we can say nothing about anything until it is seen to be a something; it can only be the subject of predicates, or an object having properties, if it is an individual first. In that sense, one is rightly associated with being; one is properly a subject; and being one is complete in itself.

Aristotle interprets Plato as a Pythagorean because Plato associates explanation with number. And indeed, as I have pointed out, the *Philebus* makes a great deal of play with the idea that Socrates is counting ones and manies, collecting them, dividing them, and generally arranging them. One interpretation of that might be[75] that Plato, in the *Philebus*, is actually proposing that things are made up of numbers—namely the one and the dyad—and that those numbers are the ultimate constituents of things; in that case Plato would indeed take on the look of a Pythagorean.

Several things, however, militate against that sort of interpretation of the *Philebus*. First, this account of the cosmological passage there makes a huge split between the later discussion of *peras* and *apeiron* in the *Philebus* and the earlier discussion of collection and division; even if the latter is about physical components, the former cannot be. Second, this misses what I have argued to be the puzzle of the *Timaeus*, which suggests that a cosmology based on the contrast between form and stuff (or limit and unlimited) may be incoherent or impossible to state. Third, if the *Philebus* is thought to suggest that physical objects are made of numbers (mediated by forms), it runs foul of the objec-

[73] At *Phil.* 23d, Protarchus misunderstands Socrates' suggestion by treating mixture, σύμμειξις, literally and by demanding a principle of dissolution. That interpretation of Socrates' cosmology would be attractive to any of the earlier scientists (and to the chaps who are overexcited about one/many puzzles at 15e). But then if Protarchus has got it wrong, perhaps we should infer that Socrates is not trying to offer a physical account at all. If Aristotle, by assimilating Plato to the Pythagoreans, is treating him like a pre-Socratic, he has got it wrong too.

[74] Cf. ch. 4, sec. 3; and ch. 6, sec. 2.

[75] Cf. Sayre, *Ontology*.

tions of the *Parmenides* and the *Sophist* that "one" cannot be treated as a component part and still retain its unity.

All of this, however, comes from the ready assumption that when Plato speaks of numbers as the principles of things he means that they are component parts; that is not necessarily so. Think, after all, of Aristotle's own analysis of number: "Number is said in two ways—we call both what is counted and is countable, and that by which we count number" (*Phys.* 219b6–7).

Thus, for example, we can distinguish between the cows in the field and the number five by which we count them. Both are five, but in different metaphysical ways. Now although, on Aristotle's view, one is not properly a number (but the unit from which numbers are made up),[76] we can only start to count when we have some grip on the unit, whether it be a monad, a mongoose, or a mistake. Number, then, depends on individuation, on sorting out the ones in the many. In what sense, then, might Plato suppose form to be number, or imagine forms to be analyzable into the one and the dyad?

Go back to the *Philebus*. I have suggested that there the principles of limit and unlimited are designed to explain individuation; by means of those principles we can determine the individual units that are to be counted. So the principles of *peras* and *apeiron* are thus the means by which we count (the limit gives us each one among the many of the unlimited), and the third class consists of what is counted—actual individuals.

. Where does that leave forms? What are the individuals that are counted by this means? The entire discussion of *peras* and *apeiron* is tangled just because it is never clear what sort of thing Socrates is talking about. Sometimes he seems to be talking about particular physical objects (as at *Phil.* 26c ff.); sometimes he seems to be talking about types of physical (or more or less physical) objects (such as musical sounds or cows); sometimes he suggests that the topic is transcendent forms (as at *Phil.* 15b, confirmed by Aristotle's remark about forms being numbers); and sometimes that they are universals —either actual classes or perhaps only concepts. And at the beginning of the passage he refers, bafflingly, to henads and monads. What is he talking about? How desperate is the muddle of Plato's ontology?

Recall Aristotle's remark that forms are numbers. This conclusion is derived from the thesis that forms have the one and the dyad as their elements. Are the forms, then, numbers in the sense that they are what we count with (like the Pythagoreans)? Or are they what is counted? If forms are monads— and if, as such, they are separate, independent objects—then they are, presumably, what is counted—individual entities. But then forms cannot be understood as transcendent and separate on the austere model of the *Phaedo* since collection and division would entangle them in an impossible plurality. On the other hand, if *peras* and *apeiron* explain what forms are, how do they also explain what physical objects in the sensible world are? How could there

---

[76] Cf., e.g., *Phys.* 207b5ff.

be the same analysis of forms as there is of particulars? And how, furthermore, can we tell—or resolve—whether Plato is talking about types of physical objects, or tokens? And does any of that matter?

On a traditional interpretation of the *Philebus*, it does. For on a traditional interpretation, these sections of the dialogue are fundamentally concerned with ontology, with detailing what entities there are, and allowing us to include in our ontology forms and monads and particulars and universals. But in that case, there is a radical problem, once again, of coherence. How, then, can the pair *peras/apeiron* be anything but equivocated?

I suggest that What is Plato's ontology? is the wrong question, because it is posterior to the one Plato is asking in this passage, as in the others I have discussed. Plato supposes, as Aristotle sees, that counting, or individuating, is a necessary condition of determining whether something is (anything at all). The business of individuation comes *before* the business of counting up all the individuals there are. The historical Socrates complained that we cannot determine which actions were holy until we know what holiness is. In like manner, Plato could object to the traditional views of his later dialogues (that they offer various ontologies); his interpreters, he might complain, assume that we can count individuals before we know what it is to be one. Instead, what Plato offers us is an analysis of individuation; let ontology wait until that is complete.[77]

There is, then, no proper answer to the question, What entities are under consideration here?—just because the analysis of how to count individuals must be free of assumptions about which things are individuals anyway; for individuation must come first. So anything that can be counted on the scheme of *peras* and *apeiron* will be an individual, whether it be form, particular, universal, or class. Anything that is anything will turn out on this scheme to be a something; only thereafter can we decide how it is such.[78]

9. COLLECTION AND DIVISION AND THE MESH OF IDENTITY

"What is there?"—"Individuals, countable basic entities, self-identical and different from others." As soon as the question is posed, the further question arises: "How do *we* understand what there is?"

In the middle period basic entities were assumed to be individuals, one by

---

[77] Consider, for example, the original dispute, from *Phil.* 12c to 15c.

[78] This account of Plato's strategy might be thought to run up against Geach's "Socratic Fallacy" ("Plato's *Euthyphro*"). If we do not know the scope of "individual," and have no way of deciding what things are individuals, how can we ever arrive at an understanding of what it is to be an individual? But notice that I have not painted Plato into that corner. For it is one thing to deny that we can decide marginal cases of universals, and another to say that we can have no intuitions about central cases at all. I have allowed Plato to have intuitions about central cases (he never seems to deny that individual physical particulars are in fact individuals), which then force him to rethink the marginal ones.

one. Understanding, however, was a complex matter, in the ideal case a structured and systematic grasp of what is known. There was, I suggested, a tension between the "one by one" view of basic entities and the systematic nature of understanding (stressed, especially, in both parts of the *Parmenides*). But now, I submit, the complexity of knowledge and the contextual account of individuation go hand in hand.

Plato insists, in several of the later dialogues, that he has discovered a new and stunning "method" of dialectic: collection and division. This, Socrates suggests, is the only worthwhile product of the discussion by the Ilissus—to show how someone might be able "firstly, by seeing them together to bring into one idea things which are scattered all over the place, so that by defining each one he might make clear whatever he wants to explain. Secondly he should be able to chop it up again according to its forms at the natural joints (not carving any one of those forms into parts, like a bad butcher). . . . As for me, I am a lover of these collections and divisions, Phaedrus, so that I might be able both to speak and to think" (*Phdr.* 265d–66b).

The *Sophist* emphasizes the way in which this "method" (*methodos, Soph.* 219a)[79] may allow us both to count kinds and to determine what each one is (217a–b); and to that end the ES gives us an exhausting demonstration (using angling as an example; 218b ff.). By using the same technique we may be able to move beyond merely having the name "sophist" to *understanding what it is* (218c). If we begin with a single general idea (e.g., "art"), we can subdivide that into forms (*eidē*) or parts (*merē*), taking care not to be deceived either by the complexity of the subject (223c) or by the similarities between two divisions (226d; 231a); the process terminates when we reach some form that is indivisible (229d). The *Politicus* reiterates the need to get the divisions in the right place (*Pol.* 262d). Some people get it wrong, ". . . dividing "Greek" off as one separate from everything else, and calling all the other races, which are indefinite and unmixed with each other and incompatible with each other by a single name "barbarian" they expect this too to be a single kind by virtue of the singularity of its name; or else someone might think that dividing number into two forms he might cut off the myriad from the rest, and then by giving a single name to what is left, he might suppose that by that very act of naming he had one kind different from the first" (*Pol.* 262c–d).

The trouble with words, these passages suggest, is that they allow us to see divisions where none really exist—names mislead us into thinking we have properly described the nature of things, when we have not done so. Instead, the divisions by name must correspond to the divisions by nature, if the method is to be sound. What is divided is reality, not just language.

The good thing about words, on the other hand, is that they allow us to see

---

[79] Is the process of collection and division a method? It is described as dialectic (*Soph.* 253d; *Phdr.* 266c), but it is difficult to see how "Just collect and divide!" could be the solution to Meno's paradox of inquiry. Collection and division offer, not a method of inquiry, but a system of understanding, a way of structuring our explanations. Dialectic, on that view, is science, not the troublesome anxieties of the philosopher.

how the nature of things is structured; for that occurs by sameness and difference, by the assimilation of two forms under a single term, and their differentiation within it. The discussion of the angler in the *Sophist* makes it clear that a proper (naturally articulated) division can be expected to produce genuine individual (atomic) kinds, countable and describable, explained in terms of their location in the collection and division as a whole. So both reality and language can be understood in terms of the relations between things: individuation, on either count, is contextual.

In the *Philebus*, Socrates flaunts the puzzles of earlier dialogues. In the *Parmenides*, or in the *Theaetetus* or the *Timaeus*, the trouble with individual objects was often expressed as their conflation of one and indefinitely many. I have characterized this as the tension between the austere and the generous conceptions of individuation. Now, however, such a conflation is positively invited—the things that are said to be are *naturally composed* of the one and the many, the definite and the indefinite. Why is that composition no longer paradoxical?

When we collect and divide, each item is one because it is counted (we need to know how many there are). It is many, on the other hand, because it is part of a complex structure (one among many); and its presence in that structure is determined by its interrelation with other items in the same complex. But its being countable (one) is a consequence of its being contextualized in the structure of the divisions (many or infinite or indefinite). On an earlier story, that would have made the item in question contradictory, since its being same as itself, different from the others, would have pluralized it and canceled out its unity. Now, however, the danger of pluralizing that comes from relations seems to be past. Why?

In the earlier dialogues Plato supposed that relational properties were superadded to the relata, parts of them that impaired their unity (relational properties, that is, "pluralized"). So a relational account of the identity of individuals was impossible without threatening the individuals themselves; hence the dilemma between austere individuals and their generous counterparts. The achievement of the *Sophist* and the *Philebus* is to resolve this dilemma by rethinking relations; individuation, consequently, can be understood relationally.

This move had, I have argued, five stages:

1. Individuals are basic; well-formed speech and properly structured reality are founded on individuals. But individuals are not just isolated objects. Instead,

2. The terms "same" and "different" establish the identity of something in relation to everything else. To say of something that it is the same as itself and different from anything else is necessary for identifying it.

3. Sameness and difference are thus primitive: any identity gives an entity.

4. What is identified is individuated, too; for this contextualizing procedure generates principles for counting.

5. And once we can count, our individuals can have properties, too.

Now because relations are no longer understood as properties of the relata, but rather in terms of the connections between the relata, this contextual account of individuation seems to escape the dangers of pluralization.

In the *Philebus* and the *Sophist*, strikingly, Socrates moves freely between discussing conceptual structures to analyzing their real counterparts in the outside world. Imagine a set of interconnected ideas, meshed together in a series of complex relations—my ideas of justice, equality, and liberty, say. Each can be understood in terms of its relations with the others (justice, for example, needs to take account of equality and liberty), but those relations need not reflect any real features of the world. Because my thinking is abstracted, detached from reality or nature, then the relations between my ideas need not be affections of those ideas, even if they can be defined only in terms of that relational context. Relating one idea to another, that is, does not obviously pluralize it. After all, an item in some conceptual structure (perhaps like a tree of collection and division) is not pluralized (as forms once were) just by virtue of being enmeshed in those structures. But then it may be the same for the world. Real objects are not pluralized by being different from other real objects, just as relational change may not be real change, but merely Cambridge change. Becoming known may not be a causally significant affection of what is known; likewise, changes in the identity or the properties of one individual in a context may not affect the identity of the rest. Frameworks of reality, therefore, may perhaps locate the individuals therein; they need not, however, be extra pieces of reality within which the individual items occur.[80]

Is this, we might ask, an idealist account of the relations that individuate? Are the items in a context only individuated if someone sees them or thinks them to be so? The *Philebus*'s comparison between the structure of what is understood and the structure of individual particulars in the world might lead us to suppose that now relations like sameness and difference are merely mind-dependent, no longer features of the world at all. However, that the structure of the world is isomorphic with the structure of universals does not imply idealism. Instead, Plato may simply be suggesting a more sophisticated metaphysical arrangement in the world itself. Some items are real and causally efficient (individual objects, properties): changes here are real changes. Some items—relations in particular—may not be causally efficient in the same way, even if they are still real: and here change is merely Cambridge change. So there are the physical objects of the world, enmeshed in a context that determines just what they are, and there is the context itself, which is not some extra entity over and above the things that appear in it, nor yet no entity at all, but, perhaps, supervenient on the individuals it explains (or *subvenient in them*, more appropriately, for something understood on the model of place).

How far does Plato's strategy differ from Aristotle's? Aristotle individuates

---

[80] Any more, to return to Zeno, than a place is something in a place; contrast *Phys.* 210b22ff.

by sorting, Plato by determining one item in a complex classification. The traditional view would be that Plato has offered us, for example, a biological classification, which will thereafter enable us to say "one rabbit," "one soft-shelled crab." Plato, on this account, is merely anticipating Aristotle's fully worked out theory for sorting individuals into kinds.

But that does not fit, for example, the later discussion of *peras* and *apeiron* in the *Philebus*. There, I have argued, individuation was a matter of determining a location (the *peras*) on a continuum (the *apeiron*). The individual that we get at the end of collection and division is the nexus itself ("rabbit," "soft-shelled crab," not particular rabbits or crabs), determined by its place in the whole context. The individual that we get from musical analysis is a note (type or token), which is the one note it is because of its place on the continuum of sound. The individual we get from cosmological analysis is a particular sensible individual, which can be picked out as such because of its context and its place within it. The crucial things here are not the sorting terms, but the way the meshing or sorting is done. It is the superordinate terms (same different, one many) that matter, for it is those general terms that determine individual identity.

How would that work for the limiting case of sensible individuals? It is, perhaps, easy to see how individual concepts are determined by their relations with other concepts, and thus how concepts are individuated by context and place. It is far harder to understand how this might be true for concrete objects, which seem to be individuated by their stuff—"they are just there," irrespective of their context which, after all, changes as they move around the physical world, and the world around them.

Imagine that an armadillo lumbers into the room. What makes us say that it is one thing? We might be thoroughly Aristotelian and argue that it is one because it is sorted by the class "armadillo." Or we might, conversely (in ignorance, perhaps, of its class, or of any classes at all), imagine it to be one because it moves through its background. Its independence from the things around it (it can move around) and its relativity to its place (it is wherever it is) allow us to call it one thing. This, if you like, is to offer its spatial coordinates, and its temporal ones, too, if we imagine our armadillo walking around over a period of time. This individual is an individual just because it is contextualized; this thing is just one, before it is an armadillo, or a collection of bones and scales. And that account of individuation meets Plato's constant criteria: being one, being just one, comes first.

But reflection may suggest that this explanation of individuation is too thin for comfort. The context may explain how something is one something such that we can count it—it is a unit. But can the context explain the unity of any something? Only, I suspect, in a rather limited way (as self-identity). Such units are rather austere, after all. Instead we might ask for a wider, more generous notion of an individual—and then we need to know, What makes it one?

Consider, therefore and finally, a special case—the unity of persons. Here the problem is not one of counting, but rather one of identifying persons by seeing their principles of coherence, both at a time and over time. To explain *someone* makes radical demands on our account of unity and individuation; here again, Plato tells a rich, and even a likely, story.

The Unity of Persons

"THE ONE AND THE MANY" had Plato worried. How could an individual have many parts or properties and remain an individual? Contrariwise, how could it be specified as an individual without allowing it to have parts? This, at any rate, is the trouble he has with individual objects. Does he have the same difficulty with persons? Can the analysis of individual objects that he gives be applied, *mutatis mutandis*, to individual persons?

Some of the difficulties that beset individual persons are indeed the same as those that beset individual objects: how are they to be individuated and identified at a time, and how can we say that they persist over time? For persons, no less than for things, we might worry about synchronic unity (Is John Major the same person as Margaret Thatcher?); and for persons no less than for things, we may worry about their persistence through time (Is this the genius I met yesterday?). And for persons no less than for things, such questions might be understood as a problem about self-identity (I have described this as absolute individuation from within: "Is this one whole person?") or as a problem about difference from others (here we have relative individuation from without: "Is this one person as distinct from others?").

But persons are trickier than things. The questions that we can ask about "being one something" (as I have suggested Plato to understand the problem of individuation) are far simpler than the questions we can ask about "being someone." At least in a post-Cartesian world, there seems to be something special about "I" (and thereafter about anyone like me).[1]

There may be, first of all, an epistemological point about "I"; I think that I have direct and privileged access to what I think and experience. While I may be skeptical about anyone else, at least I have some confidence in my own cognitive goings on; and while I may be suspicious of anything else, I seem secure in my own view out onto the world. Moreover, this specialness has an ethical counterpart. I care about what happens to me in a particular and special way. I have, it seems, an interest in my own survival and well-being that is deep and effortless compared to my interest in the survival and well-being of others. And yet I do also see that others might be special too; thus, I can readily suppose that they think, too, and that they, too, have ethical interests. So I talk to other persons rather than to the lamppost; and I hold others responsible for what they do just because they are persons (I do not blame the lamppost when I bump into it). This could be understood as a special sort of

---

[1] Cf., e.g., Shoemaker, *Identity, Cause and Mind*, or Nagel, *The View from Nowhere*.

basicness—persons are, we may readily suppose from introspection, irreducibly basic.

How far does Plato recognize the argument that persons are special? How far can we explain what it is to be an individual person in terms of what he says about individual objects? His account of the unity of persons, I shall suggest, is complex and important; and it complements his account of the individuation of things in a surprising way. In particular, while the mesh of identity allows us to count simple entities (very like the austere individuals of my original problem), Plato's account of the unity of persons shows how a complex entity may cohere, without suffering from hopeless generosity. He deals, that is, both with unity (the unity of consciousness) and persistence (personal identity over time). For persons, this rich account of individuation and identity is vital to preserve our intuitions about the specialness of "I."[2]

Socrates asked, "Who will you become [sc. if you visit the sophists]?" (*Protagoras* 311b). This formula, I shall suggest, captures something of Plato's account of persons; and it shows him not lagging far behind Descartes. For he does have an account to give of the first person; but the context in which it is given pushes him toward the view that being a unified person is not something I can take for granted (once I start to focus on my own intellectual activities) but rather something to which I aspire. Being a unified person is for Plato an honorific title; hence, the proper question to ask is indeed, Who shall I become?

1. Immortal Souls

Of course, Plato concedes that persons are moral agents (and lampposts are not); what is more, he talks about how a moral agent turns out to be one, when he talks about souls.

The *Phaedo* is a discussion of the immortality of the soul that takes place just before Socrates drinks the hemlock. What Socrates (or his friends) are worried about is survival after death; and they are anxious to be convinced that death is innocuous. Why? Because they want to survive; but they want to survive as individuals—they are afraid that by the next day there will be no more Socrates (not no more souls). So it would hardly be a consolation to them to show, for example, that the form of soul is deathless. Plato must demonstrate that Socrates' soul is immortal, that we go on and on as individuals, not as a generic soul, or even as part of some reservoir of psychic stuff. In the face of death, individual survival is what matters.[3]

---

[2] It could be argued—cf., e.g., Burnyeat, "Idealism"—that this is an anachronism, and that we owe our interest in "I" to Descartes. I think that the Platonic evidence shows otherwise. I also think that this interest in the identity of persons goes back to that proto-Cartesian, Parmenides; cf. Mackenzie, "Parmenides' Dilemma."

[3] Hence, perhaps, all the fuss in the modern literature about split brains and clones, fission and fusion. Cf., e.g., the papers collected in Perry, *Personal Identity*; Rorty, *The Identities of Persons*; Hofstadter and Dennett, *The Mind's Eye*.

Two different arguments take the strain: the argument from Recollection; and the affinity argument.

1. *The argument from Recollection (Phd.* 74ff; cf. *Meno* 79ff.). When we are confronted with cases of equality—this stick is equal to that stick—we appear to understand "equal" despite the fact that the sticks are just as much cases of inequality as they are of equality. So we must have known what equal was all along (and likewise known our entire conceptual structure); and we must have got that knowledge before birth.

This argument, of course, says little about survival after death; but it does lay claim to the prenatal existence, and thus to the persistence of the soul over some time, if not all time. The soul's persistence is guaranteed by its being able to remember (in a queer way) what it has experienced before; this memory is a guarantee that this soul is the one that was around in the underworld before it was born.

So far so good. Saying that I persist because my memories form a connected chain is a popular move in the discussion of personal identity, employing as it does the idea that my memories are special to me; they are personal, mine, inaccessible to anyone else (debarring the anomalous cases of interfering scientists and deceptive computers). But Socrates' Recollection is only remembering in a queer way: for two connected reasons.

First of all, this memory is a complete system, which informs the activities of mind in the soul's incarnate existence; it does not occur piecemeal or haphazardly as ordinary memory does. After all, the theory of Recollection explains our access to truth that is fixed and objective, unaffected by its being relative to persons.[4] If this innate system of ideas[5] marks off one person from another, then I am marked off from you by where my system ends and yours begins—even though the systems are exact clones of each other, reflections of "all of nature" that is akin. So (despite Plato's protestations) Recollecting is not the same thing as remembering; rather, it is the whole collection of ideas innate in the soul, latent from birth and only subsequently, if at all, activated. In that case, we may wonder whether Recollection does the work of guaranteeing personal continuity that modern appeals to memory exploit.

Second, we might say that this system is programmed into the soul. Does a program guarantee personality? The modern objection might be that these are machines, not minds: does Recollection fit our intuitions about minds? After all, this memory is not personal—far from it. What I am programmed to Recollect (even if I do not succeed in actually recalling it) is exactly the same as what you are programmed to remember; there is nothing private or special here about me.

Nonetheless, the recollection argument does provide a criterion for individuating souls; for if what I am programmed to Recollect is a complete system, then an individual will be just who can or does Recollect the system whole.

---

[4] This is so, at least, until Plato comes up against the objection that becoming known is dangerous for what is objectively true; cf. ch. 3, sec. 7.

[5] Cf. above, ch. 3, secs. 1, 3.

This supposes that the location (actual or potential) for a completely Recollected system is a single mind. The difference between one mind and another will be just where one Recollected system ends (could end) and the next begins. But of course the Recollected systems are clones of each other (each system is true, and truth is unique); so the minds in which they occur will be clones of each other too. They will be distinct from each other, but their nonidentity will be numerical, not qualitative. There will be nothing special about either.

This has three important consequences for Plato's account of who I am. First, it is thoroughly intellectual. I am nothing but what I think; how I feel, or how I behave, whether I am virtuous or disgraceful, makes no difference to my coherence as a person (even if it may make a difference to my happiness or to others' opinions about me). Second, in one sense, being a person is just having the regular collection of innate ideas, the same collection as everyone else. In another sense, however, being a person is actualizing that potential, bringing the ideas to the forefront of my mind (and in that respect one person may differ from another). But then the difference between persons is understood in terms of their relative intellectual success. If my personal identity or coherence is a matter of intellectual success, then "being one" turns out to be an honorific title. I may aspire to personal identity, but I do not have it all along. Third, however, does an intellectual criterion of identity like this one hold out any hope of explaining what it is to be *me*; can Plato's intellectualism accommodate the subjectivity that seems to make being a person so special? The individuation of persons devolves onto the individuation of systems of knowledge, and this then needs analysis in just the same way as the individuation of objects. Persons, here, are just specially good objects, not different from objects because they are special.

2. *The affinity argument* (*Phd.* 78b ff; 100b ff.). Souls are incomposite and invisible. Forms are incomposite and invisible. So souls are like forms. But forms are eternal because they are incomposite—they are thus not subject to change. Souls, therefore, insofar as they are incomposite, are not subject to change either—so they are eternal, too.

Once again, this argument (from incompositeness to persistence) is a popular one (from the ancient atomists onward). But from Plato's point of view it has disadvantages; and from our point of view, too.

From Plato's point of view, if souls are like forms, they will be just one and not many in any way. This conception of the unity of forms (what I have called the austere conception of unity) precludes, Plato seems to have thought, coming up with any account of what makes the unit unified (since, austere as it is, it can have no character, no properties, stand in no relations to anything else). So if forms get into trouble as individuals (and they do), then souls do, too. Moreover, if souls are as austere as forms are, then it is difficult to see how they can do what souls are supposed to do; indeed, they cannot do anything or be affected by anything without interfering with their own austerity. But surely, is not the good thing about having a soul that it can do things? If I am my soul, and you are yours, I do not want either of us to be austere; ethics is not the only baby to go out with this bathwater. From Plato's point of view, this conception of souls as individuals must fail.

From our point of view, it will fail no less. If souls are like forms, they lose any personality. But (as I argued) the reason we want our souls to be immortal is because they are, or have, personality. So to argue that souls survive because they are incomposite gives us no consolation for dying. Avoid the hemlock, then, at all costs.

2. COMPLEX SOULS

In the *Republic*, Plato takes a different tack. Here the issue is not survival, but virtue and action. Indeed, he seems to take the point that an incomposite austere soul is no good as a moral agent; for, famously, he offers an argument for the complexity of the soul from the complexity of action and choice.

Republic IV provides an analogy between the soul and the state, on the basis that what is said of the soul is also said of the state, so that we can look at the state (writ large) to understand the soul (writ small). We can see that the state is a complex entity, since different parts of the state have different functions; likewise, different parts of the soul have different functions, and the soul is a complex entity, too. This can be seen from obvious cases of ethical and practical conflict, which can only be explained in terms of different sources of impulse—reason, spirit, and desire.

But both souls and states, if they are complex entities, must have unifying principles; indeed, it is vital that they should do so, in order to see what constitutes happiness for whole souls and whole states (*Rep.* 420b). What makes a soul or a state one?

Perhaps there is a teleological explanation. The state should be like a statue, whose parts are fitted together with a view to the integrity of the statue, not the beauty of the individual parts (*Rep.* 420c). So the city's parts should be in harmony with each other (423a); and the city as a whole should be compact enough for unity—if it is too big it collapses into a heap (or a bundle! 422e8). Each citizen, then, should perform his natural task; thus, if one man does one job, the city itself will have the same character, and will be one (423d).

But if the state is like this, then the souls of the citizens will have the same character (*Rep.* 435e), because it is the citizens who make the state. So the expressions that characterize citizens can be used in the same way as for states, since character is transmitted from citizen to state. And it turns out (after a lengthy consideration of action and conflict) that persons have exactly the same parts as the state; persons, therefore, will be unified in the same way, when the parts are in harmony and reason rules (443c ff.); then each will be one, act as one, and constitute a part of the unified state as well.

There are several oddities about this account of the unity of states and persons.

1. To be one is treated (once again, and with emphasis) as an *honorific* title; being one is a virtue of the soul, so that when the internal order is disrupted the soul will degenerate into many, not one, and the state will cease to function as such. You can, then, aspire to being one, but you may not be one all along, or ever. Will that do as an account of personal identity? On this account there may never be any persons, only bundles aspiring to personhood; will that do? Contrariwise, can we see that it will not, without appealing to the specialness of persons, or to the extraordinary status of "I"?

2. "One" is understood here as a *complete* expression, not dependent on something else to qualify it. Hence comes the idea that the "oneness" of the citizens (each to one job) is a character of the citizens that they can then transmit to the state. So to be one is to be just one, whatever that involves; being one is basic. This means, for example, that unity is not parasitic on a kind (one sloth, one table, one person); rather, each kind is realized in a proper whole (hence "one" tends to be treated as honorific).

Recall Plato's strategy for explaining the unity of the cosmos in the *Timaeus* (30c ff.).[6] If the intelligible universe is to include all its parts, there can be no other universe. Why not? Because it is whole, and thus all-inclusive and exhaustive. That assumption works if "whole" is treated as a complete expression (the universe is just whole) rather than as a modifier demanding completion from a substantive (whole universe, whole sock, whole cake). So (on Timaeus's view) we cannot say that this is a whole universe, but not a whole galaxy; for if it is whole, it is complete, *just* whole. But in that case, it exhausts all there is, and so it must be unique—just one (and there is no other). Thus "one" is a complete expression, too. The universe is not one something or other (one universe but not one galaxy)—it is just one, exhaustive and complete.

Aristotle objected that Plato handles "one" all wrong. In particular, he complains, Plato's account of the unity of the state misses the features of being one that Aristotle regards as fundamental: that it is syncategorematic; and (therefore) that it is systematically ambiguous. Socrates in the *Republic* makes a mistake: "I mean in supposing that being one is the best thing of all for any state; for he offers this hypothesis. And yet it is clear that as the state advances towards becoming more and more one, it will no longer be a state; for a state is by nature a plurality, whereas it is a household that evolves as one from a state, and a man from a household . . . and a state should be not only composed of many men, but of men differing in forms; for a city cannot come into being from men who are all alike" (*Politics* 1261a15–24).

The unity of the state, Aristotle goes on to argue, is derived from its natural form (what it is to be a state); and it is this derivation that makes unity parasitic on natural kinds. Instead, he objects to Plato that Plato treats unity as if it were uniformity; and thus Plato fails to explain what makes the state a whole.

6 Cf. ch. 6, sec. 2.

Aristotle has missed the point of Plato's analysis. Plato wants an organic, nonuniform account of unity here—for states, for souls, and for parts of souls; thus, he understands being one as a matter of the interrelation of the parts of the whole. But where Plato and Aristotle really part company is in their understanding of what comes first. For Aristotle, forms are basic; for Plato, individuals are. (By individuals, I mean here any individuals, not just putative individuals of the physical world.) So for Aristotle, we understand what something *is* first, and then what individuates it is obvious (namely, *what* it is); for Plato, we understand *being one* first, and the explanations of the natures of things come afterward. The consequence of that, I suppose, is that we cannot look to our understanding of persons to determine the particular sort of unity that persons have; instead, persons may be thought to aspire to proper unity, which is the same whatever your kind. Not surprisingly, such an account of unity will suppress any special features of being a person in favor of the individuals' being basic, being just one. Are the special features of being a person this insignificant?

3. Nonetheless, being one is treated as a matter of the coherence and compatibility of several parts (the soul is no longer incomposite).[7] Here, as with individual objects, Plato still needs to tell us how the bits hang together. Is their coherence an additional feature of the soul? Or of the parts? Think about this in terms of virtue. The soul hangs together, Plato suggests, when its parts all have the virtues of self-control and justice. But what is it to have such a virtue? There are two ways of looking at it. These may be virtues of each part, as they are virtues of the whole (by the composition principle); or they may be virtues that are constituted by some special relation between the parts. That Plato has difficulty, at this stage in his thought, in seeing relations as supervening on (or contextualizing) the relata (and sees them, instead, as real properties of the relata) is witnessed by his reluctance to treat the relations of the parts as the definientia of justice and self-control. Instead, he suggests that each part will have those virtues, just as the whole does, and just as the state, of which the whole is a citizen, will. So for unity as for the virtues: the unity of the state is explained by the unity of its citizens, and the unity of the citizens by the unity of their psychic parts. But, at the same time, Plato insists that unity writ large is just the same as unity writ small (hence, his claim that the state is a suitable analogue for the soul). So the unity of anything is explained by the unity of its parts; and the explanation is regressive.

This may look unsatisfactory (many commentators have complained);[8] and it has one important consequence for the individuation of persons. Plato's account of the parts of the soul treats parts as being themselves organic entities (which themselves have some kind of cognition, witnessed by the propositional content of their desires; and some kind of desire; and the vigorous

---

[7] Cf. Burnyeat, "Grammar," p. 34: in the *Republic*, the"proof and expression of autonomy is conflict."

[8] E.g., Annas, *Plato's Republic*, ch. 5; Vlastos, "Justice."

impulses associated with spirit). Each complex soul, then, is a complex of homunculi, which need explaining in turn. The individuation of states is pushed back to souls, of souls to their parts, and of the parts to the parts of the parts. The regress endangers any explanation of the character of the psyche as a whole, since its very unity is under threat.

We might be forgiven for complaining that Plato's account of personal identity is hopelessly archaic. In explaining persons as souls, and in explicating psychological unity in the various ways he does, he misses the interesting, and urgent, questions about the unity and persistence of persons as opposed to any other complex organism. He misses (somone might suppose) the specialness of being me, or you, or Socrates. He can tell us about agents, but not about "I"; about the place of individuals in the state or in the cosmos, but not about the slanted view I have from in here out on the state, or on the cosmos, or on any other person.

But that interpretation of Plato remains surprising, after all. Consider two of the great influences on Plato—Socrates and Parmenides (influences that significantly, come together in the late dialogues). Socrates was famous for insisting "know thyself"; Parmenides used the thesis "you think" as a crucial premise in his argument for monism.[9] Both "know thyself" and "you think" figure prominently in dialectical contexts; and they trade on the self-consciousness they create in the interlocutor. Is it then reasonable to suppose that Plato missed the specialness of persons?

3. SOPHISTIC SOMEBODIES

"Man is the measure of all things—of the things that are, how they are, of the things that are not, how they are not," says Protagoras (*Tht.* 151ff). Socrates thinks that Protagoras is wrong; in particular, he thinks that Protagoras is wrong to claim as a consequence of "man is the measure" that everything is true, and that contradiction is impossible. Protagoras is wrong, and his truth must be false.[10]

Protagoras (or Plato's version of him) wants to show how "it seems to me that p" gives each of us a privileged access to the truth. The canonical case of "it seems to me that p" is taken to be a case of perception. Suppose that each episode of perception is private because it is relative to the perceiver. This is because the perception of, say, a quality takes place exactly when the perceiver and the perceived object interact. The perceived quality, then, is neither a feature of the object nor of the perceiver, but an event generated by their interaction. So whenever I say, "it seems to me that p," for a perception, my remark is incorrigible, and might as well be true.

But suppose, further, that the scope of "seeming" is widened to take in any

[9] Cf. here Mackenzie, "Parmenides' Dilemma," "Ignorance."
[10] See Chapter 5 passim.

judgment. Then any judgment we make is a distinct episode, and private to the judge. Each time I say, "it seems to me that p," I make a different judgment from one made at any other time by me, or by any other person. Hence, just as my perceptions are private and incorrigible, so are my judgments; and both will thus be true (if anything is).

This account of perception and judgment gives a mechanical account of how each perception/judgment is episodic, private, and disconnected from any other perception of the same perceiver, let alone the perceptions of other perceivers. And that is thought to justify "man is the measure" as a theory of truth. But it also seems to lead to a Heraclitean theory of flux: "Nothing is one itself by itself, nor could you correctly call it something, or something of such and such a sort. But if you call it large, it will also appear small and if heavy then light and everything likewise, since nothing is one or something or suchlike. For everything that we say is, we describe wrongly, since it comes into being through motion and change and mutual mixture; nothing ever is, but always becomes" (*Tht.* 152d).

This, you will recall, follows from the theory of perception: "nothing is one itself by itself, neither the agent (the object perceived) nor the patient (the perceiver) but from the relations between both they give birth to the perceptions and the perceived; the latter become such somethings, the former perceive" (*Tht.* 182d).

Now, as I have argued, this is lethal to the individuation of objects; for they turn out to be bundles of perceptual episodes, with nothing to tie them together. It is equally lethal to the individuation of persons. No one is somebody, since every episode is new. There are, then, only stages, not persons for the stages to constitute. Individuals fall apart.

But this suits the sophists. If "my" perceptions and judgments are peculiar to their own now, they occur as momentary episodes (like old-fashioned cinema film). Because they are episodic, they will be separate from any other episodes (whether they purport to belong to "myself" or to "someone else"). Now, first of all, none of my judgments will be vulnerable to contradiction by anyone else, because they are private; nor, second, will they be vulnerable to contradiction by myself. If all my judgments are true just because they are all momentary episodes, no judgment can be shown to be either consistent or inconsistent with any other. After all, each episode is separate from any other; so there are no superepisodes in which I might compare two common or garden episodes for consistency or coherence. I could say "the elephant is pink" and "the elephant is aquamarine" without a qualm, since my first remark has no bearing on my second. Contradictions simply fail to occur. But then consistency does not matter. If no statement is comparable to any other, then no statement can be consistent or inconsistent, either now or next week. There will be no link at all between one sentence and another, or between my last paragraph and my first. Indeed, there will be no paragraphs at all— sequence, with consistency, goes out the window. And in that case, there is no consciousness that persists from now to now: there are only the momentary episodes. Are we really to affirm that a person is just such an episode? And could we (within an episode) affirm any such thing at all?

The sophistic strategy of disintegrating persons and suppressing consistency may well have been a commonplace. Compare two arguments from the *Euthydemus*.

> "Well now," said Dionysodorus, "you say that you want Cleinias to become wise?" "Certainly." "But is Cleinias wise now or not?" "Not yet . . ." "But you want him to become wise, and not to be ignorant?" "Yes." "So you want him to become (someone) who he is not, and no longer to be who he is now?" [Consternation] . . . "Surely, if you want him no longer to be who he is now, you want him to be destroyed, it seems?" (*Euthyd.* 283c–d)

Any change is death, and there can be no persistence of who you are through change. This argument is often diagnosed as a fallacy of equivocation; but its affinities to Protagoras's more carefully developed thesis should not escape notice.[11] For a Protagorean, no persistence across judgmental episodes is possible; in particular, when episodes of measuring follow on one another, no measure can persist through them, because change is death to the measure. There is, then, no account at all of who you are through time, no persistence of the person through change.

And consistency does not matter to these sophists either, as Socrates points out:

> "If we never make mistakes in action or in speech or in thought, in that case, by Zeus, whom have you come to teach? Did you not say just now that it is best of all to hand over virtue to whatever man is willing to learn?"
>
> "Well, Socrates," said Dionysodorus interrupting, "you are an old-stick-in the-mud, when you remind me of what I said earlier, and you would even recall what I said last year, even if you have no answer to the point I am making now." (*Euthyd.* 287a–b)

The sophists of the *Euthydemus*, like Protagoras, insist on an episodic or temporally qualified account of truth and consistency; what they say now is irrelevant to what they said before. Consistency over time is vacuous.

Aristotle observed that contradictions can occur if you fail to put in the right temporal qualifiers (*Met.* 1005b19ff.). "Your wages are jam and no jam" jam" looks contradictory, but "jam tomorrow" is not inconsistent with "no jam today." Now a sophist extends this point to the psychological dimension of belief. We may say that I cannot (as a psychological matter of fact) believe propositions I know to be inconsistent—but the sophists do not need to worry about that. If Dionysodorus argues for *p* now where he argued for not-*p* before (and he has not changed his mind), this still does not commit him to believing (*p* and not-*p*) now. For if discourse is episodic and discontinuous,

---

[11] I discuss this further in McCabe, "Persistent Fallacies."

all utterances are believed just when they are uttered; belief, like truth, is momentary.

Returning to the *Theaetetus*, consider the following exchange, which recalls the theory of perception and its consequence, the disintegration of the perceiver:

> "Let us now repeat the same argument about me and you and everything else. Take 'Socrates healthy' and 'Socrates ill'; is one like the other, or unlike?"
>
> "Do you mean 'Socrates ill' taken as a whole, compared to 'Socrates well' taken as a whole?"
>
> "Exactly so."
>
> "One is unlike the other."
>
> "But if unlike, then different?"
>
> "Necessarily."
>
> "And likewise for 'Socrates asleep,' and so on?"
>
> "Yes." (*Tht.* 159b–c)

Socrates goes on to insist that since each episode of perception is distinct, each perceiver is different from the next as well (*Tht.* 159e ff.); thus, "I" will never be the same as myself, from episode to episode. Lest it be thought that here Socrates' argument rests on a hopeless equivocation on "same" and "like" (as Dionysodorus's seemed to), the challenge should be understood in terms of the complete absence of any relation between one episode of Socrates' and the next, or between two simultaneous episodes, either. "Man is the measure" has exhausted all the cognitive possibilities. But then the fact that Protagoras's theory allows no context wherein the episodes might be interrelated (because the "measure" doctrine exhausts all the possibilities of judgment) makes the theory lethal to any of our intuitions about the continuity and the integrity of the self. The non-identity of the stages of a person (whether or not they are qualitatively different) is enough to raise the challenge about personal identity.

Compare Protagoras's account of "person-stages" with the analysis of individual objects in the *Sophist* and the *Philebus*.[12] There, each object was "one something" because it fitted into a context. It was individuated, I suggested, relatively, from without. But Protagoras denies even this minimal account to his person-stages; and for that reason he can explain neither identity over time nor synchronic unity for the persons the stages might make up.

So if beliefs are momentary, what happens to the persons who believe them? Plato points out that Protagoras's theory makes not only the objects of perception but also the perceivers themselves incoherent bundles. Who am I? For an episodic relativist I am just what I think or feel now. But then is there a self there to think or feel at all? Is there a subject? What ties the bundle of perceptions together to make a "someone who believes"? This is the focus of

---

[12] Cf. ch. 8, secs. 2, 7.

Plato's attack on the sophists. "Who will you become if you are taught by sophists?" asks Socrates (*Prot.* 311b). "I need to know myself, I need to make sure I do not contradict myself" (cf. *Gorgias* 482c; *Charmides* 166d).

It is here, in the defense against the sophistic attack on consistency, that Plato comes to see, and to set out, the specialness of persons. And in the *Theaetetus*, I shall argue, this allows him to confront four different questions that arise about the unity of persons. The first is about the *persistence* of persons over time: "What makes this Socrates the same as the philosopher of yesterday?" The second, Cartesian question is about the subject and its *first personal perspective*: does "I think" or "I feel" have a different status for me than "you think" or "she feels"? The third concerns the *unity of consciousness*—"What makes it one subject who thinks?" The fourth is about the *autonomy* of the subject in its dealings with the external world—"How far are these words my creation, and not the result of the workings of the world out there upon me?" Only after resolving these issues can Plato offer us a full account of the unity of persons.

4. Persistence: Memory and Continuity

Socrates begins by arguing that the judging subject has some continuity over time. If Protagoras is right (in his version of knowledge is perception), is there such a thing as memory? How does the immediacy of the "Measure" doctrine accommodate the continuity over time that memory offers? If I smell garlic now, then I measure the smell of garlic in Protagoras's way; "I smell garlic" must be true. But if I remember the smell of garlic, without smelling it now, what status does "I remember the smell of garlic" have within Protagoras's theory? He could, of course, say that any proposition, uttered (by me) now is true for me now; if I say, "I remember the smell of garlic," then it must be true that I remember the smell of garlic. But Socrates' objection is that this account of "remembering" is vacuous. For we suppose that memory is knowledge that we have and keep; we remember because we have that knowledge. Protagoras, though, means us to remember just as we perceive—immediately. If the immediate memory (on the analogue of perception) is missing, then we do not remember at all; so we do not know (Protagorean-wise) what we know (in the ordinary sense of remember). The immediacy of measuring rules out the continuity of memory; and that, Socrates suggests, is absurd (*Tht.* 164b).

Is this merely a verbal victory (*Tht.* 164c)? Socrates follows up his attack on the continuity of consciousness over time with a question about the integrity of consciousness at a time. Suppose that knowledge is perception in a narrow sense. Suppose that I see that sloth, then cover up one eye, and see it with one eye and not with the other. Surely, then, I am seeing and not seeing what I see; I know and do not know the same thing at the same time. That, on Socrates' view, is absurd. Why? We might say that Socrates gives us a trivial and silly example. Protagoras need not say that my closed eye is an issue in any judgment at all, so that there is no danger of the absurdity Socrates threatens. However, the absurdity runs deeper. Protagoras cannot even see that there is an absurdity, because on Protagoras's view, there is no connection between one eye and the other; any judgment delivered by either is true. Why is this not then a contradiction? There are no contradictions, since there is nowhere for them to confront one another; there is, on Protagoras's view, no "I" to contain both judgments and risk their conflict; hence, the defense that Plato gives to Protagoras: "Do you think that anyone will agree that the present memory of some experience is the same as the past experience itself? Far from it. Or would you shrink from saying that the same person can both know and not know the same thing? Or, if you are afraid of that claim, surely you would not grant that someone who changes is the same person as he was before he changed? Instead of saying that someone is this [person] we must say that there are these [persons], and infinite in number at that, coming into being as the change takes place" (*Tht.* 166b–c).

Socrates makes a parallel point about the future. Protagoras has claimed that there is still some point in looking to the experts—because they can improve the perceptions of laymen, and make them better (nicer, more pleasant). But that means that the experts must be measures for the future (*Tht.* 178a). Does "Man is the measure" imply that anyone "has the criterion in himself" of the future, so that what he says will happen, does happen? If not, if there are experts, then surely there is such a thing as making a mistake (by a layman, about the future). And then we do not measure the future; we are not measures of our own interests.

Protagoras could protect himself against this objection by arguing that momentary episodes are still true. However, the argument about the future complements the argument about memory, since the person who is a measure for Protagoras exists only in the present, and cannot extend his memory into the past or his interests into the future. Why not? Because this person has no continuity at all; no history, no projects, only this moment now, isolated from any other. The measure doctrine cannot, on this view, persuade *us* at all.

Socrates, then, argues for the continuity of persons over some time by appeal to memory and to our attachment to our own future projects. This sort of argument was revivified by Locke[13] and has been under attack ever since. (For example, eschewing science fiction, if I am just who remembers my past life, who am I if I think I remember the past life of Napoleon as my own? If I suffer amnesia, is my personhood severed? Or if I undergo a radical conversion, are my future projects the projects of the same person I am now?) But notice what Socrates has not said to Protagoras. He has not claimed that memory is sufficient for personal identity, nor that my having memories is evidence that I am a single and unified individual. Plato's argument for personal continuity is milder than Locke's has been interpreted to be. For Plato wants only to argue against the episodic view and for some persistence of the

---

[13] John Locke, *Essay Concerning Human Understanding* II.27.

person over some time; and not for continuous memory or future interests as the sole criteria of personhood (he has, I shall suggest, a different account for that). And notice what claims Socrates is making for memory and future projects—that they are personal, mine, relevant to my own and private purposes. This makes the question of memory relevant to Protagoras's account of person-episodes; and it ensures the importance of the personal perspective in Plato's argument.

5. CONSISTENCY AND THE ARGUING SUBJECT

Protagoras's measure doctrine, I have suggested, threatens not only the continuity of persons, but the consistency of anyone's beliefs, by suggesting that consistency is a logical relation that is vacuous. Socrates, on the contrary, had always insisted that consistency matters, for logical, psychological, and ethical reasons. Two passages from the *Gorgias* may illustrate this. In the first, Socrates is insisting that Callicles put up with the rigorous examination of his theory that "might is right." Socrates disavows responsibility for the refutation himself; it is not Socrates, but philosophy who speaks. Philosophy (unlike Alcibiades) always says the same thing: "and so either refute her, as I was saying just now, and show that doing wrong with impunity is not the worst of evils; or, by the dog, if you leave this unrefuted, then Callicles himself will not agree with you, Callicles, but he will be out of harmony with you for the rest of his life. And I think, my friend, that I prefer to have my lyre out of tune, or any chorus I might pay for, and for most men to diagree with me and contradict me than for me, one man as I am, to be out of harmony with myself and contradict myself" (*Grg.* 482b–c).

The Socratic elenchus works by exposing the inconsistent beliefs of the interlocutor, and leaving him in a state of aporia. In that state, uncomfortable though it may be, he will at least be consistent with himself, and thus better off than he would be with unnoticed holes in his psyche. This is, notoriously, rather a depressing way of carrying on (not to mention liable to long drinks of hemlock); but there is a positive thread running through these accounts of the personal importance of consistency.

Socrates suggests that the Callicles who believes that might is right is in fact at odds with the real Callicles who, underneath, believes something quite different. Once again, this is a commonplace of Socratic rhetoric; but it is given a philosophical explanation earlier in the *Gorgias*. Here (*Grg.* 466a ff.), Socrates is arguing, against Polus, that tyrants and other apparently powerful men do only what they think best, and not what they want. For what they (really) want is happiness; what they think best is to be tyrannical, violent, and uncontrolled. Since the tyrannical life is in fact bad for them, they do not really want it (they only think they do). They have, therefore, no power at all, since they cannot pursue what they want.

Now this argument rests on an intellectual contrast between what we think we want (and are mistaken about) and what we really want, which is determined by the goal's actually being in our interests. That is, Socrates offers two levels of desire: shallow desire, where we get it wrong, and deep desire, which is for what really is in our interests. The difference beteeen the two is a cognitive one (depending on whether we get it right about the actual desirability of the objects of our desire). This then allows Socrates to assume that there are two corresponding cognitive levels: shallow belief and deep belief. Shallow beliefs are what people just happen to say; these are subject to refutation because they are liable to be inconsistent (among themselves and with the deep beliefs). But deep beliefs, it seems, are always right, and so are always consistent.

But then reflect on how Socrates expresses this notion of deep belief: that is the true Callicles, the true Polus—the deep level where what we believe is consistent and true. Deep beliefs, that is, cannot be refuted; if they cannot be refuted, they must be consistent (Socratic refutation is fit only to expose inconsistency, not positively to reveal truth). And deep beliefs constitute the real person.

Now some of this we may find immediately plausible. If it is to count as an inconsistency to say "I believe that p" and "I believe that not-p," it must be the same "I." Contrariwise, if there are no persons, perhaps there is no such thing as inconsistency (If I believe p and you believe not-p, it doesn't matter at all). If it is the same "I," it is, of course, entirely possible that I might believe both p and not-p, without noticing their inconsistency; but (barring perhaps anomalies like the puzzle about fallibilism) I cannot explicitly and overtly believe both to be true at once. And suppose that I change my mind, that change of mind itself is to be understood in terms of consistency, since I have dropped p to accommodate not-p. (If *I* believe p and *you* come to believe not-p, *I* have not changed *my* mind at all.) On this view, consistency can help to answer some of the questions we have about personal identity. For example, I am just the person who cannot believe p and not-p overtly, without changing my mind; conversely, if when I have believed p I then come to believe not-p, it is *my* mind that *I* change, not someone else's. Inconsistency only threatens me as a relation between my beliefs (it does not, for those purposes, matter what someone else believes).

Now two consequences seem to me to follow from this account of consistency. The first is that the importance of consistency in argument is—as one might say—one-sided. That is, if you and I are having an argument about something, the charge of inconsistency will not stick against your and my views considered together (the argument takes place because we cannot agree, but there is nothing logically vicious about that). But if one party to the debate contradicts himself, that in itself is likely to undermine his position. Second, if we think of consistency in the context of argument or debate, and if we think of it in terms of what can be believed, it seems clear that retaining consistency is a personal matter; that is, a matter that engages each of the parties to the debate insofar as they take themselves to be continuous thinking persons. If consistency matters because it is a mark of personhood, then those who deny the importance of consistency in an argumentative context will have their identity under attack, too. And this, I suggest, is exactly what happens in the *Theaetetus* when Socrates tries to show that Protagoras's measure doctrine refutes itself. (We should not forget, of course, that to try to refute someone who stoutly denies the importance of consistency may be rather like having a conversation with a cauliflower, or with someone who insists that the law of noncontradiction is false.)

The so-called "self-refutation" (*Tht.* 169d–171e)[14] falls into three parts: the description of the argumentative setting (169d–e; 171c–d), the first phase of the argument (170a–171a), and the "cleverer," second phase (171a–c). Consider the direct passages of arms first.

The first phase reminds us that Protagoras has difficulty (unfortunately for his own job description) in explaining how anyone can be an expert, and consequently in showing how anyone could teach anyone else, when everyone is right all along. And yet people generally believe that there are experts and teachers, for they believe both that they themselves can be right and that they can (at other times) be wrong. What is more, if I think *p* is true (for me), you do not then immediately concede that *p* is true (for me, for you, or for anyone else). Instead, we often disagree. In particular, we disagree about the measure doctrine itself. How can we explain this disagreement? Is it that *M* is true for me and false for thousands of other people? Does that make *M* more false than true (171a)? (I leave the diagnosis of this argument to one side; suffice it to say that I think it can be rescued from a crude slide from relativism to subjectivism.)[15]

The second (cleverer) phase shifts from a consideration of relative *truth* to discussing the nature of *argument*. Protagoras, by virtue of the measure thesis itself, must concede that his opponents are telling the truth (even if it is relative to them). So then he agrees that when they say that something is false, it is true for them that it is false. To what, Socrates asks, does Protagoras's *agreement* amount?[16] The measure doctrine allows that we may measure not only our direct sensations, but the views of others also (*Tht.* 170d). What happens, then, when Protagoras agrees that his opponents tell the truth (for them)? His agreement, Socrates claims, implies that his doctrine is false not only for his opponents, but for himself as well.

Is that right? Is Protagoras's concession of the relative truth of his opponents' disagreement lethal for him after all? At first sight, it seems not. Protagoras can simply continue to insist on the relativity of any truth and can remain immune from either the first objection that his doctrine is more true than it is false or the cleverer objection that he himself must concede its falsehood. He can continue to insist on relative truth, that is, provided he

---

14 See Burnyeat, "Self-Refutation."
15 Again, cf. Burnyeat, "Self-Refutation," for a clear defense of Plato's argument.
16 Notice the emphatic repetition of ὁμολόγειν, and its cognates.

continues to insist on the privacy of truth, on the insulation of my world, measured by me, from yours, measured by you. Protagoras can retain the measure doctrine by paying the price of solipsism.

But then the setting of the argument indicates what a high price that is to pay. Socrates and Theodorus open their discussion of Protagoras's doctrine— that "everyone is self-sufficient in wisdom" (*Tht.* 169d5)—by wondering whether they have the authority to present a defense of Protagoras's views: "For if he were present himself to agree, instead of our having to make concessions on his behalf, we should have no need to take up the issue again and strengthen it. But now someone might complain that we have no authority to make agreements on his behalf. So we had better make a clearer agreement about this matter; for it is not insignificant whether it is so or not" (*Tht.* 169e).

Then, once the formal argument is complete (in which Theodorus plays the role of Protagoras), the man himself intervenes; he pops his head out of the ground to laugh at Socrates' refutations, at Theodorus's agreements, and then runs away and disappears. Protagoras's mythical intervention focuses on the assumptions that Socrates and Theodorus have made in order to get the self-refutation going—that Protagoras will stay still to be refuted, or to be prevailed into agreeing with something that Theodorus has said. Instead, Protagoras refuses (like Euthydemus and Dionysodorus) to agree to anything; his remarks are themselves momentary episodes; they never remain to be refuted at all. Protagoras himself is *only a bit of himself*; he only appears from the neck up. For Protagoras denies that consistency matters, and laughs at the notion of agreement just as he ridicules the sequence of a refutation. For Protagoras, there are only the episodes; neither agreement nor refutation can happen, for there is no context for the consistency on which they rely; Protagoras is, literally, unanswerable. But then to be a measure is not to be anything but each episode; the measure itself (like Protagoras, or any object in flux) never stays the same, never sticks together into a coherent person. But then the measure cannot agree to anything (for that takes time), nor can a measure be responsible for its position in an argument. For that, we should be true to ourselves and insist on saying always what seems to us to be true (*Tht.* 171d). There is, after all, some time (some "always") across which we can be true to ourselves.

And yet Plato and Protagoras do perhaps have something in common. Protagoras's measure doctrine (as his opponents were fond of pointing out) is indifferent to who does the measuring; it may be a man or a god, a pig or a baboon (cf., e.g., *Tht.* 162c). Being a measure is about being a person, not about being a member of a particular natural kind. The important thing, on that view, is to understand the special capacities of persons, capacities that distinguish them from individual objects; and not to sort them out into "god-persons," "parrot-persons," or even "mechanical-persons." The notion of being a person, on that account, takes priority over the natural kind to which the person belongs. The question is, "Who am I?"

Reflect once again on the Cartesian question. Does this account of the self (to whom we may be true) show any understanding of the perspective of the subject, of the specialness of "I"? Like Descartes, Plato and Protagoras insist on the personal features of thought and argument, and on our reflectiveness on our own mental states. In order for this to be effective, it is vital, for Plato no less than for Protagoras, that our mental states (our beliefs and opinions) be our own. We should be in charge of our own agreements and disagreements; it is ourselves to whom we should be true. As a consequence, as the self-refutation of Protagoras shows (we can now see how aptly it is named), the relations between my beliefs are vitally connected to who I am; so that reflection on my own beliefs necessarily involves me in a first-person perspective. So far, so Cartesian. But Plato differes from Descartes in one fundamental respect—his account of the coherence of the person is not set against the background of doubt. For Plato, it is enough to show the importance of the consistency of parties to an argument. He never faces (as perhaps Protagoras should have done) the possibility that I and my mental states may be unique; he never comes to grips with the question whether there are other minds at all, nor with the serious asymmetry that Cartesian doubt shows to exist between the first-person perspective and the perspective of the second or third persons. It is the absence of doubt, therefore, that marks Plato off from Descartes, not a deficiency in his account of what it is to be a person.

6. SYLLOGIZING SOULS AND THE UNITY OF CONSCIOUSNESS

Is knowledge perception? After routing Protagoras, Socrates directly attacks Theaetetus, with a three-stage investigation of the deficiencies of perception. As we have seen,[17] perception fails because its objects are inadequate for knowledge (it "fails to grasp being"). It also fails because it gives too narrow an account of the knowing mind. Socrates focuses on the capacities of soul.

1. The theory of perception advanced at *Theaetetus* 154 plausibly suggested that any perception is a real event, caused by the interaction of the perceiver with the object perceived; and thus perceptions are veridical. But this claim will only do if "perception" is understood in a properly narrow sense, to describe pure sensation (the raw feels that come at us from the outside world; vide Socrates' concession at *Theaetetus* 171e). If perception includes all judgment, as Protagoras suggested it should, then every judgment is true and knowledge turns out to be vacuous. So Socrates needs to distinguish between "perception" in the narrow sense and perception of the sort that constitutes judgment. He needs to show that not all judgments are true, in order to establish that some judgments, the judgments that may constitute knowledge, are true after all.

His first problem seems to lie with the causal assumptions of the theory of

17 See ch. 5, secs. 1, 5.

perception. For if perception is just caused by the outside world, it is hard to see how it can be other than veridical (and from this intuition flowed the earlier difficulties with Protagoras's view). So judgment, to be distinct from perception (and suitably fallible), must be explained differently.

Suppose that perception is veridical because it happens to the perceiver. But perhaps there is more to being a perceiver than just being a receptacle for perceptions. Socrates turns his attention to the nature of the mind and argues that even perception is not merely received, but actively thought by the mind.

Are we to say that we see with our eyes or through our eyes? If we see with our eyes, the senses will lurk inside us as within a wooden horse, never reaching as far as the mind. Rather, we should say that the soul perceives through each sense; perception cannot be reduced to a bodily event (*Tht.* 184b–e).

> Socrates: It would be a strange thing, my child, if there were many senses sitting in us as if in a wooden horse, and if all these things did not converge on one single form[18]—the soul or what you will. By virtue of this we perceive whatever is perceptible through the senses as if they were instruments.
>
> Theaetetus: This seems to me to be a better option than the earlier one.
>
> Socrates: That is why I insisted on precision with you, asking whether it is by virtue of something, one and the same thing, that we reach black and white through our eyes, other perceptible things through other senses. And in answer would you want to refer all things to the body? (*Tht.* 184d1–e2)

Why is a person not a wooden horse? There are, I think, two separate points here.

For a start, wooden horses are *not alive*; they are (treacherous) machines, mere objects. The vigor of the wooden horse comes from the warriors within it; in itself the horse is nothing.[19] Minds, contrariwise, do actively think. So however the mind is characterized, it must be as an active thinker, not merely a passive one. So minds cannot be reduced to bodies.

Moreover, wooden horses are liable to be full of *competing* warriors; the warriors are not unified at all, except by the accident of their being inside the same receptacle. And yet, if we insist on the passive account of perception, the mind will be just a wooden horse. For if perception is narrowly understood as sensation, then the raw data will come into the horse and sit there; but they will never be coordinated or compared; and they will never be converted into active judgment, just because they are, by their very nature, effects of the outside world on the mind.

Now first, we may grant that each sense offers its data independently and privately to the soul; then the soul thinks each special sensible separately. But

[18] Cf. Burnyeat, "Grammar," p. 30; this expression "is used quite non-committally and carries no reference to Platonic forms." Burnyeat translates "a single kind of thing." But n.b. the reappearance of the same expression at 203c5–6 in an attempt to describe the unity of the syllable: the use of the same expression is, on my account, no coincidence.

[19] Cf. Burnyeat, "Grammar."

then, what is the contribution of the mind to thinking about the special sensibles? Socrates insists that the correct description for the relation between mind and sense is that the mind perceives through the sense; and this makes two different points. First, this allows the soul to coordinate the senses (so that they are not totally disconnected; 184d3). Second, it allows Socrates to speak of the perceiver, no longer as the patient of the perceptual event, but as the agent of perception, as the perceiver.[20] These two points allow "I see that white" and "I taste this bitter" to be said of the same "I."[21]

2. Still, the soul's perceptions remain piecemeal, since "white" and "bitter" are the objects of different senses. What if the soul "thinks something about both" (i.e., an object of one sense and an object of another; *Tht.* 185a–186a)? For example, suppose I say (minimally) "white and bitter." That (joint) thought could not be accomplished by either sight or taste just because white is only seen, bitter is only tasted. Nonetheless, we do think (judge) that two such items[22] are "both," each different from the other and the same as itself. Then we can count them, register their similarity, and so forth. How? We must do so either through some third sense or in some other way:

> Socrates: Through what does the capacity work to show you what is common to everything including the case of two objects of the same sense, by virtue of which you apply[23] the expression "is" and "is not" and the others I just mentioned? What sort of an instrument would you posit for all of these through which our perceiving feature perceives each?
>
> Theaetetus: You mean their being and not-being, likeness and unlikeness, sameness and difference and again one and number? Clearly you are asking about odd and even and everything else that follows from these—through what instrument of the body do we perceive all these with the soul? (*Tht.* 185c4–d4)

We cannot make these judgments of what is common through any of the senses, since what is being thought or judged is common to (the objects of) them all. What is more, even comparative judgments about the objects of a single sense will involve some common terms: "is and is not," "likeness," "sameness and difference," "number." There is, then, no organ or perception that can grasp these common features. But they must be grasped—and by a

---

[20] Cf. Burnyeat, "Grammar," on the rich idiom of Plato"s preposition "through" (διά).

[21] Here, my interpretation of the passage is indifferent to whether the first stage involves a judgment or not; the important point, I claim, is that Plato is now investigating the activity of the mind and the unity of consciousness. But cf. ch. 5, sec. 5.

[22] This, as I have already observed (ch. 5, sec. 5), is ambiguous between the color and the colored thing.

[23] Cf. Cooper, "Sense-Perception," on the text here. Plato is talking about the way in which the common expressions are applied to special sensibles; he is not, as Cornford, *Plato's Theory of Knowledge*, suggests he is, reintroducing the ontological distinction between the physical world and the world of forms. Burnyeat, "Grammar," makes the point that Socrates here eliminates the possibility that another sense judges what is common, for what is common will be so across the senses.

single subject. We must conclude that the soul, therefore, thinks the common terms (as they are applied to the object we perceive) itself by itself (*Tht.* 185e).

What exactly have Socrates and Theaetetus established here? There must be more to thinking than the special sensibles; this can be shown by comparison both between senses and within the objects of a single sense. So the terms to be found in judgments are not only those given by sensation, but also the common terms discovered by the soul—notably, the terms we use to establish identity.

So far so good. Socrates is talking about the source of the terms we use; by contrasting the input of perception and the output of the soul, he has succeeded in establishing the soul as an active thinker (it operates "itself by itself"; *Tht.* 185e1, or, more emphatically, "we perceive with the soul through the senses," 185d3). But he is still limited to a picture of thinking that is piecemeal, term by term, or concept by concept, or even object by object. The soul can think "is" or "equal," even if those common terms are not derived from sense-perception. But so far, thinking is no more complex than that; there is, for example, no room here for the logical connections between one thought and another. Thinking, on this account, will be at most proposition by proposition. And that—the Plato familiar from the *Republic* might argue—is bound to be an inadequate account of knowledge. For if to know is to understand,[24] because knowledge means being able to explain, then knowledge must be complex, not simple, for it must connect propositions together, not merely enunciate them one by one.

3. However, there follows a further move (*Tht.* 186a–e). Theaetetus agrees with Socrates:

> Socrates: . . . you have done a good job in saving me a long argument, if it seems to you that the soul considers some things [terms] itself by itself, and others through the capacities of the body. For that was what seems right to me; and I wanted it to seem right to you too.
> Thaeatetus: But it appears so . . . (*Tht.* 185e)

The agreement between the two persons, Socrates and Theaetetus, has (paradoxically) a Protagorean flavor. Recall that Protagoras, too, was committed to (unassailable) episodes or monads of judgment. Yet that view ruled out both agreement (what Socrates and Theaetetus have here) and any coherent account of the person. The third stage of Socrates' arguments builds on the anti-Protagorean agreement of the second to produce a sketch of the complex activity of the soul. To counter Protagoras's monadic episodes, we need some sort of complexity in judgments; to produce an account of the person, we need complexity of the judge. Socrates argues that the soul (is a whole because it) has a characteristic activity—and that characteristic activity is the making of complex judgments, or the comparison between judgments.

[24] See ch. 3, sec. 3.

Being, sameness and difference, identity and nonidentity, and value are all common terms. Oh yes, agrees Theaetetus: "These [values?] are the things where most of all the soul compares their being, calculating in itself the past and the present with relation to the future" (*Tht.* 186a9–b1).

Socrates recapitulates. Some things are directly perceived through the sense organs—the hardness of what is hard, for example. But in order to determine "the being [of hard or soft items] and that they are, and their being opposites, and the nature of their opposition, the soul itself rising up and comparing them tries to make a decision [to judge] for us. . . . So it is possible for men and for beasts, even straight at birth, to perceive some things, things which reach as far as the soul through the body.[25] But the calculations about them, about their being and their utility, come [when they do] with difficulty and over time and through much experience and education" (*Tht.* 186b–c).

But these calculations, he suggests, are a necessary preliminary to arriving at truth: "But no-one can get hold of truth without getting hold of being; and no-one can be knowledgeable if they miss the truth. . . . So there is no knowledge in the affections of the senses, but only in the comparative reasoning [*sullogismos*] about them . . . (*Tht.* 186c–d).

Notice that Socrates is not talking about comparing two sense data here; nor is he describing our grasp of the objects of the phenomenal world. Now he speaks of comparing common terms (in this case values) in relation to each other. The discussion continues to insist on the comparative, judgmental element of this part of the soul's activity: "it judges comparing them to each other" (*Tht.* 186b8); it makes "calculations about being and utility—with difficulty and over time and with a great deal of activity and education" (186c3). Because it can get at being, the soul can get at truth; and only with truth can the soul be a knowing soul (186c9); so knowledge lies not in the affections of soul, but in its syllogizing about those affections.

This account marks a new stage in the business of thinking. For now truth is arrived at by further reflection on and comparison of the common terms that the soul thinks itself by itself. And truth, Socrates emphasizes, is not just what turns up when we make judgments about being and not-being, or sameness and difference. Instead, he suggests, truth is made possible by comparative reasoning (*Tht.* 186c6, d4), just as, through training and experience, successful judgments about utility, which require comparisons of the past, the present, and the future, may eventually be made.

So this account of the activities of soul goes beyond the simple derivation of the common terms in the second phase of the argument. For now Socrates speaks, first, of the comparison of nonsensible terms; and second, of the derivation of truth from the judgments about being. How is truth derived from comparative judgments about being? Several answers might be possible here—ranging from a traditional view, that truth is about reality,[26] to a more

[25] Cf. Burnyeat, "Grammar," p. 42, n. 39.
[26] Cornford, *Knowledge*.

cautious semantic claim, that any true proposition must be reducible to a subject-predicate pair, connected by the copula ("being").[27] I have argued (ch. 5, sec. 5) that Plato's complaint here rests on the notion that I cannot think about the objects of the world by means of the senses alone. But think now about the insistence not on being, but on comparison ("comparing and calculating," *analogizomenē*; "comparing together," *sumballousa*; "comparative reasoning," *sullogismos*). Why is truth a matter of comparison? This is hardly how we should describe the correspondence between a true proposition and a state of affairs. But it is how we should describe the condition that collections of true propositions should be consistent with one another.

But then, why should consistency matter so, in the context of this argument about knowledge? Surely Plato is not suggesting that knowledge is just a coherent collection of propositions? But, as we have seen, the logic of consistency does tie in with the development of an argument for the nature of the thinking soul; consistency has a great deal to do with persons.

Socrates, Theaetetus, and Theodorus earlier faced the dangers of the sophistic view that contradiction is impossible. Instead, they insisted throughout on consistency and agreement—both anathema to a sophist. In the beginning, there was Protagoras who, by denying that there are persistent persons, removed the context wherein beliefs might turn out to be consistent (or not). Ranged against that view will later come Socrates' anxiety to show that there is such a thing as false judgment; but Socrates will find himself in difficulties because any diagnosis of false judgment appears to commit the judge to an inconsistency; and that, for a persistent person, appears to be absurd. When Socrates confronts Protagoras, he assumes the importance of consistency where Protagoras denies it; where Protagoras says that there are no persons, Socrates denies it.

On a Socratic view, consistency can help to answer some of the questions we have about personal identity. For example, I am just the person who cannot believe {*p* and not-*p*} overtly, without changing my mind; conversely, if when I have believed *p* I then come to believe not-*p*, it is my own mind that I change, not someone else's. The relation of consistency, then, between propositions is enough to distinguish between my overt beliefs and someone else's, because inconsistency only threatens me as a relation between my beliefs for those purposes, it does not matter what someone else believes). It is also enough to show the connection between my beliefs over time—or at least to show the potential connection between them, since inconsistency can remain unnoticed. And consistency is a necessary condition for knowledge, if knowledge is to be understood as a systematic collection of beliefs (as understanding must be).

Here Plato's interest in the question What is knowledge? coincides with his interest in the persons who do the knowing. To syllogize is to think about the interrelations of "pieces of knowledge"; to grasp the whole structure of inter-

---

[27] Cooper, "Sense-Perception," is tempted in this direction, I think.

relations is to understand (as Socrates will later suggest). And this must be done within a single consciousness.[28] Understanding, then, is the grasp of a coherent logical system.[29] But this is an account of the soul, just as much as an account of the system of what is known, because logical or epistemological coherence has a psychological counterpart; rather, logic and psychology go hand in hand, because it is the psychological importance of consistency/coherence that explains why we are committed to a consistent logical structure —as we shall see. The focus, then, of Plato's account of the soul is on consistency.

Return to the attack on "knowledge is perception" in the *Theaetetus*. I have suggested that Socrates' argument falls into three parts, corresponding to three separate points that he needs to make against the Protagorean view of persons and perception.

1. The *objects* of judgment. Sensation is different from judgment (even if sensation is veridical, judgment is not). In particular, the simple data of sense-perception fail to supply the common terms that judgment needs. So we need a different source for these common terms than sensation provides, a different causal account of our being able to say "is" or "different."

2. The *activity* of judgment. Sensation is different from judgment because while sensation is an affection of the soul through the bodily organs, judgment is an activity of the soul. Theaetetus's thesis fails to explain how knowledge is something we do, not something we suffer; instead, we need a proper account of the active mind.

3. *Unity*. In the first place the central faculty of the mind unifies the disparate affections of sensation. So one of the first objectives of the argument was to show how the mind is a single faculty. In the last place, knowledge, determined as a complex matter that compares judgments and perceptions in order to arrive at a consistent structure of beliefs, will end up as a unified whole—complete understanding.

Protagoras was dominated by his desire to show that "everything is true" and "contradiction is impossible," so that he emerges with an account of persons as disconnected and self-contained (if even that expression is permissible) episodes. What Plato sees to be missing here is the requirement that the episodes should be connected into a whole. How can Plato explain whole persons without falling foul of the puzzles he himself has raised? When it comes to objects, he wants neither an austere nor a generous account of what it is to be an individual object. But, as the confrontation with Protagoras insists, neither austerity nor generosity will do for persons either. On Protagoras's view, on the one hand, persons are atomic, disconnected episodes. Here, there is no way of impugning the unity of an episode, since each turns up

---

[28] Keith Hossack objects to me that machines could do this, too, even if wooden horses could not. Plato's account of individuation may be unable to distinguish minds from very clever computers—though he does, perhaps, have some account of self-consciousness that might help here; cf. Mackenzie, "Ignorance."

[29] On Plato's/Socrates' view, there is only one such system; cf. Vlastos, "Elenchus."

on its own; each is just a single episode, one by one—each is austere. And by the same token, there is no way of contextualizing any episode. Protagoras's account of perception allows us to suppose that the (individual, atomistic) data of perception are true. Then those data are isolated from each other, and persons become correspondingly austere. But the reader (and the author) may protest. Surely we are not just episodes of disconnected perceptions, not merely cognitive events. But if we are not, how are our cognitive events to be connected? And how are comparative judgments about them to be made? And how are those judgments themselves to be organized? These seem to be problems for epistemology to deal with; but they are also problems for metaphysics. If persons are just individual episodes, how can there be a sound notion of personhood at all? Are persons more than bundles of beliefs?

On the other hand, the *Republic* suggested that persons are whole souls, complex and interconnected entities. But—as the *Theaetetus*'s account of the problem about wholes and parts suggests—how are these wholes to be connected without making them more complex still? What is a "whole soul"? Recall the difficulty about the parts of the tripartite soul—they are either inexplicably simple or themselves complex wholes: homunculi. If whole souls are collections of homunculi (and so are the homunculi), they degenerate into hopeless generosity.

Plato approaches this as a problem in the philosophy of mind; and in the end his account of the individuation of persons owes whatever success it has to his account of the unity of the mind. His program follows the three moves from the sketch in the *Theaetetus*. First, how are we to understand these common terms that are not available to perception? Second, how are we to justify the notion that the mind is active, not passive? Third, how is the active mind to be unified?

7. COMMON PROPERTIES

Protagoras and Heraclitus suggested that anything we can say corresponds to an actual feature of the (flux-ridden) world; thus, anything we may say of something represents a real feature of the something. This will be true of relations and values no less than for directly perceptible properties. But Plato once shared this view, to the extent that he supposed relations and values naturally to inhere in their objects. Now one way of understanding just why Plato thought that would be to suppose that he was puzzled by just how we might get the idea of some nonperceptual property (equal, perhaps, or same, or beautiful). He was puzzled, that is, both by how we ever come to have the idea at all (how does "equal" ever feature in my judgment?) and, more immediately, by how we come to notice this nonperceptual property now. Both puzzles could be understood as problems for the mind. For we need to know how the mind, unbidden, comes to know what equal is; and how the mind, unprovoked by a visual image of equality, comes to think of equality now.

In the first place, Plato is tempted to answer these difficulties by proposing a causal account of the activities of mind: Recollection. First of all, the mind comes to have an idea just because it has been affected by the (independent) form; and the mind is the receptacle in which the idea is retained. Second, the mind comes to say "equal" now because the equal objects of the world out there affect it now. Both stages represent the mind as passive, the world as active; and this account works for nonperceptual properties just because Plato thinks that they are real features of the physical world, as well as actual intelligible objects.

So what happens when Plato changes his mind about this account of relations? In the *Sophist*, he broke the chains of natural inherence and suggested that the central relations of individuation can be understood as features of the context in which things are found, rather than as properties of the things in themselves. This seems to correspond to the *Theaetetus*'s promise that being and not-being, sameness and difference, are understood by the mind "itself by itself," comparing and contrasting the sensible objects with which it is faced. We might, perhaps, imagine this as someone learning the alphabet:

> We know, I suppose that when children have just learned their letters—
> What?
> That they are well able to recognise each of the letters in the shortest and easiest of the syllables and they are able to tell the truth about them.
> How not?
> But then again they may be in doubt about the very same letters in a different syllable, and make a false judgment or a false statement.
> Certainly.
> Now isn't this the easiest and best way of educating them in the things that they don't know yet?
> How?
> First bring them to the letters among which they have judged these same letters correctly; and then put those beside others they have not learned yet and by comparing show them that there is the same likeness and nature in both the combinations until the letters they have right have been shown and compared to all the ones they do not know, and when they have been shown, they thus become paradigms, so that the teacher makes him say of each one of all the letters in all of the syllables that this different one is different from the others, and this same one is always the same in the same respects as itself.
> Altogether.
> So we have grasped this sufficiently that a paradigm comes into being whenever [something] is correctly judged to be the same in [something] different and scattered/disparate and has been compared in each case so that it produces [just] a single true judgment about each [case of the same thing] that they are both [the same thing]? (*Pol.* 277e–278c)

The *Politicus* is about coming to know, since it is about philosophical method and the travails of Socrates' eponym in dealing with the intricacies of collection and division. In particular, it is about how we may come to understand a particular item when it is enmeshed in a collection of others, as letters are. The ES suggests that while each letter may be simple and individual, it is found separated out from the others by the mind's insistent activity; it is the mind that isolates the letter *A* by showing how it is distinct from all the others and compatible with many of them in various combinations. But this individuation attributes "sameness" and "difference" to a letter just because the mind (the student of the alphabet) sees the context in which the letter fits.

But then it is vital that Plato dissociate the mesh of identity from the causal features of the perceptible world. I have argued that his position is not an idealist one (that is, he does not suppose that the mind *invents* sameness and difference).[30] But, as the *Theaetetus* shows, he is equally anxious to deny that sameness and difference *derive* from, for example, redness or bitterness. He also does not argue that these are grasped by the mind just by inference from perception. Instead, they are the objects of the mind's activity "itself by itself"—they are the special objects of the mind.

So does that mean that these things (sameness, difference, being, and so on) are, after all, Platonic forms, the transcendent objects of the mind? I think not. In the last chapter I suggested a comparison with the old Eleatic puzzle about place. Every something is in a place; place is a something; so place is in a place; and its place in a place, and so on. Not so, Plato may retort at last; place, instead, is an ordering of things, just as the context in which things are found to be individuated is not another thing, itself needing individuation, but rather the mesh of identity within which things are found. Now this does not imply that place is unreal, nor that to understand "place" we need to look to the transcendent realm. Instead, place is a different order of reality that underlies the individual physical pieces of furniture in the world. This means that sameness, difference and so on are not to be derived from perception; nor yet are they mental constructs or separate entities in the intelligible world. For they are inextricably bound up with the physical world; they are necessary to prevent the physical world collapsing into indeterminacy, and they are also necessarily themselves nonphysical, on pain of the paradoxes of austere individuals. So they are graspable not by perception, but by the mind operating itself by itself:

> But I think that many fail to notice that indeed there are many natural likenesses available in perception for those who are anxious to learn easily about what there is; and these are not difficult to point out in answer to someone asking for an uncomplicated explanation but without reasoning. But for those greatest and most important things there is no image clearly made for men which you could show someone who inquires and satisfy his soul. So we must practise being able to give an account of each thing, and to accept one. For non-physical things, the most beautiful and the best, are shown by reasoning alone and in no other way;

[30] Cf. ch. 8, sec. 9.

and it is for the sake of these that we have said everything that we have said. (*Pol.* 285e–286a)[31]

The ES underlines the difference between definition by ostension and definitions that are strictly intellectual, capable of being given in an account and in no other way. Now definition is given by the mind itself by itself. The soul turns out to be actively engaged in intellectual pursuits and is not the passive recipient of the sensible properties of the world.

8. ACTIVE MINDS

Meno's paradox first raised the question of how the mind works. The puzzle about how we inquire is a puzzle about the causal mechanisms of the mind: how on earth, unless I already have a clear intention to inquire into something I do not know, can I ever develop an intention to inquire? How can inquiry start from nothing? The theory of Recollection suggested that inquiry never does start from nothing; instead, the mind is full all along, and learning is simply the bringing of what has been forgotten to the forefront of the memory—so learning is simply the recovery of what you knew already. But this account of learning—or of any cognitive activity—was depressing for three reasons. First, it suggested that the mind is merely the receptacle of what it knows, the place where all knowledge is stored, ultimately to be recovered by our accident-prone relations with the outside world. Second, it denied the interesting possibilities of falsehood; this sort of mind is just full of what is true, and there is no possible explanation of mistake, of fiction or of falsehood at all. This sort of mind is entirely passive, never creative (or interesting). Third, if minds are individuated by the collection of ideas innate in them, personal identity is (again) a dull affair, since our minds are clones of each other, each full of what it Recollects of "all of nature [which] is akin."

If there is an essential connection between being a mind and being a person—as Plato's intellectualist account of the self in the *Theaetetus* suggests—then we may need some account of how the mind is distinct from the external world. In particular, corresponding to the first-person perspective, we may feel the need for some account that disjoins the causal relations of the external world from the causal relations within the soul; we need, perhaps, some account of the autonomy of the mind. (Notice again that this is not, or is not necessarily, the idealist's question; the question is not whether the mind supersedes, or even creates, the world that appears to be around it,

---

[31] Owen, "Undepictable," disputes Skemp's translation, *Plato's Statesman*, ad loc., rightly, in my view. Owen argues that these "incorporeals" are not separate paradigmatic forms; and I agree. The point of this passage is explicitly to bring us back to the discussion of letters and syllables at 277e, and to explain how, while ostension is one way of getting to grips with the world, reasoning is better, because even if it is difficult, it is about what matters most. This is precisely what the long series of puzzles about individuation has shown.

but rather whether the mind can be counted as an entity on its own, in addition to all the entities in the world all around it.)

Protagoras had raised the nightmare possibility that everything is true; and his claim was refuted (I have suggested) by showing how it rides roughshod over our intuitions about personal identity. But still, has Plato shown that falsehood is possible?

Suppose that Pachycephalus judges that the earth is flat, when in fact the earth is round. So Pachycephalus' judgment is false. Now the possibility of falsehood is problematic in two different ways:

1. The *logical or scientific* problem. If the earth is in fact round, then the sentence "The earth is round" is about the roundness of the earth. What, then, is the sentence "The earth is flat" about? Is it about something, or nothing? And what (something or nothing) makes that sentence false? (The *Sophist*, as we have seen (ch. 7, sec. 1), tackles this problem).

2. The *psychological* problem. Since the earth is not flat, but round, how did Pachycephalus come to believe that it is flat, not round? How did the idea of the flatness of the earth (since the flatness of the earth does not exist) get into his head? How could he think that?

Falsehood is interesting—from the psychological point of view—just because it does not come directly from the outside world. There are no falsehoods lurking "out there" to affect or infect our thinking. So where do they come from? Perhaps we make them up. It looks as if falsehood, like imagination, is up to us in a way that truth, like perception, is not. But then we need some account of who we are who can make mistakes in this interesting and creative way. This puzzle also is in play in the *Theaetetus*.

Is it? Did Plato see that there are two puzzles about falsehood? Characteristically he opens the discussion of falsehood with a paradox—that false judgment is impossible. This is for two separate reasons:

a. Either we know what we judge, or we do not. If we know it, we cannot get it wrong; if we do not know it, we cannot even have it in mind—so it cannot figure in the judgment at all (and thus we could make no mistake about it; *Tht.* 188a–d).

b. False judgment is about what is not. But how can we make any judgment about what is not? Surely any judgment must be about what is—so that any judgment is true (*Tht.* 188d–189b).[32]

The second reason bears the mark of Plato's difficulties with individual objects. Since it is about what is judged (on the analogy of what is seen or what is perceived), it reflects what I have called the logical difficulty in explaining falsehood. The first reason, on the other hand, is about the judge—and about how he can get these putative falsehoods into his head at all (*Tht.* 188b9). Socrates needs to tackle not only the logic of falsehood, but its psychology as well.

---

[32] Cf. ch. 5, sec. 6; and Fine, "False Belief"; Annas, "Knowledge"; Burnyeat, *Theaetetus*, on diagnosing the difficulty.

Notice, first of all, that the objects of falsehood (at 1 and at *b*) are understood in austere terms: these objects are just simple entities, so that it is difficult to explain how they could be confused with each other (they cannot, if they are simple, be identified under different descriptions). The subjects who judge falsely (in *a*), however, must be complex, on pain of Protagoreanism. If minds must be the location of consistent (or even inconsistent) beliefs, they must be whole and composite entities and not simple ones. But then minds risk being a collection of beliefs, generously assembled higgledy-piggledy. What, to ask the question once more, makes the mind a unity, now and over time? One answer is that it is unified by virtue of its activity—minds, unlike wooden horses, *do* things on their own: in particular they believe their own falsehoods (can machines do that?).

Socrates' first attempts to explain falsehood fail notoriously (*Tht.* 188b–191a), because he has no way of plausibly asserting that "the morning star ≠ the evening star " when in fact "the morning star = the evening star". The two propositions contradict each other; it would be absurd for anyone to believe them simultaneously, and absurd for both to obtain in the world. Falsehood seems to occur; and yet its occurrence seems only describable by a blatant (and transparent) contradiction, which we could never believe. Somehow the contradiction must be rendered innocuous—or at least opaque.[33] One way of obscuring or qualifying the contradiction might be to locate the (contradictory) propositions in different places—thus, "the morning star = the evening star" appears in the world; "the morning star ≠ the evening star" appears in the mind of the false judge. But in order for this to work, we need some account of what it is for a proposition to appear in a mind; and for that, we need some grip on what a mind is.

At *Theaetetus* 188a, Socrates explicitly set aside discussion of learning, remembering, and forgetting. Then at 191c3, he reintroduces them; and we should recall the significance of the issue of remembering and forgetting in the discussion with Protagoras, who denies there could be any such thing. Someone who remembers (or forgets) is someone who persists over time; to give an account of memory is to present some angle on personal identity. We have, Socrates suggests, wax tablets[34] in our souls (191c8), varying in character and receptiveness, which retain the imprints of our perceptions and our thoughts: "We say that it [sc. the wax tablet] is the gift of Memory the mother of the Muses, and on this we mark impressions of whatever we want to remember—whether we saw it, heard it, or imagined it for ourselves—holding it under

---

[33] Cf. C.F.J. Williams, "Referential Opacity."

[34] Myles Burnyeat objects to me that my use of the expression "tablet" instead of his preferred "block" imports into Plato's theory the idea that the impressions made in the wax are proto-linguistic, whereas the image may simply be of images pressed into wax. I persist in "tablet," not only because I find "block" an uncongenial expression, but also because it seems to me that Socrates' suggestion that the imprints are made in wax has immediate appeal just because we, and even more the classical reader, think straightaway of wax tablets when we think of imprints in wax.

our perceptions and thoughts we seal [it], as it were, with the stamp of a signet ring. And whatever is impressed on the wax we remember and know just so long as the imprint remains; whatever is wiped off or cannot be impressed we have forgotten or do not know" (*Tht.* 191d).

These imprints constitute our memories; and our mistakes can be explained by the mismatching of some present perception and some imprint on the wax tablet. For example, Theodorus is before me; but his image is wrongly fitted into the Theaetetus slot in my wax. This mismatch evokes "Theaetetus" incorrectly, and the mistake is made. The mismatch can occur because the difference in cognitive location (out there in the world vs. already in the wax tablet)[35] allows me to muddle something I know (have in my wax tablet) with something else (known or unknown, but at any rate perceived).

But this account of mistakes has two drawbacks.

1. The first drawback is its unclarity about the psychological account to be given even of mistakes of this kind. When a perception becomes wrongly allotted to an imprint, how did the wrong allocation take place? At times Socrates suggests that the mind itself makes the mistake (*doxa* did it, *Tht.* 194a), by picking the wrong imprint. In that case, the wax tablet is simply a memory store, a tool to be used by the mind in effecting its judgments. But then, has the psychology of the mistake been explained at all? How did the mind come to *choose* the wrong imprint, since it had the right one in its memory bank all along? Perhaps, instead, the wax tablet itself provides the explanation—our mistakes take place *because* the wax tablet is grubby or woolly or sloppy. The wax tablet may be not an instrument of the soul, but itself a part of the soul (so that who I am is partly determined by my memory; my intellectual character is determined by the character of the wax, 194d); then perhaps the mistake is just the bad fit between percept and imprint, occurring mechanically in the transmission of the percept to the interior of the soul (in the same way as mirror images are automatically reversed, 193c7).

We might now tell two different stories about the psychology of falsehood. There is, on the one hand, an intentional account; here my mind uses the tablet, but makes the mistakes by itself. Or, on the other hand, there is a causal account, wherein the mistakes occur by a failure of the mechanism of the wax tablet to work properly. But the wax tablet is undecided between an intentional and a causal account of the psychology of falsehood. And so it cannot explain how complex theoretical mistakes can be made (such as "5 + 7 = 11") not only because of what the mistake is about, but also because it is difficult to see how the *judge* could make *either* an intentional mistake here (*Tht.* 196b) *or* a mechanical one (196c). Consider Socrates' suggestion that it is the judgment itself that does the wrong matching. How? Perhaps we ourselves make the mistake (cf. 194d). Perhaps I see Theodorus, judge him to be Theaetetus, and allot my perception of him to my Theaetetus imprint. But then it is in me (my judgment) that the mistake is made, not in my wax tablet;

---

[35] Burnyeat talks about a difference in cognitive routes, *Theaetetus* p. 65ff.

and my false judgment still remains to be explained. Or perhaps I just am the wax tablet, so that the mistake is not judgmental but mechanical—a slippage of the Theodorus percept from its proper place into the Theaetetus slot next door. But how is such a mechanism sufficient to explain false allocations if it also explains true ones? What is responsible for the falsehood?

2. This theory of mistake only explains simple mistakes. If the wise are those who are good at allotting percepts, the stupid are those who are incompetent, Socrates counts himself among the latter (*Tht.* 195c). His disdain for his own theory invites us to ask whether the mechanical acount of thinking will do: or whether there is not a better and richer story to be told of "Socrates' ignorance" (195c1). For the wax tablet can only explain—if indeed it can explain—mistakes of a present perception, and mistakes of a monadic kind (whether they be whole propositions or logical atoms): "In short, it is impossible, so it seems, to make mistakes or have a false judgment about something one does not know and has never perceived—if what we have just said is sound. But in cases where we both know and perceive—just in those cases judgment turns around and vacillates between true and false: true when it connects the impressions straight across and gets the proper imprint, false when it gets opaque or crooked imprints" (*Tht.* 194a–b).

The wax tablet can only explain perceptual mistakes because it relies on the difference of cognitive location to qualify the contradiction (the contradiction that would rule out the possibility of any mistakes). No theoretical mistakes are explained. It can only explain monadic mistakes because the mechanism of mistake is seen as one of mismatching, or wrongly swapping, one item with another. No complex muddles are allowed. So we still have no account of complex or theoretical mistakes that cannot be reduced to a perceptual mismatch. What then of mistakes like "5 + 7 = 11"?

Socrates interrupts his own conclusion (*Tht.* 195c) and proposes a different account, designed to replicate the difference of cognitive location (in the wax tablet, between the perceptible world and the apparatus of the mind) within the mind. This—he hopes—will then allow for cognitive mismatches within the different places in the mind. The emphasis now has changed. In the wax tablet, Socrates focused on the mechanics of mismatching (195d); the tablet allows for a causal explanation of mistake (the incoming perception hits the wrong imprint). Now, however, Socrates wants to know whether anyone can think that eleven is twelve, or that seven plus five equals eleven. What is it to be a false judge (195e ff.)? In response Socrates moves away from discussing cognitive events to analyzing cognitive states (and thus supposes that there are persons to be in those cognitive states).

There is a difference, Socrates argues, between possessing knowledge and having it. Imagine a hunter who catches birds and puts them in an aviary to keep them. He possesses the birds in the aviary because he has power over them; it is, after all, his aviary, and he has the power to catch them again at will, or to let them go (*Tht.* 197c7). Just so, every soul has in it an aviary, which becomes filled with birds as we learn and discover things: that is possessing knowledge, and the knowledge we possess is determined by which (collection of) birds we have in our aviary (knowledge of arithmetic, for example, will be determined by our having arithmetical birds). But the birds we possess are not necessarily immediately to hand (or to mind) (198d8); instead, we are able to recover some particular knowledge from within our souls by catching the appropriate bird. This is what it is to have power over the birds.

There are, then, two different cognitive locations—one inhabited by the birds within the aviary, the other inhabited by the hunter outside who is able to catch any of his birds at will. The aviary itself is a cognitive state just because the birds continue to be held in it: the knowledge we possess persists. The hunter, on the other hand, has a more active capacity—the ability to catch a particular bird; this, then, is a cognitive faculty. Therefore, the difference in location is now cashed out as a difference in cognition; and that, Socrates hopes, will solve the paradox of falsehood. For we can both know something (have it in our aviary) and not know it (have it in hand outside the aviary), if we possess (a piece of) knowledge but fail to use it. In this way we may (without absurdity) be said to make conceptual mistakes.

But how? How does the mistake occur? To activate knowledge (grab the appropriate bird) must be to get it right. How does our attempt to recover the bird that is our knowledge of "12" produce the wrong answer (*Tht.* 199d)? Like the wax tablet, the aviary offers us a choice: either there is something wrong with the bird we grab (Theaetetus's suggestion—it is an "ignorance" bird), or there is some mistake being made by the grabber (Socrates' objection—what is the birdcatcher's thought about what he is doing?). Neither the causal nor the intentional model appeals.

> We have come a long way round to get back to our first difficulty. That expert in refutation will smile and say: "Oh excellent people, do you think that someone who knows both, the knowledge and the ignorance, will suppose that one of the things which he knows is another of the things which he knows? Or, when he knows neither, will he judge what he does not know to be something else he does not know? Or that he knows one but not the other, and thinks the one he knows to be the other which he does not know? Or vice versa? Or—back to the beginning—will you tell me again that there is knowledge of the knowledges and the ignorances which a man might get and keep in yet more ludicrous aviaries or fictitious bits of wax, so that he would keep them so long as he has them, even though he does not have them to hand in his soul? And thus you will be forced to circle back to the same place ten thousand times and never make any progress."
> (*Tht.* 200a11–c4)

Theaetetus might suppose that the eleven-bird can figure as either knowledge or ignorance—or else that there is an "ignorance-eleven-bird" and a "knowledge-eleven-bird." On that account, the mistake occurs by accident (or perhaps by coincidence, as a consequence of a causal sequence), depending on which bird happens to be grabbed. Socrates is no better off than

Theaetetus, for he must suppose that the grabber makes a mistake about which bird to catch. But then the problem recurs; does the grabber know what he is doing, or not? This is the problem with which we began (as Socrates points out), but which is asked now of the fictional population of the mind.

A further feature of this argument now becomes clear. When both the aviary and the wax tablet are proposed, Socrates suggests that we have these pieces of apparatus (the tablet and the aviary) in our minds. But the Protagorean discussion of sensation should make us wary of supposing that memory (or knowledge, or forgetting) are adjuncts of the mind, or instruments of the soul—apparatus that we have. For that assumption leaves untouched the question of *who we are*. Instead, we should suppose that the tablet and the aviary are themselves parts of the soul—parts of who we are—intrinsic, not instrumental, to our personhood. Who then is the "I" who wields the wax tablet ot catches the birds in the aviary? Not I, but some part of me, distinct from the aviary or the tablet. However, this part of me does seem to have the special attributes of personhood—notably intentionality (the grabber decides which bird to catch) and the ability to carry those intentions out (the grabber can catch a bird at will). So while the aviary and the wax tablet are part of the furniture of the mind, the tablet wielder (e.g., at *Tht.* 194d5) and the birdcatcher are part of its population—they are homunculi.

In that case, the discussion of false judgment canvasses two different models of the mind: in one, the mind is a machine; in the other, it is a person. But then the impasse with which the discussion concludes offers us an impossible choice: between the assumption that we can be analyzed away into a collection of mechanisms and the assumption that the specialness of personhood cannot be analyzed at all, since it always reintroduces persons (homunculi) at a lower level of analysis. That choice becomes interesting just when (and only if) Plato has understood about the specialness of persons. And that resides, on this analysis in the activity of mind, in its autonomy, its being able to think at will—and to make mistakes.

In one sense, the wax tablet and the aviary fail, because they do not provide a fully articulated account of the mind. In another sense they succeed, for they make vivid to us the intuition that minds have some claim to autonomy, to some kind of independence from the causal workings of the world out there. But the peculiar thing about the discussion of falsehood is that—unlike an account of mental autonomy based, for example, on idealist assumptions—it rests on the private nature of mistake. That is to say, the autonomy we display when we make mistakes, or when we imagine, or when we invent a poem, is special to the individual who does it. This sort of autonomy is incurably personal, just because it *fails* to reflect the true state of affairs in the world.

Compare the *Theaetetus*'s analysis of false judgment with a different account of the way the mind imposes itself on the external world—the *Philebus*'s account of false pleasure (*Phil.* 36e ff.). Imagine that tomorrow you will watch your favorite football team win a vital match. Imagine it with vim and vigor, so that you really enjoy the prospect. Tomorrow, sadly, your team suffers a dismal defeat. What has happened to all the pleasure you had in anticipating victory? Surely, Socrates argues, the pleasure was false—not false just because the belief that sustained it was false, but because the pleasure was false in itself.

Against an unconvinced opponent Socrates tries to defend this claim by offering an elaborate account of the mind, once again populated by homunculi. There is the scribe, who writes down our beliefs (he represents the fact that we believe them), and there is the painter, who paints in stunning technicolor the emotions that go along with our beliefs (he represents the pleasures that we feel).[36] Between them, these persons within us make a mistake and create a wish-fulfilling pleasure that never turns up in the real world. Is that a false pleasure? Perhaps it is. Perhaps the very act of imagination, and the enjoyment that goes with it, do count as false independent of the belief that describes the pleasure, and on which the painting is parasitic. Socrates, at any rate, thinks so. But for our purposes, the crucial thing about false pleasure is that here the mind is represented not only as autonomous over its beliefs, but autonomous over its emotions as well. Emotional as well as cognitive imagination is an exercise of the soul "itself by itself"; and it is this rich life of the soul that rightly lays claim to an account of personal identity.

9. THE UNDERSTANDING MIND

Plato repeatedly hints that the individuation of a mind can be understood in terms of the connectedness of its conceptual system. For this point he needs to establish that thinking has a feature of connectedness (rather than merely being piecemeal).[37] He also needs to establish what that feature of connectedness is. That account is the "method" of collection and division.

In the late dialogues Socrates' influence becomes prominent again; and this is to be seen in the reappearance of the maxim "know thyself." In early dialogues, this had the air of a venerable adage, appropriately brought in by Socrates to justify both his aporematic method and his peculiar way of life.[38] But in later dialogues, "know thyself" turns up at precisely those moments when Socrates is discussing the unity of the soul, the problem of consistency, and the possibility of systematic understanding.

At *Phaedrus* 229a ff., Socrates and Phaedrus are discussing the interpretation of myth. Socrates eschews clever mythologizing (he says) because he thinks that to concern himself with the affairs of others, when he does not even know himself, would be absurd. For he does not even know what sort of a creature he is: is he a Typhon (a complicated beast), or a simple animal? Any soul, indeed, may be simple or complex (as the aspiring orator must know).

---

[36] The interpretation is disputed; cf., e.g., Gosling and Taylor, *Pleasure*; D. Frede, "Rumpelstiltskin."

[37] This takes us back to the problem of logical atomism.

[38] Cf., e.g., Critias's remarks at *Charmides* 164d ff.

But souls, then, are like speeches. For although speeches can be thrown together any old way, they should be arranged properly, like an organic whole (*Phdr.* 264c). True rhetoric should follow proper principles of arrangement (265d). In particular, it should be based upon collection and division: "Perceiving them under a single form, to bring together the things which are scattered all over, so that by defining each thing it may make clear the subject of its teaching. As in the case of the speech just now attempting to define love—whether it was well or badly made—it was on this basis that the speech had clarity and agreed with itself" (*Phdr.* 265d).

The dialectician, of course, is the man who can do all this—as he will be in the *Sophist*. But the dialectician is the same person as the true orator—and his business is to understand the souls of his audience, as well as the speeches he should make. The two, souls and speeches, apparently correspond. (*Phdr.* 271d ff.)

Speeches are unified and consistent when they follow proper scientific principles. Is the same true of souls? Souls, to be properly unified, must at least be consistent—and at most they must know. The properly coherent soul is the soul of the dialectician who has the whole system of ones and manies inside his head.[39] So unified souls must be understanding souls; and they must possess the systematic knowledge given by the structures of collection and division: "Surely we shall say that it is the task of the science of dialectic to divide by kinds, and not to think that one form is the same as another, nor another the same as it. . . . Therefore the person who is able adequately to distinguish a single form spread out over many distinct items, and many forms different from each other embraced from without by a single form, and a single form, again, collected together into a one through many wholes, and many separated altogether apart" (*Soph.* 253d).

This may, of course, be an elegant conceit. Recall the way in which the theory of collection and division provided a context for the individuation of objects. There, individuation could be explained by fitting each item into the context of others (and they into a context that included it). Now the context itself, as a complete system of understanding, explains the coherence of the understanding soul. This account of individuation is *absolute*, not contextual, explained as it is by the *internal* constitution of the individual soul.

Plato insists on intellectualism. He allows that the incoherent soul may be overcome by anger or pleasure: such a soul is ignorant, too.[40] But once reason rules in the mind of a man, his soul is in harmony, unified and whole. That state of mind is one to which we may aspire; and it is the state of mind of the dialectician. His systematic understanding is just what makes his soul cohere: his beliefs are fully consistent, and his understanding is complete. His soul will properly be one.

The dialectician's soul is unified by knowledge; in a similar way, the soul

[39] Cf. ch. 8, sec. 9.
[40] Cf. Mackenzie, *Plato on Punishment*, chs. 9 and 10.

that is able to Recollect is unified by the knowledge of "all nature," which is latent in it. Likewise, the soul that is consistent in its beliefs is held together as a single person by the consistency of its beliefs. But, I suggested, neither Recollection nor the consistency of deep belief give us any notion of the specialness of persons. Does the new account, of persons held together by the systems of collection and division, fare any better? The dialectician, like the philosopher-king, is bound to be right. Has he ever suffered from the falsehood elaborated in the *Theaetetus*? And—perhaps paradoxically—if he has not, does his knowledge retain any of the subjectivity made so interesting in Socrates' encounter with Protagoras? And if the dialectician's knowledge is all about objectivity, with no room for the subject, is he interesting as a person?

Return, for the last time, to the *Theaetetus* and the problem of the wooden horse. Socrates argued that the soul is not a wooden horse, not only because the information given by the senses is transmitted to the soul, but also because the soul has the capacity to coordinate all its cognitive activity. Imagine that I have two sensations, one of hard, the other of smooth; or two more, of hot and bitter. Those sensations will be merely physical episodes unless there is some central capacity to which they can be referred. Unless I can coordinate the sensation of hard and the sensation of smooth, I can never rise above the moment or perception. Unless I can connect the input of two different sense organs (to sense hot and bitter), I can never say that I have two sensations, or even begin to think that they might be the properties of the same object. Unless I can compare one sensation now, and another in ten minutes' time, I can never determine whether anything in the world persists at all. And in order to do all of that, there must be some central feature of the soul with the capacity to register unity, and the persistence to identify individuals in the world. That capacity itself is sufficient to establish the coherence of the person who does the individuating.

So, as it turns out, the individuation of persons is parasitic on the individuation of objects, in rather an unexpected way. For the individuation of persons occurs at two levels. In the first place, persons are just those whose sensations are compared by a single mental capacity. Having the capacity to compare is what unifies me, what makes sure that I am this "I," both now and over time. This will be a feature of all persons, as such; and it is reflected in my ability to pick out individuals in the world. But second, there is what we may call the philosophical unity of those whose system of understanding is itself complete and coherent. Persons like this—dialecticians and philosopher-kings—have the sort of unity that is reflected in the contexts where we find individuals in the real world; for them "unity" is an honorific title, the complete state to which their mental capacity may aspire.

Meno's paradox raised two questions about inquiry: How do we begin? and How do we reach a recognizable end? The theory of Recollection answered these questions by focusing on the way the mind may be affected by what it knows; and therein, I suggested, Plato offered us rather a dismal account of what it is to be a person. By the late dialogues, however, the situation is different. For now the crucial features of persons—albeit still conceived in an intellectual model—are vitality and autonomy. Persons are one because they are able to identify individuals, and watch them persist over time—and that cannot be done without the central capacity of mind. And persons are one when they can make a system of understanding come together by reason; then their souls are complete and coherent—they are honorably One.

Locke, perhaps, would be disappointed. Aristotle would be amazed. Being one, on this account, is something to which we aspire; "one" is an honorific title. The inquiry that leads to that unity, however, is an inquiry conducted by the active mind, the syllogizing soul endeavoring to maintain consistency in its beliefs and to produce proper explanations. Socrates' encounters with the sophists make it clear that this process is done by persons—by "me," "you," and all the rest (not, of course, by parts of persons, or lumps of soul—Protagoras down to the neck is inadequate for inquiry). The process is difficult, piecemeal, and beset by falsehood; and the person who carries it out may be more like a monster than a simple creature. Self-identity and unity are what we aim for, but subjectivity is the character of the search. True to his Socratic origins, Plato insists that "know thyself" is the first imperative of the philosopher.

Conclusion

1. Plato's Changing Metaphysics

Plato confronts the physical world before us and its objects. Some of the properties of those objects, he argues, are only instantiated at the same time as their opposites in the same object (this is the compresence of opposites). So the appearances of such properties in the phenomenal world are cognitively unreliable. To provide the explanations they need (since Plato does not, in the end, resort to skepticism), he postulates, first, transcendent forms. He supposes there are two kinds of entity: particulars and forms.

Particulars (the middle-sized objects of the sensible world) are individuals: not least because they are the single entities in which properties inhere (they are "one under many"). Forms are individuals too, for they are the singular entities that underpin explanation (they are "one over many"). So both forms and particulars are basic individuals.

But if particulars are one, they are also hopelessly many. For Plato supposes that having a property is having a part: this is true for relations and values as well as for other, more ordinary properties (this I have called the assumption of natural inherence). Consequently, particulars are composite entities and are liable to destruction just where their properties hang together. But then they are dissoluble just where the relational properties that hold them together are attached to the composite whole. If relations, values and any other attributes of a particular are parts of that particular, it seems to be absurdly complex, hopelessly many.

If, on the other hand, forms are one, they are thought to be entirely simple, incomposite entities (and thus immune to dissolution). But such simple entities are in trouble when they are, or when they become, related to anything else; for such a relation impugns their simplicity (again, if relational properties are parts of the relata). And then, of course, simple transcendent forms cease to be useful explanations, for they cannot enter into a significant relation with their explananda. The theory of forms, on this count, fails as an explanation.

Forms and particulars could, I argued, be characterized as individuals of two extremely different types. Forms are pure and simple, austere individuals; particulars are complex and composite, generous individuals. After the criticisms of the forms in the *Parmenides*, I contend, Plato's metaphysical attention turns away from the theory of forms to a more general focus: the problem of individuation itself, for any entity at all (forms, particulars, monads, numbers, kinds, whatever). Hereafter Plato develops the contrast between austere and generous individuation as a quite general difficulty for any putative individual. Either it is specified austerely, apart from its properties, or it is specifiable generously, by virtue of its properties. In the former case, the individual is prior to its properties—understood, perhaps, as the possessor of properties, and not defined by them. In the latter case, the individual just is its properties, they constitute what it is to be this individual. In the *Theaetetus*, the *Timaeus*, and the *Sophist*, Plato canvasses various arguments to explain a something prior to its properties (stuffs, lumps) and concludes that a bare something is unmentionable. Likewise, he considers how something might be just a collection of its properties (a bundle, a slice): here its constitution is so generous that it is indeterminate. So in neither case, it seems, can we arrive at a satisfactory account of what being an individual is (just one individual, a unit and a unity).

Two connected problems seem to lie at the heart of these puzzles. The first is the view that having a property is having a part, so that any property pluralizes what has it. The second is that the formal conditions for establishing identity and individuation are just properties of the identifiable individual. This means that to be an individual is to have the property of being an individual; and the property brings plurality and compromised individuation with it.

Plato's strategy is to rethink both the status and the function of the terms for individuation. First of all, he suggests that there is a set of privileged relations that determine identity: being, being one, being the same and different, and being able to possess properties (this last, I have argued, is indicated by the kinds Motion and Rest in the *Sophist*). This I called the mesh of identity. Second, Plato seems to deny that these relations pluralize their relata; they are no longer understood as real properties. Instead, they provide the context within which individuation takes place. So to count individuals, we locate them in a context; individuation is context-relative, and so no longer subject to the generous/austere paradox.

This account gives us individuals, all right, but individuals of an exiguous kind—bare units. But Plato has a deep and rich account of unity to offer as well. For his philosophy of mind—as it is developed in the *Theaetetus* and other late dialogues—shows how persons can be seen as (aspirants to) a complete system of understanding. They have unity from within, and are individuals in themselves. Here, in the obverse of the context-relative account, Plato's metaphysics, his epistemology, and his ethics cohere in an account of the activities of mind—autonomous, complex, and, in the best of all possible worlds, one.

2. Plato's Account of Individuation

That, I have argued, is how Plato's thinking about "What is there, really?" developed. Consider now the salient features of his account in its developed form. In the critical dialogues he investigates five different aspects of the problem of individuation:

1. What is a basic object?
2. How is identity to be understood, either at a time or over time?
3. How is being related to being one?
4. How are individuals countable (units)?
5. How are individuals unified?

His answers to these questions constitute, I have argued, his theory of individuation; it has, as I shall suggest, grounds to be considered a rival to Aristotle's theory of sorts.

1. *What is a basic object?* A common sense approach to the natural world might encourage the belief that physical objects are basic. After all, physical objects seem to be the possessors of properties (not the other way about)— and that appearance is confirmed by the way in which these objects underlie changes of properties. Plato, I suggested, subscribes to this view. Consider, for example, the last argument of the *Phaedo*: that the properties of things may be lost, while the thing itself persists (see ch. 2, sec. 4). That view of the physical world contains two different assumptions: that the world is asymmetrically arranged (into objects and their properties); and that the objects are basic (or more basic than their properties) because they endure through change.

The second of these assumptions is developed into a deeper discussion of what is basic to change in late Plato (perhaps under pressure from something like the "Theseus' ship" problem). Thus, the *Timaeus* suggests that beneath change there may be a substrate that just is what underlies change (and nothing else can be said of it; see ch. 6, sec. 5). But in that case, what there is is so basic as to be unmentionable—and that conclusion is an uneasy one.

In reverse, there may be nothing to underlie change. Instead, perhaps Heraclitus was right to suggest that change is all there is, and that it is constant. Or rather—as Plato represents Heraclitus in the *Theaetetus* (see ch. 5, sec. 4)— there is only this momentary episode, and then this, and then this, and so on . . . a succession of nows replaces change and leaves us with nothing to underlie it. This view of the world as a staccato series of episodes is no less impossible to maintain than the "basic stuff" view; and it will not sustain a coherent theory of the structure of the world.

There must be, then, some basic objects; but they should not be so basic that they defy description, nor be so affected by change that they do not really persist at all. To support this account of what is basic, Plato deploys the grammatical prejudice (ch. 1, sec. 3; ch. 6, sec. 6; ch. 7, secs. 1, 2; ch. 8, secs. 1, 2, 3). Our ordinary speech reflects an asymmetric arrangement; there is, on the one hand, what the speech is about (the subject), and there is what we say about that subject (the predicate). As Plato investigates the question of just how the structure of what we say reflects the way the world is arranged, and as he investigates the problem of falsehood, he comes to insist that there is a significant contrast between reference and predication, which reflects the way the world is structured. There is a difference in speech between "this" and "such"; in the world, the same differences obtain. (Indeed, this contrast, between the subject and the predicate, the object and its properties, is the contrast that underpins the contrast between austere and generous conceptions of individuation.)

But the fact that speech mirrors the world allows Plato to conclude that successful speech requires reference to some real object (whether or not we attribute the right properties to the object; see ch. 8, secs. 2, 3). So the world can be divided up into "somethings" and into what may (or may not) be true of those somethings; the somethings, on this account, come first.

Why? Underlying Plato's insistence that the syntax and the structure of the world rely on an underlying order of somethings is a strong epistemological claim. The world, first of all, is somehow susceptible to reason (even if we need to postulate transcendent entities to explain it; see ch. 2, sec. 3, and ch. 3, secs. 2, 3). And what reason does is explain; and explanations produce understanding when they are systematically arranged. Plato's assumption, throughout, is that the system on which understanding and explanation are based itself reflects an order in the way things are; and so the way things are must itself be systematic. It is so, according to the principles of grammatical arrangement— objects come first. And in that case we need to be able to understand just what is a something.

2. *How is identity to be understood, either at a time or over time?* If the notion that objects are basic rests on the idea that they persist through change, then they had better be seen to have some kind of systematic identity over time. If, on the other hand, successful speech depends on picking out, identifying, some "this," the basic objects of the world had better have some principles of identity at a time.

a. *Identity at a time.* Plato first tackles these questions of identity by wondering whether the terms in which identity is described are properties just like any other (see, e.g., ch. 4, sec. 5). His arguments make it clear that if the principles for establishing identity are common or garden properties, then they fail to do the identifying job at all. For not only do they pluralize the objects they purport to identify, but they also make a mess of the identifying relations themselves (so that, for example, something may be deduced to be both the same as itself and not the same as itself; see ch. 4, sec. 5). Now this difficulty, often diagnosed as a failure on Plato's part to distinguish the "is" of identity from the "is" of predication, lies, as I have argued, far deeper than that (see ch. 7, sec. 3, and ch. 8, sec. 2). Rather, Plato's suggestion seems to be that identity should be a formal matter, on two counts. First of all, the conditions for identity are both all-pervasive and specific—limited, that is, to just those terms that do indeed convey or display identity. Second, the concepts that explain identity should not be thought to correspond to some (material or other) part of the object identified. For otherwise, identity can only be a matter of the thin speech of the late-learners; "man," "good" (or "man is man" etc.) can be uttered, or perhaps pointed to, but no more can be said (see ch. 7, sec. 4).

To meet these requirements Plato proposes that there are generic relations of identity,

(1) that are all pervasive (so much so that they are conditions for everything from temperature to philosophical classification; see ch. 8, sec 4) and

(2) that do not feature as properties of their relata. The all-pervasive terms cover identity, individuation and the ability to possess properties (being, sameness, difference, unity, motion, and rest; see ch. 6, sec. 6, and ch. 8, sec. 2).

b. *Identity over time.* If Heraclitus and Protagoras are wrong, then objects are not just bundles of momentary episodes. Instead they do (and if speech and thought are to be successful, they must) persist through time; they must do so, moreover, without running foul of the puzzles of the *Parmenides*, that something will become older and younger than itself (see ch. 4, sec. 5). Persistence through time is a matter of determinate identity through time, and not simply a proliferation of entities at every moment (or every "suddenly," as Parmenides has it, see ch. 4, sec. 5).

In the matter of identity over time, once again Plato presses the consequences of two different demands—the first of reason, the second of necessity. First, reason demands that, in order to avoid foolish Protagoreanism, there must be entities that survive property change. Second, those entities must be able to tolerate aspect change as well; they must, that is, remain unaffected by Cambridge change, impassive to the changing relations of the rest of the world. Finally, those entities must persist through elemental change, through the depredations of physical change and the dangers of flux. These entities must persist just because reason fails without them; and theories that deny such entities are themselves unreasonable.

But, at the same time, it seems difficult to see how such entities may be made determinate. Timaeus's account of the receptacle of becoming is dictated by the necessity of finding what underlies any change at all. But this reductive analysis produces an entity that is so indeterminate that it is impossible to understand. So, once again for explanation to be possible, the entities we postulate must be determinate. In that case, the mesh of identity must give us the conditions for any entity to be a something. And this, I have argued, Plato construes as the demand that basic entities must be individuals.

To identify, we need to postulate entities that are determinate at a time and over time; and entities that persist through change or difference of aspect. These entities will be basic.

3. *How is being related to being one?* These basic, identifiable objects are, I have suggested, entities. However, my argument throughout has denied that Plato is concerned with the notion of existence (nor with the attendant problems of the verb "to be"; see ch. 4, sec. 8; ch. 7, sec. 3; ch. 8, sec. 9). Instead, his attention focuses on identifiable individuals, just because individuals,

ones, are what is basic and identifiable. The problems of "being," therefore, are attached to whether, and how, we can determine that something is an individual; and whether that can be done without precluding its being the possessor of properties as well. So being is being one something, in the first place; and only somethings can be such—only determinate individuals (so the theory goes) can be the possessors of properties.

But Plato also makes three significant assumptions about the way in which the expression "one" and its instances work:

    a. "One" is a complete expression, and not parasitic on some other (especially some substance) term.

    b. So being one is a basic, irreducible feature of whatever is one; individuation is primitive.

    c. Nonetheless, being one can be understood in two rather different ways— either as "one among others" or as "one in itself." Something may be one from without, in the context of others; or from within, in terms of its internal structure.

So for Plato individuation is basic; but it may be understood in two different ways—from without, contextually, as a matter of counting; or from within, as a matter of determining unity.

4. *How are individuals countable (units)?* Plato's final analysis of how we count individuals is determined by our ability to locate those individuals in a context. Here, therefore, the connection between individuation and identity becomes fundamental; for something is individuated in the context of other individuals when it is determined to be different from them and the same as itself. I argued that the canonical example of this context-relative counting occurred in the discussion of the great kinds in the *Sophist*; but that it occurs again in Plato's account of classification and in his use of the analogy between spelling and the structure of the world. For he can understand the notion that individuation may be context-relative only when he comes to see that the order in which the letters appear in a word correctly spelled is not itself another letter, or another part of the word, but rather some feature that supervenes on the whole word, without thereby making the word, absurdly, longer than it was in the first place. Likewise, syntax matters when we speak; even if the words we use are the same ones, the order in which they appear (or their function in an inflected sentence) affects the meaning of the whole, even if their order is not itself another word. So, when it comes to the structure of the world, there are just the entities in it that there are; but their individuation is determined by the way they fit into the context of the whole. That fitting does not add to the number of entities we must deal with, nor is it a property of the entities themselves; instead, and irreducibly, it is the context, the relations in which they appear. That is what allows us to count without running the risk of a Zenonian regress.

5. *How are individuals unified?* This account of individuation is, I suggested, rather too thin for satisfaction. Moreover, it fails to explain what might make something not a bare unit, but a unity—a coherent whole. So, I

argued, in the case of individual persons Plato focuses not on their difference from other persons, but rather on their integrity and coherence (ch. 9). And that—we should readily concede—is what we need from a theory of personal identity, since I shall not favor an account that tells me that I am who I am just because I am different from someone else. Nonetheless, the unity of persons is complementary to the contextual individuation of things. For Plato's account of personal unity is thoroughly intellectualist, based, I argued, on his claim that consistency is a condition of soul; and it reflects his assurance that the world itself is structured and susceptible to understanding. But in that case, we may see, also, why he treats "being one" as an honorific. We may aspire to unity, just as we may aspire to understanding—but we may never get there; nonetheless, our account of who we are is determined by the aspiration itself. Persons have identity just because their souls could be fully consistent; but like the philosopher-kings, there may never be anyone like that.

3. PLATO AND ARISTOTLE

Aristotle claims that I can only pick out individuals by virtue of the kinds to which they belong: being one is being one of a kind. For Aristotle, therefore, kinds or forms or essences are basic just because the structure of the world and our understanding of it depend on them (especially in the case of natural kinds). Plato (perhaps surprisingly, on some accounts of the theory of forms) does not consistently claim that the world is sorted by kinds. He maintains, rather, that being one is irreducible and basic—individuals, not kinds of individuals, are the basic items for metaphysics to study. Consequently, as I have argued, Plato offers both a minimalist acount of individuation (context-relative) and a correspondingly rich account of the identity of persons. In both matters he is at odds with Aristotle; for in neither the context-relative nor the structural account of individuation does Plato relax the claim that "being one" is a complete expression just because individuation as such is primitive.

Aristotle would (and did) argue against Plato that his acount of "one" is fundamentally misguided. Plato claims that "one" is a univocal expression, and irreducible; Aristotle, that it is syncategorematic because it is parasitic on the term that follows it. For, on Aristotle's view, we have no grip on "one" on its own; we always, both for counting and for considering organic unity, need to know "one what?"

Plato could, however, mount a counterargument. Suppose, with Aristotle, that we sort the world into kinds: in particular into classes of whole organisms. How, without knowing what makes any organism whole, can we tell which organisms fall into what kinds? Plato might with reason say, Does not sorting presuppose individuating (the putative members of the kind)? If the sort is to classify objects, we need some a priori notion of *an object pure and simple* before we start to classify; and if the sort is to classify whole organisms, we need some a priori notion of *whole organisms* before we start to classify. (It is, of course, no response for Aristotle just to claim that the kinds are given in nature. Plato may simply say that it is individuals, not kinds, that we are presented with first.) In either case, Plato could argue, individuation comes first; for it is individuation that provides us with the principles for determining what is basic (objects), what is a unit (an object), and what is a unity (a whole object). If metaphysics is to be well formed, we must address the fundamental questions first. Individuation, as Plato argues over and over again, is the most fundamental question of all. Being some kind of something is a later issue; being one something comes first.

On the Order of the Dialogues

IN THIS BOOK, I have claimd that particular lines of argument can be seen developing throughout Plato's work. But then I am forced to take a stand on the dating and ordering of the dialogues (and of course I am vulnerable to the objection that my view of the ordering of the dialogues, depends on my finding this thread of argument therein). For the relative placing of some dialogues I have argued elsewhere (cf. Mackenzie, "*Cratylus*," "Impasse and Explanation"); otherwise, it is my contention that the ordering of the dialogues can only be understood by means of thematic and argumentative continuity. Consequently, if I am right about the sequence of arguments on individuation, the order in which I have treated the dialogues is the correct one from the chronological point of view.

Now this (particularly, I suppose, when it comes to the dating of the *Timaeus*; notice the vigor of the debate between Owen, "*Timaeus*," and Cherniss, "*Timaeus*") runs counter to the modern revival of interest in stylometric and stylistic tests (cf., notably, Brandwood, *Chronology*, whose deplorable analogy, p. 249, fails to persuade; and Ledger, *Recounting Plato*). I assume, first of all, that stylometry does not tell us all there is to know about the order of the dialogues: it is an imprecise science (if it is a science at all) that fails to take account of the deliberation with which Plato may well have altered his stylistic tricks. Stylometrists assume that some literary devices must be unconscious (and so reflect development); while this may well be true, I remain unconvinced that anyone can show which particular devices are the unconscious ones.

Some have claimed, for example, that the avoidance of hiatus is one such device—and that all the late dialogues are characterized by hiatus avoidance. The presumption is that at some point in his literary career Plato became aware that hiatus is ungainly; after that point he avoided hiatus as much as he could. Now this suggests that his use of hiatus was unconscious, his recognition of its ugliness conscious, and his subsequent avoidance of it conscious. This supposes that Plato could reflect on the nature of hiatus; it also implies that he could have, had he wished, reverted to a literary style that used hiatus, rather than eschewing it. Therefore, there is, I suggest, no way of telling whether Plato's use of hiatus was unconscious (before his recognition that it was ugly) or conscious (after that recognition, in deliberate pastiche of his own early style). The same argument applies to any particular stylometric test; none of them can rely on the unconsciousness of the use of the style in question, just because Plato is such an able imitator of himself (compare, after all, the Socratic pastiche in the *Theaetetus*). This does not show, of course, that all the features of Plato's style are conscious; but it does cast doubt on which of them should or could be used as evidence for his literary and thence his philosophical development. In that case, the basis for collecting stylometric data remains obscure.

I assume, secondly, that connected arguments, in different dialogues, reflect the order of composition: similar arguments are likely to have been written close together, similar puzzles puzzled about the same time. Once again, this assumption is the basis of the development I find in Plato's treatment of individuation. He proceeds, I argue, from an unclear and object-specific view of his problem (in the middle period, especially in the *Phaedo* and the *Republic*), to a clear and general synopsis (in the critical period—the *Parmenides*, the *Theaetetus*, and the *Timaeus*; here, we may include, also the *Cratylus* and the *Euthydemus*), and finally to a solution (in the *Sophist* and the *Philebus*). If I have the problem right, this order of its development seems the right one, too.

So let us divide the dialogues, as tradition recommends, into three groups— Socratic, Platonic middle, and Platonic critical. The Socratic group (characterized by the use of the elenchus in the search for definitions) contains *Crito*, *Euthyphro*, *Apology*, *Charmides*, *Laches*, and *Protagoras* (in no particular order). Then there are three transitional dialogues, where the shift away from the Socratic elenchus and toward Platonic epistemology, metaphysics, and psychology can be seen: *Meno*, *Lysis*, and *Gorgias*. The middle period contains at least the *Phaedo*, the *Symposium*, and the *Republic* (in, I think, that order). Finally the late, critical period is introduced by the *Parmenides*, and is then followed by the *Theaetetus* and the *Timaeus*, along with the *Cratylus*, the *Euthydemus*, and the *Phaedrus* (at some point in the critical group). (The *Laws* I take to be a late work, possibly a compilation; I do not discuss it here.) The *Sophist*, the *Philebus*, and the *Politicus* represent, I shall argue, the culmination of Plato's painstaking attempt to rethink his own metaphysics.

Arguments from First Principles

ONE MAY TAKE Plato's dialogues to be exegeses of Platonic doctrines; or one may take them to be more tentative and argumentative. But if they are argumentative, we might hope to find in them arguments that appeal not to the paid-up Platonist, but to any reader in any age. In that case, some Platonic arguments may start not from Plato's own assumptions, nor from the conclusions of other arguments, but from first principles. Consider two, in particular, the evidence of which may uphold my claim that the puzzles about individuation of the late dialogues are intended as general metaphysical challenges to the reader—to any reader, to me and to you.

The Plato of the *Phaedo* is, an opponent will insist, clearly a dogmatist. For here, Socrates starts his argument by picking up what he said about forms earlier (*Phd.* 65–66) and reiterating the doctrine that there are such entities, transcendent and all. So when Socrates says, "We say, don't we, that there is such a thing as the equal itself" (74a), "we" are the exclusive group of those who believe the theory of forms; and "there is such a thing as the equal itself" refers us to that existential claim.

This interpretation, however, ignores the context in which the argument is put. Socrates is talking to Cebes and Simmias about the arguments for the immortality of the soul—to Cebes the convinced Pythagorean/Socratic; and to Simmias, the philosophical duffer. At *Phaedo* 72e, Cebes (an irritating man to meet, no doubt) reminds Socrates that if learning is recollection, then the soul must preexist its incarnation; this, after all, was shown by the "most beautiful argument" that people use mathematical reasoning to solve puzzles, even if they have never had any formal training in mathematics. This reference to the argument of the *Meno* (81b–86b) is one that strikes the reader; but Simmias is still in the dark. "I cannot remember the arguments," he complains (*Phd.* 73a5–6); and what follows is addressed to Simmias, in an attempt to raise in him recollection of what went on on that other occasion—or at least recognition of its concluding truth, that learning is Recollection.

The argument within the dialogue, therefore, is addressed to Simmias; but the reader, who does recall what Simmias cannot (if, that is, the cross-reference does reach him), is outside the magic circle of Socrates' admirers. This reader (you or I) is not committed one way or another to what Plato wrote in the *Meno*; and by deliberately activating the reader's recollection, Plato invites our critical scrutiny of what follows. So, both because Simmias needs the argument stated afresh, and because you, the reader, cannot be assumed to assume the theory of forms, we should expect an argument from first principles here. What is more, that is exactly what we get. For in the next

stage Socrates discusses the phenomenon of remembering—not Platonic Recollection, but remembering of the ordinary sort—the sort that Socrates did
when Cebes reminded him of the *Meno*, the sort that Simmias cannot quite
manage, and the sort that I did when I read the passage and recalled Socrates'
encounter with the slave boy in the *Meno*. So perhaps this extends to the entire
argument: the argument from recollection, on that account, is an argument
that invites the scrutiny of the nonpartisan reader; it is an attempt to argue
from what we will accept to the conclusion that there is Recollection, and that
Recollection is of forms.

I have argued that the middle dialogues propose a problem about particulars that is felt to be compelling enough to force us to postulate the theory of
forms. In the *Phaedo*, this strategy is appealing just because this is what shows
that philosophy provides a consolation for death; and if that claim is to
persuade the reader, then the arguments must do so as well. But then Plato
must persuade us (a) that there are forms and (b) that souls are like them. For
this discussion in this context, Plato cannot simply assume that there are
forms; he needs to argue for them. In particular, he needs to argue against a
reductionist view (such as materialism, *Phd.* 96c ff.) that the world we see is
the world we get, and to show that there are (there must be) extra transcendent entities. For (a), then, he needs to demonstrate that physical particulars
do not exhaust all there is. So he starts with what is obvious—physical
particulars, and by demonstrating their inadequacy, works up to what is
unobvious.

This sounds like Aristotle, not Plato, an objector might say. It is Aristotle
who works from the data to the theory; Plato, by contrast, offers us the theory
first. Plato had—on this view—a metaphysical insight, that there are supra-
sensible entities, the forms, which explain the physical world, an insight
arrived at, perhaps, in response to Socrates' quest for definitions. Plato supposes that definitions are given by real transcendent entities. The forms are
quite different from the sensible entities of the physical world, which are pale
imitations of the forms. The theory of forms underpins his arguments, which
are (therefore) addressed directly to someone who already accepts Plato's
metaphysics; his arguments, thus, are articulations of the way this original
insight may be deployed in epistemology, in metaphysics, and in ethics. There
is—again on this view—no argument for the theory in the corpus, only
arguments from the theory.

Is that right? Compare the argument about the difference between knowledge and belief at *Republic* 476e ff. In the *Republic*, Socrates argues that the
philosophers should rule. Why? Because they love to contemplate the truth;
they alone are able to steer the ship of state with true moral judgment. They
are awake, while everyone else is merely dreaming; they see "the beautiful
itself," and are able to distinguish between that and the things in the physical
world that participate in it. These philosophers know; everyone else only
believes (*Rep.* 475c–476d).

This conclusion provokes an imaginary protest from one of these dreamers, from the person who is said only to believe. The believer, after all, is the person who cannot see the forms, cannot acknowledge that they exist if he is shown them (*Rep.* 476c), and obstinately clings to the assumption that his own state of mind is entirely adequate. The argument that follows is intended to calm him, to explain to him that his state of mind is in fact only second-rate; and to persuade him that Socrates' account of the matter is in fact the true one (476e). So the argument that follows cannot be addressed to the committed Platonist. On the contrary, we should expect what follows to offer some kind of explanation, from generally acceptable premises, that Plato's epistemology, based as it is on the contrast between forms and particulars, is the right one. Now this, of course, does not exclude mention of the forms; but it does mean that if the argument is to be read as it is presented, it has no business using the theory of forms (which the believer does not believe) as a premise.

In the case of these two arguments, then, Socrates begins from first principles —the sort of principles that any reader at any time might be ready to accept; and he argues from them for the difficult and extravagant theses of the theory of forms. If this is correct (especially, if this is correct for these two arguments, canonical as they appear to be in the middle period), then we may readily expect Plato to construct other arguments based not on the esoteric assumptions of Platonism, but instead on the ordinary assumptions of any reader. In that case, two consequences may be thought to follow. The first is that we may read his arguments *as arguments*, and not just as statements of doctrine; this means that they can be assessed according to the canons of argument, and criticized accordingly. The second consequence of this way of reading Plato is that it allows us to understand the questioning and the puzzles of the late period as such, and not as a coded defense of his middle-period metaphysics.

Ackrill, J.
  "Plato on False Belief: *Theaetetus* 187–200." *Monist* (1966): 383–402.
  "*Sumplokē eidōn*," in Vlastos, ed., *Plato* I, 201–9.
  "Plato and the Copula: *Sophist* 251–59," in Vlastos, ed. *Plato* I, 210–22.
Allen, R. E.
  "Participation and Predication in Plato's Middle Dialogues." *Philosophical Review* (1960): 147–64.
  Plato's Parmenides (Oxford, 1983).
Allen, R. E., ed.
  Studies in Plato's Metaphysics (London, 1965).
Annas, J.
  "Forms and First Principles." *Phronesis* (1974): 257–83.
  "Knowledge and Language: The *Theaetetus* and the *Cratylus*," in Schofield and Nussbaum, eds., *Language and Logos*, 95–114.
  An Introduction to Plato's Republic (Oxford, 1981).
Archer-Hind, R.
  The Timaeus of Plato (London, 1888).
Barnes, J.
  The Presocratic Philosophers (London, 1979).
  "Aristotle and the Methods of Ethics." *Revue Internationale de Philosophie* (1981): 490–511.
Bedu-Addo, J.
  "Sense-Experience and the Argument for Recollection in Plato's *Phaedo*" *Phronesis* (1991): 27–60.
Bestor, T.W.
  "Plato's Semantics and Plato's *Parmenides*." *Phronesis* (1980): 38–75.
Binder, G., and L. Liesenborghs.
  "Eine Zuweisung der Sentenz (*ouk estin antilegein*) an Prodikos von Keos," in C. Classen, ed., *Sophistik* (Darmstadt, 1976), 452–64.
Bolton, R.
  "Plato's Distinction between Being and Becoming." *Review of Metaphysics* (1975): 66–95.
Bostock, D.
  "Plato on 'Is Not.'" *Oxford Studies in Ancient Philosophy* (1984): 89–119.
  Plato's Phaedo (Oxford, 1986).
  Plato's Theaetetus (Oxford, 1988).
Brandwood, L.
  The Chronology of Plato's Dialogues (Cambridge, 1990).
Brisson, L.
  Le même et l'autre dans la structure ontologique du Timée de Platon (Paris, 1974).
Brown, Lesley
  "Being in the *Sophist*: A Syntactical Enquiry." *Oxford Studies in Ancient Philosophy* (1986): 49–70.
Burnyeat, M.F.
  "Protagoras and Self-Refutation in Plato's *Theaetetus*." *Philosophical Review* (1976): 172–95.

"Plato on the Grammar of Perceiving." *Classical Quarterly* (1976): 29–51.

"Examples in Epistemology: Socrates, Theaetetus and G. E. Moore." *Philosophy* (1977): 381–96.

"Socratic Midwifery, Platonic Inspiration." *Bulletin of the Institute of Classical Studies* (1977): 7–16.

"Conflicting Appearances." *Proceedings of the British Academy* (1979): 69–111.

"Idealism and Greek Philosophy: What Descartes Saw and Berkeley Missed." *Philosophical Review* (1982): 3–40.

The Theaetetus of Plato (Indianapolis, 1990).

Burnyeat, M. F., and T. Honderich, eds.

Philosophy as It Is (London, 1979).

Castaneda, H.-N.

"Plato's *Phaedo* Theory of Relations." *Journal of Philosophical Logic* (1972): 467–80.

Charlton, W.

"Aristotle and the Principle of Individuation." *Phronesis* (1972): 239–49.

Cherniss, H.

"The Relation of the *Timaeus* to Plato's Later Dialogues," in Allen, ed., *Studies in Plato's Metaphysics*, 339–78.

Cohen, S. M.

"The Logic of the Third Man." *Philosophical Review* (1971): 448–75.

"Plato's Methods of Division," in Moravcsik, ed., *Patterns in Plato's Thought* 181–91.

Cooper, J. M.

"Plato on Sense-Perception and Knowledge (*Theaetetus* 184–86)." *Phronesis* (1970): 123–65.

Cornford, F. M.

Plato's Theory of Knowledge (London, 1935).

Plato's Cosmology: The Timaeus *of Plato* (London, 1937).

Plato and Parmenides (London, 1939).

Crombie, I. M.

An Examination of Plato's Doctrines, II (London, 1963).

Davidson, D.

"Mental Events," in Burnyeat and Honderich, eds., *Philosophy as It Is*, 213–38.

Denyer, N. C.

Language, Thought and Falsehood in Ancient Greek Philosophy (London, 1991).

Descartes, R.

Discourse on Method and the Meditations, trans. F. E. Sutcliffe, (London, 1968).

Dover, K.

Greek Homosexuality (London, 1978).

Dybikowski, J.

"False Pleasure and the *Philebus*." *Phronesis* (1970): 147–65.

Fine, G.

"Plato on Naming." *Philosophical Quarterly* (1977): 289–301.

"Knowledge and Belief in *Republic* V." *Archiv für Geschichte der Philosophie* (1978): 121–39.

"Knowledge and *Logos* in the *Theaetetus*." *Philosophical Review* (1979): 366–97.

"False Belief in the *Theaetetus*." *Phronesis* (1979): 70–80.

"The One over Many." *Philosophical Review* (1980): 197–240.

"Separation." *Oxford Studies in Ancient Philosophy* (1984): 31–87.

"Plato on Perception." *Oxford Studies in Ancient Philosophy Suppl.* (1988): 15–28.

Foster, J.

The Immaterial Self (London, 1991).

Frede, D.

"The Final Proof of the Immortality of the Soul." *Phronesis* (1978): 24–41.

"Rumpelstiltskin's Pleasures," *Phronesis* (1985) 151–80.

"The Soul's Silent Dialogue: A Non-Aporetic Reading of the *Theaetetus*." *Proceedings of the Cambridge Philological Society* (1989): 20–49.

"The Philosophical Economy of Plato's Psychology: Rationality and Common Concepts in the *Timaeus*." Forthcoming.

Frede, M.

"Bemerkungen zum Text der Aporienpassage in Platons *Sophistes*." *Phronesis* (1962): 132–33.

Prädikation und Existenzaussage (Göttingen, 1967).

Essays in Ancient Philosophy (Collected Papers) (Oxford, 1987).

"Individuals in Aristotle," in M. Frede, *Essays in Ancient Philosophy*, 49–71.

"Being and Becoming." *Oxford Studies in Ancient Philosophy Suppl.* (1988): 37–52.

Furley, D.

"The Rainfall Example in *Physics II*," in A. Gotthelf, ed., *Aristotle on Nature and Living Things* (Bristol, 1985): 177–82.

The Greek Cosmologists I (Cambridge, 1987).

Furth, M.

"Elements of Eleatic Ontology." *Journal of the History of Philosophy* (1968): 111–32.

Gallop, D.

"Plato and the Alphabet." *Philosophical Review* (1963): 364–76.

Geach, P.

"Plato's *Euthyphro*: An Analysis and Commentary." *Monist* (1966): 369–82.

God and the Soul (London, 1969).

Gill, C., ed.

The Person and the Human Mind (Oxford, 1990).

Gill, C., and M.M. McCabe, eds.

Form and Argument: Studies in Late Plato. Forthcoming.

Gill, M. L.

"Matter and Flux in Plato's *Timaeus*." *Phronesis* (1987): 34–53.

Gosling, J.

"*Republic* V: *ta polla kala*." *Phronesis* (1960): 116–28.

"Similarity in *Phd.* 73b ff." *Phronesis* (1965): 151–61.

Plato (London, 1973).

Plato: Philebus (Oxford, 1975).

Gosling, J., and Taylor, C.C.W., eds.

The Greeks on Pleasure (Oxford, 1982).

Hartman, E.

Substance, Body and Soul (Princeton, 1977).

Heinaman, R.

"Self-Predication in the *Sophist*." *Phronesis* (1981): 55–66.

Hicken, W.
  "Knowledge and Forms in Plato's *Theaetetus*." in Allen, ed., *Studies in Plato's Metaphysics*, 185–98.
Hofstadter, D.
  Godel Escher Bach (New York, 1979).
Hofstadter, D., and D. Dennett, eds.
  The Mind's Eye (New York, 1981).
Holland, A. J.
  "An Argument in Plato's *Theaetetus*." *Philosophical Quarterly* (1973): 97–116.
Irwin, T. H.
  Plato's Moral Theory (Oxford, 1977).
  "Plato's Heracliteanism." *Philosophical Quarterly* (1977): 1–13.
  Aristotle's First Principles (Oxford, 1988).
Jordan, R. W.
  Plato's Arguments for Forms (Cambridge Philological Society, 1983).
Kahn, C. H.
  The Verb "to Be" in Ancient Greek (Dordrecht, 1973).
Kerferd, G. B.
  The Sophistic Movement (Cambridge, 1981).
Keyt, D.
  "The Mad Craftsman of the *Timaeus*." *Philosophical Review* (1971): 230–35.
Kirwan, C.
  "Plato and Relativity." *Phronesis* (1974): 112–29.
Kneale, W., and M.
  The Development of Logic (Oxford, 1962).
Kraut, R., ed.
  The Cambridge Companion to Plato (Cambridge, 1992).
Kripke, S.
  "Identity and Necessity," in Burnyeat and Honderich, eds., *Philosophy as It Is*, 467–514.
Lear, J.
  Aristotle, the Desire to Understand (Cambridge, 1988).
Ledger, G. R.
  Re-counting Plato (Oxford, 1989).
Lee, E. N.
  "On the Metaphysics of the Image in Plato's *Timaeus*." *Monist* (1966): 341–68.
  "Plato on Negation and Not-Being in the *Sophist*." *Philosophical Review* (1972): 267–304.
  "Hoist with His Own Petard: Ironic and Comic Elements in Plato's Critique of Protagoras," in Lee, Mourelatos, and Rorty, eds., *Exegesis and Argument*, 225–61.
Lee, E. N., A.P.D. Mourelatos, and R. Rorty, eds.
  Exegesis and Argument (Assen, Netherland, 1973).
Leibniz, G. W.
  New Essays on Human Understanding, trans. P. Remnant and J. Bennett (Cambridge, 1982).
Lesher, J.
  "Aristotle on Form, Substance and Universals." *Phronesis* (1971): 169–78.

Lewis, F.
"Foul Play in Plato's Aviary: *Theaetetus* 195b ff.," in Lee, Mourelatos, and Rorty, eds., *Exegesis and Argument*, 262–84.
"Plato on 'not.'" *California Studies in Classical Antiquity* (1976): 89–115.
Locke, J.
An Essay Concerning Human Understanding (London, 1961).
MacDowell, J.
Plato: Theaetetus (Oxford, 1973).
"Falsehood and Not-Being in Plato's *Sophist*," in Schofield and Nussbaum, eds., *Language and Logos*, 115–34.
Mackenzie, M. M. (see also McCabe).
"Parmenides' Dilemma." *Phronesis* (1981): 1–12.
Plato on Punishment (Berkeley, 1981).
"Paradox in Plato's *Phaedrus*." *Proceedings of the Cambridge Philological Society* (1982): 64–76.
"Putting the *Cratylus* in Its Place." *Classical Quarterly* (1986): 124–50.
"Heraclitus and the Art of Paradox." *Oxford Studies in Ancient Philosophy* (1988): 1–37.
"Impasse and Explanation: From the *Lysis* to the *Phaedo*." *Archiv für Geschichte der Philosophie* (1988): 15–45.
"The Virtues of Socratic Ignorance." *Classical Quarterly* (1988): 331–50.
Mackie, J. L.
Ethics: Inventing Right and Wrong (London, 1977).
Mates, B.
"Identity and Predication in Plato." *Phronesis* (1979): 211–29.
Matthen, M.
"Perception, Relativism and Truth: Reflections on Plato's *Theaetetus* 152–60." *Dialogue* (1985): 33–58.
Matthews, G.
"Accidental Unities," in Schofield and Nussbaum, eds., *Language and Logos*, 223–40.
Matthews, G., and S. M. Cohen.
"The One and the Many." *Rev. Met.* (1968): 630–55.
McCabe, M. M. (formerly Mackenzie).
"Myth Allegory and Argument in Plato." *Apeiron Supplement* (1992): 47–67.
"Persistent Fallacies," *Proceedings of the Aristotelian Society* (1993): 73–93.
"Arguments in Context: Aristotle's Defense of Rhetoric," in Furley and Nehamas, eds., *Aristotle's Rhetoric* (Symposium Aristotelicum) (Princeton, 1994).
Meinwald, C.
Plato's Parmenides (Oxford, 1991).
Mignucci, M.
"Plato's Third Man Arguments in the *Parmenides*." *Archiv für Geschichte der Philosophie* (1990): 143–81.
Mills, K.
"Plato's *Phaedo* 74b7–c6." *Phronesis* (1957): 128–47; (1958): 40–58.
Modrak, D. K.
"Perception and Judgement in the *Theaetetus*." *Phronesis* (1981): 35–51.
Moore, G. E.
Principia Ethica (Cambridge, 1903).

Moravscik, J.
"Learning as Recollection," in Vlastos, ed., *Plato I*, 53–69.
"Forms and Dialectic in the Second Half of the *Parmenides*," in Schofield and Nussbaum, eds., *Language and Logos* 135–53.
Moravscik, J., ed.
Patterns in Plato's Thought (Dordrecht, 1973).
Morrison, D.
"Separation in Aristotle's Metaphysics." *Oxford Studies in Ancient Philosophy* (1985): 125–58.
Morrow, G., and J. Dillon, trans. and eds.
Proclus' Commentary on Plato's Parmenides (Princeton, 1987).
Nagel, T.
The View from Nowhere (Oxford, 1986).
Nehamas, A.
"Predication and Forms of Opposites." *Review of Metaphysics* (1973): 461–91.
"Plato on the Imperfection of the Sensible World." *American Philosophical Quarterly* (1975): 105–17.
"Self-Predication of Plato's Theory of Forms." *American Philosophical Quarterly* (1979): 93–103.
"Participation and Predication in Plato's Late Dialogues." *Review of Metaphysics* (1982): 343–74.
"*Epistēmē* and *Logos* in Plato's later thought." *Archiv für Geschichte der Philosophie* (1984): 11–36.
"Meno's Paradox and Socrates as a Teacher." *Oxford Studies in Ancient Philosophy* (1985): 1–30.
Nussbaum, M.
"Saving Aristotle's Appearances," in Schofield and Nussbaum, eds., *Language and Logos*, 267–94.
O'Brien, D.
"The Last Argument of Plato's *Phaedo*." *Classical Quarterly* (1967): 198–213; (1968): 95–106.
Osborne, C.
"Topography in the *Timaeus*." *Proceedings of the Cambridge Philological Society* (1988): 104–14.
"Space, Time, Shape and Direction: Creative Discourse in the *Timaeus*," in Gill and McCabe, eds., *Form and Argument*. Forthcoming.
Owen, G.E.L.
Logic, Science and Dialectic (Collected Papers), ed. M. C. Nussbaum (London, 1986), including:
    "Eleatic Questions," 3–26.
    "The Place of the *Timaeus* in Plato's Dialogues," 65–84.
    "Notes on Ryle's Plato," 85–103.
    "Plato on Not-Being," 104–37.
    "Plato on the Undepictable," 138–47.
    "A Proof in the *Peri Ideōn*," 165–79.
    "Logic and Metaphysics in Some Earlier Works of Aristotle," 180–99.
    "Aristotle on the Snares of Ontology," 259–78.
    "*Tithenai ta phainomena*," 239–51.
    "Inherence," 252–58.

Patterson, R.
Image and Reality in Plato's Metaphysics (Indianapolis, 1985).
Peck, A. L.
"Plato versus Parmenides." *Philosophical Review* (1962): 159–84.
Penner, T.
"False Anticipatory Pleasures: *Philebus* 36a3–41a6." *Phronesis* (1970): 166–78.
The Ascent from Nominalism: Some Existence Arguments in Plato's Middle Dialogues (Dordrecht, 1987).
Perry, J., ed.
Personal Identity (Berkeley, 1975).
Quine, W.V.O.
Word and Object (Cambridge, Mass., 1960).
Ways of Paradox (Cambridge, Mass., 1976).
Robinson, R.
Plato's Earlier Dialectic (Oxford, 1953).
Essays in Greek Philosophy (Oxford, 1969).
Rorty, A.
The Identities of Persons (Berkeley, 1976).
Russell, B.
"Knowledge by Acquaintance and Knowledge by Description." *Proceedings of the Aristotelian Society* (1910/11): 118.
Ryle, G.
"Letters and Syllables in Plato." *Philosophical Review* (1960): 431–51.
"Plato's *Parmenides*," in Allen, ed., *Studies in Plato's Metaphysics*, 97–147.
Plato's Progress (Cambridge, 1966).
"Logical Atomism in Plato's *Theaetetus*." *Phronesis* (1990): 21–46.
Sainsbury, R. M.
Paradoxes (Cambridge, 1988).
Sayre, K. M.
Plato's Analytic Method (Chicago, 1969).
Plato's Late Ontology (Princeton, 1983).
Schofield, M.
"A Displacement in the Text of the *Cratylus*." *Classical Quarterly* (1972): 246–53.
"The Antinomies of Plato's *Parmenides*." *Classical Quarterly* (1977): 139–58.
"The Denouement of the *Cratylus*," in Schofield and Nussbaum, eds., *Language and Logos*, 61–81.
"Likeness in *Parmenides*," in Gill and McCabe, eds., *Form and Argument*. Forthcoming.
Schofield, M., and Nussbaum, M. C., eds.
Language and Logos (Cambridge, 1982).
Scott, D.
"Platonic Anamnesis Revisited." *Classical Quarterly* (1987): 346–66.
"Socrate prend-il au serieux le paradoxe de Menon?" *Revue de Philosophie* (1991): 627–41.
Sedley, D.
"Is Aristotle's Teleology Anthropocentric?" *Phronesis* (1991): 179–96.
Sellars, W.
"Vlastos and the Third Man." *Philosophical Review* (1955): 405–37.

Shiner, R.
  Knowledge and Reality in Plato's Philebus (Assen, 1974).
Shoemaker, S.
  Identity, Cause and Mind (Cambridge, 1984).
Silverman, A.
  "Plato on Perception and 'Commons.'" *Classical Quarterly* (1990): 148–75.
Skemp, J.
  Plato's Statesman (London, 1952).
Sorabji, R.
  Time Creation and the Continuum (London, 1983).
  Matter Space and Motion (London, 1988).
Strang, C.
  "Plato and the Third Man." *Proceedings of the Aristotelian Society Supplement*
    (1963): 147–76.
Strawson, P. F.
  Individuals (London, 1959).
Taylor, C.
  Sources of the Self: The Making of the Modern Identity (Cambridge, 1989).
Taylor, C.C.W.
  "Forms as Causes in the *Phaedo*." *Mind* (1969): 45–59.
Teloh, H.
  The Development of Plato's Metaphysics (Pennsylvania, 1981).
Teloh, H., and D. J. Louzecky.
  "Plato's Third Man Argument." *Phronesis* (1972): 80–94.
Vlastos, G.
  "Anamnesis in the *Meno*." *Dialogue* (1965): 143–67.
  "The Third Man Argument in Plato's *Parmenides*," in Allen, ed., *Studies in Plato's
    Metaphysics*, 231–63.
  Plato's Universe (Seattle, 1975).
  Platonic Studies (Collected Papers) (Princeton, (1981) including:
          "Degrees of Reality in Plato," 58–75.
          "Justice and Happiness in the *Republic*," 111–39.
          "The Unity of the Virtues in the *Protagoras*," 221–69.
          "Reasons and Causes in the *Phaedo*," 76–110.
          "An Ambiguity in the *Sophist*," 270–322.
          "Plato's 'Third Man' Argument: Text and Logic," 342–65.
          "On a Proposed Redefinition of 'Self-Predication' in Plato." *Phronesis*
            (1981): 76–79.
          "The Socratic Elenchus." *Oxford Studies in Ancient Philosophy* (1983):
            27–58.
          Socrates: Ironist and Moral Philosopher (Cambridge, 1991).
Vlastos, G., ed.
  Socrates (New York, 1971).
  Plato I: Epistemology and Metaphysics (New York, 1970).
Waterfield, R.
  "The Place of the *Philebus* in Plato's Dialogues." *Phronesis* (1980): 270–305.
Waterlow, S.
  "Protagoras and Inconsistency." *Archiv für Geschichte der Philosophie* (1977):
    19–36.

White, F. C.
Plato's Theory of Particulars (New York, 1981).
White, N.
"Aristotle on Sameness and Oneness." *Philosophical Review* (1971): 177–97.
Plato on Language and Reality (Indianapolis, 1976).
"Plato's Metaphysical Epistemology," in Kraut, ed., *The Cambridge Companion to Plato*, 277–310.
Wiggins, D.
"Sentence Meaning, Negation and Plato's Problem of Not- Being," in Vlastos, ed., *Plato I*, 286–303.
Sameness and Substance (Oxford, 1980).
Williams, B.
"Cratylus' Theory of Names and Its Refutation," in Schofield and Nussbaum, eds., *Language and Logos*, 83–93.
Williams, C.F.J.
"Referential Opacity and False Belief in the *Theaetetus*." *Philosophical Quarterly* (1972): 289–302.
Woodruff, P.
Plato: Hippias Major (Indianapolis, 1982).
Zembaty, J. S.
"Plato's *Timaeus*: Mass Terms, Sortal Terms and Identity through Time in the Phenomenal World." *Canadian Journal of Philosophy Supplement* (1983): 101–22.

difference, 3–4, 112–21, 125–26, 128–31, 138–39, 143–47, 151, 160, 166–75, 178–79, 181, 189–92, 200, 201, 205, 210–11, 216–17, 221, 223–43, 258–61, 273, 282–84, 286, 288–90, 302, 305–7

elenchus, 20–21, 276
empiricism, 55–58, 134
essence, 15–18, 38, 49, 51n.58, 63, 85n.55, 90, 107, 110n.27, 184, 193, 212, 223n.4, 232, 247, 255, 307
examples, 26–29
excluded middle, law of (LEM), 122n.46, 132
existence, 59–60, 61, 64, 75, 84n.52, 94, 97, 104, 111, 113n.32, 121, 124–30, 152, 161, 162, 199, 203, 206–7, 216, 229n.4, 242, 244nn.42, 43, 255, 305
explanation, 26–29, 33, 45n.44, 50, 53–94, 99, 115, 127, 159, 173, 176, 178–79, 183, 184, 186–87, 243n.38, 244n.47, 247, 249, 250n.62, 252, 253n.70, 255, 258n.79, 269, 294, 300–305

falsehood, 153–57, 193, 197, 213–15, 241n.33, 278, 290–96, 299, 300, 303
flux, 7–9, 26, 30n.12, 39, 44, 49, 92–93, 120, 133–49, 175–89, 203, 204, 205, 214, 221, 238, 271, 279, 287, 305
forms (Platonic), 4, 25, 34, 36, 41, 46–48, 51–52, 53–94, 97–99, 101–2, 104–5, 107, 110, 127, 130, 132, 158, 172–75, 178, 179n.26, 181, 182n.29, 183–84, 190, 202, 204–5, 213n.51, 214n.55, 222n.1, 223, 226–27, 229, 232, 235, 240n.32, 241, 244, 250, 253–57, 259, 260, 264, 266–67, 281n.18, 282n.23, 288, 289, 290n.31, 301, 307

generous individuals, 4, 51–52, 66, 74, 78, 86, 93, 97–132, 148, 161, 167, 185, 186, 191–92, 193, 216, 224, 241, 242, 259, 260, 262, 286, 292, 301–4
glue, metaphysical, 13–18, 185
god (the demiurge), 79, 90–94, 163–91
grammatical prejudice, 9–11, 148, 152, 157, 160–61, 181–82, 187, 189, 216, 303

homolomereity, 14–18
identity, 53, 90, 91, 108–21, 122, 125, 126, 128, 131, 132, 133, 139, 140, 144–45, 151, 160, 160–67, 168, 170, 175, 182, 184, 185, 189–91, 204–5, 206–12, 213, 217, 221, 223–34, 237, 242, 253, 260–

61, 264–70, 273, 275, 277, 302–6. *See also* identity, personal; mesh of identity; nonidentity; self-identity
identity, personal, 263–300, 307
ignorance, 53–60, 70–72, 162, 262, 294–96, 298
illusion, 25, 26, 34, 40, 120
immortality, 29, 36, 56–60, 264–67
imperfection, 41–42. *See also* perfection
incomposite entities, 30, 74–78, 95, 266–69, 301. *See also* composite entities
indefinite, 97, 103, 107–8, 112, 125, 128, 130, 131, 164, 213, 238, 244–49, 259
innate ideas, 56–60, 265–66, 290. *See also* unlimited
interpredication, 77, 83, 88, 100n.2, 110, 118n.39

kinds, 221–24, 240–43
knowledge, 29, 38n.31, 53–60, 68–75, 90–94, 129, 133–37, 140–41, 146, 149–52, 156, 157–58, 162–63, 203, 239, 258, 264, 266, 274, 280, 283–86, 290, 294–96, 298–99

language, 5, 123, 131, 145–46, 154, 157–58, 190, 205–19, 237, 259
Leibniz' law, 108–11
limit, 174, 233, 243–62
lumps, 5, 133–61, 186–88, 191, 215–16, 229, 300, 302

masses, 76, 166, 178–79, 183, 185, 224, 246, 248
memory, 265, 274–76, 290, 292, 293, 296, 311–12
Meno's paradox, 34n.21, 53–60, 67, 68, 69, 154, 258n.79, 290, 300
mereology, 50n.57
mesh of identity, 5, 189–91, 224–34, 257–62, 289, 305
methods of philosophy, 8, 18–21, 311–14
mind, 5, 53–60, 61–62, 70–74, 82, 118, 149, 151, 154–56, 250, 261, 263–300
monism, 80, 97, 98, 104, 108n.20, 109n.25, 166n.11, 200–2, 204, 213, 221, 244n.45, 270
myth, 56, 162–63, 184–88, 247n.55, 279, 297

names, 79–80, 89, 92, 158, 185, 193, 199, 200–202, 208, 209, 212, 213–15, 225, 239, 244, 259, 280